CONDENSED CAPITALISM

CONDENSED CAPITALISM

CAMPBELL SOUP
AND THE PURSUIT OF
CHEAP PRODUCTION
IN THE TWENTIETH
CENTURY

DANIEL SIDORICK

ILR Press
an imprint of
CORNELL UNIVERSITY PRESS
Ithaca and London

Copyright © 2009 by Cornell University

First published 2009 by Cornell University Press

Printed in the United States of America

Library of Congress Cataloging-in-Publication Data

Sidorick, Daniel.
  Condensed capitalism : Campbell Soup and the pursuit
of cheap production in the twentieth century / Daniel
Sidorick.
      p. cm.
  Includes bibliographical references and index.
  ISBN 978-0-8014-4726-6 (cloth : alk. paper)
  1. Campbell Soup Company—History.   2. Soup
industry—New Jersey—Camden—History.   3. Soup
industry—Employees—Labor unions—New Jersey—
Camden—History.   4. Industrial relations—New
Jersey—Camden—History.   5. Production management—
New Jersey—Camden—History.   I. Title.

    HD9330.S624C367   2009
    331.88'164—dc22   2008043693

Cornell University Press strives to use environmentally
responsible suppliers and materials to the fullest extent
possible in the publishing of its books. Such materials
include vegetable-based, low-VOC inks and acid-free
papers that are recycled, totally chlorine-free, or partly
composed of nonwood fibers. For further information,
visit our website at www.cornellpress.cornell.edu.

Cloth printing   10 9 8 7 6 5 4 3 2 1

For my mother and in memory of my father
and
for Sharon

✹ Contents

 CONDENSED CAPITALISM

Introduction
Global Strategies, Hometown Factories

Everyone in the United States knows Campbell's Soup, "America's Favorite Food" according to the title of the company-sanctioned history of the firm.[1] The famous red-and-white cans line shelves in kitchens fashionable and humble, most people recognize the "Mm, Mm, Good" advertising jingle, and Andy Warhol's arguably most famous paintings are his pop-art reinterpretations of the equally well-known soup cans. The quintessential comfort food for many Americans, according to numerous memoirs and blogs, is "a bowl of Campbell's Tomato Soup and a grilled cheese sandwich." The transformation of Campbell's Soup into an icon of American culture was carefully guided by company publicists through the use of streetcar signs at the beginning of the twentieth century, and then with advertisements in magazines like the *Saturday Evening Post* and sponsorship of the most popular programs on radio and television, including *Amos 'n' Andy* and *Lassie*. Campbell's marketing and public relations efforts were spectacularly successful, creating a myth of a product and company as wholesome as hometown America yet at the forefront of scientific and hygienic modern food production. Corporate critic Jim Terry has argued that "some companies have been so successful in creating a wholesome, 'apple pie' image that the myth clouds the reality.... One corporation that has been particularly successful in creating and maintaining such an image is the Campbell Soup Company."[2] On a financial level, the Campbell Soup Company today has annual revenues over seven billion dollars, and the profits resulting from its almost total dominance of the condensed soup industry have made the Dorrance family one of the wealthiest in the United States.

Despite the iconic status of the company's flagship product, however, most people are unaware of what was behind Campbell management's success at generating wealth that started with the company's founding in 1869 in Camden, New Jersey. Even more invisible are the people in the soup plants who pared the vegetables, blended the ingredients, and ran the labeling machines—without whom there would be no Campbell's Soup.

The company's management philosophy was set in place by the inventor of condensed soup, John T. Dorrance (1873–1930), who ran the company with a stern zeal during the crucial first three decades of the twentieth century. Other members of his family, and later, others schooled in the Campbell way, continued his approach. Dorrance believed that only by tightly controlling his supply chains, production, and marketing could he succeed. At the starting point of the canned-soup operation, company agronomists grew the seeds for the painstakingly developed varieties of tomatoes ideally suited for tomato soup, then provided young plants to farmers under strictly monitored contracts. The culmination of the process was equally controlled. The company's marketing department demanded specific placement of its advertisements in magazines and refused to negotiate its pricing policy with grocers.

But it was at the center of the life cycle of the canned soup business, in production, that Dorrance paid closest attention in his attempt to scientifically manage the Campbell Soup Company. Making soup was a difficult process to automate, and many procedures remained manual for as long as Campbell made soup in Camden. Dorrance simply took this problem as another challenge that he would overcome. He refused for years to raise his soup's selling price of ten cents a can and counterbalanced rises in other costs by relentlessly pushing down the costs of production. The people on the receiving end of his efforts—the production workers—did not congenially accept speedups and intensification of work, and decades-long trench warfare ensued. Individual workers found ways to beat the system, and small groups were able to undermine foremen's efforts to increase output. But the company was equally imaginative in countering opposition to its designs. Eventually workers strengthened their position by organizing a militant union in 1940 (after a seven-year campaign), and for about three decades the two sides faced each other more or less as equals.

These contending forces—management's drive for low-cost production and employees' attempts to achieve some control over their working lives and livelihoods—are the focus of this book. In particular, I examine the obstacles faced by management in keeping production costs low and the strategies it used to overcome these problems, from Campbell's adoption of scientific management practices in 1927 through the plant shutdown in 1990. These hurdles were not unique to Campbell Soup; they are, in fact, faced by virtually every firm in a capitalist economy, although they acquire special prominence at certain times. The push to lower costs that started as a solution to the economic crises of the 1970s and continues into the twenty-first century has accelerated the drive to work intensification, outsourcing, "offshoring," and deindustrialization. Yet these methods of lowering costs have a much longer history than most popular accounts acknowledge. The most well known of the recent corporate cost-cutting strategies is the movement of production to low-cost regions with weak or nonexistent union traditions, as exemplified, for example, by Campbell's neighbor across Market Street in Camden, RCA. Historian Jefferson Cowie (in his book *Capital Moves*) has described how RCA began moving its assembly work in 1940 to a series of new locations in its never-ending "quest for cheap labor."[3]

But the particular industry that Campbell was in precluded—or at least made unappealing—any solution that included moving the soup plant far away. For, while workers in Bloomington or Juárez could assemble television receivers as well as anyone in Camden, the tomatoes ripening in South Jersey fields had to be processed into soup within hours of their harvesting. In the food-processing industry, location near agricultural inputs is critical, but Camden had other attractions that prevented management from seriously considering leaving any time in the company's first century. For distributing its finished products, Camden was ideally situated in the core northeast corridor of the United States with direct access to rail and marine transport. And the Dorrance family, which watched over the giant company with the attention a small proprietor might pay to his family business—for it was the family business—could not allow the company's flagship plant to be moved out of the family's reach from its base in Philadelphia's wealthy Main Line suburbs. As a result, Campbell Soup became even more than an icon of consumerism in southern New Jersey. By the mid-twentieth century it had become a bedrock institution of the region as well. Older residents reminisced about scrambling among the long lines of farmers' trucks piled high with baskets of ripe Jersey tomatoes. Tens of thousands had, at some point in their lives, worked at the sprawling soup plant, and everyone driving across the Benjamin Franklin Bridge from Philadelphia knew they were in Camden when they saw the red-and-white Campbell's Soup-can-painted water towers rising above the factory.

Figure 1.   Industrial Camden. In foreground, Campbell Soup Company Plant No. 1. In center, from upper left to lower right, RCA. On the river between RCA and the bridge, Campbell Plant No. 2. At top, the Benjamin Franklin Bridge and Philadelphia.
Temple University Libraries, Urban Archives, Philadelphia, Pennsylvania.

Campbell Soup Company thus faced a quandary in being unable to run away from the problems that, as we shall see, made its achievement of financial success such a challenge, for the basis of that success by necessity lay in Camden and its surrounding farmlands. In this way it had much in common with many other firms that do not always have the luxury of moving production on a whim, a point missed by those who see capital flight as a viable strategy for any corporation. When RCA ran from militant unionized workers and communities supportive of those workers, Campbell had to stay in Camden and fight, or at least find other ways to keep pushing production costs down. Because the capital flight option was off the table for most of its first century, Campbell can be viewed as a veritable test case for exploring those other options that corporations used—and still use—to minimize costs and maximize profitability.

Though the Campbell Soup Company faced many of the same problems as RCA, its experience and tactics were markedly different for each of the workforce-related obstacles to profitability that RCA overcame by relocating production. Campbell's actions over several decades were complex, but they can, for the most part, be categorized as direct responses to three impediments to profitability:

Cost of production. Rather than moving to an area with cheaper labor costs, Campbell held down wages by dealing harshly with wage demands, often refusing to deal with the union at all, and by searching out those groups of workers who would accept low pay. Further, the company kept down production costs by constantly revolutionizing the production process, using automation, "scientific management" techniques, and piece rates.

Increasing sense of entitlement, solidarity, and militancy of workers. Again, instead of running away from united and assertive workers, Campbell implemented practices to minimize or actively defeat unity. Piecework promoted individualism, the company split the workforce between year-round workers and a large contingent of seasonal workers, and, before other employers in Camden, it hired female, African American, and Puerto Rican workers, then funneled them into distinct and inferior job classifications.

Community support for workers. One effect of Campbell's labor market recruitment strategies was to undermine the community solidarity that drove other manufacturers to seek new locations. As Camden's major provider of low-wage industrial work, Campbell brought into the city's neighborhoods workers from groups without a long history there. Some older, more established residents had little sympathy for the aspirations of Campbell workers and even blamed Campbell for the "decline" of Camden. Higher-paid employees of neighboring RCA and New York Shipbuilding sometimes resented the migrant workers that Campbell attracted, who often stayed in the area after their work contracts were completed and even "took over the neighborhood."[4]

Campbell's multifaceted response to these obstacles fell into four broad categories. The company directed its greatest efforts toward the control of production, with the aim of reducing costs and maximizing efficiency. The techniques it used ranged from the adoption of the Bedaux system of scientific management in the 1920s to the widespread encouragement in the 1980s of quality circles (a management technique imported from Japan to encourage "voluntary" worker groups that discussed workplace improvement), and they always included the aggressive mechanization of work processes to replace labor with technology. Campbell's second strategy grew out of the peculiarities of its labor force requirements: the segmentation of the workforce into permanent and seasonal sectors was further exploited by splitting job categories along gender, ethnic, and racial lines. The company's third strategy, a vicious antiunionism combined with anticommunism, reached its height during the McCarthy era but persisted into later decades. The final strategy, the movement of production to low-cost, rural sites, started to become a viable option in the second half of the twentieth century as mechanization of tomato harvesting in California, the interstate highway system, the growth of trucking, and deregulation changed the economics of the food-processing industry. For Campbell, this strategy began on a limited basis in the 1950s and culminated in the transfer of the remaining work in Camden to the ultramodern plant in Maxton, North Carolina, in 1990.

Campbell's strategies and techniques for keeping down production costs and workers' militancy worked well enough for it to stay in Camden—while remaining highly profitable—for decades, but this was not a one-sided history. Throughout Campbell's long tenure in Camden, workers responded in various ways to company strategies, sometimes gaining the upper hand, sometimes accommodating company wishes, sometimes suffering defeat. For example, when RCA workers were succumbing to company tactics of encouraging multiple, competing unions in the 1940s, Campbell's Camden workers were solidly united with workers at the Campbell plant in Chicago; however, by the end of the decade, Campbell managers joined with the ascendant anticommunist Congress of Industrial Organizations leadership to split Camden workers from their union brothers and sisters in Chicago. Yet most efforts to divide the workers failed. Women working the vegetable inspection tables surreptitiously helped each other subvert the production incentive system. Black and white shop stewards stood up against tyrannical foremen regardless of the workers' race. And the union membership returned a leader (an Italian remembered as "a Martin Luther King" by a black worker) to office by a landslide vote two months after his conviction under the anticommunist provisions of the Taft-Hartley Act.[5]

The Campbell experience demonstrates that many strategies of late-twentieth-century capitalism had precursors earlier in the century. Many components of Campbell's strategy, surprisingly, are as typical of today's neoliberal globalizing economy as was RCA's escape to a Mexican export-processing zone. The Campbell Soup Company made heavy use of contingent labor, increasing its workforce by 50 percent during tomato harvest season, then laying these workers off eight weeks later, just as multinational corporations today hire various types of nonstandard workers to handle specific tasks and add to flexibility. Campbell Soup was an eager advocate of transnational labor migration, importing thousands of workers from Puerto Rico, Mexico, and the English-speaking Caribbean to fill certain functions, just as immigrants fill niches in today's "global cities." The corporation used migrants in another way, similar to today's clothing retailers who deny any responsibility for the working conditions of sweatshop laborers officially employed by subcontractors. The firm paid suppliers prices that left them little choice but to exploit largely immigrant farm laborers to the furthest limits possible. The company constantly revolutionized production methods, employing technology and "scientific management" techniques to replace workers and lower costs, and even experimented with practices remarkably similar to many of the features of today's "lean production." Over time, Campbell implemented a few limited paternalistic elements to its dealings with its workers but mostly resorted to an adversarial position toward the unions they organized. The firm had a reputation, especially from the 1930s through the 1960s, as the most antiunion of Camden's "Big Three" employers, foreshadowing the "get-tough" policies toward unions common in the 1980s and 1990s. Finally, when structural changes in the food supply system finally made it possible, Campbell joined RCA in abandoning Camden as a production site, over a century after Joseph Campbell began the company in that city, the last act in the deindustrialization of Camden. The fact that it resisted relocating production for so long makes Campbell Soup an excellent case for studying the other techniques available to corporations, and its long history may hold important lessons about the consequences of such strategies.

Of course, the story of the Campbell Soup Company is complicated by many other factors beyond those highlighted here. These include the family ownership of the company (it was privately held until 1954, and the Dorrance family continued to hold a majority of the stock well into the 1990s). The types of production at Campbell—a combination of continuous-process but mostly small-batch production—differed from the assembly work at RCA. And, perhaps most important, this company and its employees worked out their history within the ever-changing context of an American and global capitalism that transcended even the dynamics of the food-processing industry, while external events (such as World War II) had enormous impacts on that history. Yet even in the heyday of the Campbell Soup Company its experience was far from unique among American businesses. All companies sought to keep production costs low, and the strategies depicted in this book were duplicated, to varying degrees, across the American corporate landscape.

As with most firms in America, the organization of production at Campbell was tied in a complex manner to assumptions and expectations about gender, race, and ethnicity. In the early decades of the twentieth century Campbell was the primary local employer of recent immigrants from southern and eastern Europe—mostly Italians. Long before other major manufacturers in Camden hired nonwhite workers, Campbell employed African Americans and Puerto Ricans. But the company placed African Americans in only certain jobs and departments, and brought in Puerto Ricans, initially, only during the peak processing months. Similarly, most jobs were strictly gender-segregated, with women earning significantly less than men. Furthermore, the contingent nature of work at Campbell left most employees unsure of the stability of their jobs: the company's boast that it was able to "offer year-round employment to three-quarters of its employees" was not very reassuring to its workers.[6]

The Campbell Soup Company tapped into the same labor markets used by truck farmers in New Jersey (and more generally in Atlantic coastal agriculture) for virtually all of its recruitment efforts. It thus played a critical role as a transition point for agricultural laborers moving into the industrial sector. Historian Cindy Hahamovitch has documented the growth of a migrant stream of farmworkers along the Atlantic seaboard, starting in 1870. She found that this agricultural proletariat drew from Italians in South Jersey and Philadelphia and African Americans from the upper South; later it included African Americans from the lower South, Puerto Ricans, Jamaicans and other Caribbeans, and even German prisoners of war during World War II. Remarkably, Campbell used exactly the same groups to fill its factories.[7]

In addition to segmentation of the workforce, automation and continuous redesign of the work process were central premises of the Campbell strategy to remain at its original site. For decades the company relied on the "Bedaux system," a variant of Taylorism developed by Charles Bedaux (later a Nazi collaborator). Throughout their existence, Campbell's Camden plants operated on a combination of hourly rates and wage incentive premiums for exceeding targets.

The men and women who processed the tomatoes and chickens, cooked the soup, manufactured the cans, and did the myriad other tasks in the Campbell enterprise did not passively accept the company's strategies. For the most part they performed their often difficult jobs well and adapted to management's demands and experiments, but they also helped each other circumvent management plans, organized unions, went on strike, conducted unauthorized slowdowns, and in some cases sued the company. Alongside militant and sometimes violent strikes at Camden's other large companies, Campbell's workers staged walkouts in the mid-1930s, but they won their first union contract only in 1940. Through the next decade they built a remarkably democratic local of the left-leaning United Cannery, Agricultural, Packing and Allied Workers of America (later renamed the Food, Tobacco, and Agricultural Workers, or FTA). A vicious red-baiting campaign destroyed the FTA, but the United Packinghouse Workers of America (UPWA) local that took the place of the FTA local in the 1950s had many of the same activists as members and a similar dedication to racial and gender equality and unity.

Despite continuous automation and rationalization of work processes, increasing demand for its products kept from four to five thousand workers employed year-round at Campbell's Camden plants from the late 1930s through the 1950s. However, by the end of the 1960s, Campbell's automation, early attempts at "lean production," and the growth of plants elsewhere led to a decline in the number employed to about three thousand. The reductions continued steadily through 1986, when management announced a three-year, thirty-seven-million-dollar modernization program for Camden that would further reduce the number of workers from 1,700 to 1,250 though, the company promised, "over the long term, the size of the workforce at the plant may return to and even exceed its [then] present level." Nevertheless, three years later the announcement came that all production would cease the following year in Camden, with the work moving to newer plants such as the highly automated ones in Paris, Texas, and Maxton, North Carolina (see table 1).[8]

Table 1. Year-Round Production Employees, Campbell Soup Company, Camden, New Jersey, Plants

	1886	1934	1942	1946	1950	1958	1962	1968	1979	1986	1990
Male			2450	2547		2100		1941			
Female			1554	2284		2000		740			
Total	25	2400	4004	4831	5000	4100	3000	2681	1850	1250	0

Sources:

1886: Mary B. Sim, *History of Commercial Canning in New Jersey* (Trenton: New Jersey Agricultural Society, 1951).

1934: "Dorrance Defines Issues in Strike," *Evening Bulletin* (Philadelphia), April 6, 1934.

1942–1946: U.S. Department of Labor, Mediation and Conciliation Service Records.

1950: "Campbell Union OKs New Pact," *Philadelphia Inquirer,* March 21, 1950.

1958: Minutes of Canning Conference, May 18, 1958, UPWA Papers.

1962: Douglas Bedell, "Camden: A Case Study in Urban Economic Problems, *Evening Bulletin* (Philadelphia), July 8, 1962.

1968: "Campbell Soup—Camden," January 17, 1968, AMC Papers.

1979: Eileen Stillwell, "Campbell Cans 300 Employees," *Evening Bulletin* (Philadelphia), April 21, 1979.

1986: Campbell Soup Company, press release, January 27, 1986, *PR Newswire,* retrieved August 10, 2008 from Lexis-Nexis.

Note: Some sources did not break numbers down by gender; only a total is given in these cases.

Scholars, journalists, and activists have warned about the strategies and effects of neoliberal capitalism at the beginning of the twenty-first century, including not only the globalization of production but also the rise of unstable, contingent work, the growth of "lean production" and other methods that intensify work, and the increasing use of low-paid immigrants to fill various niches in the economy.[9] Often, however, these analyses have lacked any historical depth—they seem to imply that these features of the early twenty-first century are entirely novel. Cowie's *Capital Moves* has demonstrated that plant shutdowns and moves to cheap labor areas were already a common corporate strategy before World War II. This book expands the examination of the historical precedents of neoliberal capital's strategies to look at the full range of those strategies—not just capital mobility—and, just as important, to uncover the varieties of labor's responses and evaluate their relative effectiveness.

The impacts of recent corporate strategies have led some to conclude that the world of the new millennium is being transformed by the "manic logic of global capitalism." Prime among the helpless victims of globalization and post-Fordism, in this view, is labor. Many proponents of neoliberalism, and even some leftists, emphasize the weakness of labor resulting, apparently inevitably, from trends in the global economy since at least the 1970s. Other scholars and activists, however, see the mobility of capital and the changes in production characteristic of post-Fordism as far more complex and contingent, and they challenge the notion that labor's current weak state is predetermined. These alternative approaches revitalize the project of studying the full range of capitalist strategies vis-à-vis labor and reject the inevitability of labor's decline, instead proposing questions about which strategies on the part of workers are most successful in countering capital's hegemony.[10] In the case of Campbell, the relative success its workers had in countering corporate strategies during the militant and united social-unionist period of 1940 to 1968, and their relative failure later may provide evidence on the likely effectiveness of alternative labor strategies today.

The structure of this book is basically chronological; such an organization most clearly reflects the historical and dialectical development of the company and its workforce. However, the four dominant management strategies—continuous production redesign; the use of contingent labor and workforce segmentation; antiunionism and anticommunism; and movement of production—took on varying levels of importance over the course of this history. Certain chapters will thus go into more depth on one or another of these strategies.

Chapter 1 sets the context for the rest of the book. Critical features of the firm, from its founding in 1869 through its almost total dominance of the industry by the 1930s, included the invention (or at least the first mass marketing) of condensed soup, the pioneering use of advertising, the division of the workforce into permanent and seasonal sectors, and the introduction of the Bedaux system of scientific management in 1927.

The next three chapters, which carry the history of the Camden plants from the mid-1930s through the mid-1950s, have much in common, but each focuses on a different management strategy. Chapter 2 counterposes Campbell's attempt to wrest complete control of the shop floor, through the use of scientific management, mechanization, and the old-fashioned "drive system," with workers' efforts to resist this move by organizing a union. World War II, the period of chapter 3, pushed the company to cast its net ever wider to find recruits for its low-wage, and especially its seasonal, workforce. A massive campaign to bring in workers from Puerto Rico (imported with help from the War Manpower Commission) and elsewhere, and the union's demands that the company drop its ban on hiring black women, led to a labor force more diverse than ever, with important implications for both company and union. Company, government, and a union splinter group's attempts to break the Left-led union in the late 1940s and early 1950s (the period for chapter 4) bring into sharp relief the antiunion and anticommunist strategies that were always present at Campbell. The company's failure to separate the Camden workers from their union and its leadership demonstrates the other side of this complex period. Local 80 navigated the turbulent times remarkably well, affiliating with the antiracist UPWA after its national Communist-led union was destroyed.

The man who brought together all of Campbell's production strategies during his presidency of the company from 1953 to 1972 was William Beverly Murphy (1907–1994). Chapter 5 explores the period during which this hard-nosed anticommunist expanded the company's efforts to consolidate control of production and fought the inclusion of an antidiscrimination clause in the union contract, while building new plants in the South and in rural Ohio. Chapter 6 examines the pivotal event in the history of company-union relations: the 1968 strike. Unions at all Campbell plants, in an unprecedented experiment in unity, waited until the start of tomato season, then all struck together, with the goal of winning coordinated bargaining and a common contract expiration date. Unfortunately for the union, that summer also saw the demise of the UPWA and its merger into the conservative Amalgamated Meat Cutters (AMC). The weakened union front was no match for the unyielding stance of Murphy, and the ensuing period witnessed a shift in Local 80's orientation from militant social unionism to a business unionism focused on maintaining wages and benefits.

The final two chapters deal with the period in which changes in transportation, demographics, and food-processing technology made it possible, finally, for the Campbell Soup Company to consider moving production out of Camden. With divided and increasingly ineffective unions, the company was free to experiment with newer and better ways to control production and replace workers with machines, and then to abandon Campbell's original soup plant in 1990. Though some union activists in Camden and Mexican migrants in the Farm Labor Organizing Committee continued to challenge the company, the national AMC merged into the even less assertive United Food and Commercial Workers. In spite of promises to the contrary, Campbell finally joined RCA and Camden's other industries, imploding Plant No. 1 in 1991 and moving production to automated plants in the low-wage South, as incoming president David Johnson proclaimed a new era of higher profits and more cost cutting. However, the shutdown did not herald uninterrupted smooth sailing for the company. In October 2001, seven hundred workers at the Paris, Texas, plant walked off their jobs and the company responded with a lockout; this dispute was resolved, but it demonstrated that the conflict between the corporation and the soup makers continues.

One final word about what *Condensed Capitalism* is and is not. This book is an exploration in political economy that takes the form of a business history and a labor history. It uses the lens of one important company to get at questions of the relationship of capital and labor, the changes both have undergone throughout the twentieth century, and the strategies they have used to accomplish their goals. Though the people and the stories that emerge in this exploration are important in their own right and are often fascinating, this is not an ethnographic study nor a social history of Camden (nor, as mentioned earlier, an analysis of Campbell's marketing and distribution innovations). Others have produced or embarked on such projects, and many more are waiting to be written. One essential work that must be mentioned is Howard Gillette's *Camden after the Fall*. This insightful exposition of the transformation of Camden from industrial powerhouse to defeated city must be read to understand the context of Campbell's experience.[11]

For Campbell's former workers in Camden, the story did not end on a bright note. But the food products they made, the families they raised, and the communities they built have become a deep-rooted part of the American landscape. Even more important for later generations, their trials, tribulations, and victories hold crucial lessons for how working people can confront global capital and, sometimes, win.

CHAPTER 1

Making Campbell's Soup

Camden, 1869–1935

"Campbelltown: A Foretaste of Industrial Utopia": thus did the Philadelphia *North American* introduce its readers in 1915 to the "model workman's colony" where John T. Dorrance planned to move production of his famous Campbell's soups. Campbelltown was never built, and Campbell's main production facilities remained in the city of the company's birth, Camden, New Jersey, until they vanished in a spectacular planned implosion in 1991. Yet the motivations behind the imagined model town, despite the sudden decision to abandon it, reveal much about the core business philosophy of Dorrance and his successors.[1]

In many ways, the idea of Campbelltown was a radical departure for the Joseph Campbell Company. Even twenty years later, the company had made only the feeblest attempts at paternalism, and *Fortune* magazine considered its philosophy "the purest laissez faire." But in 1915 the Progressive impulse attracted even Campbell president Dorrance during a visit to Britain. Inspired by Port Sunlight, the Lever Brothers' model workers' town in northwest England, he returned to Camden fired with an idea that would solve many of the problems unleashed by the remarkably rapid growth of the industry launched by his "invention" of condensed soup in 1897. The unplanned proliferation of buildings in Camden to handle the increases in production and the improvised access to rail and marine transport were obstacles that a planned facility would eliminate. Further, he believed, the workers in the model town four miles south of Camden on the Delaware River would be rescued from the "depressing city," and the refreshing air and recreational opportunities would make for contented employees (and, no doubt, ones less susceptible to the lures of unionism).[2]

The special attraction of the Campbelltown idea to Dorrance, however, lay in its potential to lower production costs through extracting greater productivity from its workers. The Joseph Campbell Company had pushed its way into a relatively secure niche in American industry by innovative use of advertising for a product that consumers did not previously realize they needed. The cornerstones of its marketing campaign were product quality and low cost—for decades the price of a can of Campbell's soup remained at ten cents. So strong was management's commitment to this price that company executives allegedly "knew that the psychological effect of raising their prices to 11 cents a can would prove disastrous to their business. So they decided to keep the price fixed at a dime and cut down expenses somewhere else." This "somewhere else," according to the latest tenets of scientific management, could be found in more rational direction of the workforce, more efficient design of production facilities, and increased use of technology to mechanize operations. Even the workers themselves could be made more productive. According to the calculus of Dorrance, the congested, saloon-filled streets of Camden had a measurable impact on the company's bottom line: "I figure that drink weakens a man's efficiency 10 per cent; and we are moving to Campbelltown soon because we want added efficiency."[3]

Dorrance's short-lived dream, had he carried through with it, might have provided a solution to most of the problems he was encountering in controlling production in a company rapidly advancing into the forefront of America's food industry, and Dorrance wanted to control every facet of producing Campbell's soups. To eliminate the problem of unreliable and innumerable suppliers of tomatoes and other ingredients, Campbelltown would have surrounded its factory and workers' homes with model farms turning out controlled quantities of consistently high quality ingredients. In place of the jumble of multistory buildings in Camden whose labyrinthine transport devices were subject to frequent breakdowns, the new plant would have been based on a radically new design: "All manufacturing floors will be on the same level, so constructed that the raw material will come in at one end and the filled cans will go out at the other." Prophetically, the ultramodern Maxton, North Carolina, plant that replaced the six-story Camden plant seventy-five years later would utilize exactly this plan.[4]

𝒮 The Creation of an Industry

In 1869, little of the company's remarkable future would have been obvious to anyone, including Joseph Campbell and Abraham Anderson. Anderson, a tinsmith, had opened a small cannery in 1862. His partnership seven years later with Joseph Campbell, a purchasing agent for a produce wholesaler, formed the basis for one of the many companies turning Camden into an industrial powerhouse. The transformation of the Village of Camden of the early nineteenth century into a city of twenty thousand by 1870 was due largely to industrial growth and its fortuitous location just across the Delaware River from Philadelphia. The industrialization of Camden proceeded at an even faster pace during the final decades of the nineteenth century and the beginning of the twentieth, with the establishment of many factories at the forefront of American industry, including Victor Talking Machines and New York Shipbuilding. The Camden County Chamber of Commerce went so far as to claim that Camden was, by 1931, "truly New Jersey's most highly industrialized city and it leads the entire Nation in the proportion of its population engaged in industry."[5]

Though the late nineteenth century was a time of explosive growth for American manufacturing as a whole, with production increasing sixfold between 1859 and 1899, food industries grew a remarkable fifteenfold during the same period. As the population of the United States urbanized, an increasing number of food-processing functions moved off the farms and out of the consumer household. Furthermore, whole new categories of food products were created. Nicolas Appert's invention of a method to preserve food for Napoleon Bonaparte's armies gave birth to the canning industry, and the American Civil War created a demand that propelled the industry forward in the United States. The firms that emerged as the best-known American canning companies—Campbell's and H. J. Heinz—were both founded in the aftermath of the war in 1869.[6]

Anderson sold his share in the new Camden business to Campbell in 1873, and the last association of the Campbell family with the company ended in 1900 with the death of Joseph Campbell, but an earlier reorganization of the partnership in 1882 brought in Arthur Dorrance, whose family would continue to play a leading role in the company into the 1990s. The most well known product of the Joseph Campbell Company was its canned South Jersey "beefsteak tomatoes," but it also sold a wide variety of other products, including ketchup, mincemeat, and preserves. South Jersey began acquiring its reputation as the best location for the cultivation of tomatoes in the 1840s, as its climate and soil proved to be ideal for this relatively recent addition to the American diet. The demand brought on by the Civil War persuaded more growers and canners in the area to specialize in tomatoes, and new varieties were developed that were better suited to canning. Very quickly South Jersey became the top tomato-growing region in the nation. Though canners in the area soon came to specialize in tomato products, their product lines were extensive. The small market for canned soup was dominated by the Franco-American and Huckins companies, which produced ready-to-eat varieties selling for an expensive thirty-five cents per bulky thirty-two-ounce can, though Campbell also sold a small amount of ready-to-eat tomato soup.[7]

Arthur Dorrance succeeded Joseph Campbell as president of the firm then known as the Joseph Campbell Preserve Company in 1894, and three years later he hired his nephew, John T. Dorrance, allegedly with some reluctance, to set up a laboratory, on the condition that his nephew fit out the lab at his own expense. Much has been made of the fact that the younger Dorrance, just returned from the University of Göttingen with a Ph.D. in chemistry, was paid only $7.50 per week, but as the scion of a wealthy family he was hardly concerned by the size of his salary. In any case, he set about with a passion to revolutionize the way soup was manufactured, sold, and consumed in the United States. His central concept—"the only basic idea that anyone in the Campbell Soup Co. ever had," according to a 1935 *Fortune* magazine article—was to remove most of the water from canned soups. This process drastically reduced the amount of water the company needed to ship around the country, and housewives could reconstitute the soup in their own kitchens simply by adding a can of water. Condensing soup may not, however, have been as original an idea as *Fortune* and the company maintained. According to food historian Andrew F. Smith, Joseph Campbell's original partner (and later competitor) Abraham Anderson was producing several varieties of "concentrated soup" at the time of Dorrance's "invention," and the Campbell company was likely working on condensing soups even before Dorrance arrived. Regardless of the provenance of the idea, the reduced shipping and warehousing costs enabled the company to sell ten-and-one-half ounce cans of condensed soup for ten cents. This the company did, and by 1900 Campbell soups were awarded a Gold Medallion at the Paris Exposition, and John T. Dorrance, at the age of twenty-seven, was elected a director.[8]

Dorrance was born in 1873 in Bristol, Pennsylvania, the grandson of John Barnes Dorrance. The elder Dorrance had amassed a fortune before the Civil War in flour mills, lumber, shipping, and railroads. His illustrious career as owner of Bristol Mills was capped by the construction of the Dorrance Mansion, completed in 1863, its "elegant style represent[ing] the lavish life of the early Victorian industrialists making Bristol their home."[9] His son Arthur continued the family's tradition of investing in new businesses with high growth potentials when he became a partner in the Joseph Campbell Company. Arthur's brother John, however, hoped for a more genteel life for his offspring. He sent his son—John T. Dorrance—to Rugby Academy and the Massachusetts Institute of Technology, and was pleased when Cornell University and Bryn Mawr College attempted to recruit him on his return from Göttingen. Though the father was disappointed when his son went to work in Camden, John T. Dorrance quickly demonstrated brilliant business acumen.[10] Cornell may have lost a potential chemistry professor, but the university did ironically provide a key ingredient for the construction of the future consumer icon: the famous red-and-white colors for the soup-can labels. While company executives were mulling over label designs for their new product, company treasurer Heberton Williams attended a University of Pennsylvania–Cornell football game. Impressed by Cornell's smart red-and-white uniforms, he suggested that Campbell adopt the same colors. In January 1898 the first of the legendary red-and-white soup cans began rolling out of the Camden factory.[11]

Though the idea of condensing soups was essential to the future success of the firm, the fledgling soup company needed next to do something even more challenging: create a market. Combined sales of canned soups for all companies totaled a mere one million cans per year at the end of the nineteenth century. Part of the problem was that soup was not an important part of the American diet, and most of the soup that was eaten was generally prepared by women in their own kitchens, not bought in stores. Campbell undertook a pioneering advertising campaign, first on cards in streetcars, then in magazines and newspapers. In some of the early advertisements, the company attempted to create and encourage insecurities in women about their roles as mothers and homemakers in a changing environment of modernity, a predicament that could be at least partially ameliorated by the purchase and use of Campbell's soups. In 1904 the company introduced the "Campbell Kids," who quickly became the firm's ubiquitous mascots. Historian Susan Strasser has demonstrated how the new mass-production, mass-distribution companies of the late nineteenth and early twentieth centuries began to convert "a population used to homemade products and unbranded merchandise... into a national market for standardized, advertised brand-name goods," often by making people want things that they did not previously realize they needed. Campbell was an early master at this enterprise. The firm quickly became the archetypal example of a brand-name consumer-products company. Unlike its competitor, H. J. Heinz, which maintained a large sales force, Campbell relied almost entirely on appealing directly to the consumer through extensive advertising and, in effect, virtually ignoring middlemen and retailers. Campbell's soup, in fact, became "the most highly advertised *single* food product" in the United States. Through its early marketing campaigns, the Campbell's Soup brand became so well-known and trusted that no grocers could afford not to carry the renowned red-and-white cans. By 1904, Campbell alone was selling sixteen million cans of soup.[12]

The company fell more and more under the control of Dr. Dorrance in the ensuing years. He became general manager in 1910, and in 1914 succeeded his retiring uncle as president. He then quickly moved to sharpen the focus of the company to condensed soups, closing down production of preserves and other distractions. In 1915, while contemplating the ambitious move of the entire operation to his "industrial utopia" of Campbelltown, he bought up all the outstanding shares of company stock he could. Two weeks after the *North American* article on Campbelltown appeared, his uncle sold him all his remaining stock and John T. Dorrance became sole owner of the Joseph Campbell Company. Now able to control every aspect of the company's production, marketing, and future direction, he quietly abandoned his plans for Campbelltown (though he never revealed his reasons) but did not relinquish the objective of turning his company into a scientifically run enterprise, with every element running smoothly under his expert guidance.[13] Over the next several decades, Campbell Soup Company (the name adopted in 1922) financed its way to the top echelons of America's corporations solely through its own earnings (as did Henry Ford's motor company), rarely becoming indebted to anyone or anything outside the control of the Dorrance family.

Though Dorrance led Campbell's rise to its position as one of Camden's "Big Three" industries—along with RCA and New York Shipbuilding—he and the company remained curiously aloof from the civic activity that the city's other business leaders enthusiastically took up. RCA's Eldridge Johnson joined retail, real estate, and banking executives in forming the Greater Camden Movement (GCM), Camden's experiment in business-friendly Progressive Era reform. In another installment in the city's quest to escape from the shadow of Philadelphia, they promoted good government, led patriotic organizations during World War I, and campaigned to build the world-class Walt Whitman Hotel (in 1925) to provide a proper home for business meetings and visiting executives. The GCM's greatest achievement was the construction of the Delaware River Bridge in 1926 (later renamed the Benjamin Franklin Bridge) linking Camden and Philadelphia. Promoters claimed the bridge would lead to further growth for Camden and pave the way for the city's ascendance into the first rank of American cities. For a few years the predictions seemed to be coming true. The million-dollar Stanley Theater opened the same year as the bridge, followed by several major department stores and some new manufacturing enterprises. Other consequences, such as the severing of North Camden from the rest of the city and the newfound ability of South Jersey suburbanites to speed past Camden on their way to Philadelphia would only later begin to raise questions about the impact of the bridge for Camden's future. Yet throughout this swirl of activity, Dorrance avoided the boosterism of his fellow industrialists and kept his focus single-mindedly on making soup and building his company.

🐌 Making Soup

The rapid growth of the market for canned soup demanded massive expansion of soup production in Camden. Dorrance tackled this task in his accustomed systematic manner, but the nature of soup production and the way the business grew resulted initially in a curious mix of mass-production practices, creative processing techniques, and the most rudimentary manual labor. Dorrance's management methods were similarly an eclectic combination of classic nineteenth-century hard-driving factory management practices, the latest "scientific management" fads, and even some innovations in production that were remarkably similar to "lean production"—the Holy Grail of global manufacturing philosophy launched by Japanese automobile makers much later in the century.

The Campbell factory spread out from its original location on Front Street near Market Street in Camden to a hodgepodge of interconnected buildings covering three large city blocks by the first decades of the twentieth century. "Plant No. 1"—the term applied to the three-block agglomeration—remained the largest production site for Campbell Soup through the 1980s. An observer walking through the plant in 1990 (just before the implosion of the plant) reported that the nineteen buildings still standing were so interconnected that, due to the removal of many interior walls, "it is hard to discern where one building ends and the other begins."[14]

Despite these changes over the years, the manufacturing model for Plant No. 1 (and for all early Campbell plants) remained that of a simple gristmill. First, raw ingredients were transported to the top floors of the plant. As each step in the manufacturing process was completed, gravity transports carried

FIGURE 2.   Conveyor belt carrying tomatoes into Campbell Soup plant.
Temple University Libraries, Urban Archives, Philadelphia, Pennsylvania.

the partially processed product down to the next level until, on the ground floor, the canned and labeled soup was packaged for shipment. Campbell workers turned raw ingredients into finished products in three main stages: ingredient preparation and inspection, blending, and, finally, can filling and processing. This manufacturing design remained virtually unchanged from the time of the invention of condensed soup in 1897. What did change was the rationalization of the work process and the replacement of many manual steps by machinery, though a significant proportion of the work remained manual due to difficulties in automating many of the operations. This factor prevented the implementation of a continuous-flow process for any product other than tomato soup and tomato juice, which were manufactured on a semicontinuous-flow basis.[15]

The largest amount of work, employing the biggest segment of the workforce, was taken up in ingredient preparation. This ranged from inspecting, sorting, paring, and dicing vegetables to the poultry disassembly line, where "workers (mostly women)...in fifteen different operations, singed, slashed, skinned, decapitated, and eviscerated" chickens, which were then cooked and deboned by hand.[16]

In the blending step, all ingredients were brought together in 115-gallon kettles (650-gallon kettles for tomato soup). In the final step, cans fed on an overhead system from the Continental Can Company (which had built a plant next door in order to supply Campbell) were filled with the blended soup. Workers then loaded metal baskets with the filled cans and took them to cookers (or retorts) for processing. Workers using machines put labels on the cans, which were then packed in cases and finally dropped through the bottom floor to the warehouse.[17]

Despite constant efforts to streamline soup making, many processes stubbornly resisted automation. Some, such as poultry processing, were still manual operations when Plant No. 1 closed in 1990. Other parts of soup production were automated only after decades of experimentation: eventually electronic eyes replaced women in inspecting rice, and, even later, blending machines took over from men who had used oars to stir large cauldrons of soup.

Ironically, two parts of the soup-making process as practiced at Plant No. 1 recalled some of the original inspirations for mass production as perfected by Henry Ford. According to historian David Hounshell, the developers of the assembly line first conceived of the idea after seeing "disassembly lines" used to butcher beef in Chicago packinghouses. Another Ford engineer was also apparently familiar with one of the few assembly lines in use before Ford's—a can-making line also in Chicago.[18] Though Campbell was never able, in Camden, to move production to the automated ideal of the assembly line, Dorrance went as far as he could in constructing the edifice of his soup-making operation as an "uninterrupted production process" using a complex mix of machines, humans, and conveyance mechanisms. He came close, in his own way, to achieving the objectives of the proponents of the assembly line "by organizing and integrating the various operations." In historian Sigfried

Giedion's classic characterization, "[The assembly line's] ultimate goal is to mold the manufactory into a single tool wherein all the phases of production, all the machines, become one great unit. The time factor plays an important part; for the machines must be regulated to one another."[19] At Campbell, five thousand humans were integral parts of this "one great unit."

Notwithstanding the addition of buildings to Camden's Plant No. 1, which, according to a *Fortune* magazine reporter writing at the time, "proliferate farther back into that depressing city almost every year," the exponential growth of the condensed soup market and the costs of transporting the finished product to consumers across the country pushed the company to begin opening new plants. The first new plant was also in Camden: Plant No. 2 on the waterfront went into operation on a seasonal basis in 1928, to handle the processing of tomatoes and a few other seasonal vegetables. Its construction was part of a huge expansion campaign; at its conclusion, operations at Campbell Soup Company required one-third of the entire water supply of the city of Camden. The next year Campbell constructed a large plant in Chicago to supply its growing Midwest market. When a tariff hike in 1930 made shipment of food products to Canada unprofitable, the company opened a small plant in Ontario in 1931, Campbell's first venture outside the United States. Yet Camden remained the center for most soup production for the next several decades.[20]

🐚 The Soup Makers

Two overarching requirements determined much about the workforce at Campbell Soup Company from the very beginning through the shutdown of the Camden plants. First, the low-cost production that would be a hallmark of the company demanded a low-cost yet productive labor force; second, the highly seasonal nature of soup production depended on the seasonal availability of a supplementary labor pool. These conditions resulted early on in Campbell's reputation as the lowest paid and least desirable of Camden's large employers. Further, some longtime city residents came to blame many of the city's problems, such as crime, poverty, and overcrowded housing, on Campbell for attracting African Americans and, especially, immigrants—initially from Italy, and later from Puerto Rico.[21]

Camden's business leaders extolled the city's "contented industries" and its solidly "American" workforce, advertising the fact that over 82 percent of city residents were native born and that 93 percent were white. Campbell Soup president Dorrance proclaimed Camden an "excellent labor market," yet for the most part his company filled its requirements for production workers from groups outside this preferred circle.[22] By the 1920s most employees were immigrants or the children of immigrants, and the lowest jobs were filled by African American men. In 1935 journalist Martha Gellhorn reported that at Campbell Soup, "most of the labor here is Italian, Polish, or very illiterate negro."[23]

In the 1920s and 1930s the largest number of production employees came from the Italian community that spread out south of the plant for a mile and a half, "all the way from Federal Street to Sacred Heart [Catholic Church]."[24] By 1930 Italians constituted the largest immigrant group in New Jersey, and the census that year recorded 5,508 Italian-born residents in Camden and many more children of immigrants. On almost every block throughout this section, people of all ages worked at Campbell Soup (as well as at New York Shipbuilding, RCA, and dozens of other workplaces).[25] In many families more than one member worked at the soup plant. Joseph Gallo's father started working at Campbell in 1907, four years after arriving in the United States, and Joseph followed in his footsteps years later; high school student Johnny Tisa worked there during tomato seasons while in school, joining his mother, Maria Tisa, who was a lifelong worker on the chicken line. Every morning hundreds of workers, mostly women, walked up Third Street to both Campbell plants.

Well over half of Campbell's production workers in the 1920s and 1930s were women. Exploiting gender stereotypes that saw food processing as women's domain, the company hired only women for most of its low-paying food preparation positions. Further, "inasmuch as Camden was then a mechanized northeastern industrial city employing mostly men in such labor-intensive industries as . . . shipbuilding and radio-making, the Campbell Soup Company was able to take advantage of an available (and undoubtedly cheap) female labor force."[26] Despite their numerical dominance in the plant, most women were limited to certain lower-paying jobs. Most worked in the labor-intensive areas of food preparation, sorting, and inspection. Inexplicably, some much heavier jobs were also designated as women's work, such as certain jobs on the can line and in a few other classifications. Notably, Campbell had another gendered category of worker: a different set of well-defined jobs was open to "boys," males up to the age of twenty-one, who were paid much less than "men" were, but a couple cents above what women were making.

The most distinctive feature of the workforce at Campbell Soup, however, was that it doubled in size every year at the start of "tomato season" in August, then returned to its year-round number of some four to

FIGURE 3. Lines of trucks loaded with tomatoes waiting to unload their cargoes at Campbell Soup.
Historical Society of Pennsylvania, *Philadelphia Record* Collection, C. James.

five thousand workers in October. The ripe tomatoes Campbell used for its largest-selling product—tomato soup—needed to be processed as soon as they were picked from the vine, and the company devoted herculean efforts each year to completing tomato processing. At the peak of the season, close to one thousand tomato farmers' trucks lined up at the Campbell receiving platforms every day, stretching down Second Street for over nine miles. Most of the trucks came from the hundreds of South Jersey farms contracted to the soup company, though Campbell also bought fresh ingredients from nearby Pennsylvania farms as well. The entire city of Camden was heavy with the smell of ripe tomatoes, children grabbed tomatoes from the backs of trucks, and, it was said, "the streets ran red" with tomatoes. In addition to doubling its workforce, Campbell required all employees to work seven days each week—twelve hours per day from Monday through Saturday, and five hours on Sundays. In much the same way that "contingent labor" is used at the turn of the twenty-first century, Campbell's use of seasonal labor allowed it to size its workforce to fit its needs at any given point

FIGURE 4.   Women sorting tomatoes at Campbell. Most women employed by the company worked in preparatory operations.
Historical Society of Pennsylvania, *Philadelphia Record* Collection, C. James.

in time, and the presence of large numbers of eager temporary employees played an important disciplinary role in the company's personnel strategies. Tomato-season workers were paid a few cents less than year-round workers, and their employee badges bore a large "T" that immediately differentiated them as temporaries. Yet almost all permanent employees began their career at Campbell Soup as tomato-season temporary workers. At the conclusion of the season, foremen would select a small number of the hardest workers to join the company as permanent employees; some of these workers made the transition only after working a number of seasons as temporaries. The division of the workforce into permanent and seasonal sections went back to the very beginning of the company. In 1895 Campbell provided full-time employment for only twenty-five workers, but the labor force swelled to 300 during tomato season.[27]

The temporary employment route was how Italians first broke into Campbell in large numbers, and it also drew hundreds of African American migrants from the South for two or three months each year. Black men

FIGURE 5. Unloading trucks during tomato season. African American men were hired for these jobs and a few others before World War II.
Historical Society of Pennsylvania, *Philadelphia Record* Collection, C. James.

worked as laborers and in a few other categories but were excluded from most production jobs; a few were hired on as permanent employees, but only as laborers, janitors, or washroom attendants. No black women were hired by Campbell for any type of work through the 1930s, and the limited opportunities for African American men did not extend to the new plant in Chicago. One of the responsibilities of a young management trainee who sat at the front desk there was to inform black applicants that Campbell Soup did not hire African Americans.[28]

The extraordinary labor requirements during tomato season, combined with the low pay offered workers, made the Campbell Soup Company the conduit into industrial employment for many groups excluded from better paying jobs in the Camden and Philadelphia area. In addition to recent immigrants and African Americans, the soup company, especially in tomato season, recruited many others viewed as marginal to the industrial economy, such as housewives and students. High school students who worked there during summers frequently became permanent employees a few years later. The tight integration of Campbell production into the agricultural economy also made it the first step into industry for many recent Italian immigrants in South Jersey and Philadelphia, as well as for African American migrants, who worked as agricultural laborers on the farms of South Jersey.

Jobs at Campbell were not only low-paying and often temporary; they were grueling, hot, noisy, and sometimes dangerous. Even sixty years later, some former employees recall the Campbell plant as a "slave house," where foremen drove workers relentlessly to keep up with production lines. Workers feeding labeling machines rushed to load over a hundred cans per minute all day long, and those in other departments faced similar demands. Leona Laird, a slight 104-pound teenager, had to drag heavy carts loaded with hot, filled soup cans to the retorts for processing. She remembered having to "peel" her work clothes off after a long day's work because sweat made them stick to her body. The heat forced Joe Morrison to change his shirt three or four times a day. The first job for many "boys" and "girls" was rapidly picking up hot filled cans, seven or eight at a time, to load the retort baskets. The flimsy gloves provided by the company did nothing to prevent painful burns and blisters. New employees soon learned from more experienced workers to wrap cardboard around their fingers over the first pair of gloves, then hold the cardboard in place with a second pair. Several areas of the plant were especially notorious for their oppressive heat, and the few large fans the company provided only blew the hot air around.[29]

Another vivid memory of people who worked there was the incessant noise; many workers suffered permanent damage to their hearing. The can line was especially noisy. Thousands of cans collided with machinery, and conveyors made a "ceaseless roar like a tin waterfall."[30] Samuel Calabro, who worked on a canning line, had to shout to communicate with his coworkers because of the racket from cans flying by over their heads. He and several other workers won suits against the company decades later because of significant hearing loss.[31]

A striking number of workers suffered industrial injuries, ranging from fingers cut off in filling machines to burns and scalds from hot cans to back injuries and hernias from lifting heavy loads. In 1927 Louis Spiewak was hired to lift heavy cages all day, though he was rated as a "boy." After suffering a severe hernia he was dismissed from his job. The same year a truck ran over Alos Dapas's leg, preventing him from continuing in his job. The company maintained an on-site medical department, but they could do little for the most tragic injuries. Among other fatalities at Campbell, Edwin Lloyd died a month after an accident at the plant in 1924, and Aubray Claborn survived only a short while after another industrial accident in 1928.[32]

The unremitting pressure to produce took its toll on the lives and health of Campbell workers. Foremen remembered as "slave drivers" pushed workers to their limits, but in the 1920s production employees had few choices other than to comply with the demands of the job or quit. Given the nature of the work and the ready availability of replacements, it is also no surprise that no one seriously considered organizing a union at the plant. But the "drive system" was not the only cog in the wheel that manufactured the massive fortunes of the Dorrance family.[33]

Making Soup Scientifically

Though Dorrance's dreams of total control over the production of Campbell's soups faded along with the blueprints for "Campbelltown" in 1915, his drive to organize every facet of production along scientific lines never abated. In this, in many respects, he was a man of his times. Just across the Delaware River in Philadelphia, Frederick W. Taylor had perfected his "Principles of Scientific Management," which entranced the management of American industry in the early decades of the twentieth century. Even more than most of his counterparts, Dorrance saw himself a scientist as well as a businessman. He had, after all, earned a Ph.D. in chemistry, and he insisted on being addressed as "Dr. Dorrance."[34]

The long process of making Campbell's products began on the farms that raised the tomatoes and other raw ingredients that went into Campbell's soups. While Dorrance was never accused of paternalism toward his workers, it was said that he lavished a "paternalistic care" on the tomato. At his house in Cinnaminson, New Jersey, he devoted 176 acres to developing the perfect tomato for his company's needs, and he and his scientists bred a number of important new varieties. Plants grown from seeds from Cinnaminson were provided to farmers under strict contract to Campbell; the farmers were closely monitored by company inspectors and were forbidden from selling to anyone else.[35]

It was in the Camden plants, however, that Dorrance determined to apply his "scientific" methods most absolutely. He employed a chief inspector to ensure that everything was done according to plan. The chief inspector, keeper of the closely guarded *Formulas and Procedures Book,* tracked any deviations in his weekly "Formula Violations Report" and "Procedure Irregularities Report." Bookkeepers checked expenditures down to the penny every day in every department.[36]

Dorrance was clearly already embarked on organizing production in a structured and "scientific" way when he was approached in the mid-1920s by an industrial consultant pitching the advantages of "scientific management" as represented in the Bedaux system. Dorrance was not immediately convinced, but he studied the system closely and read all the materials from the International Bedaux Company. These materials not only appealed to Dorrance's penchant for the scientific but also described how companies could rapidly implement the Bedaux methods and reap profits almost immediately.[37]

The Bedaux system was unique among the many scientific management systems that sprouted from the initial work of Frederick W. Taylor. It wrapped its instructions, calculations, and methods in pseudo-scientific jargon to bolster its claims of authority and accuracy, yet its relatively quick implementation made it more attractive than Taylor's original schemes, which required long and difficult study of every work process and mandated that each workman be assigned to the particular job for which he was suited. After several meetings, Dorrance decided to give the Bedaux system a try in his Campbell plant in 1927. It was a momentous decision that would play a significant role in the company's efforts to hold down production costs, and in the growth of resistance among the "fowl eviscerators and beef dicers and potato peelers" who would be subject to the system's disciplines.[38]

On the level of theory, the system purported to have solved "the problem of the proper measurement of labor." It discovered this secret in 1911, and used this understanding to construct the "B unit," a metric that gained almost as much notoriety as the system's founder, Charles Bedaux. He defined his unit rather formally: "The Bedaux Unit, or B, is a fraction of a minute of work plus a fraction of a minute of rest, always aggregating unity, but varying in proportions according to the nature of the strain." He illustrated the application of this concept with an example of a task that required 4 minutes of work with a 30 percent allowance for "relaxation." This task would then be worth 5.2 Bs (4 minutes of work plus 1.2 minutes for rest). If a worker performed this task 15 times in an hour, she would have accumulated 78 Bs (15 times 5.2). The basic wage rate was to be given with the expectation of 60 Bs per hour, and a further calculation figured a bonus in proportion to a percentage of the Bs in excess of 60.[39]

This short excursion into the mathematics of the Bedaux system is necessary to introduce a small part of the complexity—and scientific veneer—that confronted both management and labor at Campbell. The vast number of different jobs (due in large part to the thorough rationalization of the production process by Dorrance and his aides) and the daily variation in ingredients made setting consistent B values for each job a monumental and contentious problem. Against the objections of the people who actually did the work Campbell managers insisted that the "rate structure is correct" and was set "on a very scientific basis." After all, according to plant manager R. E. Worden, "There are 17 different variables that we study and take into consideration for the different jobs in our plant."[40]

Yet critics from the beginning had a very different view of the system. British union activist W. F. Watson argued that "Bedaux is no more scientific than any other system":

> After wading through a mass of explanatory literature, couched in scientific terms, accompanied by algebraic equations, charts and graphs that are bewildering, one fails to discover the precise scientific method used to measure human effort and assess relaxation values, nor by what process laws governing strain are applied to ascertain the exact amount of energy expended on a job.[41]

Not only was the theory based on shaky foundations, the implementation of the system was also highly suspect: "'It is a common sight to see a Bedaux...engineer, without any knowledge of the factory operations, solemnly approving or disapproving a time analysis made by a recent graduate engineer who also knows nothing of the work.'"[42]

According to historian Steven Kreis, "By the standards of Taylor...Bedaux was little more than a quack or charlatan."[43] For all the subsequent criticisms of Frederick Taylor, he had been committed to understanding the production process, with the goal of removing the mental component of work from the worker and placing it in the new planning departments of the companies he worked with.[44] Bedaux, on the other hand, dispensed with any efforts to understand and redesign the work process, and got down quickly to the bottom line: lowering costs by speeding up labor, though the whole exercise was, to be sure, wrapped in scientific trappings. Dorrance and his successors, though, were intensely engrossed in continually redesigning the production process, but they saw the Bedaux system as a complementary technique to measure the labor component of each process and maximize output. Charles Bedaux was just as happy to accommodate such an application of his system as he was when textile mills used it simply to implement speedup and the "stretch-out," for his greatest asset was that "he was a master salesman" who brought the "principles of scientific management down to earth" and promised immediate results.[45]

Bedaux's literature claimed that the system's engineers had a "sympathetic understanding of the workers' point of view" and that "labor's ultimate reaction to Bedaux is favorable," though it also warned that "more care should be exercised when the working class is antagonistic."[46] Yet workers from the very beginning attacked the system as little more than a speedup scheme. Joseph Gallo said that in Plant No. 1, "I saw guys working their heads off and didn't make any bonus, the standards were so high." Workers on the "chain gang" had to push one heavy truck with one hand and pull another with the other hand and almost race in order to make the premium. Before Bedaux, twelve men loaded 28,000 cans onto the labeling machine lines; afterward, just five had to load 31,500 cans, with the additional assistance of only the Bedaux incentive system. Philadelphia *Evening Bulletin* reporter Vivian Shirley was amazed at the pace of work she observed in 1932: "'What makes them work so hard?' I asked. Up came that mysterious phrase, the wage incentive system."[47] Resentment against workers who rushed to make their "*B* hour" sometimes led to fights with others who were then held to similar standards. Yet the system sometimes had contrary effects on the workers. Leona Laird could not make her *B* hour on the vegetable preparation line, so women on both sides of her surreptitiously helped her out. Others found means of beating the system in various ways—even changing the meter used to count cans.[48]

One of the most common complaints concerned the complexity of the system. Many workers never knew how much they had to produce to make the premium. The company's Labor Standards Department constantly adjusted rates on some jobs due to variations in materials; for example, one day the Preparation Department might be peeling smaller onions than usual, and another day potatoes might require more paring than on average. Other than for ingredient variations Bedaux rules decreed that the rates could not be changed for a given job—unless the production method changed. This loophole provided managers an easy solution when they wanted to change job ratings. Labor standards engineer Edward Cheeseman recalls going to the Methods Engineering Department to request that they change a process, and in other cases bringing in a new piece of equipment when management was unhappy with a job rating. "Then we would 'restudy' the job" and lower the rate.[49]

Overall, the introduction of Bedaux at Campbell did greatly increase productivity. The results were similar to those at most Bedaux installations: the system brought "increased output and lower unit costs, largely at the expense of the workers' mental and physical health."[50] Until the system's abolition in the final years of the Camden plants, it played a large part in the achievement of low-cost production there. Paradoxically, over many decades it was also the most tenacious grievance and organizing issue for the soup workers.

🐌 *Kaizen* in Camden?

Dorrance was a pragmatic businessman. Though he had a clear goal in mind for his company, he experimented with many different techniques to achieve that goal, and he was not averse to combining practices from quite different schools of management philosophy. Thus his "slave-driver" foremen pushed workers to yield the last ounce of effort in a classic example of the "drive system." At the same time, his industrial engineers were carefully measuring and redesigning each production detail in a massive experiment in "scientific management." But Dorrance's experimentation was not bounded by the well-understood tenets of these schools of "old" and "new" management. Since the late twentieth century another school of management, dubbed "lean production," has become fashionable. Perhaps not surprisingly, a number of Dorrance's innovations foreshadowed important aspects of lean production and coexisted easily with the better-known methods of his time.

Lean production was the term given by some American enthusiasts to the Toyota Production System (TPS) developed in the 1950s by Taiichi Ohno and others in Japan. The popular management literature on lean production and the TPS is vast, and it is impossible to settle on a precise definition that fits every application to which the terms have been applied. At their core is the concept of *kaizen,* or continuous improvement, in which flexibility, just-in-time production, work teams, and close relations with suppliers result in higher productivity and responsiveness to customers. Proponents also claim greater worker satisfaction and empowerment, though critics decry its methods as "management by stress." Here I will point out just a few of the intriguing similarities between the Campbell factory of the 1920s and the "lean" plants of the early twentieth-first century. The purpose is not to claim that the system existed in complete form in Camden eighty years ago, but to highlight Dorrance's unorthodox approach to running his business and to suggest that not everything ostensibly new really is.

"Ruthless Elimination of Waste"

According to Taiichi Ohno, "the basis of the Toyota production system is the absolute elimination of waste." At least twenty years before that system was born, one of Dorrance's cardinal principles of operation was the "ruthless elimination of waste."[51] For both men, "waste" meant anything that did not contribute value to the final marketed product. Ohno was especially concerned with time "wasted" by workers, whether by performing a task inefficiently or waiting for any reason. Dorrance used his Methods Engineering and Labor Standards Departments to remove any slack from work processes, calculate exactly how much effort each job required each minute, and force workers to produce at a rate that ensured they expended that amount of effort and wasted no time.[52]

Low Inventories/Just-in-Time Production

One "pillar" of the Toyota system according to Ohno was just-in-time (JIT) production, which removed the necessity of the "waste" of maintaining excess parts inventories and prevented a glut of final products. The particular nature of most of Campbell's ingredients—the fact that they were perishable—prevented the stockpiling of any inventories of these ingredients that could not be processed immediately. When tomatoes ripened, the Campbell plants worked around the clock to turn them into canned tomato soup (and later tomato juice) before they spoiled. Dorrance was just as determined to avoid the waste of storing massive quantities of canned soup, essentially forcing wholesalers to relieve Campbell of the product by offering a deal they could not refuse. During the eight weeks of tomato season the firm gave its customers two cases of soup free for every ten ordered before September 1, with "the result that by the time the pack is finished, 80 per cent of it is already in the freight cars on its way to the warehouses of wholesalers all over the U.S."[53]

Immediate Detection and Resolution of Problems

Ohno called the other pillar of the TPS "autonomation." His neologism simply referred to machines equipped with detectors that would shut down a machine in the event of a defect, with the intention that workers on the production line would immediately trace the problem to its source and resolve it. The concept also referred to any methods for detecting and resolving problems, including cords that workers could pull to stop the production line in the event of a defect. Workers at Campbell were able to shut down production lines (former employee Leona Laird recalls doing so), but they were not encouraged to do so. However, even in certified lean establishments lines are very rarely shut down; at one of Toyota's premier plants, "every worker can stop the line but the line is almost never stopped." While this is purportedly due to "relentless attention to preventing defects," the system's tendency to expose and magnify failures, as authors and activists Mike Parker and Jane Slaughter point out, may make some workers reluctant to use this power.[54] Beyond worker or machine ability to stop production in the event of a defect, Campbell had other ways to rapidly detect and resolve any problems. Management implemented its maxim that "eternal vigilance is the price of good soup" in its daily tasting ritual. Company managers, including the president, tasted samples of the company's products every day without fail. In the event any soup violated standards of quality or consistency, this "solemn ritual" had "immediate and practical consequences."[55] The problem was immediately traced to its source, any defective product was discarded, and the error was expected never to recur. Thus, rather than accepting some percentage of defective product as "normal" (allegedly 25 percent of mass-production hours were spent in repairing defects), Campbell's management insisted—as much as any advocate of lean production—on "zero defects" and tolerated no deviation from this standard. Dorrance's successor William Beverly Murphy also referred to "errorless work" as one of the core concepts of high productivity.[56]

Continuous Improvement

At the heart of lean production is *kaizen* (Japanese for "continuous improvement"). In the lean plant, it is everyone's duty to continually revolutionize the production process, to lower costs, and to improve product quality. Once an improvement is suggested, accepted, and implemented, the process begins all over again. "Continuous improvement" is also the best short description of the philosophy of Dorrance and his successors. Observers always remarked on Dorrance's single-minded focus on subjecting every detail of production to close examination with the object of eliminating waste and "constant quality improvement." His obsession even extended outside the soup plants; for example, throughout his life he never finished his quest to create a better tomato, leading company scientists in a "ceaseless study to improve tomato breeds."[57]

Work Teams and Job Rotation

Rather than interminably performing the same task all day long, lean production workers rotate jobs, fill in where needed to keep production running smoothly, and in general have a strong commitment to the success of their "team" and ultimately to the company. The degree to which Campbell employees could be better characterized as team members or as isolated individuals varied widely throughout the plants, but the company's high productivity was dependent on a highly flexible workforce whose members were frequently rotated, worked in teams, and were very conscious of their importance to the success of their work groups. Not only was Victor DeStefano acutely aware that his success in earning a sizable incentive bonus, as a label operator, was dependent on the success of his team (operator, assistant, and "packer girl") but he also performed routine repairs on his machine rather that waiting for a mechanic. In true kaizen fashion the company then eliminated the assistant operator position and three other positions in the Labeling Department with a "utility group" whose members could be moved to wherever they were needed in the department throughout their shift. Al Paglione, a "lineman on beans," bragged that he could work "anywhere—on any line," as well as on packing jobs. During the tomato season, beef trimmer Rose Sangarlo worked in the tomato shed and sometimes in the cafeteria, and scaleman Joseph Ambrose put aside his normal job of cutting and weighing pork to unload trucks and dump baskets in the tomato shed. The job with the title of "leader" in almost all Campbell departments was directly analogous to that of Toyota's team leaders, and leaders at the soup company filled in working on the line when needed. When the plant was later unionized, this position was made a union job so that leaders could perform production work, but even foremen often filled in during loosely defined "emergencies." Rather than following the stereotypical mass production role of mindless automatons endlessly repeating the same task, most Campbell employees worked in teams and often rotated job assignments to assure that production would continue flowing smoothly.[58]

Flexibility/Small Batch Production

Rather than the mammoth runs of a single product characteristic of Fordist factories, lean plants typically turn out small batches of multiple models and implement rapid setup and die changes to enable such product flexibility. At Campbell, a normal workday saw numerous product changes, as workers completed production of one soup variety, quickly washed out the cauldrons and other equipment to get ready for the next, and switched to blending and cooking another of Campbell's many soups. In addition to rapid setup, such flexibility also required an adaptable workforce. At Campbell and twenty-first-century lean plants, this meant having both permanent workers who could perform multiple jobs where needed and a pool of contingent workers who could be added as needed.

Relations with Suppliers

In contrast to mass production companies' competitive market-based supplier system, lean companies like Toyota build long-term relationships with their parts suppliers, and both sides share information with each other. Campbell took precisely this approach when dealing with its main raw materials suppliers. The firm sought to engage the farmers who grew its tomatoes and other ingredients in long-term relationships for reasons that went far beyond guaranteeing the soup company a predictable and low price for its raw materials. Campbell itself developed the tomato varieties it wanted at its labs and experimental farms, raised seed plants to produce seeds for some fifty million plants, and then provided these plants to its contracted farmers. It also organized events where its contractors showed off their tomatoes (with the best being awarded prizes by the company) and farmers listened to government and company agricultural experts lecture on the proper way to grow tomatoes. Company inspectors visited contractors' farms throughout the growing season to ensure that farmers were applying proper amounts of fertilizer and pesticide. The company took a similar approach to obtaining the cans in which it packaged virtually all of its products. Campbell arranged with the Continental Can Company to build a facility next door to Plant No. 1 in Camden and later bought out the can-making operation. Long-term supplier relationships, not the free market, characterized the Campbell way of acquiring what it needed.[59]

"Management by Stress"

Most of the characteristics of lean production listed above are accepted by both advocates and opponents of lean practices. But a growing number of academics, labor activists, and workers in lean plants have drawn attention to a less rosy side of the system, captured in their redefinition of the term *kaizen* as "management by stress." Continuous improvement in production methods means that workers cannot rest when they achieve any advance in productivity, but instead must start all over again to discover and eliminate any other "waste" in the time they spend in the production process. And in the TPS, management has an important new ally in enforcing this never-ending quest for zero-defect, high-output production: the employees' fellow workers. In a properly running lean plant, team members have absorbed the ethos of responsibility to their team and the company, and provide help and pressure to any team member not living up to his or her part in ensuring the success of the team. Lean promoters tout their assertion that "most people...will find their jobs more challenging" but admit that "they may find their work more stressful." Less positive are the assessments of those who have experienced lean work on the shop floor and complain of exhaustion, psychological pressure, and high levels of stress.[60] Similar characterizations filled depictions of work by Campbell's soup makers, and company management even seemed to take a perverse pride in the fact that only certain employees could handle the pressures of working there. Many critics of the TPS argue that supervision in lean plants is far more authoritarian and oppressive than is described by promoters who often interview only managers for their studies. One study concluded that "the mutual-interest, worker-centered image of lean production . . . is a myth grafted on to a fundamentally oppressive production system." The distinction between the "drive system" and the lean plant is sometimes clouded in the real world.[61]

Continually Declining Costs/Workforce Reduction

Throughout his influential work on the TPS the system's founder Ohno repeatedly reiterates the motivation for changing to lean methods: "The criterion of all decisions is whether cost reductions can be achieved," as well as the means to accomplish this end: "Manpower must be reduced to trim excess capacity." Unlike later Western advocates of lean production who soft-pedal negative impacts of the system on workers, Ohno was frank: "A vague statement that waste should be eliminated, or that there are too many workers, will not convince anybody. But with the introduction of the Toyota production system, waste can be identified immediately and specifically. In fact, I always say production can be done with half as many workers. . . . At Toyota, we set a new goal—to reduce the number of workers."[62] From John T. Dorrance in the 1920s to William Beverly Murphy in the 1960s, Campbell's chief executives were just as single-mindedly focused on cost reduction. When such efficiencies introduced new production methods or newly mechanized processes, layoffs were often the result. By the final decades of operations in Camden, far larger quantities of food products were leaving the warehouse doors of plants employing far fewer people than had been the case earlier in the century.

When Campbell was faced with labor insurgency in the 1930s, it did not respond by moving production to a place where workers were more docile and costs were low. By that time it had already put into place an alternative strategy to remain a low-cost producer in its home city. Just as with Dorrance's marketing techniques, his approach to production was innovative and unconventional, combining aspects of the classic "drive system," the Bedaux variant of scientific management, and even features of what could be called "lean production."

🎾 The Dorrance Dynasty

Through constant minute attention to efficiency in every aspect of manufacturing, as well as toughly bargained contracts with raw materials suppliers and aggressive and innovative marketing, the Campbell Soup Company generated enormous wealth for John T. Dorrance and the Dorrance family. *Fortune* magazine estimated that, in 1923, the company made a profit of six-tenths of one cent on every can of soup. At the peak of the tomato season, the Camden plants turned out some ten million cans per day. By the 1930s, over a billion cans were produced per year, generating some six million dollars in profits annually.[63]

All these numbers are estimates, because the Campbell Soup Company was privately held. Among all private corporations, only the Ford Motor Company exceeded Campbell in the size of its assets. Unlike Henry Ford, Dorrance was a very private man with, it was said, only two concerns in life: his family and soup. After his one son and three daughters were born he moved his family from their house in the midst of the tomato fields in Cinnaminson (several miles from Camden) to the Woodcrest mansion on Philadelphia's elite Main Line. The Dorrance parties, usually held at the lavish Bellevue-Stratford hotel in Philadelphia, became legendary. Dorrance's daughter Eleanor's debutante ball in 1926 cost him $100,000 and included an orchestra led by jazz luminary Paul Whiteman with singer Bing Crosby. *Fortune* magazine described one Dorrance party at which there were "rare flowers and foliages, and hundreds of live macaws and toucans and cockatoos and parakeets and birds of paradise in cages, and showers of rose petals falling pinkly on the dancers." When Dorrance died unexpectedly in 1930 he left a fortune of $120 million, at that time the second largest estate (after that of Payne Whitney) ever sent to probate in the United States.[64]

Though the inventor (or, at least, champion) of condensed soup was gone, the Dorrance family continued in its ownership and management roles for most of the twentieth century. John Dorrance Jr. was but eleven years old when his father died, though his father's will made clear that an important role was to be reserved for him in the future. The elder Dorrance's four daughters were never considered eligible for running the business; all married into other families at the pinnacle of Philadelphia society, cementing alliances among Philadelphia's leading capitalists. So John's brother Arthur

Dorrance, twenty years his junior, followed him as president in 1930, and he continued in the footsteps and the management philosophy of his brother. The company remained the private property of the Dorrance family.[65]

The year 1930 would be significant in other ways for the Campbell Soup Company beyond the passing of Dorrance. The ambitious expansion campaign was almost completed, and the Bedaux system had taken hold in the plants. More ominously, the United States was just entering the most severe depression in its history, one that would bring not only great economic dislocations but also a vast movement of resistance and organization from within the industrial workforce of the country.

Camden in the Great Depression

The 250th anniversary of Camden County fell in the unfortunate year of 1931. The Chamber of Commerce tried to put the best face on a deteriorating situation in its commemorative history, painting in glowing terms a picture of the "new Camden," the "city of contented industries." Ten months after the stock market crash, local newspaper headlines had assured their readers that "Recovery Is Now General," as Campbell Soup and RCA enlarged their workforces. Yet Camden was descending, along with most other industrial cities, into the worst depths of the Great Depression. Even more than most, Camden was dominated by a handful of large companies; layoffs or shutdowns in any of these had an immediate and devastating impact on the city. Campbell Soup was—relatively, at least—the one exception. It continued to sell its products throughout the Depression, though even canned soup became too expensive for many Americans. Production dropped sharply by 1932, but recovered somewhat by 1935. Campbell continued providing employment for thousands of Camden residents, but the company took advantage of the availability of large numbers of unemployed to speed up and intensify work for those lucky enough to have jobs.[66]

One of the most insightful and heartbreaking accounts of Camden during the Depression appears in a letter of Martha Gellhorn to New Deal administrator Harry Hopkins. Hopkins, the director of the Federal Emergency Relief Administration (FERA), had asked sixteen reporters in the fall of 1933 to investigate conditions and tell him the unvarnished truth: "I just want your own reactions, as an ordinary citizen." Gellhorn's letter summed up the tragedy that was Camden in 1935.[67] Her most striking observation was of the despair of the unemployed who had given up hope of any improvement in their condition. "Young men say, 'We'll never find work.'... This is like

the third year of the war when everything peters out into gray resignation."
A twenty-eight-year-old man said people gave up looking for work after a
few months: "What's the use, you only wear out your only pair of shoes and
then you get so disgusted." The demoralization pushed some people over the
edge; hospitals for mental diseases in Camden County saw their patient loads
increase by over one thousand in three years. Others merely "[sank] into a
resigned bitterness.... 'I generally go to bed around seven at night, because
that way you get the day over with quicker.'"[68]

These impacts on the spirit arose from very real material causes. The lack
of decent clothing led not only to a rise in pneumonia among malnourished
and poorly clothed children but also "[cut] these people...out of any social
life. They don't dare go out, for shame." Camden's housing, "never a thing
of beauty," was now "unspeakable." At one Unemployed Council meeting
that Gellhorn attended,

> the high point of the evening was a prize drawing: chances were a
> penny apiece and the prizes were food: a chicken, a duck, four cans of
> something, and a bushel of potatoes.... These people had somehow
> collected a few pennies... [and] waited with passionate eagerness while
> the chances were read out, to see if they were going to be able to take
> some food home to the family.[69]

The paltry relief provided by the FERA did more to help some private
industries than the residents of Camden, who viewed it "as a mere sop
to starvation." To seasonal industries like Campbell Soup, the FERA provided "a fine labor market," enabling companies to "casually lay people off
knowing they can always get them back when they need them." Campbell,
in fact, was the only company thriving, according to Gellhorn. She was
told the soup company was earning a profit of ten million dollars, but only
by implementing "a grueling speed-up...put[ting] two men on a job that
requires four."[70]

Others backed up Gellhorn's observations about the soup company:

> In the Spring time miles of farm trucks piled high with red toma-
> toes string outside the dingy building, and you get that rich heady
> smell of fruit and vegetables...but a block down the street is the plant
> employment office, and if you don't know what a slave auction block is,
> drop in there sometime and see one. The room is filled with men and
> women who want work, and simply have to have it, and the auctioneer
> knows it, because he comes out and says: "Who'll work for 35 cents

an hour?" and everybody steps forward with upraised hand and says eagerly "I will!" and he looks them over stonily ... and then says, "Well, who'll work for 30 cents an hour?" and again everybody says, "I will," but not so eagerly, because if you say no somebody else will get the job, and you need it, you really need it. And the auctioneer keeps beating the price down ... to 18 cents an hour.[71]

Camden had always been a hardworking town, and for a while the shock of the Depression took people by surprise. But in various pockets of the city people began regaining a sense that they deserved better and started pooling their efforts to fight the effects of the Depression. Laid-off workers started the Unemployed Union of New Jersey, and its president Frank Manning presented a resolution to city commissioners at the end of 1932 pushing for the city to "finance construction of homes to be owned and rented by the city."[72] Those still working at RCA and New York Shipbuilding began to believe they could, to some degree, control their own economic futures, and they organized unions and went on strike. And, in early 1933, workers at the largest soup cannery in the country, for the first time in its history, began talking to each other about the possibility of starting a union.

✄ CHAPTER 2

Bedaux, Discipline, and Radical Unions

The Great Depression provided the opportunity for Arthur Dorrance and the management of Campbell Soup Company to move closer to the complete mastery of production envisioned by his late brother, John T. Dorrance. Behind the Norman Rockwell images in the *Saturday Evening Post*'s Campbell Soup advertisements stood a company that reaped enormous profits by squeezing every penny from the work of its employees. From the hungry thousands of men and women desperate for work in Camden, New Jersey, the company's hiring boss could pick out the most qualified. When these workers entered the soup plants they were shunted into carefully defined positions within the great machine of production. Forced to work at a pace set by men with clipboards and stopwatches, they labored for as long as it took to get the day's work done. The very language of work in the soup plants evoked a world of tight control: "pushers" and "overseers" drove men on the "chain gangs" and women on the prep lines to keep up with the relentless rhythm of production; workers recall some foremen as "slave drivers" and the plant as a "slave house."[1]

Yet at the very moment when widespread unemployment in Camden drove the bargaining power of Campbell workers in the labor marketplace to its lowest point, a remarkable rebellion erupted in 1934, when two thousand men and women struck the soup company and demanded an end to the Bedaux speedup system and a return to pre-Depression wages. Wages and working conditions were a central impetus for the first major strike in Campbell's sixty-five-year history. But other factors also played a crucial role in sparking the revolt. Prime among these was the growing Left-led movement among workers and the unemployed in the nation, and, especially, in the city of Camden and surrounding South Jersey. Workers at the city's other large employers were simultaneously engaged in strikes and other job actions, and the leader of the new Canners' Industrial Union Local 1 was a socialist who had previously led Camden's Unemployed Union. In the truck farms surrounding Camden that supplied canners with tomatoes and other ingredients, leftist organizers and migrant farmworkers were establishing agricultural union locals among the same groups that made up Campbell's workforce, particularly Italian immigrants and African American migrants from the South.[2]

Campbell responded to this threat to its authority and control with a wide range of tactics, ranging from firings of strike leaders to the creation of a company union, and it succeeded, temporarily, in warding off the union challenge. But a renewed organizing drive later in the decade, allied with the innovative and militant United Cannery, Agricultural, Packing, and Allied Workers of America (UCAPAWA), led to victory and the establishment of Local 80, the organization that would represent Campbell workers for fifty years.

Neither union drive succeeded in eliminating the Bedaux system or any of the other components of the company's strategy for controlling how soup was made. However, they did place the issue of control squarely at the center of management attention, and the contestation that ensued over the next decades shaped the contours of the history of Campbell Soup Company and its workers.

Bargaining Power: Marketplace and Workplace

Historical sociologist Giovanni Arrighi has postulated two types of bargaining power possessed by workers: labor marketplace bargaining power and workplace bargaining power. In the absence of any internal or external controls, workers' marketplace bargaining power varies inversely with the size of the labor pool relative to the need for labor; thus, a labor market with a large number of unemployed workers (the "reserve army of the unemployed") corresponds to low bargaining power for workers seeking jobs.

FIGURE 6.   Men queueing up for tomato season jobs, 1939.
Temple University Libraries, Urban Archives, Philadelphia, Pennsylvania.

Skilled workers who are able to limit the size of the labor pool for their occupation through control of entry to the craft can significantly increase their marketplace bargaining power. Workers in relatively unskilled occupations, conversely, have very little power in bargaining with potential employers during times of high unemployment. In such a situation, hiring agents for companies like Campbell were able to choose the strongest and ablest new employees at pay rates barely above subsistence levels.[3]

FIGURE 7. Women waiting to be hired for tomato season jobs, 1939. Before 1942, no African American women were hired by the Campbell Soup Company.
Historical Society of Pennsylvania, *Philadelphia Record* Collection.

As Arrighi points out, however, the new mass-production industries of the early twentieth century that gave rise to giant factories filled with easily replaceable employees were, ironically, acutely susceptible to another kind of power held by their employees in those factories: workplace bargaining power. Since workers were an essential and thoroughly integrated part of the complex structure of mass production, strikes or job actions could have immediate and devastating impacts. In fact, a slowdown or work stoppage in even one critical department of the plant could rapidly bring all production to a halt. Campbell's plants were filled with such integral segments of production. "Boys" unloaded tomatoes from farmers' trucks onto conveyor belts; "boys" and "girls" ceaselessly filled retort baskets with hot, filled cans ready for processing; men on the chain gangs pushed loaded racks from one location to another; and women kept the can lines running at high speed to the filling machines. If work in any one of these stopped, the entire plant very quickly ground to a halt.

Campbell management attacked the potential threat from the growing workplace bargaining power of its labor force by employing all four of its long-term low-cost production strategies. It maintained its rigid segmentation of the workforce into permanent and seasonal sectors and divided jobs among men, women, and "boys." It threatened repeatedly to move production out of troublesome Camden to a more compliant location. But it focused during the 1930s on two of its strategies: wresting control of production from its workers, and forestalling the threat to its monopoly on power from any incipient attempts at unionization.

❧ Scientific Control of Production

Above all, Campbell management sought to consolidate its authority on the shop floor. Its central tactic in this campaign was the Taylorist project of separating the knowledge of production—its "mental" component—from the operation of production. Workers were simply to perform their tasks as instructed. Without this monopoly on the knowledge of production, Dorrance and his managers felt themselves at the mercy of employees they considered lazy or incompetent, as well as "troublemakers" who organized slowdowns or other job actions. With the mental component of manufacture in its possession, Campbell management believed it could understand exactly how much time and labor were required for each of the thousands of steps in the production of canned soup. Once it accomplished this goal, managers would be able to detect any budding problems and replace any "defective" workers. It would also be in position to meet Dorrance's demands in the drive to keep costs low. From each ten-cent can of soup, Dorrance expected six-tenths of a cent in profit. Yet sizable proportions of the total revenue stream were designated for raw materials, marketing, and other costs. His industrial engineers were charged with determining how to split the remaining two and one-half cents per can across the myriad tomato inspectors, butchers, retort operators, and warehousemen with virtually no leeway for errors or unplanned variances.[4]

Starting with John T. Dorrance himself, Campbell's leaders were almost fanatical about delineating and grading every part of every job. The introduction of the Bedaux system in 1927 turned this campaign of categorization into a scientific mission. The procedures book grew into a seven-inch thick tome spread across two volumes that assigned a name and numerical value to every process in the plant. One of the geniuses of the Bedaux system was that, in claiming to have found the true measure of work, it provided a simple method for comparing widely disparate tasks, by assigning each a "B" value. With this number, management could judge whether each worker was performing at the proper pace, for the "average good workman" was expected to turn out 60 Bs per hour, regardless of the job. Thus, the retort operators who cooked canned soup packed in large baskets were allocated 5.1 Bs for each basket of tomato soup. When processing oxtail soup they were credited with 7.8 units per basket, while pepper pot brought 9.7 units. One of the more peculiar of the myriad Labor Standards Bulletins, No. 63, issued on January 1, 1938, assigned values to be earned by workers preparing calves' heads (used in mock turtle soup):

Preparing Calves' Heads

Base Rate	Occupation	Bs/Head
.65	Skinning Face	2.60
.61	Splitting Skull	2.30
.61	Removing Teeth	2.29
.61	Scraping Nostrils	2.36

Std cost/1000 Bs = $10.58

Since the job "Skinning Face" received 2.6 Bs per head, a worker would be expected to process twenty-three heads per hour to reach the minimum 60 Bs. Similarly, those working on "Removing Teeth" needed to process twenty-six heads per hour.[5]

The planning department that Frederick Taylor envisioned as the repository for the "mental component" of production was fully realized at the Campbell Soup Company. A staff of some twenty-five employees (most of whom were trained on the job), supplemented by outside Bedaux consultants, worked to systematize all aspects of soup production. Within the Industrial Engineering Planning Department, Materials Engineering ensured uniformity and quality of raw materials and monitored the waste stream, Methods Engineering designed the work process and pioneered the introduction of technology, and Labor Standards Engineering set the B ratings for every job in the plant.[6]

Despite the questionable foundations of Charles Bedaux's methods—for his consultants never were able to explain how they came up with their numbers beyond some pseudo-scientific hand waving—his metrics were useful in management's battle for control. They also served an important disciplinary role. Hundreds of workers were discharged each month for failure to make their B hours.[7] Further, the "speedup system" (as the Bedaux system was called by some employees) drove workers to push themselves even harder to earn the elusive bonus for output in excess of 60 work units per hour. Observers (and even other workers) were amazed at the relentless pace of the women at the "high-efficiency tables" that the company set aside for the fastest preparatory workers. In another section of the plant, a new hire who was assigned to the line removing meat from cooked chickens could not believe the speed of the women on the line: "They did it so fast!" Each month the company published the names of workers who had achieved the highest *B* hours. In March, 1937, Emili Langelotti turned out an astonishing 110 *B*s per hour, at a time when others were being fired for their inability to reach 60.[8]

The purpose of scientific management has been the subject of debate since Taylor's writings on the subject first appeared. The debate was reopened in the 1970s with the publication of Harry Braverman's seminal *Labor and Monopoly Capital*. Braverman cogently argued that the overarching goal of Taylor and his corporate sponsors was control, not merely an increase in the speed of production or a decrease in production costs. Control was the reason for removing the mental component of the job from the worker. Braverman's insights unleashed a wave of new investigations into the labor process, many of which challenged some of his arguments. Industrial relations scholar Craig Littler has noted that Taylor and Braverman both were concerned primarily with *skilled* work (though, as Taylor's famous story of the laborer Schmidt indicates, it was not his exclusive focus). For skilled jobs, implementation of scientific management meant deskilling, as the jobs were rationalized into their component parts and unskilled or semiskilled workers took over the fragmented jobs that resulted. However, in less skilled mass-production environments like Campbell there was little left to rationalize or "deskill." In these companies, in such industries as textiles and meatpacking, the Bedaux version of scientific management was especially popular. It was almost always introduced with the goal of increasing the speed of production and lowering costs, often by reducing the size of the workforce. Thus, the resistance to Bedaux at Campbell came less from the threat of degraded work than from opposition to speedup and fear of unemployment at the nadir of the Depression.[9]

Though the Bedaux system set the framework within which the Campbell plants functioned, and erected an unbending bar that every worker had to pass in order to hold his or her job, it was not the only disciplinary tool used by Campbell. Especially during the years of low marketplace bargaining power for workers in the 1930s, the company made it clear that it expected strict adherence to work rules, punctuality, and willingness to "help out" above and beyond standard job descriptions. The company presented Gailon Walter Holmes, an African American hired in 1919 to repair crates, as an example for emulation. It pointed out that he was never late to work and that he had "a theory about his success": "I've always tried to do a quality job and carry out instructions to the letter." His efforts were rewarded by promotion to the position of shipper. Beyond following instructions to the letter, all employees were also expected to work until the day's production was completed, not for a fixed eight or ten hours. Harry Nelson described arriving at 7 A.M. when the blending operation started (preparation had begun about two hours earlier): "We'd work until we filled the orders," often until 7 or 8 P.M.[10]

The replacement of labor by machinery was management's preferred solution to the "labor problem," but efforts to automate had reached something of a plateau by the 1930s. Dorrance and his successors had aggressively pushed both rationalization and the application of machinery from the start, and what remained manual—still a large proportion of the process of soup making—stubbornly withstood automation. No machine yet invented was able to pare the widely variable daily influx of potatoes as expertly as the women who performed this task, and mechanical agitators still could not keep the soup in the large blending kettles as evenly dispersed as could experienced men who stirred the soup with large oars. Management never gave up on its attempts to automate almost everything, but there were few significant breakthroughs in the 1930s and little incentive in an era of cheap and plentiful labor. With the lull in new technological advances in this period, the company relied more than ever on rationalization and discipline. Foremen and plant managers employed a harsh, sometimes almost vicious, style of supervision. Sixteen-year-old Leona Laird's first assignment was on the can line. When she could not keep up with the furious pace of the line, she did the unpardonable: she shut down the line. "The boss yelled at me, and the next day they sent me to peel carrots." When foremen, who were dependent on workers' abilities and willingness to cooperate, became a little too soft in the eyes of upper management, they were quickly brought into line. Franklin Williams remembers a "decent foreman" named O'Neill who ran afoul of a plant manager who had a reputation for "terrorizing foremen." "[He] would get up in [O'Neill's] face shaking his finger in his face, you could see O'Neill shaking." When Campbell expanded into Chicago in 1929, opening its first plant outside of Camden, it carried with it its tough management practices. Veronica Kryzan recalled "penitentiary conditions" there, with bosses who even refused to grant workers relief periods to go to the washroom.[11]

Through the use of discipline, rationalization, and scientific management, Dorrance's leadership team was moving forward quite successfully in its consolidation of control of production, especially after the introduction of the Bedaux system in 1927. The Campbell Soup Company was so confident in its ability to succeed, especially in light of its enhanced position in the labor marketplace, that the company did not pursue any of the techniques of welfare capitalism, even before the onset of the Depression. Management wielded the stick, but had little use for the carrot. To be sure, there was a company-sponsored baseball team, but there were no pensions or sick benefits: "[Campbell's] philosophy reduces to the purest laissez faire."[12] The company had no need for frills to encourage its employees to follow the Campbell way to the letter. It thought it could run its plants in the way it wanted, by brute force alone.

Canners' Industrial Union, Local No. 1

Thus it came as quite a shock to Campbell management when it learned that another entity was about to challenge its heretofore undisputed monopoly on power in the plants. In the fall of 1933 loyal employees reported that some workers were meeting and intending to form a union. The disgruntled workers had many complaints, but they had two overriding grievances. The first was the precipitous drop they saw in their pay envelopes. This resulted from the short hours they were working in 1933 due to both the falling off of orders and the work-spreading scheme encouraged by the National Industrial Recovery Act (NIRA). The other grievance was the Bedaux system and the speedup that followed its implementation. That workers would risk their jobs in the depths of the Depression, when thousands of Camden's unemployed would take any job out of desperation, was a measure of both the gravity of their grievances and the hope born of a reawakening labor movement and the slim yet encouraging promises of early New Deal programs. Section 7A of the NIRA had, for the first time, placed the federal government timidly on the side of supporting the right of workers to organize unions. Further, the rhetoric of president Franklin D. Roosevelt and his director of relief, Harry Hopkins, encouraged some to believe that steps were being taken in Washington, D.C., that might lift the country from its economic nightmare. Even more crucial to raising the hopes of Campbell's workers were the examples they saw around them of their neighbors taking things into their own hands and demanding justice. Socialist Frank Manning, organizer of the Canners' Industrial Union at Campbell, had earlier led a march of thousands of Camden's unemployed in demands for relief. Those holding jobs at other city firms were also organizing in unions and, in a few important cases, going on strike. Camden residents' newfound sense of entitlement was best demonstrated by a strike among those receiving relief payments. Relief clients were given a 20 percent bonus for performing "work relief." But recipients in Camden no longer looked at themselves as needy benefactors of charitable programs. Instead they felt "that society owes a man a living and that he has a *right* to relief... his relief food order is not a gift, it's his inalienable heritage."[13] Both the employed and the unemployed in Camden were fed up with an economic system that had enriched company owners while providing no safety net for the people who created the wealth through their labor.

When confronted by workers asking to negotiate wages and discuss the Bedaux system, Dorrance and his managers reacted in disbelief. A flustered Dorrance argued that his company "paid 16 per cent. above the wages paid in similar industries" and "It has increased the hourly wage 44 per cent. over last June [1933]. The union wants as much as the workers received in 1929, when they worked 53 hours, although they now work but 35 hours." The company's counsel warned that as a result of the workers' actions, the "business will be ruined, and, perhaps, not still in the city of Camden."[14] The company belatedly introduced some limited fringe benefits and set up a puppet employee organization, but also used every weapon at its disposal to destroy the fledgling union. As historian Howell Harris has argued, unionism was considered dangerous because it "introduced another center of power and loyalty" that carried the "potential for disruptions" and that could "interfere in other ways with management's 'pursuit of efficiency.'"[15] Campbell had invested much in consolidating control of production, and the Depression had lulled it into an overblown belief in its own strength by destroying what minimal marketplace bargaining power its employees possessed. It had not anticipated that those workers could invoke another type of power—workplace bargaining power—that they possessed because of their critical roles throughout the sprawling plant.

The organization of a union at Campbell apparently surprised the workers almost as much as the company. Virtually no preparation had been done before the organizing drive, and no AFL or other existing union was involved. At the beginning of 1933's tomato season Manning and several others began signing up members for an independent union they later named Local 1, Canners' Industrial Union (CIU). Yet the campaign spread rapidly, and in November they attempted to meet with company management, claiming to represent a majority of the production workers. The company responded clumsily at first, meeting with the union on a couple of occasions but conceding nothing. As it began to formulate a response to the new threat, management decided to do what many other companies had done years earlier: set up and recognize a friendly company union. In January 1934 they aided "loyal" workers in forming the Employees' Representation Plan (ERP), even providing office space on company property. The Campbell Soup Company officially recognized the organization on March 14. The ERP went through the motions of presenting a number of "requests" to the company on March 26;

on the next day the company "conceded" and granted all the wishes of the ERP. Little was done to hide the ERP's role as company puppet.[16]

Meanwhile, the newly emboldened members of the CIU took their case to the National Labor Board that had been created as a result of Section 7A of the NIRA. The board promised to hold an election at the Camden plant, but in the absence of any statutory power (and in an environment of challenges to its very constitutionality) the board stalled, waiting hopefully for some positive response from Campbell management. But by early 1934 that management had regrouped and came out fighting any attempt by "outsiders" to challenge its authority. In frustration over the Labor Board's inaction, a thousand members of the new union met on Saturday, March 31, to plan their next step. The overwhelming sentiment was that only a strike would force the company to bargain with them. They drew up a list of demands, including the return of wages to 1929 levels and recognition of the union. They then voted, by secret ballot, 600 to 28 to strike the next day.[17]

🌿 The 1934 Strike

Because the next day was a Sunday, there was only a handful of workers at the plant who, nonetheless, walked out. But on Monday a massive strike shut down all production. Over 80 percent of the Depression-reduced number of 2,300 production workers joined the walkout, and the union quickly organized pickets to cover the eight main entrances to the enormous plant. Both company and city officials moved to keep a tight rein on the strike, but the company went so far as to exasperate even a local magistrate who rejected its attempt to arm forty loyal employees. The employees had been deputized by Camden mayor Roy Stewart to protect company property and defend strikebreakers.[18]

The Campbell walkout, in common with other strikes convulsing Camden in the mid-1930s at RCA, New York Shipbuilding, Congress Cigar, Radio Condenser, and elsewhere pitted an intransigent management against a young, idealistic union. The new union grew out of and represented a working class just awakening to its entitlement to a better life and to its power to do something about it. The predictable result was a bitter and sometimes violent confrontation. Perhaps equally predictable was the unsteady course taken by the new union. With many grievances but little experience, participation by Campbell employees waxed and waned, soaring to heights of spontaneous militancy during the strike but declining to a handful of activists after some union missteps and company repression.

From April 1 to May 5, 1934, however, the movement was at its high point, with most workers staying off the job and actively discouraging the few still willing to work from crossing picket lines. The Camden and Philadelphia newspapers were filled with sensational headlines: "Police Crush Riot of 2000 Strikers at Camden Plant"; "Soup Co. Plans 'Armed Defense'"; "500 Soup Plant Strikers Storm Camden City Hall." While most newspapers highlighted the alleged violence of strikers, the company was far more intransigent than union leaders and as determined to break the strike as the workers were to stay off the job until victory. Dozens of strikers were arrested for disorderly conduct and for assaulting strikebreakers. For example, Ralph DiPaoli was brought before a grand jury for assault and battery on a strikebreaker getting off a bus, and Carolina Glass was one of many strikers charged with disorderly conduct for picket line activities. Company loyalists were also not averse to engaging in violence. Plant manager Harry Kelleher and foreman William Fauver were arrested after allegedly going to the union headquarters and attacking two strikers.[19]

With few exceptions, however, the city administration sided with the company. Strikers, in turn, expanded the targets of their protests to include city hall. Police Chief John Golden personally took charge of his men guarding the plant on the second day of the strike. Prepared with fire hoses and tear gas bombs, the police succeeded in dispersing a large crowd of strikers and supporters only by driving motorcycles onto the sidewalks to push them back, then securing the area with fire ropes. Three weeks later, a committee from the union met with the mayor to protest "manhandling" of the pickets by police. That day, several had been arrested "without reason," according to the committee. "After the arrests, the strikers, nearly 1000, formed a parade. Waving American flags, they marched through the central section of Camden, singing." After another incident when seven pickets were arrested, over five hundred strikers marched the few blocks to the Camden city hall to demand their release. Strikers rushed into a rear entrance of the building in an attempt to reach the office of the mayor. Driven back outside by police, they gathered outside the basement entrance to the police department, shouting "We want justice!" and "Release the prisoners!" Motorcycle policemen were again used to disperse the demonstrators.[20]

Though the union spokesmen who were quoted by reporters were American-born white men, the overwhelming majority of strikers fit no part of that profile. Most of the strikers whose names were reported in the press, and most of those arrested, were Italian immigrants or first-generation children of immigrants. However, African American men were also active participants in the strike. Two of the lengthiest sentences handed out to arrested strikers were given to two black workers, James Thompson and Walker Rollins, for assault and battery on a black strikebreaker, Henry Warner.[21]

Another characteristic of the strikers was that a large proportion were women. Estimates of the number of women participants varied widely, but probably a little over half of those who walked out were female. Perhaps even more significant than their numbers was the level of militancy of the women strikers. The year before, female strikers at the Congress Cigar Company had "caus[ed] riotous conditions in South Camden." In the Campbell strike, many of those arrested were women, and, according to police and reporters, women were involved in a number of violent incidents. Police were said to be "maintaining order, except in the case of angry women." The strikers who "stormed" City Hall "included a great number of women." In other cases, two male strikebreakers "were badly mauled by 15 women who attacked them," and Anna Rozka was charged with temporarily blinding two policemen by throwing pepper—from her lunch—into their eyes.[22]

Campbell's labor force policy funneled different groups of workers into different jobs and at different pay scales. Yet in 1934 none of the employment-related distinctions imposed by the company along racial, ethnic, and gender lines prevented workers from uniting in a common cause. The timing of the strike, months before tomato season, meant that the effects of another great divide—between permanent and seasonal workers—would be untested. Only in later decades would an even more elaborate segmentation of the workforce begin to have some complicating effects on labor unity.

Though the battle between Campbell Soup and over two thousand of its workers was taking place in Camden, it was attracting attention far beyond the borders of that city. Emboldened by the NIRA, workers across the United States were forming unions and going on strike. Over 400,000 textile workers from Maine to Florida walked out in the largest strike in U.S. history to that point, and the strike wave spread to many other industries. Because the legal standing of the new unions and their actions in light of the NIRA was not yet settled, many unionists were keenly interested in the outcome of the Campbell battle. When the company sought an injunction against the union, a Philadelphia *Evening Bulletin* reporter described the spectators at the court hearing as "five hundred in the courtroom (and 500 others outside), sixty lawyers as spectators, photographers, movie cameramen, reporters, representatives of other unions who might be affected by the Court's ruling."[23]

The judge repeatedly postponed a decision, effectively allowing the union to continue picketing and other strike activities. In Washington, early New Deal agencies were trying to find their footing and test their authority during a restive year that saw many strikes and much violence. Yet the NIRA, while giving moral support to the right to organize, had little power to enforce its decisions. And, in Camden, confusion reigned about the proper roles of the U.S. Conciliation Service, the National Labor Board, and its regional boards in Philadelphia and New Jersey. In the end, the more experienced Conciliation Service, through its commissioner P. W. Chappell, conducted the negotiations between the parties. Only toward the end of the strike did Chappell pass the tentative settlement on to the Labor Board for action by that body. During the negotiations Chappell was hamstrung by both the intransigence of the company and his lack of enforcement power. He complained repeatedly about the uncompromising stand taken by Dorrance and feared a "flare of violence" from the workers, despite the accommodating approach of their leaders. In reports to his superiors, he characterized the company as "obdurate" and "adamant" while he had "found the Committee of the Canners' Industrial Union co-operative and conciliatory in its effort to secure an adjustment." Chappell's troubles were compounded by the confusion over what authority he had. He complained to his supervisor about his lack of power and of the difficulty of working with Dorrance. At heart he was a civil servant who was concerned deeply about the people on whose behalf he labored: "There are still over two thousand employees on strike. The situation of some of them is becoming desperate. I feel early action alone can prevent great suffering."[24]

On the union side, the inexperienced leaders quickly abandoned demands related to the Bedaux system and union security. They asked Chappell to propose to Dorrance that if he granted a 10 percent wage increase they would end the strike, even without formal recognition of the union as bargaining agent for production workers. Dorrance, however, rebuked the offer. Instead, he "injected [the Employee Representation Plan] into the picture," claiming that most workers did not support the CIU. The nominal leaders of the ERP continued to take direction from Dorrance. For example, when ERP representatives told Chappell that a representation election should not be held until at least ten days after all had returned to work, the commissioner wryly noted that the ERP "chairman naively remarked that Mr. Dorrance had called this to their attention."[25]

Given the hard-line position of the company and the increasingly desperate situation of the strikers, on May 5 CIU leaders accepted Chappell's proposal of proportional representation for "a joint committee to be set up for the purpose of bargaining." The company also granted all employees a 7 percent wage increase. Though well over 80 percent of production workers stayed out of work throughout the strike, support for the union began to decline after workers returned and the company reasserted its authority. In direct violation of one section of the agreement, the company announced that those who had remained at work would be given seniority preference over all those who had joined the strike. By the time the Labor Board held an election that summer, 1,200 voted for the CIU, and 1,000 for the ERP.[26]

✌ The Aftermath of the Strike

Under the rules adopted under the Wagner Act a year later, this result would have meant that the CIU would be the exclusive bargaining agent for production workers. But things were very different under the NIRA regime. The combined committee that resulted from the vote—twelve representatives from the union, ten from the ERP—still might have been able to bargain with the company, for the CIU held a majority of seats. However, Dorrance insisted that any decision by the committee should require a two-thirds vote. The union objected, but Chappell convinced them that they should accept this rule. Once they did, no decision ever emerged from the committee.

Virtually ignoring any entreaties from Department of Labor personnel, Campbell management embarked on a campaign to destroy any remnants of genuine unionism in its plants. When workers were elected to positions in the CIU, the company fired them, sometimes on the very next day. While almost the entire leadership of the CIU was laid off, no ERP members were. Frank Manning, executive secretary of the union, wrote frantic letters to the new federal conciliator assigned to the case, then to the director of that division, and finally telegraphed Frances Perkins, Roosevelt's secretary of labor, pleading for help. He described a company campaign that went beyond the firing of union members:

> Through allowing company union representatives to hire new workers; through intimidation; through preference in the matter of continuous employment to company union members; through remarks of foremen and foreladies . . . they are effectively battering down our Union and it is our hope that you will cooperate with us before it is too late. . . .[27]

Finally the Labor Board agreed to hold hearings on the union's complaints. Hearings began in March, 1935, but, before they were concluded, the NIRA was declared unconstitutional by the Supreme Court and no decision was ever rendered.

The CIU, which had seemed so full of promise in early 1934, declined to a handful of activists. When Martha Gellhorn visited Camden during this period, she noted that "there were about 1800 Union members in

Campbell's." She continued, "I should be surprised if any of these peo-
ple had work there within six months—at least, if all of them stick to the
Union—which they won't for the basic and cogent reason of hunger." The
few remaining union members were concentrated in the Maintenance
Department, where hard-to-replace skills provided some limited protection.
But overall the union entered a period of dormancy; about its only action
was its application to affiliate directly with the American Federation of Labor
(AFL). The AFL granted it a charter as Federal Local 20224.[28]

The ERP, meanwhile, continued to play its role as nominal representative
of Campbell's workers (after CIU members abandoned any efforts to work
in the combined committee). The organization continued to hold meetings
on company property, with its leaders acting as "petty foremen and fore-
women," despite Wagner Act proscriptions of company unions. To appear
somewhat more independent of the company, the ERP changed its name in
1938 to the "Campbell Soup Workers' Independent Union Local No. 1" and
moved off of company property into an office of its own.[29]

Despite the temporary defeat of unionization at Campbell, the campaign
was extraordinarily important in redefining relationships inside the plant and
in setting a precedent for a revived movement five years later. For the first
time, the soup makers had demanded the right to have a say in what they
were paid and how the plant should be run. Just a few years earlier, Dorrance
had introduced the Bedaux system to consolidate management's control of
Plant No. 1. Now, instead of meekly accepting their places in the system,
workers were demanding an end to that system, or at least a say in how it
was administered. Carmen Parente, who was hired in 1933 as a packer boy,
recalled that "in 1934 we struck to get rid of the incentive plan....I was
only seventeen years old, but that was one of the things they were pounding
in my ear all the time, let us get rid of the incentive plan."[30] Numerous complaints about Bedaux's tendency "to sweat too much production out of the
individual worker" were submitted to the Labor Board during the conflict.
No longer could the company convince itself that its control was unchallenged. A Philadelphia labor newspaper heralded the "revolt" of the "docile
workers whose exploited labor built the monstrous fortunes of the Dorrance Campbell Soup family." Company executives tried to minimize the
significance of the union campaign, blaming the strike on "an 'infection'
of Communism." They also regretted their ill-advised attempt at a good
deed early in the Depression, when the company opened soup kitchens for
the unemployed that "invited to Camden many a laboring undesirable."[31]
Though its claim of outside agitation as the cause of the strike was patently
false, a number of its employees, in the turbulent atmosphere of the 1930s,

had begun questioning capitalism in a more fundamental way, and some even joined socialist and communist organizations.

Rank-and-file Campbell workers were at the heart of the 1934 strike, as they would be in every conflict at the soup plant over at least the next thirty-five years. But committed activists who emerged from that rank and file played a crucial role in organizing and focusing the grievances and the energies of the workers. In many cases, especially in the critical first two decades of unionization, these leaders joined the Communist or Socialist Parties. This factor was often of great importance, for it provided activists with an ideological framework and a long-term vision to sustain their day-to-day work. While this usually worked to the benefit of their organizing efforts, it also carried the potential for problems. The "party line" might conflict with local needs, and these organizational affiliations provided a target for enemies of the union. The early unionization drives, however, would likely not have succeeded without the dedicated participation of these leftists. Two points should be made about these activists at Campbell: first, there was always a wide spectrum of political ideology and affiliation among them; and, second, they were, in almost all cases, "homegrown" activists whose political commitment grew out of their experiences as workers in the Campbell plants.

One important activist whose commitment to socialism predated his involvement at Campbell was Frank Manning. As South Jersey organizer for the Socialist Party, he had earlier led the Unemployed Union in Camden. By late 1932 the union had lined up support from a number of city organizations for an ambitious housing program. Their proposal to the city commissioners was the first step in what later became a successful housing program in Camden, the Public Works Administration–supported Westfield Acres. A month after their presentation, Manning and the Unemployed Union organized a mass march to Convention Hall, where five thousand unemployed men and women heard James Maurer, who had been the Socialist Party candidate for vice president the previous November. Maurer compared the Depression— "a five year plan instituted by the capitalists"—unfavorably with the Soviet Five-Year Plan, "designed to put every man and woman at work." Forty marshals wearing red armbands coordinated the march. Banners and signs announced the neighborhoods of the marchers along with political slogans, from "Nationalize the Banks" to "Beans Three Times a Day—Oh, Boy!" Though the march was led by the Socialist-led Unemployed Union, it was joined by the Communist Party–influenced Unemployed Council of Camden County. Though some tensions would later become evident between supporters of the two parties, for the most part they kept the expression of their differences to a minimum.[32]

Manning and the Socialists were also the most visible leaders of the Campbell strike in 1934, though several rank-and-file participants later became active in the Communist Party. According to one newspaper report, a Communist speaker was pulled from a soapbox as he began to address the strikers, though no other reports indicated any factionalism among strike supporters. Communists were also active in other industries in Camden, and especially in rural areas surrounding the city. The Communist Party–affiliated Trade Union Unity League (TUUL) organized several locals of the Agricultural and Cannery Workers' Union and its affiliate for small farmers, the United Farmers League, in South Jersey. Despite the difficulties in organizing largely seasonal Italian and African American workers in a hostile environment, their efforts met with significant success, most notably at Seabrook Farms, the site of violent union-company-vigilante confrontations in the spring and summer of 1934. After the dissolution of the TUUL in 1935, the small South Jersey locals joined the AFL as federal (directly affiliated) locals. Together with the remnants of the Campbell union, now also a federal local, they were among the first groups to join together in 1937 as the UCAPAWA-CIO.[33]

✶ The UCAPAWA and Campbell Soup

In its short thirteen-year existence from 1937 to 1950, the UCAPAWA (known from 1945 on as the Food, Tobacco, and Allied Workers, or FTA) gained a remarkable reputation for organizing the most downtrodden workers, those who had been abandoned by more mainstream unions. From Chicana cannery workers in California to African American tobacco workers in North Carolina, from oyster shuckers to cemetery diggers, the UCAPAWA's members formed the most diverse union in the United States. Women and minorities rose to top positions of leadership locally and nationally. Historian Vicki Ruiz called the UCAPAWA "a woman's union," for women made up half the union's membership and, more important, a significant proportion of its leaders. In the northeast region between 1937 and 1950, 51 percent of principal local union offices (president, vice president, secretary-treasurer) were held by women, and 74 percent of shop stewards were female.[34] According to historian Robert Korstad, the FTA's heroic efforts to organize mostly black tobacco workers in Winston-Salem in the late 1940s laid the foundation for a labor-based civil rights movement. And in Memphis, according to historian Michael Honey, "UCAPAWA organizers dared to do what others had failed to do: organize blacks in the sweatshops of some of the city's most plantation-minded manufacturers and begin interracial organizing."[35]

In working to organize those considered beyond the pale of inclusion by the traditional labor movement, it encountered fierce opposition. Vigilante groups and the Ku Klux Klan attacked UCAPAWA organizers and members in numerous locations. However, only when company, government, and church opponents of the union allied with anticommunist factions in the labor movement itself was it finally destroyed. The FTA was one of the eleven Left-led unions expelled by the Congress of Industrial Organizations (CIO) during the Truman-McCarthy era.[36]

In the late 1930s, however, the UCAPAWA was breaking new ground in organizing agricultural and food-processing workers. This task was far more difficult than that faced in other industries, for the Wagner Act of 1935 specifically excluded (at the behest of Southern Democrats) agricultural and domestic workers, the two occupational bases in which the majority of African Americans and Mexican immigrants worked. Further, canneries, though included within the purview of the act, were permitted a fourteen-week exemption from its provisions and another fourteen weeks of limited coverage. States such as New Jersey also drastically reduced the protections afforded workers when it came to the canning industry, claiming that the perishable nature of the material being processed precluded its workers from enjoying the protections extended to other workers in America. A further difficulty for organizers, especially in the small truck farms of the East Coast, was the fact that agricultural workers were dispersed in small groups throughout far-flung rural areas. The final factor complicating the UCAPAWA's job was the seasonal nature of its targeted industries: most agricultural workers and about half of cannery employees worked seasonally, making it difficult for organizers to establish stable locals.[37]

Nonetheless, the tiny remnant local from the Campbell Soup Company and others from rural South Jersey joined with peanut mill, citrus, and turpentine workers' locals in Florida, among many others, at the Denver founding convention of the UCAPAWA in July 1937. The leading force in pulling these locals together was Donald Henderson. Expelled from his teaching position at Columbia University because of his communist affiliations, he led the Seabrook Farms organizing campaign and strike in 1934. Seabrook, the largest farm in New Jersey, was located thirty-five miles south of Camden. At one point during the campaign Henderson was nearly lynched by farmer vigilantes. Attacks on those trying to form a union at Seabrook, however, generated a wave of support for the agricultural union. More than three hundred representatives of religious, union, and unemployed organizations, as well as communist and socialist activists, met in Cumberland County, home of Seabrook Farms, to express their solidarity.[38]

The early efforts of the UCAPAWA met with notable successes in some cases, but the difficulties of organizing dispersed agricultural workers prevented any big increase in the numbers of new members in the first few years of the union's existence. The number of UCAPAWA contracts increased from thirty to sixty-five between 1937 and 1938, but the number of workers covered by these contracts increased only slightly, from 7,035 to 9,003. The financial toll on the union that resulted from attempting to organize innumerable isolated locals over vast agricultural areas pushed union leaders to change their organizing strategy. Rather than focusing on agriculture, the union decided to target large food-processing and related industries, often in large cities. The UCAPAWA formally adopted this change at its Third National Convention in 1940. The Campbell Soup Company's fledgling local was the main beneficiary on the eastern seaboard of this change in direction, for union activists considered the largest soup cannery in the United States the key to the union's future in the food processing industry.[39]

✄ The Birth of Local 80

Seventeen-year-old Joseph Gallo began his career at Campbell in the tumultuous year of 1934. Though his first job was packing hot cans into baskets, he soon had the good fortune to begin an apprenticeship that prepared him for a coveted job in the Maintenance Department. John Tisa, who lived in the same close-knit Italian neighborhood a few blocks from the factory as Gallo, had worked tomato seasons while in high school and had enthusiastically participated in the 1934 strike. Unlike Gallo, he lost his job at the soup plant but continued working on union activities there. His developing political orientation veered sharply to the left, and while Gallo was learning the mechanical trades, Tisa headed off to Spain to battle fascism as a member of the Abraham Lincoln Brigade.[40]

These two young men represented the two streams of workers that revived the dream of a union in the late 1930s and worked to achieve a resounding victory for the UCAPAWA in Camden. Gallo was one of the confident skilled mechanics who could afford to continue his membership in the tiny AFL local that survived the 1934 strike without fear of reprisals. Tisa, like many others, was radicalized by his strike experience and began moving in Unemployed Union, socialist, and communist circles. The goals of these two groups in the organizing campaign—the protection of the interests of skilled tradesmen, and the advancement of industrial social-justice unionism—would later lead to serious rifts among Campbell unionists. But in the late 1930s, their common enemy, the giant Campbell Soup Company, easily united them in the organizing campaign.

The two groups in the vanguard of the new organizing drive had much in common. Both emerged from the rank and file: the initial organizers were all Campbell employees. Thus, they were an organic part of the people working in the plant and living in the neighborhoods surrounding it. Furthermore, they were intimately aware of the complaints, problems, and frustrations of working for Campbell. Though members of these groups were the first to step forward—maintenance men because they could, radical activists because they were ideologically committed to doing so—their actions gradually unleashed a massive movement of support for the union drive among almost all sections of the workforce.

Armed with a new charter from the UCAPAWA-CIO as Local 80, union members began slowly spreading the union idea by talking to their coworkers. The Maintenance Department became a solid bastion of union support, and, when Tisa returned from Spain fervently committed to a vision of a new world, he pulled together a group of like-minded leftists, including workers like Anthony Valentino, a charismatic young "leader of the kids in packing."[41] A similar scenario was working itself out in factories and mills across America in the turbulent 1930s, as different groups of workers took up the crusade of unionization for often quite different reasons. Just as leftists and maintenance mechanics were the "spark plug" unionists at Campbell, the same two groups were responsible for organizing most of the early locals of the United Electrical Workers, and similar groups could be found in numerous other industries.[42]

UCAPAWA's decision to refocus its efforts on large food-processing plants, and in particular on the Campbell Soup Company, provided the boost that turned Local 80 from a "passive" to an "active" chapter of the organization. District 7 of the union covered fourteen locals in 1937, including Tree Surgeons Local 19, Basket Workers Local 54, and Oyster Workers Local 163. But the district located its headquarters in the same building as Cannery Workers Local 80 in Camden. The UCAPAWA also committed resources to organizing Campbell's new plant in Chicago. The union sent full-time organizers to both cities to support union members inside the plants who were doing the difficult work of signing up members. When the company discovered activists engaged in union activities, they fired them, and the union filed charges with the National Labor Relations Board (NLRB) on their behalf. But even work on the outside was sometimes dangerous. Several International organizers[43] who were handing out leaflets to workers leaving the Camden plant were arrested and charged with "illegal distribution of circulars" and disorderly conduct. Their sentences of fifteen days in jail were thrown out when a Superior Court judge overturned their convictions.[44]

Within the plant, organizing picked up speed, though it proceeded unevenly depending on the department and the people doing the sign-up work. The can-making department joined Local 80 en masse, though they technically were employees of Continental Can Company. Because they were not employees of Campbell, the union petitioned the NLRB for an immediate election for the can workers. Before the election could take place, Campbell responded by buying out the can unit and merging its workforce into the Campbell employee pool. The election petition was withdrawn, but the action gave Campbell only a temporary reprieve from having to deal with Local 80, for the department became an active advocate for unionization of the entire plant. In other departments, workers were more timid about showing their support; one worker remarked that "people wanted a union, but were afraid to come out."[45]

Women had been among the most ardent participants in the 1934 strike, but some organizers had a more difficult time signing them up this time. Joseph Gallo, the Maintenance Department union stalwart, recalls that there were "a lot of women" in the plant, but "we had a hell of a time with them" when he tried to get them to join the union. The experience of the other group of early union activists, the leftists, was quite different. Evidence from the 1939–1940 organizing campaign, as well as women's participation in union activities before and after, suggests that Campbell's social-justice unionists placed a high value on actively involving women. Verna Gillan, who later became president of Local 194 at the Chicago plant, began signing up people from her job in the cooked chicken department. She recalled that "right from the beginning women began coming into the union equally as fast as the men," and accounted for a majority of those who signed union cards. Back in Camden, John Tisa's mother Maria also worked on the chicken line. She "asked for and got the Number One union dues payment book of Local 80." At an organizational planning meeting in September 1939, members of the local debated ways to sign up more of the workforce. They reached a decision that suggests both the challenges they faced and their resolve to overcome divisiveness in the plant: to "concentrate more on organizing women workers, spend more time on the Italian workers, [and] reach the Negro workers."[46]

The situation facing those organizing the Chicago plant was a bit simpler than in Camden. Only ten years old in 1939, the Chicago plant had few of the complexities that had developed over the previous seventy years in Camden. Despite an attempt to spread the 1934 strike to Chicago, it had remained a Camden affair, and there was no company union in the new location. The workforce was more homogeneous, comprised of almost all European immigrants (mostly Slavic) and no African Americans. And there were no long-standing craft traditions in its Maintenance Department. Thus the main body of organizers in the plant came not from the skilled trades group, but from left-oriented immigrants. Not surprisingly, the organizing drive there proceeded even more quickly than in Camden. The NLRB ordered an election for October 22, 1940 in Chicago, and the mandate of the workers was clear: 1,139 for the UCAPAWA and 439 against. Under Wagner Act rules, Local 194 became the exclusive bargaining agent for Chicago production workers.[47]

The situation in Camden was more complicated, and UCAPAWA organizers as well as rank-and-file activists planned carefully and worked diligently to organize what they repeatedly referred to as "the largest cannery in the world." International president Donald Henderson came to Camden and participated in the planning. The UCAPAWA's most astute move was to appoint John Tisa as "organizer representing the International" but "working under the direction of the Executive Board of Local 80"—that is, under the leadership of people working in the plant. Though Tisa no longer worked at the plant, he had ongoing connections: he still lived in the plant's neighborhood and his mother still worked there. The Spanish Civil War veteran was the ideal person to advance the social-justice unionism of the UCAPAWA in a way that understood and respected the experience and knowledge of the workers the union sought to represent.[48]

The union pulled out all the stops in the campaign in Camden. It lined up active support from other CIO unions in South Jersey. The local's sound truck circled the plant at lunchtime exhorting workers to sign union cards. In the plant, union activists began taking up workers' grievances and acting as unofficial representatives in dealing with foremen. In a few cases, company management even met with CIO committees to resolve problems. As Campbell workers began believing that a union victory was actually possible, they became more daring in confronting the company. Early in 1940, the company had fired retort operator James Morris and four others for union activities. But after six more months of organizing, workers like Mike Tomasetti and Joseph Pirolli were even giving up their lunch breaks to stand outside company gates defiantly signing up new members. Maintenance Department men began holding departmental union meetings and circulating petitions to oppose the company practice of having them work seven hours a day, five days a week, then come in on Saturday to work at straight time to make up their forty hours.[49]

If union supporters were going all out for their cause, the company was working equally hard to stymie the campaign. One side of the company strategy led to increased vigilance against union activity and the disciplining or even firing of "troublemakers." The other side, however, was another halfhearted attempt at benevolence. Though Campbell Soup was a master at presenting itself to the public as a wholesome company attentively preparing nutritious food for America's families, it had some difficulty putting on the same face toward its employees. The company did organize a number of social functions for employees and increased support for its athletic association. When it also began playing music in the workers' cafeteria, however, many workers believed the union's assertion that the only reason was to drown out the union sound truck and "keep the workers from talking union." The union also claimed credit when the company granted an across-the-board pay increase of one to three cents an hour.[50]

When Local 80 requested a representation election to determine the will of the majority, the company at first agreed—on the condition that the company union (or "Independent") also be on the ballot. Though Local 80 was presenting a confident front, it apparently was not entirely sure of the outcome, so it rejected the offer. When in the fall of 1940 the union finally agreed to inclusion of the company union on the ballot, the company changed its position and withdrew acceptance of any election. The new company position was that "it would grant exclusive rights to neither [the UCAPAWA nor the Independent] until one or the other was certified by the [Labor] Board, but that it would not consent to an election."[51]

By this time, Local 80 had presented the NLRB with 1,400 signed union cards and 649 signatures on a petition authorizing the CIO to bargain for them, and the NLRB ordered an election. Again the union appeared to have doubts about the certainty of its victory and delayed the election temporarily. This latest hitch had to do with the departments to be covered in the bargaining unit and, thus, eligible to vote. The company insisted that guards and timekeepers be included, but the union argued to the NLRB against the inclusion of these groups, suspecting that they would likely be company supporters and vote for the Independent.[52]

The union, as it turned out, had little reason to fear the outcome. Of the valid ballots cast, 1,918 went to Local 80, with 886 for the Independent and 105 for neither. As of December 20, 1940, Campbell production workers in Camden were represented by the UCAPAWA-CIO. A short time later, guards, who had at last been excluded from the ballot, voted overwhelmingly to affiliate with Local 80. Flush with victories in both Camden and Chicago, the UCAPAWA went on to organize many other groups on the peripheries of American industry: farmworkers in Arizona, salmon cannery workers in Alaska, and tobacco workers in North Carolina, among others.[53]

In Camden, the win meant a shift in the work of union activists. From organizing new members they turned now to negotiating a contract and working out the union's place in the day-to-day life of the plant. A strong shop-steward system became the most visible manifestation of the union in the plant, and direct action the hallmark of their presence there. Slowdowns and walkouts became the means of enforcing both the written and unwritten contracts for Campbell's workers. Over the next three decades, top management at Campbell facilities in both Camden and Chicago complained bitterly about the job actions that became a constant reminder of the battle over who would run the plant—Campbell management or Campbell workers. In August 1941, "the entire plant walked out in support of the warehousemen" in Chicago when they were excluded from a plantwide pay increase. Three months later in Camden, the company allegedly provoked militant shop steward Federal Marino into an argument, then fired him. "The following morning," according to Local 80 president Anthony Valentino, "the third floor where Marino worked pulled a complete shut-down affecting more than 1000 people. The sit-down lasted three quarters of an hour and was settled by reinstating Marino."[54]

The thorniest problem for the union, however, remained the Bedaux system. The company clung to the system more resolutely than ever and refused to entertain any idea of abolishing it. For the workers, Bedaux continued to symbolize the dictatorial control exercised by Dorrance and his managers. The union alternately proposed abolishing the system, modifying it, and turning it into a jointly administered union-management project. The company fought hard against every improvement sought by the union in negotiations, but eventually gave in, to some degree, on wage increases, vacations, and pensions. But the best the union was able to wring out of the company on Bedaux was a joint advisory committee to help the workers "understand" the system better and resolve disputes about correct B ratings. More effective, from the workers' perspective, was the same kind of guerilla tactics that worked in dealing with abusive foremen. Spontaneous work stoppages and other hit-and-run job actions kept the Bedaux system from ever being the all-powerful tool that would guarantee management's monopoly on control in the soup plant. The lines of the resulting stalemate shifted back and forth over the next decades, permitting Campbell to continue low-cost production but always with some uncertainty as to the limits of its power.

World events, however, soon turned the attention of everyone in Camden to the eruption of the war that was engulfing the world. The transformation of the home front during World War II brought dramatic changes to the Campbell Soup Company as well. Not only would the company turn more than half its production over to the manufacture of C rations and other canned food for the war effort, but the workplace itself also underwent dramatic changes. While daily struggles with the new union continued, both labor and management focused their efforts on maximizing production for the war effort. At the same time, the company went to unheard-of lengths to staff its plants with workers who would accept its low wages and hard work at a time of acute labor shortages. The groups brought to Camden to fulfill this goal became the focus of the next strategy Campbell employed to continue making its products cheaply, and to continue doing it in Camden.

❧ CHAPTER 3

World War II and the Transformation of the Workforce

Campbell Soup Company and its employees did their part to aid the Allied victory over Nazism in World War II. A large portion of the C rations that kept the armies fed were made at Campbell's No. 2 plant on the Delaware River in Camden, New Jersey, and the company's other food products sustained the home front. Yet Campbell also benefited from changes brought on by the war. Profits remained robust for the Dorrance family while sales doubled over the course of the war, spurred on not only by government contracts but also by war-themed advertising aimed at housewives. The continued imperative to manufacture its products cheaply, while maintaining high quality and remaining in the city of its birth, forced the company onto new ground. Simply managing production scientifically would no longer be sufficient; it now had to figure out how to keep workers from leaving its low-paying jobs. Potentially even more troublesome, it also had to deal with a union for the first time in its history.

Less than a year after the United Cannery, Agricultural, Packing, and Allied Workers of America (UCAPAWA) Local 80 won its resounding victory to become the company's official union in Camden, the war brought massive and unanticipated changes to Campbell's workers and their union. Though its impacts were many, the war complicated the new union's job in two specific ways. First, support for the war effort by union members and leaders presented unionists with a difficult conundrum: How could they reconcile their opposition to speedups and other company tactics to squeeze more work out of workers with their advocacy of doing whatever it took to defeat fascism? The no-strike pledge that the local eagerly embraced stood in sharp opposition to the direct-action tactics that both workers and the fledgling union had used effectively in their daily contest with the company. Campbell employees had supported the union drive because they saw the local as a body that consolidated their strength and was strong enough to engage in confrontational tactics when useful or necessary. Now their union was telling them not only to continue working no matter what their grievances but even to improve their efficiency and output. In reality, Local 80 played both sides of the issue, strongly supporting the war effort yet in some cases tacitly accepting direct-action tactics initiated by workers to help its position in dealing with the company.

The war also brought dramatic transformations in the makeup of the workforce at the soup company. The changes occurred during a severe labor shortage due to both increased wartime production demands and the departure of workers to the armed forces and to better-paying jobs on the home front. By the end of the war the workforce bore only partial resemblance to its prewar makeup. The company's approach to its labor shortage never was to raise wages enough to attract sufficient numbers of workers from the existing pool of labor but rather to expand that pool by adding entirely new groups who would accept what Campbell was willing to pay. At a period when the progressive ideals of the UCAPAWA led it to fight to overcome differences among workers, the company stratified its labor force more than ever. The company fought the elimination of the "boys" category and the equalization of pay between men and women. It refused to accept an antidiscrimination clause in its contract with the union and maintained segregated facilities and jobs throughout its plants. Only the combined pressures of union activists—sometimes at the expense of their popularity among some workers—and severe labor shortages broke down the company's rigid policies of workforce segmentation.

Thus, the focus of this chapter will be the contest over Campbell's use of labor segmentation and "divide and rule" tactics in an environment of compromised union capacity to enforce its position through the use of direct action. On the surface, the marked changes in the composition of the workforce appear to be the more lasting effect of the war, for the no-strike pledge disappeared with the end of the conflict. Yet there were perhaps equally long-lasting effects on the struggle over control of the shop floor; the company took full advantage of the increased production drive to enshrine its management prerogatives and the Bedaux system in the first contracts signed with Local 80.

This period of drastic increases in production and labor recruitment also brings into sharp relief the role of the state in a capitalist firm, even one noted for its laissez-faire policies. The actions of the War Labor Board in managing wages and other contract issues, the War Manpower Commission (WMC) in conducting a massive transfer of workers from Puerto Rico to Camden, and the Quartermaster Corps in placing enormous orders for food products are only the most obvious examples of government intervention in the business of the Campbell Soup Company. In reality, the state played an important role throughout the company's life in Camden, but never was it so clear as it was between 1941 and 1945.

✺ Campbell's Soup Goes to War

The advent of World War II provided many opportunities for the preeminent manufacturer of prepared, ready-to-eat food products, but it also presented the Campbell Soup Company with a number of difficulties. Some of these problems were ones that could be expected for any company during wartime, but some grew directly out of Campbell's low-cost approach to production. Thus, war-induced shortages of critical materials like tin led to minor readjustments at Campbell but were overcome fairly easily. The firm had far more trouble recruiting and retaining the low-cost labor required to keep the plants humming along during those busy four years.

Contracts to supply the armed forces proved a bonanza for the company. The participation of the United States in the war depended, to a large degree, on the continuous availability of ready-to-eat food products that could be easily transported and that would last indefinitely. Napoleon Bonaparte had recognized a similar need and had offered a reward to anyone who could devise a method of preserving food for his armies; the winner of that contest was Nicolas Appert, since then known as the "father of canning." Campbell had pioneered this industry in the United States (along with a few other companies) and now quickly expanded its product portfolio to include such products as C rations, a meat-and-vegetable hash that the company's employees produced in the millions for consumption by soldiers on the front lines. Government contracts grew to account for slightly over half the firm's business, but production for the home front continued with only minor alterations. Some soup product lines were discontinued or modified, and the looming threat of a tin shortage led the company to experiment with packaging dry soups, but Campbell's soup production proceeded without interruption. This was due in large part to a ruling from Washington that *condensed* food products should continue to receive their required allocations of tin plate, while canners of other food products, like Campbell's archrival H. J. Heinz, were severely affected by a sharp reduction in their tin supply. According to one Campbell manager, "that was Bev Murphy's doing." Arthur Dorrance had hired the young and ambitious William Beverly Murphy away from the A. C. Nielsen Company in 1938 to work on finding new ways to expand the business. Although he was being groomed to take over the company one day, he became a "dollar-a-year man," lent by the company to the War Production Board in Washington. Though it is unclear exactly what role Murphy played in smoothing Campbell Soup Company's path through Washington's bureaucracies during the war, both Murphy and the company prospered.[1]

Campbell's always-innovative marketing efforts quickly took up the theme of the war as the company donned the mantle of patriotism. Though readers of the *Saturday Evening Post* would never have suspected it, this was a mantle the company wore with some awkwardness when it came to the production side of the business. Early in the war it tried to deny that it was engaged in war work to avoid being subject to the jurisdiction of the War Labor Board. Much of its production equipment came from Germany, and a number of its engineers were German citizens. Further, the founder of the scientific management system at the heart of Campbell's soup plants, Charles Bedaux, was a Nazi sympathizer who killed himself while in U.S. military custody in 1944.[2]

Nonetheless, Campbell's magazine advertising tied the company's products directly to the war effort. Several advertisements highlighted Campbell's contribution to "the feeding of our overseas men." One featured a photograph of Secretary of Agriculture Claude R. Wickard over his quotation urging that "food will win the war." Another showed four soldiers (in an artist's illustration) enjoying their field rations after heating them "under the motor hood of [their] jeep," demonstrating how ingenious GI's were still "eat[ing] good American food, cooked the way a man enjoys it." Other ads directly targeted the home front, exhorting America's wives and mothers to "build your wartime meals around soups like these . . . for the man behind the lathe and the drill": "When your man comes home hungry, sit him down to a bowl brim-full of Campbell's Beef Soup."[3]

Between military and domestic markets, Campbell's sales more than doubled between 1939 and 1945, from just over 65 million dollars per year to over 138 million. Further, its net profits throughout the war never dropped below 10 million dollars per year. Yet this success did not come without problems. It was all predicated, as usual, on the continuation of Campbell's practice of low-cost production. But with the start of the war, several aspects of this approach came into question. How would the war, rationing, and new government agencies affect the company? How could Campbell continue to attract workers to its low-paying jobs in an environment of labor shortages? And how would its running of the plants change, now that it had to deal with its new and unwelcome partner, the union representing its workers?[4]

🎗 "Labor Will Crush Fascism": Local 80 and the War

While Campbell's new union, the UCAPAWA, had opposed military preparations in the late 1930s, charging that war profiteers would benefit at the expense of working people, its position changed dramatically by the time of the attack on Pearl Harbor. For union activists who were close to the Communist Party, this reversal had much to do with Adolf Hitler's invasion of the Soviet Union. But support for war preparations swung upward for almost everyone in Camden as the looming threat from the spread of fascism made U.S. involvement almost inevitable. Though Local 80 continued to look out for the rights of its workers during the war, its greatest exertions went into drumming up support for the Allied military effort and increasing the output of war materiel in the form of C rations and other food products.[5]

By mid-January 1942, the change in the UCAPAWA's focus was unmistakable. The union newspaper held up Campbell's Camden plant as a model to be emulated by other companies, for it had enrolled 28 percent of employees in a war-bond purchase plan that early in the war. The article was printed over a cartoon of an angry Uncle Sam captioned "YOU'LL GET IT ADOLF!" and beside another article explaining the no strike policy: "But more important than merely preventing strikes are our constructive proposals to get at the real causes of lagging defense production and to make possible the maximum output."

The war bond drive continued to be a top project for Local 80. Just five months later the union boasted that 97 percent of the combined Camden and Chicago workforces had purchased bonds, earning for the Camden plant the first "Minute Man" pennant (awarded for exceptional support of the war bond campaign) in the city. At the ceremony celebrating this achievement, Camden's Mayor George Brunner joined Local 80's president Anthony Valentino and Campbell company president Arthur Dorrance. During this gathering of erstwhile enemies, Dorrance praised Valentino and the union for their "cooperation" and declared that he "look[ed] forward to a labor-management committee to help us achieve efficiency in many respects." The irony of the occasion was overshadowed by the widespread spirit of patriotism and the UCAPAWA's determination that (as expressed in the union's newspaper) "Labor Will Crush Fascism."[6]

The Labor-Management Committee that Dorrance hinted at was formally announced in June, at the same time that the Army rations contract with the company was made public. Local 80 continued its crusade to increase production, and the joint committee was an important vehicle for that campaign. The committee quickly developed a five-point program that it publicized to all workers. The points were simple, but effectively conveyed the essence of the committee's work:

1. Improve our safety record
2. Reduce waste
3. Safeguard machinery
4. Improve efficiency
5. Avoid errors in production

Two years later the local was still encouraging its members to do all they could for the war effort. On March 23, 1944, "over 5000 Campbell Soup workers and management representatives crowded into a flag-bedecked warehouse...to receive the War Food Administration's 'A' Award for outstanding achievement in food production for the Armed Services, the home front and our allies." Union president Valentino noted at the gathering that "Union officers and Shop Stewards were always on the alert to prevent any interruption in the flow of production." Though adherence to the drive to maximize production would cause numerous complications for the local and result in some loss of support from the rank and file, union leaders did their best to combine their traditional union roles with what they considered to be their duty in the world fight against fascism.[7]

Local 80 members also supported the war effort beyond the soup plants. Many joined the armed forces and engaged the enemy in a more direct way. By June of 1942, 119 members of Local 80 were serving in the military and those numbers continued to rise throughout the war. Many were drafted, and, for numerous others, enlisting was the best way they could perform their duty for their country. For those ideologically committed to the Left, including many in union leadership, the war against Hitler was unquestionably the most important issue in the world at that time, and an extraordinary number of union leaders and activists volunteered.

A union international vice president and Local 80 member, and one of the first to organize in South Jersey, Leif Dahl enlisted on May Day, 1942, to fight in the artillery. The man with the reputation as Camden's most militant steward, Federal Marino of the Retort Department, joined to carry on the "fighting tradition of Local 80": "I'm glad to go into the armed service to wipe out Fascism, to fight side by side with the rest of the young men of the U.S.A., Britain, China and the Soviet Union."[8]

The experiences during the war of two of the leaders of the main groups behind the Local 80 organizing drive were suggestive of the differences in the stances toward the war among Campbell workers. Joseph Gallo was completing his training as a mechanic in the Maintenance Department, and repeatedly received deferments from the military draft with the assistance of the company. On a number of occasions he thought his last deferment had run out, and once he even sold his car in anticipation of being called up. Yet at the last minute he was notified of another deferment, and he spent the entire war in Camden, as did thousands of other workers in this critical industry.

John Tisa, the Spanish Civil War veteran and former Campbell employee who had been the UCAPAWA's prime organizer in Camden, on the other hand, eagerly signed up for the Army. The union organized a big send-off for Tisa, both to recognize his service and to publicize its support for the war. At a Camden banquet attended by 210 supporters, Tisa recalled the failed attempt to stop fascism in Spain, and warned that the world must not let the same thing happen again. The master of ceremonies, Carmen Parente, was a Local 80 member, but a number of notables also paid tribute to Tisa, including UCAPAWA president Donald Henderson; E. Washington Rhodes, editor of Philadelphia's African American newspaper, the *Philadelphia Tribune;* and the eighty-year-old labor and Communist Party veteran Ella Reeve "Mother" Bloor.[9] Though Tisa was anxious to go to the front, his efforts were thwarted by government officials concerned about his political history and orientation, and he spent the war in a training unit at an airfield in Oklahoma.[10]

The experiences of Local 80 and its activists who were members of the Communist Party provide an interesting case for studying how the party line worked out in practice in a wartime union local. The party's subordination of all other goals to its defense of the Soviet Union was clearly evident in the pages of the union's newspaper. For many leftists, and especially party members, the best hope for the future of world socialism lay in the success of the Soviet experiment. Thus, making the fight against fascism their top objective was not inconsistent in their minds with their day-to-day tasks of building a movement against capitalism. However, the clear-cut position promulgated by party leaders became a bit muddled when it encountered the complications of the daily struggles on the shop floor.[11]

At the start of the war there was little confusion over what course the union should take; as described above, achieving maximum production was virtually the only point union leaders talked about. This goal remained important throughout the course of the war, yet its visibility in the local certainly diminished. Tactics other than the now forbidden strike were tested, especially collective bargaining negotiations and appeals to war-related government bodies. The subject of these efforts was not how workers could be more productive, but the kinds of grievances fought over before the war: wages, the Bedaux system, and discrimination. In many cases, rank-and-file-initiated work stoppages and other direct actions kept alive a more confrontational approach to dealing with problems.

One reason for the apparent decline of Local 80's single-minded goal of doing all to win the war may have been the departure of its most dedicated leftists to the front. John Tisa was the UCAPAWA's most ardent supporter in Camden of the mission to defeat fascism, and, along with other activists such as Dahl and Marino, left early to join the armed forces. Many others committed to the union's position (like Valentino) remained, but their influence was diluted among other more "bread-and-butter" unionists, such as many of the early union supporters in the Maintenance Department.

Even Valentino's support for the no-strike pledge weakened appreciably over time. Only by juggling all-out support for the war with attention to more mundane grievances could Valentino and other activists continue successfully at the helm of the organization. Another reason for the drop in support for the no-strike pledge was the growing perception by workers that the company was profiting handsomely by supplying the war effort while they were being asked to shoulder an unfair share of the sacrifices. The net result of all these factors was a complex tangle of motivations, grievances, and actions that constituted the union at Campbell during the war.

New Tactics on the Shop Floor

Though most Local 80 members believed in the correctness of their union's primary policy of helping the war effort, that was clearly not the reason why they had voted for the UCAPAWA to represent them. The problems of wages, working conditions, and respect that were at the heart of the organizing campaign did not disappear when the war started; in fact, the intensified demands on production and government-imposed restraints on wage increases made these issues more important to employees than ever. Many of the old tactics of direct action continued, but now without the sanction of the union.

Meanwhile, Local 80 experimented with a variety of new tactics, including collective bargaining, appeals to the War Labor Board, and building its shop steward system. Its record of success was less than stellar, and it would suffer in the future for some of the compromises it accepted during this period. On the other hand, union activists creatively used many of the new institutions created during the war and did not give in to company wishes without a fight. Local 80's greatest and most lasting successes in this period were in defeating several long-standing divisive company policies and in winning support among groups of workers new to the Campbell Soup Company; these achievements will be discussed in a later section of this chapter. Here the focus will be on the shifting lines in the old war of position over who would run the plant and how the fruits of the labor expended there would be allocated.

For both the company and the union locals that represented its workers in Camden and Chicago, collective bargaining and the negotiations that led to a contract were entirely new phenomena. The company was still unhappy that it was being forced to deal with "outsiders" and the "troublemakers" who symbolized the worst element—in management's view—in its workforce. For the workers who volunteered to serve on the negotiating committee, the prospect of trying to win concessions from a notoriously antiunion company must have been daunting, but they approached company representatives in negotiating meetings as equals and argued their points without backing down. Yet the union entered the meetings with one hand voluntarily tied behind its back, for it had agreed to surrender its most potent weapon, the strike. Further, both sides vied for the title of most patriotic in advancing their positions, and the union was faced with the difficult if not impossible task of both fighting speedups and advocating increased production.[12]

Both the Camden and Chicago locals signed their first contracts with the company a few months after their election victories, in early 1941. John Tisa led the negotiating teams for the union in both cities. Compared to later contracts negotiated during the war, these first agreements brought significant improvements to Campbell workers. The hiring rate for new employees was raised twelve cents per hour, and an across-the-board increase for current employees raised their pay 7.5 percent. Further, workers received one week's vacation with pay. Most important, the contracts (Camden's and Chicago's were almost identical) recognized the important protection of plantwide seniority. When the one-year contract ended in early 1942, Tisa again led a tough campaign and even threatened to take strike action. Camden's demands included a further ten-cent-per-hour pay increase, a second week's vacation, the closed shop, and a provision "that twenty per cent of the production employees of the company be colored." Claiming that the union wanted to avoid "loss of production for defense," Tisa, in a telegram to the Labor Department's director of conciliation, warned "Situation tense" and declared that the union would strike despite the no-strike pledge. The company, however, was determined not to allow the union another clear victory in its second contract. Notably, the union perceived government intervention as helpful to its side, while the company "intimated that it would contest the jurisdiction of the National War Labor Board . . . inasmuch as the company claims it is not doing defense work." Given the public record of a $554,750 contract to Campbell to supply "unit M-2 Meat and Vegetable hash" to the Quartermaster Corps depot in Chicago, the company was forced to backtrack and accept War Labor Board (WLB) jurisdiction. An agreement was finally reached in May, granting the second week of vacation, but only a 3.5-cent wage increase.[13]

Beyond wages, benefits, and union security, negotiations during the war focused directly on issues crucial to Campbell's long-term strategies to maintain low-cost production. The union fought divide-and-rule provisions that segmented the workforce and continued its difficult struggle over shop floor control as represented by the Bedaux system. Company negotiators repeatedly and consistently refused to entertain the notion that the workers or their union should have any say in how Campbell "scientifically" ran its plants. Conversely, the union never let an opportunity go by to challenge the Bedaux plan, sometimes head on, but more often chipping away at what it considered unfair aspects of the system. More time in negotiations and hearings was spent in arguing over the Bedaux system than on all other issues combined. Beyond the very existence of the system, union activists challenged it on the basis of its complexity, the ease with which it could be abused by management, its use as a speedup mechanism, and its provision that workers received only three-quarters of the bonus in excess of 60 Bs per hour (with the other quarter reserved for supervisors and other "indirect" employees). The union's Elizabeth Sasuly argued that

> over a period of years the operation of the incentive plan and various features of the incentive plan has been a continual irritating source of grievance among the workers. . . . The accumulation of these past grievances sort of burst forth in a general demand that something be done about the incentive system. . . . The workers may be very well justified in asking for the elimination of the present plan.

Nonetheless, her negotiating team did not recommend the plan's elimination, but did argue strenuously, though ultimately unsuccessfully, for significant revisions in the system. Sasuly described tumultuous union meetings in which she and other union leaders had to argue the workers out of striking over the system, and they pledged to their members that they would work to "disconnect wages from the Bedaux [*sic*]." From the company's perspective, Bedaux meant control. It was also a wedge management could use to weaken union solidarity. The union negotiated everyone's hourly base rates, but the Bedaux company counseled its clients to avoid "group payment" whenever possible, for, it claimed, "Man instinctively seeks to distinguish himself, and his interest is defeated by submergence in a group." If the union had its way, Campbell would be forced "to upgrade people on the basis of time and not on the basis of accomplishment or production," according to its personnel manager R. E. Worden, and then "we might just as well take all the industrial technicalities that have been developed and dump them in the waste basket." This the company would never do, for Dorrance and his executives no doubt agreed with the union's national research director that Bedaux was the secret of Campbell's prosperity.[14]

By the time the second one-year contract expired in early 1943, both sides had learned how to play the game and, more important, which cards were held by each side. The union was, more or less, keeping to its promise to prevent any interruptions in production, and the company knew that the local had few other options to back up its position. The union also realized the weak state it was in and turned to its only remaining hope: the government agencies set up to regulate wartime labor and production. These agencies were a poor replacement for more direct tactics, and the union, which brought fifteen ambitious demands to the start of talks for a third contract, eventually caved in entirely on eight demands and agreed to submit five issues (including a wage increase and union security) to the WLB. The board granted a union shop and dues check-off, but rejected the proposed wage hike. Local 80 tried to give a positive spin to a minor wage adjustment that raised some rates a few cents, but it was clearly not delivering the results the workers wanted. The union members most vocally dissatisfied were the craft workers of the Maintenance Department, and the local repeatedly tried to address their concerns, including a failed attempt to get the WLB to approve an extra pay increase for the craft group.[15] The union tried to redress some of the dissatisfactions with this contract by utilizing a wage-reopening provision a year later to address many more issues beyond wages, but with only limited success. Only when the end of the war freed the union from its self-imposed restraints was Local 80 able to resume its favored tactics with relish. Less than two weeks after V-J Day (and in the middle of tomato season), a "spontaneous" work stoppage shut down the entire plant until the company agreed to an immediate retroactive wage increase.[16]

Just a few weeks earlier, however, with the war still on, the Chicago local had organized an after-hours picket to protest the firing of three workers; among the signs carried by workers was one proclaiming "We Refuse to Strike." Such dedication to the war effort cost the union in support, especially as the war dragged on. Chicago Local 194 leader Veronica Kryzan complained that "during the war we upheld a no-strike pledge and the companies took advantage of the workers which caused the Union to suffer in membership." Local 80 leader Anthony Valentino feared that union membership could slip below 50 percent at Campbell's Camden plants, threatening its very future there: "We have 2600 of those 5000 [workers] in our Local. That is barely a majority. Time after time at our membership meetings the question arose by our members, 'When are we going to get an increase in our wages? What are we paying our dollar dues for?'"[17] Campbell workers had learned in the 1930s to use the workplace bargaining power that they possessed by virtue of their ability to shut down or slow production. During the war they continued to use this power when no other avenues seemed to be open, even if they had to do so without formal union support. As workers less committed to the union slowly but steadily neglected their dues payments and dropped out of active participation in the local, the dues-paying membership dropped perilously close to 50 percent of the bargaining unit in its nadir in 1945.

Campbell employees, in most cases, tried to use the new grievance machinery that emerged as a marriage of the old practice of shop floor activists confronting foremen directly and the new formal procedures laid out in the union contracts. At the first grievance level this looked very much like the traditional methods of resolving problems, though now with legal sanction: accompanied by the departmental shop steward, the aggrieved worker or workers took the complaint directly to the foreman. In an overwhelming majority of cases, the grievance was resolved right there, for foremen had no incentive to have their departments' difficulties aired out with higher management. After all, their job was to keep production moving, not serve as human relations professionals. When the source of the problem, however, emerged from upper managerial directives—especially from the Methods Engineering and Labor Standards groups—foremen had little or no authority to modify the management position. In these cases, the union pushed the grievances up the formal grievance level chain, or workers took more direct actions themselves.[18]

In the summer of 1942, managers began replacing men operating labeling machines in the Chicago plant with women. Though the men had been paid 74.5 cents per hour, the company paid the women only 57 cents per hour to perform the same job. The union took the issue through three steps of the four-step grievance procedure without resolving the problem. In exasperation, all the women on the labeling machines told their foreman at the end of their shift on October 5 that they were going to the union office and would not return to their jobs until they were paid the higher rate. The union informed the Department of Labor that a strike was in effect, but the union officials that afternoon advised the women to return to work the next day and said they would take the issue to the final grievance step. The women returned to work, but the fourth-step meeting produced no resolution. Government conciliators advised the union just to include the issue in the next contract negotiations, which were to start three weeks later, but the union "report[ed] they [were] having trouble controlling" their members, and took the issue immediately to the WLB. There the grievance apparently died in the bureaucracy while the new contract came into effect with somewhat stronger equal pay provisions.[19]

In a dispute the following year, workers took far more aggressive actions and won a far more satisfactory and immediate result. By this time Tisa and many other union leftists had enlisted in the army, and Local 80, though not condoning the work stoppage, supported the workers and used the ongoing threat of direct action to negotiate a resolution which was clearly a victory for the workers. The issue brought together two of the factors central to understanding Local 80 throughout the 1940s: the Maintenance Department and the Bedaux system. As discussed earlier, the craft workers of the Maintenance Department were at once among the most ardent unionists and the least interested in the social-justice orientation of the UCAPAWA and its leftist leaders. Further, this department was one of the few pockets of Campbell production operations still untouched by the Bedaux plan. Despite the difficulties in enumerating the many complex steps performed by maintenance mechanics, Dorrance and his Bedaux consultants were fully confident that any work operation could be scientifically analyzed and brought within the purview of the system.

Thus, at the beginning of October 1943, managers informed the mechanics that they would henceforth be required to fill out two time cards for each job they performed instead of the one simple card they had filled out previously. The second card, unlike the first, would contain a detailed description of each operation involved in performing the job, and would be punched on a time clock at the start and completion of each step. Maintenance Department workers, claiming that this was but a transparent first step in bringing the Bedaux plan to their department, refused to fill out the cards. According to department employee and union activist Joseph Gallo, "they tried to get [the Bedaux system] in our group too, but we never bought it." The company immediately suspended all 275 department employees for two days, threatening to fire any who still refused to fill out the forms at the conclusion of the suspensions. Union leader Valentino publicly supported the workers, saying "they found this speedup system was going to be forced on them and they refused, rightly, we think, to accept it." Though he advised the workers to stay on the job pending a conference with the WLB, they refused, and gathered at union headquarters. He had more luck in keeping five thousand production workers on the job who threatened to walk out in support of the suspended workers. With the actions of the maintenance men and the threat of additional trouble backing him up, Valentino hammered out a resolution with management that satisfied the workers and kept the Bedaux system at bay. The second time card was eliminated, and the company even conceded to paying the men for one of the two days that they were suspended.

Valentino's qualified support for strike action in the midst of the no-strike pledge upset Communist Party leaders, who insisted on unswerving adherence to the war effort. Valentino, like his friend John Tisa, by that time was a party supporter, and probably a member. According to an FBI informant, Valentino was "handled gently" by the party, receiving only mild criticism "because he was looked upon . . . as a man with considerable influence among the working class."[20]

Because they were hamstrung by the no-strike pledge, union activists tried to widen and deepen their influence in new ways. The primary vehicle for this effort was the shop steward system, but this was only part of a thorough plan to consolidate the power of the union in the plants. Chicago's local enumerated its program thus: "1—a strong shop steward council; 2—union education; 3—local organization; 4—publicity; 5—political action; 6—organizing the unorganized."[21]

With ninety stewards by 1944, the union's reach extended to every part of the Camden plants. Local 80 insisted that all stewards attend union meetings, and they appear to have had a high degree of success. Education of stewards in union and more general political and economic matters was a high priority. The local sent twenty-five stewards, including many women and several African Americans, to evening and weekend classes at the Philadelphia School of Social Science and Art, a "workers' school" based on a philosophy of social-justice unionism similar to that practiced by the UCAPAWA. (Chicago stewards attended the similar Abraham Lincoln School.) Courses ranged from "The Shop Steward and the Union" and "The History of Labor" to "Art in Society." Stewards sent to the school were enthusiastic about the opportunity. Benjamin Butler reported that he could "hardly wait until Wednesday nights to attend class," and John Allender said the classes should be required of all stewards: "I am learning things I never knew about unions and duties of Shop Stewards." The local also purchased subscriptions for all stewards to *In Fact,* a muckraking journal published by maverick reporter George Seldes. For Communist union activists, who were the core of the most dedicated unionists at Campbell's in the 1940s, stewards were seen as advanced workers who were the most likely candidates for building a left-oriented progressive movement within American factories. Thus some of the educational activities went beyond shop floor issues. For example, the Philadelphia School was close to the Communist Party, and the local stocked issues of the party's *Daily Worker* for sale at union headquarters.

However, the focus of steward education was overwhelmingly concerned with how stewards could do a better job as trade unionists representing the people in their departments. One of their primary duties was to get members out to union meetings, and another was to sign up more members. In August 1944, African Americans Addie Smith and Ambler Bailey took top honors in a stewards' contest to sign up new members. Sylvia Neff had started signing up members at the River Plant during tomato season before the union was recognized; in 1944, as steward in the large Preparatory Department, she won first place in a different contest for getting 228 members to sign up for automatic deduction ("checkoff") of their dues. She noted that getting to the point where she would not need to collect dues would allow her more time to work on grievances. Beyond contests, the local recognized stewards in other ways, including articles in the local and national union newspapers. In late 1943, the local held a banquet to show its appreciation of the stewards, and honored several for outstanding service. Though the union's self-imposed restraints limited its power, it was building a strong network that served it well during the war and that made the union a powerful adversary for the company once the no-strike pledge ended.[22]

If the union was exploring new ground in its efforts to build a powerful position on the shop floor, the company was by no means sleeping during the war. Campbell managers and attorneys insisted on the inclusion of contract clauses that, if fully carried out, would have meant complete victory for the company on the issue of shop floor control. Section 10 of the 1943 contract declared that "employees...shall do everything within their power to...improve the efficiency of manufacturing." Further, the next section reserved as "sole responsibilities of the Company" such powers as the right "to lay off for failure to meet Company standards of performance" and to have exclusive authority over "the schedules of production, the methods,...processes and means of manufacturing." The contract also made clear that a joint labor-management committee set up to promote "a better understanding of the incentive system... will, under no circumstances, assume management's prerogative of establishing labor standards."[23]

Beyond their vigorous opposition to union advances in collective bargaining and their drive to strengthen the Bedaux system, Campbell executives returned to a bedrock goal of John T. Dorrance: to mechanize every part of production that could be mechanized, and thereby decrease, as much as possible, the expense and troubles inherent in employing human labor. After a rigorous effort to automate many plant operations in the early decades of the century, the difficulties encountered with the remaining processes led to a shift in attention to analysis of human work processes and "scientific management."

However, the advent of the union, the labor shortage, and the increasing intractability of workers as World War II approached resulted in a renewed interest in mechanization. By the late 1930s and throughout the 1940s, Campbell engineers and inventors designed novel machinery that both sped production and lowered manpower requirements. In 1939 Campbell was granted a patent for an improved can-filling machine invented by Erich Johannes. The fact that several of the firm's best equipment-development engineers were Germans caused the company some problems during the war. Harry Nelson, who later became manager of Campbell's pilot plant, recalled that the firm's "number one" engineer, Ernie Richter, was a German citizen. When the U.S. government threatened to withdraw a contract, the company "let him go" but paid him his full salary during the war. The investment paid off, for Richter's invention of the "pulsometer" for measuring soup revolutionized that step of production. Among other improvements approved for Campbell by the Manpower Priorities Committee in early 1945 were "can manufacturing equipment," "equipment to sort, trim, clean and wash asparagus," and "hydro-magnetic basket loaders and unloaders to increase production over hand method of handling cases of soup."[24] No amount of machinery, however, could eliminate Campbell's dependence on thousands of workers, who operated the machinery but also continued to perform the myriad operations that remained manual.

🥄 Recruiting a Segmented Labor Force

Working at the Campbell Soup Company was not for everyone. When Victor DeStefano started working there before the war with several of his friends, he was the only one who was able to "stick it out." "You had to be a real man" to do the tough work required in the Campbell "slave house." Leona Laird was hired during the war, but her girlfriends, who all worked at RCA, thought she was crazy: "How can you stand working there—when you come out you smell like soup!" Despite Campbell's reputation as a tough, low-paying employer, both came to be proud of their jobs and worked there until they retired. Yet the reactions of their friends suggest the difficulty the soup company encountered in keeping its sprawling plants staffed, a problem that reached its annual peak during tomato season, when the workforce almost doubled.

As war approached, the obstacles mounted: men and women were going off to war, and many others were finding jobs in better-paying industries. The labor marketplace bargaining power of Campbell workers shot up dramatically almost overnight. Yet the company was determined not to give in to the changed situation by offering significantly higher wages, and, unlike RCA, it was not ready to leave Camden for cheap-labor regions in the South or Midwest. Under pressure from both labor market forces and the new union, Campbell did raise wages during the war, but the company's primary solution to its dilemma was to recruit new workers, especially for its peak season, from populations which had never before been part of its employee pool. From the company's perspective, there were two advantages to this approach. It could pay these new "peripheral" workers lower wages than might be demanded by those in its traditional labor pools, and, by reinforcing the segmentation of its labor force into distinct groups performing different jobs, it could weaken the solidarity that was becoming more problematic for the company now that it had to deal with the union. From the perspective of the workers, both new and old, this strategy had other important consequences. For many previously outside Campbell's traditional labor force, these opportunities provided the first step into industrial work, and, for some, into the mainland United States. For Campbell's left-oriented union, the company's attempt to divide its workers provided a challenge the union eagerly took up to enroll the new workers and fight discrimination. The union's social activism was largely successful at overcoming the divisions, though it was not universally popular among all longtime employees. The company's goals and those of the union differed on most aspects of the new labor recruitment strategy, but they agreed entirely on its primary objective: to do whatever it took to keep food production flowing for the war effort.[25]

The many-faceted campaign to pull new groups of workers into the Campbell plants reached its height during the 1944 tomato season, but only after a frantic scramble the previous season barely saved the tomato crop. In the summer of 1943, the company, the community, and the U.S. government pulled out all the stops at the last minute to process a bumper crop of tomatoes into critical food supplies for both the war and the home front. It also awakened everyone to the need for better planning for the next year.

When weather conditions that year exacerbated processing problems by ripening the tomato crop two weeks early, only heroic efforts saved a half million bushels of tomatoes. New Jersey governor Charles Edison pleaded for all available men and women to volunteer for the duration of the emergency. On August 18, "727 truck loads stretched from the plant for a distance of five miles... [and] nearly 100 railroad cars with tons of tomatoes... awaited unloading at sidings."[26] On the weekend of August 21 and 22, it seemed as if everyone in Camden had descended on the Campbell plants:

> Barbers, butchers, lawyers, artists, accountants, band leaders, city clerks, housewives, business girls—they were all over the plant... on the filling lines, the labelling lines, pushing retort baskets towards the steam cookers. The whole working force of R. M. Hollingshead in Camden paraded down Market Street at 6 in the morning with the Mayor and a band in the lead. R.C.A. employees joined the parade. French sailors, our own seamen and coast guardsmen formed their own working brigade. A banker from the Main Line took a room at the Walt Whitman Hotel and changed from his golf clothes to overalls.... By Sunday night the situation was in hand, so that Monday morning, when 1000 soldiers certified for the emergency arrived from Fort Dix, they could take over at normal pace. As a result... the State [of New Jersey] turned out 160,728,000 No. 2 cans of tomato products last season. Sixty-nine per cent went to the armed forces.[27]

Similar hectic scenes occurred through all the tomato seasons during the war, but company and government officials gradually realized that they needed to take a more proactive approach to the annual "emergencies" beyond frenzied calls for help at the last minute. Several initiatives were undertaken in what turned out to be the busiest year—1943—and by 1944 a number of "organized migration plans" brought thousands of new workers to Campbell from the South, Puerto Rico, and the English-speaking Caribbean.

The 1943 efforts, however, were more heroic than organized. To be sure, the union assisted Campbell and WMC officials in a massive push to transport almost 500 African American temporary workers from Florida to Camden. But more typical of that year's recruitment were constant calls for help from anyone in the Camden and Philadelphia area who was available. Recruiters commandeered the Camden Police Department sound car to "broadcast throughout the residential districts asking men and women

FIGURE 8.   U.S. and Royal Navy sailors helping out at the Campbell Soup Company during the severe labor shortages of World War II.
Temple University Libraries, Urban Archives, Philadelphia, Pennsylvania.

who are unemployed to report to the U.S. Employment Service [USES] office." The USES office also placed advertisements and news items in local newspapers and on radio stations and contacted over a hundred organizations for help in recruiting temporary labor, including "the P.T.A., Federated Women's Clubs, [and] American Legion Auxiliaries." In one campaign that left no doubt about where Campbell stood in the hierarchy of local employers, the employment service combed its files and called in any men or women who might be available. The WMC area director reported that "these registrants are being called in and hired by Campbell Soup interviewers. All registrants rejected by other interviewers are sent to the Campbell Soup interviewers."[28]

One large-scale organized effort in 1943 eventually succeeded in bringing several hundred workers from the South for the tomato season, but only after an extended battle that pitted a UCAPAWA Southern organizer, Campbell managers, Local 80 activists, and WMC officials against the State of Florida, citrus growers' organizations, and the Ku Klux Klan. For years thousands of African Americans from the South had joined the migrant streams of workers who provided the labor at the base of Atlantic Coast agriculture. In winter they harvested the citrus crops in Florida, then moved in ramshackle trucks to the Carolinas by early summer, and finally provided the backbreaking labor for the potato and other harvests in New Jersey. In all cases, the work was hard, intermittent, and paid the low wages typical for migrant farm labor. Only in cases where farmers faced an impending harvest but encountered a shortage of labor were migrant workers able to use their temporarily improved labor marketplace bargaining power to gain modest improvements in pay. Growers, not unexpectedly, preferred dealing with an excess of labor and often used various means to impede the annual exodus of field workers from their regions.

It was in the heart of one of these regions, in the citrus groves around Orlando, Florida, that the UCAPAWA made one of its forays into organizing workers that more traditional union leaders thought were virtually unorganizable. Union activists, led by former Oklahoma tenant farmer Otis Nation, succeeded, at least in the short term, in recruiting several hundred laborers into the Florida Citrus and Allied Workers Union, Local 4, an affiliate of the UCAPAWA. When by early June 1943 most of these workers had been laid off (as they were every spring), Nation conceived an idea (likely with the input of union president Donald Henderson) that would benefit the war food campaign, the union, and, most of all, the new members of his local. Some had already left for the annual trek to the Carolinas to earn the meager wages available there, but, if Nation's idea succeeded, they might earn union pay in a Northern industrial plant, over twice their normal wages. He contacted the regional farm placement representative of the WMC in Philadelphia, W. V. Allen, with a proposal to provide five hundred or more Local 4 members for work at Campbell Soup during the tomato season, provided his men earned full Local 80 wages and were supplied with housing and transportation by the soup company. Allen was then engaged in trying to work out a plan to move some field workers from the blueberry harvest in South Jersey to Campbell's plants in Camden, but the needs were far greater than could be satisfied from this source. He recommended to his superiors that Nation's offer be accepted, and Campbell quickly agreed to refurbish an old factory building as a barracks and charter a special train to carry the workers north at the end of July.[29]

Plans for the exodus came together quickly, as the union, the company, and the WMC rushed to work out the details, but apparently without the involvement of local Florida officials or growers. The WMC promised to provide referral cards to any workers not currently employed in an "essential industry," with the understanding that they would return to Florida by

October 15 for the citrus harvest. Campbell chartered a train and ordered two thousand sandwiches and six hundred quarts of milk for the trip. Local 4 instructed workers to visit the Orlando office of the U.S. Employment Service to secure the necessary clearances. These visits alerted Florida officials to the plan, and, after some three hundred of the five hundred workers scheduled to make the trip had received clearances, state officials moved to stop the entire project. Influential growers had recently succeeded in getting the Florida legislature to enact the Emigrant Agent Act, which required any organization seeking to transfer labor out of the state to obtain a $1000 license from the state and a $500 license from each county where the migrants resided. The union and Campbell tried to sidestep the law by calling on the WMC to handle the recruiting. In the ensuing confusion, a local KKK spokesman threatened the Campbell personnel director, and Florida newspapers attempted to inflame public opinion against the "labor pirates." On July 31, the day the chartered train arrived, Orlando police began frisking and detaining any African American male carrying a suitcase. Hundreds of workers rushed the chartered train without getting the required referral cards, and company and union officials stayed away from the train from fear of arrest or worse. WMC representatives began a fruitless attempt to check whether each man who had boarded the train was on the authorized list, but the train engineers refused to wait, and the WMC allowed the train to depart with 434 hopeful workers headed north.[30]

Led by their chief steward, Rev. W. B. Shannon, and fifty-five shop stewards, the men arrived the next day to a heroes' welcome in Camden. As the train pulled into the station, one of Local 80's African American shop stewards, Ambler Bailey, called out to the men, "Welcome, Brothers!" For the first time in their working lives they would see the benefits of working under a union contract firsthand, including a 66.5-cent-per-hour pay rate, time and a half for overtime, and the end of arbitrary supervision, as stewards from both locals worked together to iron out problems. Union leader Otis Nation warned the workers that the growers back home feared what would happen when they returned: "They are afraid that you are coming back, and that you will bring your check stubs with you to show to some of our $7 a week boys what you've been getting up here."

Nation's prediction proved correct, and these workers returned to the citrus harvest in October with a new attitude. As citrus workers began demanding better pay and working conditions, Local 4 petitioned the NLRB for certification elections at many growers and related companies. At the beginning of December, citrus workers took matters into their own hands and went beyond what UCAPAWA leaders had in mind for them. When the Florida

Wage Stabilization Board reduced the maximum wage scale in the industry, more than three thousand workers walked off their jobs in a spontaneous strike. Union leaders scrambled to pressure the War Food Administration and the WLB to take jurisdiction in the controversy, then called meetings of shop stewards to urge a return to work. After three days the workers did return, but Shannon and other local activists kept attention focused on the urgency of the issue, and Local 4's influence spread throughout the Orlando area.[31]

Shortly after the Florida workers arrived in Camden, the growers and their Florida government allies took their vengeance on Otis Nation. He was arrested on charges of violating the Emigrant Agent Act by organizing the recruitment of seasonal workers for Campbell. Simultaneously, the KKK stepped up its antiblack and antiunion campaign in Orange County. On the night of September 24, dozens of hooded Klansmen paraded through the town of Apopka, a center of UCAPAWA organizing activity, threatening several African Americans known to be union members. The union retaliated by making Nation's defense a national issue, sending him on a speaking tour and raising funds for his legal expenses.[32]

For the UCAPAWA, taking advantage of union machinery to facilitate the employment of seasonally laid-off Southern members in Northern plants experiencing seasonal labor shortages made eminent sense. Though Congress of Industrial Organizations–affiliated unions like the UCAPAWA took the first steps in trying out innovative methods to organize new groups of workers, many AFL unions soon realized they could take advantage of prounion New Deal policies to increase their memberships as well. UCAPAWA-predecessor unions had organized Seabrook Farms and other South Jersey farms and canneries in the 1930s, but most of these locals had been disbanded by the time of the war. In their place, an enterprising local of the Amalgamated Meat Cutters, Local 56, had reestablished unions in many of these businesses. Local 56 leader Leon Schachter even worked out a deal with H. L. Mitchell, president of the Southern Tenant Farmers Union (STFU), to send idle Southern cotton workers to South Jersey farms and canneries in a plan similar to that organized by Nation. The STFU had, for a short time in the late 1930s, been an affiliate of the UCAPAWA, but differences between the strong-willed leaders of each group, Mitchell and Donald Henderson, and the UCAPAWA's new focus on food-processing plants over agriculture, led to the departure of the STFU from the CIO union. Despite the lingering animosity between the UCAPAWA and the STFU, Local 80 looked the other way when Schachter even sent some of his Southern recruits into Campbell for the tomato season, no doubt because of the primacy of the war effort to UCAPAWA leaders.[33]

With the supply of African American men from Florida; short-term help from active-duty Army, Navy, and Coast Guard servicemen; and intensive local recruiting of housewives, students, and anyone else not otherwise occupied, the 1943 tomato harvest was successfully processed. But the WMC was not going to allow this essential industry to flirt with disaster for yet another year. By the early spring of 1944, plans were in the works to assure an adequate supply of low-cost labor for the Campbell Soup Company that summer. Campbell's personnel manager, R. E. Worden, listed the company's needs for the WMC: "In round numbers, we will need 2000 full time males, 2500 full time females, 1000 full time male minors and 1000 full time female minors. In addition to this, during the peak periods of the tomato canning season it will doubtless be necessary... for us to call upon the community to furnish part-time workers.... A good estimate on this number would be 5000."[34] Worden was apparently not convinced that WMC officials realized the urgency of the situation, for he followed up less than two weeks later with another letter listing the reasons why he feared that Campbell would be unable to get the workers it needed: "We cannot see where any of this labor is coming from.... The 'Puerto Rican Deal' is apparently off. The Mexican labor is apparently not available... and apparently Jamaicans and Bahamans will not be available except on an emergency basis.... We have no assurance that migratory labor from the southern states will be forthcoming."[35]

The WMC, however, was actively working to bring in labor from most of the sources Worden mentioned, as well as others. On April 6, the WMC Regional Director reported that "1000 Family groups.... Great majority white families" from West Virginia, 300 "Colored women" from Tennessee, and 1,000 workers from Florida were available for food-processing employment in New Jersey. Two new sources, however, which had previously been only slightly tapped, became the focus of WMC and Campbell recruiting that year: men from Puerto Rico and the English-speaking Caribbean. Once again, Campbell became the entry point into industrial work for new groups of laborers, and, in the case of Puerto Ricans, the company became the conduit for migrants from the island to the heretofore tiny Puerto Rican enclaves in Camden and Philadelphia. Campbell's use of noncitizen Jamaicans and Barbadians demonstrated the harsher side of capital's employment of disposable labor who possessed virtually no legal rights, and whose resentment sometimes flared into angry confrontations.[36]

The "Puerto Rican Deal" brought together the Campbell Soup Company, the WMC, and the government of Puerto Rico in an effort to relieve both unemployment on the island and Campbell's labor shortages. It was an experiment (also involving a small number of other companies) that, though successful in meeting its primary goals, was discontinued the following year. The problem was not the productivity of Puerto Rican workers but the fact that they were U.S. citizens and thus not subject to deportation when the need for their labor ended. Instead of returning to Puerto Rico at the conclusion of their work contracts, many settled in Camden and Philadelphia; some observers even claimed that "the first...founders of the Puerto Rican community in Philadelphia came under contract to the Campbell Soup Company in Camden." As Victor Vázquez-Hernández has shown, a small Hispanic community, including some Puerto Ricans, already existed in Philadelphia before the war, but the Campbell-induced migration certainly swelled the Puerto Rican population in that city and initiated a process of chain migration that eventually led to a large Puerto Rican community there.[37]

The WMC did not directly recruit workers from Puerto Rico; instead, it "assisted employers' representatives in the recruitment," arranged transportation, and made itself available to companies in the event of "problems." The assistance of the WMC was invaluable in Campbell's case, especially in organizing transportation during the severe shortages of wartime. In assuring Campbell's Worden that the WMC was serious about the "Puerto Rican Deal," R. J. Eldridge wrote that "shipping space is available to bring in 900 about the first of August. It is estimated that the transportation cost will be approximately $50.00 per head, with delivery at New York City." The recruitment of workers on the island was done by both Campbell representatives who traveled from Camden and officials from the island government. Most migrants came to Campbell on contract (about two hundred in June and three hundred in July, 1944), though many also were recruited on an individual basis. Those coming under contract had certain limited benefits, but also were subject to more stringent controls. Workers were guaranteed employment for a specified number of months and a rate of pay "not lower than that paid by the Employer to his domestic employees." Transportation costs to Camden were deducted from workers' paychecks, but the company agreed to pay return costs "provided that the Worker requests such return transportation within ten days after...termination." The company also provided barracks, but deducted housing costs from workers' pay as well.[38]

A central focus of the contracts and the mechanisms set up to administer them, however, addressed neither conditions of employment nor the welfare of the migrants, but instead control of the workers. Contract laborers at Campbell could be identified by Social Security numbers beginning with "219-09." Campbell was instructed to inform the local USES office in the event of any termination of employment. The employment office threatened any worker considering leaving contracted work with a host of negative consequences:

> Calling to the attention of the worker the legal nature of his obligations under the contract. . . . Pointing out that the worker will forfeit his right to return transportation. . . . Reminding the worker that . . . he automatically becomes liable for a 30% withholding from his wages. . . . Impressing upon the worker that if he breaks his contractual relationship he will lose his right to deferment under the Selective Service System.

Nonetheless, the experiment was considered a failure, for of the 2,200 laborers brought under contract to Campbell, the B&O Railroad, and other employers in 1944, only about one-quarter completed their contracts and just 15 percent returned to Puerto Rico. Before the 1944 contract season was even completed, the program was discontinued.[39]

Though the program did not last, it did set in motion a process of chain migration that eventually brought many families to the Delaware Valley. Of some one thousand Puerto Rican men who came to work at Campbell during the war (under contract and individually), sixty-five were still with the company in 1961, but many more had moved on to other jobs and still lived in the region. Marcelino Benitez signed a contract and came to Camden from his native Carolina, Puerto Rico. Juan Canales came a year later but tired of working only during the tomato season and got other work. Both resided at a boarding house in Philadelphia. A worker referred to as Don Santiago was recruited to Campbell in 1944 but three years later sent for his wife and moved to Philadelphia. After his family "got established" in Philadelphia, he sent for other relatives, including his sister and her children.[40]

Campbell never relied entirely on contracted labor from Puerto Rico. When the WMC program ended, the company stepped up its own recruitment on the island. In 1945, the company's J. E. Heap traveled the island signing up workers. Jorge Melendez had moved from his father's farm in Cidra to San Juan, where he worked as a clerk in a grocery store. When Heap stopped in one day he asked Melendez if he would be interested in coming to the mainland to work at Campbell. Melendez agreed, but decided not to live in the barracks ("they were too dirty") and instead got an apartment across the street. Though his future wife also came from Puerto Rico, he met her at a dance in Camden, where she worked in a garment factory. Luz Morales had come to Camden from Ponce with a girl friend "for a better life." After her marriage to Jorge in 1946 she became one of the first Puerto Rican women to work at the soup company. She worked there ten years until her job was eliminated by automation, but her husband continued working at Campbell until retirement. Over several decades they lived and raised a family in South Jersey.[41]

Jorge Melendez's opinion of the barracks at Campbell, which housed African American migrants from the South, Puerto Ricans, and Jamaicans, was shared by most who lived there or visited. The crowding and minimal facilities made life difficult for residents, and even led to serious health problems. Oscar Braite and Warren Cala were diagnosed with "epidemic type spinal meningitis" three weeks after their arrival in the "[Puerto Rican] section of a labor barracks at 2nd and Arch St." In response, the director of the Camden Health Department ordered the quarantine of all three hundred Puerto Rican workers in that section of the barracks. Plant physician Paul Loudenslager reassured the public that there was "no cause for alarm," claiming, without further explanation, that the Puerto Rican workers "[did] not come in direct contact with the food."[42] When the disease failed to spread further, the quarantine was lifted and Campbell again took full advantage of the labor provided by its Puerto Rican workers.

From the perspective of the Campbell Soup Company, Puerto Ricans provided an excellent solution to at least a part of their "labor problem." They were more than willing to accept what most Camden workers considered low pay and tough working conditions, and managers generally gave high marks to the quality of their work. Yet Puerto Ricans carried with them a liability: their U.S. citizenship. A report of the President's Commission on Migratory Labor overstated the facts when it claimed that Puerto Ricans were "not utilized" in the "wartime labor program." But it accurately captured the sentiments of many politicians and employers when it quoted the president of a Florida growers' association: "The vast difference between the Bahama Island labor and the domestic, including Puerto Rican, is that labor transported from the Bahama Islands can be diverted and sent home if it does not work, which cannot be done in the instance of labor from domestic United States or Puerto Rico."[43] Though Campbell managers had little concern whether their seasonal help left the area or stayed after the end of tomato season, they quickly adapted to the greater availability and real advantages the firm could gain from a labor pool that could "be diverted and sent home if it does not work." It found this pool in the large numbers of temporary laborers that the WMC was providing from the English-speaking Caribbean.

As a young man in the British colony of Jamaica, Renford Glanville was excited by returnees from the United States dressed up and driving new cars. Faced with only two options during the war—joining the army or working in food production in the United States—he opted for the latter. Though his contract sent him to work at Seabrook, hundreds of his countrymen, as well as others from the Bahamas, Barbados, and British Honduras, found themselves living in Campbell's barracks and working at the soup company.

The WMC implemented a sizable program in 1944 to bring these British subjects to the United States. In the previous year, about 450 Jamaicans had been employed in New Jersey canning and food processing plants, but "in violation of the agreement with the Governor of Jamaica," causing a mild diplomatic row. Whatever misunderstandings existed in 1943 were apparently worked out, for the numbers of English-speaking Caribbeans employed in the United States increased markedly in each of the next two years. Campbell Soup employed 130 Jamaicans (and some other Caribbeans) in 1944. Though Campbell eagerly continued hiring individual Puerto Ricans the following year, the discontinuation of the WMC program to contract and transport workers from the island resulted in a sharp drop in Puerto Rican job applicants. In their place, Campbell increased its employment of Caribbean British subjects to some seven hundred.[44]

Though conditions for all new groups of workers recruited by Campbell were poor, Jamaicans suffered some of the worst conditions and treatment by bosses at the soup plant. They were given the hardest jobs, and were fired—and immediately deported—at the slightest infraction of company rules. In response, Jamaicans became known as the most rebellious and troublesome of the new workers. The U.S. liaison officer for these workers became alarmed at the petty firings and deportations, and argued that the workers "naturally become resentful and suffer the sense of being ill-treated." He was inundated with complaints from Jamaicans and Barbadians employed at Campbell: "In the event of any trouble between the employing firm and the worker the imported workers are given no formal hearing. . . . Campbell's version is simply confirmed without any chance of defending themselves." He described one case in which a worker "was sentenced to repatriation for dipping his finger into a pan of soup." One result of such treatment was the disappearance of workers charged with infractions who went AWOL rather than submit to deportation. In another case, a Jamaican cursed his foreman when he was told to work faster. The foreman hit him with a large hook, breaking his shoulder, but the Jamaican was fired while the foreman was not even disciplined.[45]

Because of the perceived difficulty in managing Jamaicans, Campbell management had mixed feelings about employing them, despite their advantages as easily disposable low-wage workers. J. E. Heap of the company's personnel department eagerly hired anyone willing to accept Campbell's wages and working conditions; he had been the company's representative in

Florida during the controversial recruitment of citrus workers, and he personally went to Puerto Rico to sign up workers. When he learned that 161 Jamaicans in Eustace, Virginia, were available for immediate employment, he signed contracts to bring them all to Camden. But when his superior, R. E. Worden, found out what he was doing, he ordered Heap not to take any Jamaicans, but was too late: Heap had already committed the company to hiring the workers. WMC officials feared that the "Jamaicans at Eustace [were] ready to riot if they [didn't] get employment" and warned Worden that the Jamaicans could sue Campbell for 480 hours pay per worker, plus transportation costs home. After conferring with Campbell's president and counsel, Worden reluctantly agreed to accept the men, and 152 boarded a special train for Camden the same night. A WMC official noted, "everybody satisfied, if not happy." Heap was apparently not discouraged, for he continued to encourage men from the British Caribbean to come to Camden (at their own expense), promising that Campbell would "be glad to accept you...as employees."[46]

When the war ended the WMC moved to repatriate all foreign laborers and replace them with returning servicemen. Yet Campbell Soup, and especially the irrepressible Mr. Heap, tried to keep its seven hundred foreign workers until the end of the tomato season in 1945. Heap argued to the WMC that "the continued employment of these foreign laborers is absolutely essential to the successful completion" of peak-season processing. Though Heap asked for an extension to October 15, the company announced on August 24 "that 700 West Indies laborers...would be released to make way for displaced war workers." Despite the difficulties in managing an allegedly intractable labor force, the company only reluctantly let go of a critical part of its overall strategy to remain a low-cost producer.[47]

With the assistance of the U.S. government, Campbell could control almost every aspect of the lives of the Jamaican workers it employed: where they lived, what they did, and whether they stayed or were sent back home. But one other group presented the company with the opportunity for total control: German prisoners of war. There had been some limited use of prisoners of war in food processing plants in South Jersey, but Campbell applied to the WMC for a massive increase for the 1945 peak season. On March 7 of that year, certifications for six hundred prisoners for Campbell were sent to the regional WMC director. Army officials insisted that the employment of such a large group would require the construction of a camp nearby, which would cost Campbell at least $25,000. Campbell had a sudden change of heart, and decided "it would not be practical" to hire such labor. Despite this one reversal, Heap, Worden, and the rest of the Campbell recruiters had tapped virtually every possible source of cheap labor, and the company met all of its production demands during the war.[48]

🍎 Division and Unity in the Campbell Workforce

Both company and union supported and actively participated in the recruitment efforts that kept soup and C rations rolling out of the doors of the Camden plants, but the two sides approached the issue from decidedly different vantage points. Management had long viewed its workforce as composed of distinct groups playing different roles in the overall manufacturing process. White men of generally Anglo-Saxon Protestant background composed upper and middle management. White men who were usually recent immigrants or the sons of immigrants cooked the soup, operated most of the machines, and filled the ranks of the craft workers in the Maintenance Department. Women from similar backgrounds worked at the many preparatory jobs and in can making. African American men performed basic labor and worked as janitors and locker room attendants. Perhaps the greatest distinction was between permanent and seasonal workers, and it was for the latter category that new groups of "peripheral" workers were hired. Such a segmented labor force strategy had worked well for American industry, and it was most clearly visible at companies like Campbell. The soup company stood at the low edge of U.S. employers in terms of pay and working conditions, and it straddled the industrial-agricultural divide, drawing from the same groups that worked the truck farms of South Jersey. Even New Deal labor law recognized the special status of canneries. Cannery workers were covered under federal and state wage and hour laws, but with large gaps exempting employers from important provisions.

That Campbell divided its workforce along gender, age, racial, and ethnic lines was patently clear. The company's actions also demonstrated that this was more than an inadvertent consequence of societal norms; leaders of the firm promoted division as part of their overall control strategy, especially after the arrival of the union. A segmented labor force made it easier for the company to keep wages low, and the small differences in pay and conditions encouraged resentment and disunity. Conversely, the social-justice unionism of the UCAPAWA/FTA led it to make worker unity a cardinal principle of its day-to-day work. As each new group of workers entered Campbell's gates during World War II, managers funneled them into distinct jobs, job paths, and even separate housing, while union activists fought to break down barriers and present a united face to the company.

Though the Camden plant had long employed African American men in a few job categories, company policy dictated that no African Americans would work at the Chicago plant. Yet shortly after the start of the war, labor shortages forced the company to open its doors to black men there as well. In neither city, however, did the company employ African American women, even as late as 1942. In fact, while the company was refusing to hire a single one of a thousand black women who filled out applications in Chicago, it was running advertisements in a local Polish newspaper for female help. In both cities the union made this a big issue and eventually claimed credit for breaking down the barriers of discrimination, though their efforts were undoubtedly aided by wartime shortages of workers. In the end Campbell conceded, but the way it did so illustrated the company's ongoing commitment to keeping its workforce divided.

In both cities, verbal agreements to begin hiring black women went unfulfilled until the union threatened to take the cases to the Fair Employment Practices Committee (FEPC). When Local 80 sent the company a letter in late 1942 detailing several cases in which the company had refused to hire black women and indicating that the next step would be a complaint to the FEPC, managers posted copies of the letter all over the plant "in order to create a division between white and Negro" workers. Though this action "created a small stir," union activists used the opportunity to discuss the issue with plant workers, emphasizing in particular that discrimination was harming the war effort, and dissention within the ranks dissipated, at least for the time being. When the union undertook a similar campaign in Chicago in 1943, the company said it would comply with the request to hire African American women on the condition that it could keep black and white women segregated. The union refused to accept this condition, even though Veronica Kryzan and other union leaders were called "Nigger lovers" for trying to open the plant to African Americans. The activists succeeded in maintaining the support of the great majority of workers, according to Kryzan, because the union had previously fought against discrimination targeted at the largely Slavic workforce in the Chicago plant.[49]

Just opening the doors to African Americans in no way ended the company's discrimination toward them nor its segmentation of the workforce, which was as rigid as ever. Even before the war, when many African American men worked at Campbell in Camden, the company enforced a separation of racial groups that approached apartheid. African Americans could be found in only the most menial jobs, there were no black supervisors, and even employee lockers were separated by race. Among the company's meager social programs for employees, African Americans were limited to an all-black chorus and the "Colored Athletic Association." In 1936 a company publication praised the record of the association's baseball team: "We are glad to hear these boys are doing so well this year."[50] The next year the Campbell Soup Company became a prime sponsor of the *Amos 'n' Andy* radio program. In this extremely popular daily (and later weekly) radio comedy, which portrayed African Americans almost invariably as lazy and either conniving or dim-witted, two white actors voiced the parts of the title characters. So it was not surprising that, after the influx into Campbell's plants of black men and women during the war, African Americans were still isolated in a handful of jobs and separated socially from white workers.

But neither these workers nor their union were willing to accept "business as usual" anymore, though the reactions of other workers were mixed. After Sylvester Akins left the Navy in 1943, he went to a vocational school to learn auto body and fender work, but soon hired on at Campbell. For three years his job consisted of cleaning the pots used in making soup on the night shift. When more desirable—and better-paying—jobs in the all-white Digester Department and the Butcher Shop opened up, African Americans were not considered for the positions. As Akins recalls, "we had to fight" to force those jobs to be opened to all. Management's treatment of African Americans went beyond a mere separation of racial groups, but was rooted in a deeply ingrained view of them—held by a number of important Campbell managers—as inferior. Reverend David Burgess, who ministered to the migrants at Campbell recruited through the STFU, said of employment director Worden, "Like other Campbell officials, he has a *very* low opinion of the Negro." In a letter to the WMC, Worden explained that Campbell would not give release letters to the migrants from Florida because they would, he claimed, lose them: "Our experience this summer in supervising the workers' Barracks confirms this thinking."[51]

The company's practice in dealing with Puerto Ricans and other groups replicated in many ways its approach toward African Americans. They were initially assigned to only certain jobs, were housed in separate barracks, and, in the rare cases when they participated in company social activities, they did so apart from other workers, as in the company's Puerto Rican Ensemble.[52]

When African Americans and Puerto Ricans joined the Campbell workforce they occupied separate and inferior locations in the structure of production. But none of these groups worked at the Chicago plant before the war, and only African American men worked at the Camden plants before 1942, and then in only a few job categories. Women, however, played an integral role in production from the beginning of Campbell Soup Company. Furthermore, Campbell used traditional views of women's work to justify paying them far less than men; in fact, the food-processing industry was built upon a gendered structure of labor. By defining the jobs women performed as "simple" and unskilled and paying them accordingly, Campbell reaped enormous profits from the labor of women over and above the substantial profits it realized from men's labor. Before the union came to Campbell, the women's starting rate averaged 72 percent of men's. Further, it was almost impossible for women to advance in their careers beyond the jobs and pay they received when first hired. Women were excluded from the majority of job categories in the plant. About 80 percent worked in ingredient preparation, peeling potatoes, inspecting rice, and sorting tomatoes—jobs similar to what women allegedly did at home and, thus, "unskilled" by definition. These workers received but one increase of a few cents a short time after they were hired, and had no possibility of progressing further, except by earning a bonus by exceeding the number of B units set for their jobs by labor standards engineers. Most men's jobs, on the other hand, continued to increase by grades over a long period of time until they reached the job's maximum rate. A single small category of women workers did receive a second small increase in pay: chicken eviscerators. Apparently the company was forced to take this measure due to the unpopularity of this unpleasant job. During contract negotiations, company representatives argued strenuously against any alteration in the company's division of labor and pay by gender. When union negotiators argued that "girls" performing a job done before the war by men should be paid the male rate, production manager J. M. Hoerle responded with alarm, declaring that paying these young women the higher rate "would throw them out of line with the prevalent rate of female labor in our plant... and completely destroy our entire wage structure," and that "this... would serve to cause more trouble in our labor relations than any single thing I can think of."[53]

The war, in fact, brought constant challenges to the mythology of the unskilled nature of women's work, for the absence of men forced the company to put women on many formerly male jobs. While most women had worked in food preparation, the war pushed the canning industry, as it did many others, to utilize women's labor in new ways. Women were, for the first time, employed in controlling retorts, operating filling and closing machines, and even heavy labor. In many cases, these changes did not survive the war. Along with women in factories across the United States, "women's work" was again redefined when men came home from war. Leona Laird remembers that "when the fellas came out of the service we started losing packing jobs" and she and other women went back to their old jobs ("that was okay with me as long as I had a job"). But women had demonstrated by their work that the company's discriminatory policies were merely an excuse to define women's work as cheap labor.[54]

The company made explicit its desire to preserve the gap between male and female workers by trying to keep any wage increases on a percentage basis. In this way, the relative difference by gender would be maintained. Company negotiators argued strongly against wage increases of a certain number of cents per hour across the board, which would tend to narrow the gap.[55]

Women workers at Campbell were divided from male workers by being limited to a narrow range of jobs and locked into a wage structure significantly lower than men's. But even among male workers a myriad of divisions existed. African American, Puerto Rican, and Caribbean men, when employed at all, occupied only the lowest rungs of the employment ladder, especially before the advent of the union. The white native-born and immigrant men who filled the full range of production jobs were further split into two groups: "men" and "boys." Until the age of twenty-one, males were rated as "boys," and, though the work they performed was often as strenuous as that assigned to older workers, they were paid at a much lower rate. In 1935, the rate for unskilled men was fifty cents per hour, while for boys it was forty cents; women received thirty-six cents in equivalent job categories. In some other years the starting rates for boys and women were the same. Just as Campbell management fought any modification of its separate and inferior categories for women, it bitterly opposed any change to its pay scales for younger men. When union negotiators demonstrated that the level of work and skill involved in jobs rated as men's and boys' were the same, company representatives fell back on the defense that all job classifications had been done "scientifically" by an outside engineering firm, and were thus not open to question. The union's Elizabeth Sasuly responded that "the main issue involved is the inequities between jobs that require at least the same amount of skill and effort, where you have a discriminatory wage, just for no reason but to enable the Company to underpay a considerable number of jobs." She reminded the company managers that "boys" of eighteen and nineteen were at that very moment, ten days after D-Day, fighting and dying as soldiers in Europe and the Pacific Theater. The company refused to budge on the issue; the intricate segmentation of the Campbell workforce was too important.[56]

Campbell's pool of workers was segmented in another way, one that cut across lines of gender, race, and age and that was present from the very beginning of the company. This division, into permanent and contingent labor forces, is one that has received much attention in the late twentieth and early twenty-first centuries as global corporations downsize their core workforces and offload many tasks to temporary and part-time workers. In Campbell's case, its contingent workforce was made up of the thousands hired during the tomato season. These seasonal workers were paid less than year-round employees, and they were marked as different—and of lower rank—in conspicuous ways. Their employee badges bore a large, black *T* across the entire emblem, and they worked as subordinates to full-timers, who were often appointed as tomato season supervisors though they normally worked at production jobs.

In addition to providing the massive amount of low-cost labor needed to process the harvest, seasonal workers were used in other ways central to Campbell's personnel strategies. Most full-timers began as temporaries. Those who worked hardest and complained the least were most likely to be hired on as permanent workers. During periods of labor trouble, like the 1934 strike, the company hired large numbers of tomato season workers to replace union supporters. Then and in other years, "good" employees were rewarded with being able to bring in relatives for the season. While seasonal work was a conduit to permanent work for some in Campbell's traditional labor pools, it was the only work that members of other peripheral groups would ever see at the soup company. Certainly no Jamaicans or Bahamians were hired on permanently in the 1940s, and Florida migrants and Puerto Ricans under contract generally left Campbell at the end of the season, especially in the early years. This section of Campbell's contingent labor force suffered the worst conditions, as described earlier, but there were no negative consequences for the company. What historian Cindy Hahamovitch has written of farm employers applies equally well to Campbell: "They have averted criticism and conflict by importing workers who can be exploited without apology or protest." Though the union made many efforts to organize and involve seasonal workers, the short-term nature of their employment made this exceedingly difficult.[57]

The UCAPAWA locals in Camden and Chicago did, in fact, make fighting the divide-and-rule tactics of the company a core component of their work. Union activists fought racial discrimination, worked to close the gap between men's and women's wages, and demanded an end to the "boys" classification. Their efforts paid off to a degree that may have surprised even them, though they sometimes had to overcome resistance from within the ranks of the union. Several of the activists most committed to building unity and ending discrimination were members of the Communist Party, but many spontaneous battles in this struggle were set off by rank-and-file workers. These were most often African Americans refusing to accept discriminatory practices, but also included some white workers, especially shop stewards, who were convinced of the need for unity.

From its beginning, the UCAPAWA strongly and openly fought racial discrimination. At its first convention, delegates adopted a resolution "condemning [this] reactionary practice," not only on the part of employers and government but also within the union movement. The union newspaper constantly carried articles on the advances won by its locals in opening up companies like Campbell to black workers. It also dealt with racial issues outside its industry, condemning the 1943 race riots and the "pro-Hitler" 1944 wildcat strike by a company union faction against the upgrade of black workers in Philadelphia's transit system. In the latter case, the UCAPAWA and Local 80 expressed support for the CIO-affiliated Transport Workers Union, which opposed the strike, and even sent a telegram to President Franklin Delano Roosevelt calling for him to send in federal troops.[58]

The UCAPAWA's stand against discrimination was not limited, however, to resolutions and pronouncements on national issues. In the daily life of Local 80 (and Local 194 in Chicago) the fight for unity came right down to the shop floor. Shop stewards, white and black, defended black workers against autocratic foremen, and ending discrimination was a constant and important part of union demands in every contract negotiation. In the 1942 negotiations, Local 80 even made the extraordinary demand for a minimum quota for black workers: "that twenty per cent of the production employees of the company be colored." Though the company adamantly refused to accept an antidiscrimination clause in the contract until the mid-1950s, African American workers, shop stewards, and union leaders fought to break down barriers in one department after another. The task of integrating Campbell was not an easy one; activists faced opposition not only from management but also from many white workers. Sadie Harris, who started at Campbell in 1944, recalled that when the first African American was hired for a job in the press room, all the white workers walked out. Under pressure from their union and threat of dismissal from management, they soon returned. Reactions in other departments were not always as overt, but sometimes made it difficult for African Americans to qualify for better jobs. Sylvester Akins remembers some white workers who "didn't want to train you" and who even went to the lengths of diluting the soup to get a black worker fired. Franklin Williams felt that whites "resented you right away if you got an operator's job.... [They] always tried to show they had more intelligence." When he started at Campbell at the end of the war, "there were only certain jobs you could get." After doing the "backbreaking work" of feeding cans on the belt, he asked for a promotion to the easier job of labeling machine operator. "They'd say, 'You don't want that job,' but they were making more money."[59]

Yet not all white workers fought the integration of their departments. Many accepted their new coworkers and even helped them learn the ropes. Sadie Harris recalls an Italian woman named Nancy who was "very nice" and trained her in her new job. Decades later most white workers recalled only good relationships among workers of all races. Leona Laird and Joe and Jenny Morrison all remember African Americans, whites, and Puerto Ricans working side-by-side without problems: "we all got along." Most black workers experienced the early years as far more conflictual, but, especially as the production departments opened up to African Americans, the work environment itself provided a material basis for overcoming divisions. For example, Victor DeStefano ran a labeling machine, but he worked with a black assistant and a black "packer girl": "We made the [Bedaux system] incentive together, or not at all." Several other workers, black and white, made the same point, suggesting that the system used to discipline and speed up workers ironically also encouraged people to work together and overcome differences. The unity that grew from working together sometimes extended beyond the workplace. When Jorge and Luz Melendez moved from Camden to an all-white neighborhood in suburban Pennsauken, some of their new neighbors began "raising hell." When the neighbors gathered to plan how they would drive out the unwelcome newcomers, one of the residents angrily denounced the plans and defended her coworker at Campbell, Luz Melendez. "They are better than we are!" she shouted. After more heated discussions, the troublemakers backed down. The Melendez family was soon accepted by their neighbors and became an integral part of the neighborhood.[60]

If the simple fact of working together contributed, in many cases, to the overcoming of long-held prejudices, Local 80's leaders went out of their way to fight discrimination and disunity as a cardinal principle of the union's practice. They fought to open up employment to black women, as did their counterparts in Chicago. Local 80's Anna Layton was the sole woman on the South Jersey Industrial Union Council's Committee Against Racial Discrimination in 1944. When Puerto Ricans began working at Campbell the same year, Local 80 activists recruited several shop stewards from among them and signed up three-quarters of the new workers as union members. While the union was not able to do away instantly with discrimination everywhere, it fought disunity on many fronts. In the case of African Americans, it broke down barriers in one department after another, until all but the craft-based Maintenance Department were integrated. In the case of women, it demanded equal pay for equal work, and negotiated higher raises for women than for men in almost every contract. Thus, while the women's starting rate was 72 percent, on average, of the men's wages before the union, the average rose to 76 percent by the second contract and 94 percent by 1950. Leading Local 80's campaign against discrimination was Anthony Valentino. Though called a "nigger lover" by some for his actions, Sadie Harris recalls him as "a fighter...he worked for all of us." Sylvester Akins adds, "he was a Martin Luther King...he really put life into the union." By facing the prejudices that many workers held head-on and by openly fighting the segmentation of the workforce that encouraged disunity, Local 80 succeeded to a large degree in building the united front needed to stand up to the company.[61]

Yet that united front never extended to every corner of the Campbell plants or to every union member. Campbell did not succeed in building a workforce that was sufficiently internally divided to make it powerless against the company's designs for control. Its divisive tactics, however, combined with prejudices many workers brought with them to their jobs, did have corrosive effects that weakened the united front and made the union's job tougher. As African Americans made up an increasingly larger proportion of the workforce at Campbell, they saw the real benefits—especially the opening up of better-paying jobs and new departments—that came from worker unity and the principled stand of their union. As a result, most became staunch union supporters, volunteering to be shop stewards and helping out in other ways. Just six months after starting at Campbell, Sylvester Akins became steward for his department—"seeing how it was a need for someone to represent the people." He later became assistant chief steward, then recording secretary of the local. For white workers, the message was less clear. Many had worked in departments that had the dubious privilege of being all white. Management could hold out the marginal rewards of slightly higher pay to various groups: craft workers over production workers, men over women and boys, year-round employees over temporaries. But the union was able to demonstrate the even larger benefits workers could realize by overcoming these differences and standing united against foremen or top management. Thus, many white workers also became active union supporters, and not infrequently a white steward could be found fiercely defending a black fellow worker against a white boss. Steward Victor DeStefano was called to the aid of a black worker fired on the spot for being found with an open can of spaghetti by a supervisor with a reputation as a "tough guy." DeStefano stormed into the supervisor's office and asked if he saw the worker opening or eating from the can. When the boss admitted he hadn't, DeStefano yelled "So give him his fucking badge back and let him go back to work!" Forced to back down, the supervisor relented, but threatened the steward: "I'll get you!" Not long afterward he caught the unionist smoking in the men's room and suspended him for five days. But the company was not able to use racial identity in this case to get a white steward to side with another of his race over another of his class.[62]

In other cases, however, white workers resented the special attention to issues of discrimination and the egalitarian ideology of the union. As mentioned earlier, the reaction of one department to racial integration was a short walkout. But only in the case of the all-white-male Maintenance Department, composed of craftsmen plying a number of trades, did the question of unity fall to the advantages of privilege. In other industries craftsmen occupied a special place, with jobs protected by limited-entry unions and pay significantly higher than that received by most blue-collar workers. At Campbell, however, maintenance mechanics always had to struggle to receive the advantages they felt were their just due. In fact, this made them among the strongest early supporters of unionization (along with the left-oriented social unionists), and their steadfastness even kept the Bedaux system out of their department. The uneasy alliance of progressives and craftsmen held together for a time, but many leaders in the Maintenance Department began to resent the fact that the union was fighting to narrow wage gaps while pushing for increases for all. Mechanic Joseph Gallo complained that "these people [leading the union] didn't favor any group.... We were always battling, fighting to get more money for machinists." Though Local 80 did attempt to win certain contract concessions to appease Maintenance, it was clearly more devoted to organizing and improving the lot of the waves of new employees coming to Campbell. Gallo recalled that, with the onset of the war, Campbell "had to hire colored" for more than the janitorial jobs they previously held, and, "once they get in, you can't get rid of them." The UCAPAWA/FTA and Local 80 had clearly decided to throw their lot with the production workers—black and white, men and women—and this portended a problematic future for those whose idea of the proper role for a union hearkened back to an exclusivist craft tradition. Management was not unhappy with this division in the union; according to Gallo, "the company was even on our side." Company officials told the Maintenance Department men in confidence that "we'd like to help you people, but we want peace," with the clear implication that the local's concern with African Americans and women was keeping the craftsmen from getting the rewards that should come from their special position. Even outside the plant gates, some long-time Camden residents who worked at white male bastions like New York Shipbuilding began blaming Campbell (and the Benjamin Franklin Bridge, which connected Camden to Philadelphia) for bringing in "outsiders" who were "ruining" the city. As the Campbell Soup Company labor force was transformed during the war, its internal fissures never developed into an open fracture. Nonetheless, these divisions, which also spread to a small degree beyond the Maintenance Department, made clear the very real negative potential of a divided workforce.[63]

The Role of the State: Campbell's Partner in Labor Segmentation

Arthur Dorrance and his management team worked hard to keep the profits rolling in during World War II. In keeping with a core component of their approach, they refused to allow their costs to rise appreciably by meeting labor market shortages with significantly higher pay. Production and revenue roughly doubled during the war, and such large increases required massive investment in plant and equipment. Campbell financed this investment—which would continue to pay dividends after the war— solely through its revenues. Such expenditures might have been expected to cut profits temporarily, but the Campbell board ensured that annual net profits going to the Dorrance family coffers continued at about eleven to fourteen million dollars each year. If company directors had reduced dividends in order to raise wages to meet labor market prices they would have continued running a reasonably profitable business. Further, the end result would still have been greatly increased company assets and the foundation for future profitability. Instead, they recruited new groups of workers who would accept the existing labor deal, and in turn keep longtime workers from using their newfound muscle in the labor marketplace to exact a better deal from the company. Despite ups and downs, they were successful in this strategy. Yet as described above, their workers and their union, UCAPAWA Local 80, were also apparently largely successful in fending off the divide-and-rule tactics of management. How, then, was the company able to succeed in its overall goal without more serious concessions to its newly organized and energetic workforce? The answer lay in its relationship with a very important silent partner: the state. In virtually every case when Campbell appeared in danger of failing, various agencies of the U.S. government came to the rescue.

The most crucial service provided by the government came in the recruitment of whole new sources of low-cost labor. Agencies including the U.S. Employment Service and the WMC brought in thousands of new workers from the South, Puerto Rico, Jamaica, and elsewhere. To keep new workers in line—and fulfilling their contracts—government officials threatened to report Puerto Ricans who left their jobs to the Selective Service. British subjects from the Caribbean were summarily sent home if they stepped out of line. To fill shortfalls, the military even granted leaves to soldiers, sailors, and coast guardsmen to keep the soup and C-ration plants running. Though the contracts and arrangements under which these new employees worked generally guaranteed them the going wage, their presence relieved Campbell from the need to revamp its entire pay structure upward to meet the realities of a tight labor market. The government was even prepared to provide large numbers of prisoners of war to preclude a labor shortage. For longtime employees who had been working at Campbell before the war and who had tasted the fruits of a union contract for the first time in 1941, other government agencies kept a lid on future wage increases. During the war, union negotiators had to surmount two hurdles to win raises for their members: they needed to wring concessions from Campbell, then get the WLB to agree to any increases. In addition, the formal grievance machinery put in place under the sanction of the NLRB became an important factor in labor control during the stricter reign of the WLB. Even before the wartime regime, the grievance process had regulated and individualized shop floor problems, which otherwise might have flared into collective direct action; the WLB attempted to guarantee that such problems would never interfere with production.

Government assistance to Campbell went beyond labor supply and control. Contracts to supply the military with C rations and various canned food products grew to about half of total production during the war, assuring a steady revenue stream. In this period of government rationing, the company also depended on administrators to allocate tin plate and other essential materials. The presence of Campbell's rising executive star, William Beverly Murphy, in Washington as a "dollar-a-year man" during the war aided immeasurably in the favorable treatment the company received.

Clearly, the role of the state in this period was central to the continued profitability of the company. Campbell's reliance on a divided workforce to keep labor costs down was successfully challenged by its new union. Yet a clear victory for labor was short-circuited by two factors: the union's self-imposed no-strike pledge, and the war government's siding with management. The end of the war eliminated the first factor and modified the second, and management and labor faced each other on a very different battlefield.

🍲 The End of the War: A New Era Begins

At the end of World War II, the Campbell Soup Company looked both the same as and different from the company that existed at the start of the war. The dreary jumble of buildings in Camden topped by the Campbell's Soup–can water towers looked much the same as it had for decades. But inside the plants new groups of employees worked alongside women and men who had lived through the introduction of the Bedaux system in 1927, the militant but abortive 1934 strike, and the finally successful unionization push of 1940. The union-company contract, which had been an untested novelty at the start of the war, had solidified into an instrument guaranteeing management rights and prerogatives in return for modest improvements in wages and benefits. The contract also substituted a formal grievance procedure for the direct-action tactics favored by militant unionists, though the rank and file never entirely gave up on combative spontaneous responses to problems.

During the war, the struggle for control in the Campbell plants entered something approaching suspended animation, for the union worked as hard as management to increase production and avoid work stoppages. That struggle reappeared with full ferocity immediately after V-J Day. Dorrance and his managers were never happy that they had to deal with a union. As Campbell was a privately held, family-owned business, they believed any rights of control existed solely with them, and they came close to enshrining such a view in the language of their contracts. The workers who made the soup felt that they had earned the right to have a say in how the plant was run and how the proceeds should be allocated. Rank-and-file workers took the lead by walking off their jobs only days after the end of the war in a demand for more money, and this time their leaders supported them. Union officials had, however, become somewhat enmeshed in the bureaucracies of wartime labor control, and they diverted the mass action into a petition to the NLRB. Their tactic was ultimately successful in winning a sizable wage increase, but only after the union made a credible threat of another strike. The unity that union activists had worked so hard to build paid off in this struggle, and the company appeared to be put on the defensive.

The two strategies to preserve low-cost production that had so far worked for Campbell had hit something of a stalemate with the union. Control of the production floor through scientific management had been successful to a degree, but was susceptible to shop floor actions like slowdowns and walkouts, and the union was again prepared to endorse such actions. The strategy of segmenting the workforce into discrete camps succumbed to the union's counterstrategy of unity. A third strategy that had worked well in 1934—a strident antiunionism—would be far more difficult in the postwar world of entrenched unions protected by the Wagner Act and even more so by their own power to shut down production. A new, more sophisticated type of antiunionism would be required in this new environment. It must realistically accept the existence of "responsible" unions, ones that would forever abandon any designs on control of the workplace or any issues beyond wages and fringe benefits. But it would also unalterably oppose and destroy any "radical" workers' movements that sought to impinge on management prerogatives or fight for social issues inimical to the continued hegemony of capitalism. The Campbell Soup Company, and corporate America in general, were handed such a strategy in the form of the anticommunist hysteria of the Cold War and McCarthyism. The FTA, as a left-led union with an ideology of racial unity and social unionism, was a direct target of this new strategy.[64]

🍎 CHAPTER 4

The Fight to Save Local 80, 1946–1953

"You started out as a Catholic, in the organiza-
tion that aside from the Army and Navy, has done most to fight communism
in this country. I am at a loss to understand how you could have gone over
to the anti-Christ." With these words, U.S. District Judge Thomas M. Madden sentenced Anthony Valentino to five years in federal prison for "falsely
telling the NLRB he was not a Communist." Valentino, one of the founders
of Local 80, became the first unionist in the nation convicted for violation
of the infamous Section 9(h) of the Taft-Hartley Act, which required union
officers to sign noncommunist affidavits in order for their unions to be
recognized by the National Labor Relations Board (NLRB). The leader of
the Campbell Soup Company's Camden, New Jersey, local was accused of
signing the affidavit while still a member of the Communist Party, though
Valentino insisted he had resigned from party membership by that time.
Another longtime Campbell worker and union official, Sylvia Neff, was
charged with perjury during Valentino's trial and also sentenced to five years
in prison.[1]

Valentino's trial took place in 1952 during the height of the anticommunist
hysteria of the McCarthy era. The media, the Catholic Church, and union
splinter groups all combined forces against the "Red infection" of Local 80,
and the federal government, through Judge Madden, U.S. Attorney Alexan-
der Feinberg, and the Federal Bureau of Investigation (FBI) orchestrated the

trial and conviction. Despite the efforts of all those arrayed against Valentino to terrorize the public about the dangers of his "great crime," the soup plant workers in Camden apparently were not convinced. Two months after his conviction they reelected him as union business agent, giving him more votes than both of his opponents combined. Rank-and-file plant workers respected the union's communist activists because they were the strongest and most dedicated unionists, fighting for better pay and working conditions and against speedup and discrimination. The policy of Local 80's communists of being less than forthright about their party membership, however, left them open to being "exposed" by McCarthyites and created confusion among union members.[2]

Despite Valentino's tenacity and the union membership's continued support for him, the postwar period was a trying one for Local 80, and external attacks and internal dissension left scars that would weaken the local in the future. Yet Local 80 emerged from the period in remarkably better shape than most of the Left-led unions of the time. When its parent union, the Food, Tobacco, Agricultural and Allied Workers of America (FTA) was expelled by the Congress of Industrial Organizations (CIO) during its anticommunist witch hunt, the Camden local, unlike the Chicago local, refused to follow the national FTA into a quixotic merger with several other leftist unions. That amalgamation degenerated into a weak union that expelled its own communists two years later. Instead, it temporarily became an independent local within the CIO, then reemerged in the United Packinghouse Workers of America (UPWA), a tough CIO union that protected its leftist activists and fought zealously against racial discrimination. The UPWA continued the campaign for racial unity pioneered by Valentino, but his resignation a month after his reelection destabilized the local leadership, and some three hundred maintenance mechanics seceded to form their own craft union.[3]

During all this turmoil, Campbell management took something of a backseat. Though it was clearly the greatest beneficiary of a weakened union, it preferred to let anticommunist zealots attempt to rip apart Local 80. Behind the scenes, company executives provided information to the FBI concerning leftist union members, and they encouraged the craft employees who were trying to split the union, but the company did not want to appear to be openly attacking Local 80's popular leader on grounds unrelated to work. Instead, while others assailed the local's leaders on charges of communism, the company provoked a strike that coincided with Neff's trial and even earlier initiated a public relations campaign portraying the union as reckless and self-serving. The Campbell Soup Company's policy of strident antiunionism, which had been muted during the period of relative cooperation during World War II, came roaring back as the foremost postwar company strategy to keep production costs low. Once again, however, the company was only partially successful, as Local 80 countered the company campaign with a greater-than-ever emphasis on unity. This chapter will examine the twists and turns of both the Campbell Soup Company and Local 80 in the postwar period.

🍲 Campbell Soup in the Postwar Era

The end of the war marked the start of a new era at Campbell in more ways than merely the reconversion to a peacetime economy. Arthur Dorrance, who had taken over leadership of the company after his brother's death in 1930, died the year after the war ended. For the first time since 1894, a Dorrance would no longer be at the helm of the soup company. The young and ambitious William Beverly Murphy was being groomed for the leadership position, but he was not yet considered ready for the top post, especially since he had spent the last three years of the war in Washington, D.C., with the War Production Board. Instead, a longtime company executive, James McGowan, was chosen as president, a post he held until 1953, when Murphy began his own long and eventful reign. McGowan's interregnum was unmarked by any momentous changes at the company, but sales and profits continued to climb throughout his term: sales rose from 138 million dollars in 1945 to 339 million in 1954, and profits more than doubled in the same period, from 11.3 million dollars to 23.6 million. Though he made few major changes, McGowan did cautiously lead Campbell into slightly more modern methods of management. Executives were no longer required to punch a time clock, a personnel department was established in 1949, and the company began experimenting with advertising on the new medium of television in 1950. The firm's television sponsorships continued to enhance the wholesome image of Campbell's Soup and included the full run of the series *Lassie,* in which Campbell products were often seen in the background in one of the earliest examples of product placement marketing. The notoriously tightfisted company (not a penny of John T. Dorrance's estate had gone to charity) even donated a million dollars in 1950 to the Massachusetts Institute of Technology for the construction of the Dorrance Laboratories of Biology and Food Technology.[4]

Like other companies, Campbell was concerned about how it would fare in the changed environment of the postwar era. Management spokesmen in organizations like the National Association of Manufacturers (NAM) warned that productivity had fallen during the war due to cost-plus contracts and lax labor discipline. Internationally, capitalism seemed to be on shaky ground, with the rise of communist and social-democratic governments in Europe and even a Labour Party victory in Britain. The NAM took a two-pronged approach to the danger, pushing for business-friendly legislation like the Taft-Hartley Act while urging corporate leaders to fight to take back management prerogatives that had been eroding since the New Deal and World War II. Campbell took on this crusade with relish, refusing to budge an inch on its "management rights"; its efforts in this arena will be discussed below. But the company also sought to trim expenses in areas beyond direct labor costs. Thus, it opened its third U.S. plant in Sacramento in 1947 to eliminate the exorbitant costs of shipping finished products to the West Coast from Chicago or Camden.[5]

In its efforts to keep ingredient prices at rock-bottom levels, however, Campbell ran into some serious problems in the late 1940s. Ingredient prices were, in fact, tied to the costs of labor not directly employed by the soup company. By setting prices for tomatoes, carrots, and other ingredients at fixed—and minimal—levels, Campbell forced farmers to extract the most labor for the least pay from farmworkers. In the case of small farmers, this meant that they themselves and their family members had to work long hours just to eke out a living. Campbell, however, could wash its hands of any responsibility for the wages and working conditions of the laborers who planted and harvested the crops that went into its soups, for it could claim that its buyers were merely being good businessmen and driving a hard bargain with suppliers. As a result, Campbell gained a reputation with farmers every bit as harsh as with workers in its soup plants. One of its most notorious practices was to refuse to deal with farmers' cooperatives; the company signed contracts only with individual farmers. Campbell disliked collective action by its suppliers just as much as it did by its workers. Not surprisingly, farmers sometimes responded in ways that created problems for the company, both in maintaining its flow of cheap ingredients and in its public relations.[6]

Throughout the late 1940s and early 1950s the Campbell Soup Company and the farmers who supplied it were involved in a number of bitter and contentious lawsuits over the terms of their contracts. The company initiated several suits to keep its raw materials flowing at the agreed-upon rates and to give clear warning to other suppliers that they would have nothing to gain by challenging the status quo. Farmers, on the other hand, resorted to litigation in the absence of any other viable weapon against their mammoth opponent. At various times since at least the 1930s, many South Jersey farmers had united in organizations like the Tomato Growers Association, the New Jersey State Grange, and the National Farmers Union, but no group ever commanded sufficient power to attempt collective action. Instead, individual farmers broke onerous contracts (and were sued by Campbell) or sued the company. In all, relations between the soup company and its growers were "worse than those of any other large canner." In fact, South Jersey residents shared "a widespread feeling that Campbell just doesn't give a hoot for its farmers."[7]

In a glaring example of Campbell's practices that was repeated hundreds of times every season, company officials contracted with the Wentz Brothers of Upper Dublin Township in Pennsylvania for the delivery of their entire carrot crop in 1947 at the price of thirty dollars per ton. The contract was a preprinted company form with a few blank lines that were filled in with the particulars of the agreement. The common provisions provided a "penalty for the farmer for breach of contract, but none for the company; and a proviso allowing the company to reject a crop but forbidding the farmer, in that case, to sell the crop to anyone else without Campbell permission." When the Wentz farm's one-hundred-ton crop was ready, the market price for the carrots was ninety dollars per ton, and the brothers refused to deliver to Campbell at the contracted rate of thirty dollars. In situations like this one, Campbell took the offending farmers to court and almost always won, for its attorneys had carefully crafted its contracts to deny any legal loophole to the aggrieved growers. In this case, however, the lopsided contracts led Judge Herbert Goodrich to find that they were so "one-sided" and "tough" as to be unenforceable "in a court of conscience." The court called the provision restricting what the grower could do with his crop if rejected by Campbell "carrying a good joke too far" and concluded that "equity does not enforce unconscionable bargains."

Such farsighted opinions were the exception, however. Though a similar contract involving Maryland tomato growers was also found to be unenforceable, most judges dutifully ordered farmers to live up to the letter of their Campbell-written contracts and paid no heed to whether their provisions were conscionable. Overall, Campbell's disputes with its farmers had very little impact on its flow of raw materials. The bad publicity that emerged from the litigation, however, was a greater worry to the company that sponsored the *Lassie* television program, and it portended difficulties in later years, when farmworkers would launch a corporate campaign and boycott that seriously tarnished Campbell's company image. Of far more immediate concern, however, was a revitalized union in its home plant, newly freed from its self-imposed no-strike pledge.[8]

🎺 Local 80—Back in Action

From the end of World War II through the end of the 1950s, Local 80 held a well-earned reputation as a militant union that would use any means necessary to win its contract battles with the company and the day-to-day conflicts on the shop floor. Despite the serious distractions of attacks by the media, the church, and the government, as well as the continued tough antiunion stance of the company, the union, more often than not, prevailed in this period. This was due primarily to forceful union leadership and the strong shop steward system that had been built before and during the war. But the union's success was also aided by conditions in the larger economy. Workers at the soup company enjoyed strong bargaining power in both the labor marketplace and the workplace during most of this period. The growing economy in American capitalism's "golden age" provided expanding industrial job opportunities (with minor exceptions during recessions), and companies in traditionally low-paying industries were hard-pressed to retain a competent workforce. Campbell was thus forced by labor marketplace conditions to respond positively, to a degree, to demands for higher wages. But even after the company had taken the steps needed to attract and retain employees, it was still subject to a different kind of bargaining power in the workplace; workers had innumerable ways of impeding production, a weapon that they brought to bear in the daily battles over control of the shop floor.[9]

Starting just after the end of World War II, the Campbell plants in Camden and Chicago were the sites of almost continuous class warfare. Every two years or so the contests focused on negotiations over a new contract; throughout the postwar decade daily skirmishes erupted from any number of shop floor disputes. The union conducted its side of the battle amid an increasing crescendo of anticommunism yet managed to keep its focus on trade union issues. As a result, most of its members continued to give the union their strong support. By 1952, however, the collusion of company, government, and media in attacking Local 80 from all sides led the union to more closely tie its contract and shop floor fights to its defense of its leftist leaders.

The first postwar dispute—a "spontaneous" walkout the same month the war ended, finally resolved by a significant wage increase utilizing a wage-reopening contract provision—was significant on several counts. To begin with, it marked the abandonment by Local 80 of its wartime pact of cooperation with the company. Further, it demonstrated the willingness of the union to once again use extracontractual means to achieve its ends, using

FIGURE 9. "Wildcat" strike. As soon as the war ended in 1945, workers walked off the job "spontaneously" to demand higher wages. Though African American women were only hired for the first time in 1942, many became active unionists. Here strikers call out to coworkers to join them.
Historical Society of Pennsylvania, *Philadelphia Record* Collection, B. McGuigan.

tactics such as "spontaneous" walkouts in the middle of a contract to put muscle behind its demands. For example, in addition to the initial walkout in Camden, four thousand Chicago workers walked out in the midst of negotiations to stop the company from reducing the number of workers in the Retort Department from seventeen to fifteen.

But most important, the first postwar dispute resulted in a near total victory for the union and especially for its strategy of unity. The FTA fought for, and won, equal pay raises (of fifteen cents per hour) for men and women, when the company had insisted on smaller raises for female workers. The company succeeded in segmenting the workers in one respect, however: the raise for seasonal workers was two and one-half cents lower than that for full-timers. The union's strategy was planned and conducted jointly between Local 80 in Camden and Local 194 in Chicago, with the active participation of national union leadership. When agreement was near, company negotiators tried to impose slightly different settlements in each city, attempting to exclude a retroactive raise in the case of Chicago and to give women in Camden two and one-half cents less than men. The union stood firm against both divisive proposals and won the same raises in both cities. After the initial walkout in Camden, leaders from both locals (including Valentino) met in the FTA national office with FTA vice president Lewis Bentzley and secretary-treasurer Harold Lane. They agreed to pursue the first step of a long-range strategy for dealing with Campbell of unified bargaining—leading eventually, they hoped, to a master agreement for both cities and organization of new plants that the company was building or had on the drawing boards. Their spectacular success in the first postwar contest convinced them of the soundness of a strategy of unity.

Campbell management, however, drew exactly the same conclusion: if the company was to maintain its low-cost labor strategy, it must defeat worker unity and unified bargaining at all costs. The wrecking of the FTA nationally, the subsequent reaffiliation of the two Campbell locals into different unions, the split-off of maintenance workers in Camden into a different union, and the organization of the new Sacramento, California, plant by an American Federation of Labor (AFL) union—the Teamsters—made future unity difficult. When years later all of Campbell's disparate locals attempted a grand strategy of unity in the momentous 1968 strike, the company's president William Beverly Murphy remembered the disastrous outcome of 1946, when he had been a junior executive, and he vowed to shut the Campbell Soup Company down before allowing a unified workforce to dictate terms to the company.[10]

✍ The Salisbury Conflict: The Red Scare Begins

The criticality of organizing any new Campbell plants into the same union that represented Camden and Chicago workers led to the first major showdown between the FTA and Campbell after the union won its first postwar pay raise. Again the union prevailed, but this conflict saw the first efforts by the company to use advertising to appeal to the public for support for its side, as well as charges that the union's actions were part of a "Red plot."

The dispute centered on a new Campbell seasonal plant in Salisbury, Maryland, that operated only nine weeks each year to process Eastern Shore tomatoes. The company had made arrangements with a non-CIO union to supply two hundred of the total eight hundred temporary workers to staff the plant in 1946 and guard against FTA-CIO organization of the new location. The non-CIO union was the same amalgamation that Leon Schachter had put together to supply South Jersey canneries—including Campbell—with migrant workers from the South during the war. Schachter brokered an agreement with H. L. Mitchell's National Farm Labor Union (successor to the Southern Tenant Farmers Union) to bring seasonal workers into his Amalgamated Meat Cutters (AMC) union for the Salisbury tomato season. According to an affidavit from a disaffected Farm Labor Union staffer, Buford W. Posey, Schachter and Mitchell met in a Memphis, Tennessee, hotel room with James Heap (of the Campbell Soup Company) to plan the Salisbury scheme; Posey was allegedly ordered to finger any CIO supporters and Heap would immediately fire them. When Posey went to the FTA with his story, the CIO union's president Donald Henderson cabled an angry telegram to U.S. Secretary of Labor Lewis Schwellenbach: "A conspiracy of the Campbells Soup Company to break up the established union...in their Camden and Chicago plants threatens to bring a shutdown of both plants at the height of the tomato canning season.... Our more than 13,000 members in Campbell plants will not stand idly by while their union is smashed and while the farmers crops are allowed to rot in the fields." The FTA threatened to shut down both major Campbell plants at the height of the approaching tomato season unless the company abrogated its agreement with Schachter's union and agreed to employ CIO workers at Salisbury. In reaction to the strike threat, the company announced the next day that it would not disburse a half million dollars in retroactive pay that was part of the settlement of the initial postwar pay dispute. The union's Herbert Kling asked, "Who is violating the agreement now? Not FTA, whose members are staying at their jobs, but Campbell's, which is withholding money rightly due to us." A strike appeared inevitable.[11]

Between the Campbell-AMC "conspiracy" revelation on July 1, 1946, and the strike deadline of August 12, both company and union scrambled to win public support for their respective sides in the dispute. Campbell still did not employ a public relations firm, but it did experiment with using its long experience with advertising to sell not soup this time, but its version of the conflict. In full-page newspaper ads, Campbell charged that Local 80 and its members would be "inflicting catastrophe upon thousands of tomato growers and serious economic loss upon the community as a whole" through a reckless and illegal strike. The company put most of its efforts into winning the support of farmers who could potentially lose everything in the event of a strike. The largest farmers' organization, the New Jersey-Pennsylvania Tomato Growers' Association, sent a letter to President Harry S. Truman signed by sixty-four farmers declaring that it went "on record as being strongly opposed to the threatened strike" and called for "prompt settlement...by Company and Union." It asked the president to order the seizure and operation of the plant "by proper government agencies" in the event of failure of negotiations. A smaller farmers' group, however—the

Eastern Division of the Farmers' Union (no relation to Mitchell's National Farm Labor Union), which had close ties to Local 80—asked to join the negotiations to prevent the ruin of tomato growers, but was rebuffed by the company.[12]

One ominous note in the Salisbury fight was introduced by Mitchell when he began announcing to the press that the strike threat was a "communist plot." He followed up his claims with a letter to the secretary of labor contending that the situation should be investigated not by the Department of Labor but by the Department of Justice, which, he argued, should look into Henderson's "activities as a member of the Central Committee of the Communist Party, USA." He asked Schwellenbach to "repudiate an attempt by a well-known agent of the Communist Party to use the Department of Labor to the detriment of our organization." Since the split of the Southern Tenant Farmers' Union from the United Cannery, Agricultural, Packing, and Allied Workers of America (UCAPAWA) almost a decade earlier, Mitchell's antipathy toward Henderson had only increased, and he used the latter's Communist Party membership as his primary focus of attack.[13]

Despite Mitchell's denunciations and Campbell's appeals to the public, the iron-clad unity between the Camden and Chicago FTA locals proved decisive. Campbell earned the bulk of its profits from products manufactured during the critical tomato season, and it simply could not afford to take a companywide strike at that time. The company bargained hard and appeared unbending in its position, but the union was equally uncompromising. Labor Secretary Schwellenbach pushed government conciliators to find a way to an agreement, and they kept both parties in negotiations for thirty-two hours, yet without reaching a settlement. Schwellenbach did win a one-day strike delay from the union, but an hour before the second deadline expired at 5 a.m. on August 13, pickets began encircling the sprawling Camden Plant No. 1. At the deadline, Herbert Kling of the union announced to the workers, "The strike is on!" Ten minutes later he received word that an agreement had been reached a minute before the deadline, and the picket line was dismantled.

The settlement represented virtually a total victory for the union. Campbell agreed to (1) terminate its arrangement with Schachter and the AFL and release the workers hired through it; (2) use the FTA to recruit workers for Salisbury; (3) use a slightly modified version of the Camden contract for Salisbury; and (4) pay the retroactive wages owed the workers immediately. A demand added during the dispute for a closed union shop in Camden and Chicago was not agreed to, but the agreement included a rider expressing the company's willingness to consider a union shop at the next contract negotiations. At mass meetings two days later, workers overwhelmingly accepted the settlement. National FTA secretary–treasurer Harold Lane told the thousands gathered in Camden's Convention Hall, "You have accomplished something the national office of our union has been trying to do for years. To demonstrate to this company the unity of the two locals.... No one is going to be able to break your union, last of all Campbell's Soup Company."[14]

That unity, and the union behind it, would be the target of an unprecedented campaign over the next eight years. While Campbell management recognized that its preferred outcome—no union—was unachievable, it concluded from the experience of the first twelve months after the war that it could not continue generating the same level of profits for the Dorrance family if it continued to face a militant union that covered all Campbell locations. In the campaign against FTA and Local 80 were arrayed Campbell Soup Company management, local and national media, the Catholic Church, and several disgruntled factions within the union. Though H. L. Mitchell had raised the specter of anticommunism during the latest dispute, it was Camden's *Courier-Post* that launched the first barrage in the campaign to paint Local 80 as a cabal of communists duping its members in the interest of Moscow. The day after the settlement that averted a strike over the Salisbury plant, South Jersey's major newspaper published an editorial calling for Campbell's employees to "oust the leaders who support the devious line of a foreign power in contradiction to the sound principles of union responsibility to the community and the country." Local 80 unionists hit back with a sharply worded letter to the editor signed by twenty-four local leaders. They denounced the *Courier-Post's* calls to purge Communist leaders and proudly reviewed their record as strong progressive trade unionists:

> This is not the concern of the Courier-Post nor any other outside factor to interfere in the internal affairs of any labor organization. That is a matter for the members alone to decide.... Our local is proud of its record over the last 10 years in bringing the benefits of progressive trade unionism to thousands of Campbell Soup workers.... Our local will continue to exercise a progressive influence in our community by fighting against racial, religious and political prejudice in whatever form they may appear.

Perhaps more surprisingly, they forthrightly acknowledged that some union leaders were Communists: "If we have Communists in the leadership of our local, and we have, it is because they have met the same high standards of honesty, integrity and loyalty to Local 80 as those leaders of other political views."

When the newspaper received the letter, they published it as a front-page exposé under the headline "FTA Officers Admit Reds among Local 80 Leaders." In the same issue they ran another editorial ("Commies out in the Open in Campbell Soup Union") in which they blasted the union for its "frank and sensational disclosure." When Valentino would not name the party members for fear they would be attacked—a justifiable concern given the newspaper's actions—the *Courier-Post* editor sneered, "Are the Commies of Local 80, like Ku Klux Klanners, ashamed to identify themselves with their true loyalties?" The newspaper again demanded the ouster of the local's leftist leaders. At the very dawn of the Truman-McCarthy Red Scare, anticommunism became the primary weapon in the fight to destroy Local 80.[15]

The use of anticommunist accusations at Campbell was not an invention of *Courier-Post* editors after the war. But in earlier manifestations it was just one of many antiunion tactics utilized by a management committed to defeating any attempts at worker organization. In the 1934 strike, the company blamed the disturbance on an "'infection' of communism," but this was merely one of a raft of charges and actions targeting the new union. The company also set up a sham company union on Campbell property, attempted to arm "loyal" employees during the strike, and fired virtually all union activists after the strike settlement. Similarly, union president Henderson had warned Local 80 members to expect "a great deal of red-baiting" as far back as 1939. In the period of growing anticommunist hysteria after the war, however, this tactic began to take on a life of its own, as a handful of right-wing zealots within the local made common cause with the rightward-moving national CIO, anticommunist media and religious organizations, and, most crucially, with the powerful forces unleashed by the federal government. As Campbell's top executives began to see the efficacy of such tactics, they became bolder in making anticommunism a cornerstone in their dealings with the union and, in fact, in their public image.[16]

As the crescendo of anticommunism rose through the second half of the 1940s, Local 80 tried to maintain its focus on the day-to-day struggles important to its activists and members. Work stoppages, slowdowns, and other job actions took place regularly to fight speedup, abuse by foremen, and discrimination. During the negotiations in the summer of 1946, the company alleged that fifty-five strikes had taken place since the last contract was signed. Though most of these "strikes" were minor departmental actions, it was true that union activists did not hesitate to use their power when they felt they needed to. Steward Sylvester Akins recalls that "if there was a need for action, we'd take action…the department would go down, if necessary maybe another department would go down…the union was strong, it had support." In some cases, the disputes mushroomed into plantwide walkouts. Increasing antagonism over the Bedaux system—called the "speedup system" by workers—led to the suspension of twelve-year veteran and steward of the Digester Department Robert Wooley. The entire plant walked out and stayed out. The company refused to negotiate the suspension unless all employees returned to work. When the union rejected that proposal and no one went back into the plant, the company relented and agreed to let the suspended worker resume his job; Wooley was the first to reenter the plant.[17]

Though it did not abandon the shop floor to the union, Campbell turned to contract negotiations and antiunion legislation to regain the initiative. Both aspects of this new direction were apparent in the bargaining that took place in early 1947. Though the old contract was due to expire on March 1, Campbell not only refused a union offer to extend it by two months but went so far as to cancel the contract outright and demand that a new agreement be worked out from scratch. Company executives were both playing hardball and playing for time while waiting to see what a new Republican congress would provide in the way of antilabor legislation. The proposals the company put forward would have resulted in an almost total rollback of gains won by the union since its arrival in 1940. Campbell demanded that company-union relations "be governed by the open shop principle," that seniority in layoffs be eliminated, and that the probation period for new employees be lengthened. In an attempt to retake the initiative on control of the shop floor, it proposed tightening up the Bedaux system, "whereby [a] worker failing to keep up...'100 percent effectiveness' will be cut to the next lowest rate until finally he reaches the hiring-in rate."

The union countered by demanding increases in wages and union security and insisted that shop floor issues like the incentive system and job classifications be subject to collective bargaining. Central to its position were demands opposing company divide-and-rule tactics: it proposed expansion of plantwide seniority and demanded that "all rates...be based on the job, not on whether the worker is a man or a woman." It concretely furthered unity by tightly aligning negotiating efforts between the Camden and Chicago locals, the core strategy in its earlier successes. As talks dragged on without progress, a strike seemed increasingly likely. Though Campbell was waiting for relief from Congress, it could not afford to wait indefinitely if it meant taking a shutdown of its entire production. The company agreed to bring in Peter Manno of the U.S. Conciliation Service, and thirty-two long negotiating sessions ensued under the guidance of the government official. A final agreement was hammered out on June 5, less than three weeks before the Taft-Hartley Act was passed over President Truman's veto, ending what

Manno described as "one of the most difficult disputes ever handled by the U.S. Conciliation Service."

The timing was auspicious for the union, and it delivered a substantial package for its members in terms of wages and benefits. Workers received a wage increase of 14.7 cents per hour and, for the first time, pension benefits. Yet on issues of control, the contract was at best a stalemate for the union. Most provisions remained as they were, with the company retaining full rights, at least on paper, to make all decisions regarding the running of the plants, including the Bedaux system. The union fared a little better in its efforts to fight divisions within the workforce, winning an across-the-board cents-per-hour increase rather than the company-preferred percentage raise (thus narrowing the relative gap between men and women) as well as maternity leave, another first at Campbell. The national union touted the economic gains that brought Campbell workers "up to the highest level in the U.S. food industry," but, as historian Howell Harris has argued, "fundamentally, [the industrial conflicts of the late 1940s] revolved around issues of control," and on that point the union had little to show. Nonetheless, the formal contract did not even slow down the day-to-day struggles in the plants.[18]

✹ The FTA Confronts the Red Scare

While Local 80 and Local 194 leaders were planning their negotiating strategy in early 1947, the national CIO received a report from the FBI on a meeting of the "leading Communists of the FTA" held on the evening of January 9. The report from this meeting, another from a CIO regional director concerning alleged political antagonisms between FTA locals and the national union, and a few other documents formed the initial basis for the CIO's plan to expel the Left-led union, along with nine other national unions. Simultaneously, the FBI began testing for weak points among Local 80's communist activists. Through threats and intimidation, FBI agents succeeded in pushing a few Local 80 members to give statements against other communists in the local—especially against Anthony Valentino. Simultaneously, similar attacks were being launched against other FTA locals, such as Local 22, which had made spectacular gains in organizing black and white tobacco workers in Winston-Salem, North Carolina.[19]

Progressive unions like the FTA were, in the postwar United States, in the unhappy position of being in the crosshairs of the proponents of the ascendancy of American capitalism from several angles. Because of leftist unions' support of the world socialist movement and the Soviet Union, Truman and other state actors saw them as threats to the security of U.S. hegemony. To corporate leaders still smarting from their loss of authority as a result of the militant unionism and New Deal legislation of the 1930s, the Left-led unions were the primary obstacle to their reassertion of their right to run their businesses—and the economy—as they saw fit. Once the campaign against the leftist unions was unleashed, numerous other groups and individuals joined the crusade, from fringe right-wing ideologues to dissident union factions. Often these true believers pushed the campaign further than its originators had planned, as in the case of senator Joseph McCarthy, and even the courts overturned many convictions under the anticommunist laws of the period. But in the meantime, the massive wave of anticommunist hysteria that swept the United States destroyed most of the Left-led unions, including the FTA.

The crucial piece of legislation that set in motion the attack on progressive unionism was the Taft-Hartley Act of 1947. Under the prodding of business groups like the NAM, the law was crafted to weaken the labor movement across the board. Since union activists committed to an ultimate goal of replacing capitalism with socialism were considered the ultimate threat to business, the act contained a provision that, its advocates hoped, would remove communists from union leadership even if union members wished otherwise. In order for unions henceforth to utilize the services of the NLRB in matters such as union certification, representation elections, and unfair labor practices, Section 9(h) of the act required union officers at the national and local levels to sign an affidavit stating that they were not members of, nor affiliated with, the Communist Party, nor did they support "the overthrow of the United States Government by force or by any illegal or unconstitutional methods." Any officer who signed a false affidavit would be subject to the penalties for perjury.[20]

Within the CIO, Section 9(h) provoked both strong opposition as well as an opportunity for those leaders on the national and local levels who had long-standing rivalries with leftist unionists. Initially, even many noncommunist CIO leaders refused to sign the affidavits on principle, but pressure from government sanctions and some members led all to eventually capitulate. A few leftist unions, such as the United Electrical workers (UE), then the third largest union in the CIO, rebuffed Taft-Hartley and went off on their own without the benefit of NLRB recognition. Most, however, dealt with the requirements of Section 9(h) in other ways. The FTA, for example, after initial refusal to go along with the law, met the narrowest definition of compliance by reassigning well-known communist Donald Henderson to the new appointive position of national administrative director while other leaders resigned party membership, then signed affidavits.

As the tide of Cold War America enveloped even the labor movement, the top leadership of the CIO moved to expel some one dozen unions tainted with accusations of communist domination. Relations between the Left-led unions and the other CIO unions, especially the United Automobile Workers (UAW) and the United Steel Workers of America (USWA), deteriorated rapidly after the war. UAW leader Walter Reuther, who had long feuded with communist activists in his own union, led the mainstream CIO into a temporarily secure, if junior, partnership with business and Truman's Cold War government. In return for a share in the spoils of advancing American capitalism, Reuther and his allies agreed to abandon demands for any say in how plants were run and to police union membership to keep out those who did not go along with the new order. As one contentious issue followed another in the late 1940s, the wedge between the Left and the Reuther-led leadership widened. The FTA and several other unions supported Henry Wallace's Progressive Party bid for the presidency in 1948 in order to challenge Truman's antilabor domestic record and the national security state he was creating to buttress the Cold War against the Soviet Union. The national CIO supported Truman. The Left-led unions also opposed the Marshall Plan as a scheme to stabilize capitalism and supported CIO participation in the World Federation of Trade Unions (WFTU). Again the national CIO held diametrically opposite positions, supporting the Marshall Plan and withdrawing from WFTU in May 1949. By that year two unions, including the UE, had left the CIO, and, in 1950, the CIO expelled nine others, including the FTA.[21]

Donald Henderson, president of the FTA until the union decided to sign the Taft-Hartley affidavits, was a lightning rod for anticommunist campaigners. His outspoken views supporting socialism and opposing discrimination incensed many, and an FBI report alluded to unspecified unfavorable "personal habits." When rivals in the CIO began mounting their campaign to oust the federation's communists, Henderson was a favorite target. Henderson's (and the FTA's) record on organizing the most downtrodden and difficult-to-organize sectors of the American workforce provided little opportunity for his opponents to attack. So instead they assailed his statements and actions supporting the Soviet Union or opposing the Cold War. When Henderson attended the World Peace Conference in Paris in April 1949, his statement that "the American working people will not be driven into a war against the Soviet Union" provoked howls of rage in the media and among anticommunist labor leaders. Jacob Potofsky, president of the Amalgamated Clothing Workers, condemned Henderson and said he "had no right to speak in the name of the C.I.O." A campaign was initiated to get various CIO union locals to pass resolutions calling for Henderson's ouster. Identical resolutions, with a blank for inserting the local's name and number, arrived at CIO head-quarters the month after Henderson's return from Paris.[22]

The drumbeat to expel the FTA from the CIO culminated in the "trial" of the FTA by a three-man panel from the opposing camp, headed by Potofsky. These proceedings against the FTA and other Left-led unions led directly to their expulsions, but FTA activists did not leave without a fight. When ordered to appear before the trial panel under conditions stacked against them—only the panel, not the FTA, could decide who could testify; no legal counsel was permitted the FTA; and the proceedings were to be closed, including to rank-and-file union members—the FTA went to court in an attempt to block the proceedings, or at least to level the playing field. The union lost on its major point, but did win the right to bring witnesses of its own choosing and to allow limited rank-and-file attendance.

The charge against the FTA was that its actions were "consistently directed toward the achievement of the program and policies of the Communist Party rather than the objectives and policies set forth in the Constitution of the CIO." The primary "evidence" consisted of a comparison of articles in the *FTA News* and the Communist *Daily Worker* conducted by William Steinberg, an anticommunist leader of a small CIO affiliate, the American Radio Association. In a few cases the parallels were, in fact, clear. For example, articles in the FTA publication during the period of the Adolf Hitler–Joseph Stalin pact opposed U.S. participation in a war; after Hitler's attack on the Soviet Union the paper, and the union, became ardent boosters of the war effort, as has been described in chapter 3. These positions did not, however, diverge markedly from the CIO stance, especially in the federation's support for the wartime no-strike pledge. In other instances, Steinberg's analysis of FTA articles demonstrated that divergence from the positions staked out by the anticommunist leaders of the CIO would no longer be tolerated. Thus, the FTA's support for the WFTU and Wallace and its opposition to the Marshall Plan became not a healthy expression of differences within a democratic federation but grounds for expulsion from it.

Henderson, John Tisa, and other FTA leaders and members used the hearings to make a careful case, answering the charges and proudly proclaiming the union's record in improving the lot of its members. Henderson alone defended his (and by extension other FTA leftists') support for socialism. He described the "terrific emotional effect" the Sacco and Vanzetti affair had on him as a student and declared he believed that "this economic institution in this country ought to be changed." He hoped that Americans would not "have to do it the way the Soviet Union did it" but declared, "I am in favor of socialism, and never made any bones about it." But all the other witnesses brought by the FTA emphasized how the organization was doing a great job in its daily trade union activities and in fighting discrimination. Further, they described the democratic governance and decision making within the FTA and attacked the growing "political dictatorship" within the CIO. Rank-and-file members Adele Ellis from Local 57 in Richmond, Virginia; Veronica Kryzan from the Campbell Local 194 in Chicago; and Robert Black from the Reynolds Tobacco Local 22 in Winston-Salem all testified to the open and democratic procedures within their locals. In the FTA's rebuttal it charged that "the trial committee, and the bringer of the charges, dare not attack FTA on its record. Therefore they ignore the record, just as they ignore the issue of freedom of speech and freedom of action in CIO." Despite mounting a serious defense, no one from either side ever had any doubt about the outcome. The three-member panel voted unanimously to recommend expulsion, and the CIO's 1950 convention rubber-stamped the decision.[23]

Local 80 Goes It Alone

The campaign to destroy its parent union began to have effects within Local 80. The national Red Scare energized a number of factions in the Campbell local that had long been unhappy with their union's leftist ties and anti-discrimination activism. One small group was led by perennial gadfly and self-described "right-wing candidate" Joseph Ward. A more serious threat to Local 80's unity was centered in the Maintenance Department and included longtime union activists; this all-white group was becoming increasingly disturbed by the growing numbers of blacks working alongside them and even beginning to take leadership positions in "their" union. The develop-ing anticommunist hysteria gave them a golden opportunity to attempt to wrest control of their local from those who had guided Local 80's pro-unity, antidiscrimination stands.[24]

In the FTA's other Campbell local, in Chicago, things were different. Local 194 had always had a unified leadership comprised primarily of left-ist activists, and there were no serious challenging factions as there were in Camden. Women played an important role in the Chicago local, and one of them, Veronica Kryzan, testified on the FTA's behalf at the CIO "trial." She described her metamorphosis from soup plant worker to union organizer:

> I was hired in the Campbell 2 plant in 1939. Our rate was 28 cents
> for women and 45 cents for men. That was before the union. We had

penitentiary conditions, I might say. We couldn't go to the wash room, had no relief periods, and the company was very adamant about any conditions being given to the workers at the time. In 1940 I was coming out of the plant and met a fellow named Harold Lane. He was passing out leaflets to organize the Campbell Soup plant. He asked me if I was willing to join the union or UCAPAWA and fight for conditions of the people in the plant, and I said if we could change the penitentiary conditions we had at the present time I would be willing to join and do my darndest to see that the people in Campbell's would be organized.

Kryzan also described UCAPAWA/FTA efforts to fight discrimination:

At that time the war began, and Campbell Soup wouldn't hire in a negro man or woman.... I was insulted and called a nigger lover and every name under the sun because we were fighting... to get our negro brothers and sisters in the plant to help the war effort. Today we have negro and white people working side by side.... this union in our cannery plants did a splendid job for all minority groups and the Slav people—our people are mostly foreign-born in the processing plants, and they are satisfied.[25]

In Camden's Local 80, conditions were a bit rockier. As 1950 began, the local faced an uncertain future: its parent union was about to go on "trial" by the CIO, negotiations were beginning on the contract with Campbell due to expire in March, and a faction opposed to the current leadership was stirring up trouble. For most of 1949, the local had continued to focus attention on the standard day-to-day issues of grievances and contract enforcement. But by December the attacks on the national FTA began to take center stage in the local's concerns. The *Local 80 Bulletin* started reporting derisively on the charges of "dictatorship" that the anticommunist wing of the CIO was leveling at the FTA. As "one of the largest locals in FTA" it challenged CIO head "Phil Murray, or any other CIO leader, to come to its Executive Board, Stewards Council or Membership meeting, and point out who make the decisions at such meetings. If they can find any dictatorship in Local 80 FTA, we will retract every accusation we have made against the national CIO." The local's publication again stressed the importance of unity in the working class: "Local 80 still believes that organized labor instead of fighting each other should unite into one solid, trade union.... If we do not, eventually the big industrialists will succeed in smashing all of us."

In mid-January, as the trial began, the local made a significant change on the front page of its newsletter. Until then, the masthead showed a male worker and a female worker facing each other with the rising sun between them; on the sun were emblazoned "CIO." Starting with the January 12 issue, "FTA" appeared on the sun in place of the initials of the once-united industrial federation. Alongside an article titled "We Are Accused [of] Being a Dictatorial Union" was another implicitly rebuffing the charge, listing the twenty-eight names of the members democratically elected to the negotiating committee for the new contract, male and female, black and white, communists and Maintenance Department representatives. In a cartoon below, a muscular worker with "Local 80 FTA" imprinted on his shirt scoffed at CIO leaders Phil Murray and James Carey, who were trying to get him into a coffin labeled "Company Union" while bosses looked on approvingly. The die was cast; Local 80, along with the rest of FTA, was going it alone.[26]

Taft-Hartley's affidavit requirement was making it increasingly difficult for nonsigning unions to compete with anticommunist unions attempting to replace them. New unions like the International Union of Electrical Workers (IUE) could offer union members NLRB-supervised negotiations and assistance in grievance resolution, while workers who stuck with the leftist UE had only their own strength to withhold their labor to rely on. One by one, most of the Left-led unions capitulated to the anticommunist provisions of the Taft-Hartley Act and signed the affidavits. As rumors spread that Local 80 was about to be raided by both AFL and CIO unions, the local announced in June 1950 that all its officers had signed. In that month's newsletter, union activists trumpeted their achievements in fighting grievances and promised to improve the lot of their members in the future—"win[ning] many aims that we were compelled to drop during negotiations"—both on bread-and-butter issues and in the "elimination of the vicious speed-up system under Labor Standards." In what would prove to be wishful thinking, the publication asserted, "While we have a small group of dissenters in our ranks, no serious attempts have materialized to wreck Local 80, thanks to the common sense of our membership."[27]

Nationally, the FTA had thrown in its lot with two other Left-led unions to form the Distributive, Processing, and Office Workers of America (DPOWA). Sociologists Judith Stepan-Norris and Maurice Zeitlin have argued that if this grouping had allied with other ousted unions to form a new leftist labor federation, the Left within the union movement may have survived and become a significant player in the future of capital-labor relations. Whether a leftist federation could have survived the onslaught of anticommunism then engulfing the United States is open to question. Yet a movement based solidly on a foundation in the labor movement may have provided the single best hope for a progressive political alternative in that dark period. In any case, due to poor decisions and poor leadership from within the Communist

Party and the ravages of McCarthyism, such an alliance was never formed. Instead the DPOWA, along with the remains of most other leftist unions (with some significant exceptions, such as the UE) gradually disappeared from the scene of organized labor in the early 1950s.

In 1950, however, the top FTA administration was doing all it could to carry all of its locals into the DPOWA. Local 194 in Chicago, under a unified left leadership, voted to follow its parent union into the new organization. In Camden, however, this issue proved to be the wedge that the right-wing faction was looking for. Local 80 activists from the Maintenance Department, led by Joseph Gallo and Daniel Harkins, along with some others dissatisfied with the direction their union had been taking, such as Herbert Kling and Joseph Colangelo, put forward a proposal for Local 80 to become an independent CIO affiliate rather than follow its ousted parent union into the DPOWA. Tony Valentino, however, and many black workers in the union initially went along with the FTA, agreeing to follow whatever decision the national organization made. John Tisa, Valentino's longtime friend from South Camden and now vice-president of the FTA Division of the DPOWA, returned to his hometown to try to keep one of the FTA's most important locals in the fold. As late as mid-September Valentino was promising to "go down fighting for the FTA union merger." He was, however, under tremendous pressure to allow Local 80 to break free of what some viewed as a hopeless cause. In the recent contract negotiations with Campbell, the company had been able to maintain a tougher stand against the union now that the NLRB had withdrawn FTA's certification, and the pressure from within the local to secede from the FTA/DPOWA was becoming overwhelming. In a union meeting on September 24, Valentino shocked his old comrade Tisa and many others by seconding a motion against the merger of Local 80 into DPOWA. With the defection of Valentino, Local 80's break with the FTA became final.[28]

Tisa and the FTA did not take Local 80's actions amicably. Claiming that the vote to secede was unconstitutional and that the FTA was still the legal representative of the Campbell workers according to the last contract signed with the company, the DPOWA sent telegrams to the local's executive board informing them that the local officers were suspended and that John Tisa had been named administrator of Local 80. Tisa continued issuing "Local 80 FTA Bulletins" denouncing "Local 80 CIO." The bitterness of the breakup, on personal as well as political and organizational bases, showed through in articles describing the "betrayal" of Tisa's old friend. It seemed that the right wing of the local had finally succeeded when Tisa, attempting to enter the union hall on October 18, was blocked by Joseph Gallo and other erstwhile union brothers. Tisa's Local 80 Bulletin and leaflets distributed in Camden denounced the CIO Local 80 leaders as "a clique of self-seekers, white supremacists, and company men" who were also "against women taking part in union affairs." Though Tisa tried to attract rank-and-file workers to "FTA Local 80" meetings, he soon gave up the attempt. If the right wing was rejoicing, however, its celebrations were premature. In a remarkable resurrection, Local 80 soon resumed its traditions of militancy, unity, and even support for leftist leaders.[29]

The newly named independent Local 80, Food, Tobacco and Agricultural Industrial Union–CIO, did not wait long to demonstrate what kind of union it would be. On October 31, the company tested its power against what it hoped would be a weakened adversary by trying to once again reassert its sole authority on the shop floor by eliminating half-hour breaks for seven women inspectors on the tin can lid line. When the women refused to work the full shift without their traditional break, the company suspended them. Immediately all five thousand production workers walked off the job, "telling the company"—according to a company press release—"how it is to operate its Camden plant press room." The plant remained shut down tight for a week until Campbell agreed to reinstate the women inspectors and not to seek reprisals against the union.[30]

The unexpected militancy of the independent Local 80 was due to a complex set of factors. The newly ascendant leadership group, based largely among craft workers, had never been able to control the local on its own; it had, since the beginning of the union in 1940, been forced to cooperate with leftist activists and with the industrial workers who made up the bulk of the workforce. With the defection of Valentino to their side in the DPOWA dispute, the independent local inherited a large group of activists—both union officers and shop stewards—who were not prepared to abandon their tradition of militancy. Further, many of these activists were African Americans and women, whose strong support for the union was tied to its outspoken stance against discrimination. As the proportion of African Americans in the union continued to increase, their insistence on the importance of the fight for equality became ever stronger. Gallo, Harkins, and friends quickly realized that recruiting most of their rivals into their camp had not been an unqualified blessing.

Local 80A–UPWA

By early 1951 another open split developed between the Maintenance Department group and its allies on one side and Valentino, Local 80's first black president Benjamin Butler, and most African American and female union activists on the other. Gallo's group soon moved to consolidate its hold on the local by proposing that the independent local affiliate with the right-wing Retail, Wholesale, and Department Store Union–CIO (RWDSU). The one large leftist branch of the RWDSU, District 65, had, in fact, left that union to become one of the founding parties of the DPOWA, the FTA's new home. The prospects for Local 80's joining the RWDSU were enhanced by the fact that the head of the CIO's South Jersey Industrial Council was also an RWDSU official. Butler and Valentino quickly searched for an alternative to the RWDSU. There were undeniable advantages in aligning their local with a large and more financially secure national union, but Local 80 had irrevocably cut its ties with the FTA/DPOWA, and none of the remaining CIO unions appeared to be a comfortable home for an organization with Local 80's leftist history and unabashed support for equality for African Americans and women.

There was one promising exception to the right-wing mold of most surviving CIO unions, however, and it, too, represented workers in the food processing industry. The United Packinghouse Workers of America (UPWA) had one of the strongest records of fighting discrimination in the entire union movement, and it continued to harbor many leftists, even Communist Party members, among its leadership. The depictions of the history of the UPWA by historians Rick Halpern and Roger Horowitz reveal an amazing number of parallels between the meatpackers' union and Local 80. The UPWA's predecessor, the Packinghouse Workers Organizing Committee, had developed in the 1930s through an alliance of leftists, African Americans, and old-time trade unionists from the skilled trades. As the proportion of African Americans in the meatpacking industry grew, the UPWA had thrown its efforts behind a strong antidiscrimination program. The companies in that industry, meanwhile, had developed many of the same techniques that Campbell had to drive costs down, control production, and restrict the power of the workers, including a sophisticated scheme to segment labor by race, ethnicity, gender, and skill. The meatpacking companies had even widely adopted the Bedaux system, the same "scientific management" scheme in use at Campbell. When the Taft-Hartley Act threatened to derail the progressive unions, UPWA first refused to sign the anticommunist affidavits. After the AFL's AMC began raiding UPWA locals, the CIO union reluctantly complied with Section 9(h) after shuffling a few people on its executive board, but it continued to protect communists throughout the union. One of these leftists was Meyer Stern, director of Region 6, the division of the UPWA that covered New Jersey. Paradoxically, both the Communist Party and the right-wing leaders of the CIO had earlier suggested that the UPWA and FTA should consider joining forces, though the CIO's version of this plan saw the UPWA raiding FTA locals. In any case, as Butler, Valentino, and the other progressives in the independent Local 80 looked around for an alternative to the RWDSU, their choice was obvious: they were to lead the fight in 1951 to ally their isolated local with the UPWA.[31]

Each side in the affiliation battle campaigned hard to convince Campbell's workers that its national union was the best choice. The UPWA openly portrayed itself as a tough union that would rely on the rank and file and fight the company without hesitation. It pointed to its history of "plant shutdowns, protest meetings, delegations to Washington and mobilized community support" as the basis for its achievements in the companies covered by its contracts. It promised to fight the wage differential between men and women and proclaimed that it "preaches and practices equality for all peoples, regardless of race, creed, color, sex or nationality." The proponents of the RWDSU, meanwhile, dubbed themselves the "Clean Slaters" and relied on negative campaigning and barely concealed appeals to racism. Their major issue was the arrest of Valentino—during the campaign—for violation of the anticommunist provisions of the Taft-Hartley Act. Several RWDSU backers, in fact, became the FBI's star witnesses in Valentino's trial. Leaflets distributed by RWDSU supporters charged that the UPWA backers "have been following the commie party line for the past 10 years" and boasted that a key principle of the RWDSU was, "No communist can hold office." Some "Clean Slaters" grumbled about the victory of a number of African Americans in recent Local 80 elections. Joseph Gallo claimed that in 1950 he had been cheated out of the post of financial secretary, a position he had held for three years: "I got beat by a colored woman, 3570 to 3550, but everybody thought it was crooked." Other RWDSU campaigners were explicit in their appeals to racism. According to worker Edward Woronka, a shop steward told him during the campaign, "Sign a Retail and Wholesale card and get rid of the niggers." The steward was stripped of his post after a union hearing, but Woronka, under severe pressure, later recanted his testimony. In the end, in a large vote turnout over three days in October, Local 80's members selected the UPWA by a large margin, 2,658 to 1,665.[32]

The UPWA's new Local 80A (rechristened because another UPWA local refused to give up its number 80) quickly moved into the forefront of that progressive union's struggle against racism and anticommunism. Its opponents, meanwhile, argued about what course to take and split into several antagonistic groups. After rightist ideologue Joseph Ward failed in a bid for union office in 80A, he joined with a handful of others in an appeal to the

AFL to raid Campbell's Camden plants. Others, for the time being, decided to go into opposition but remain members of Local 80A. The Camden local, as a result, faced a number of obstacles as it attempted to regroup and face the company in the difficult 1952 contract negotiations. Campbell's position was immeasurably aided by America's Red Scare, as leaders of Local 80A were hauled into court in the midst of negotiations and FBI agents did their best to rip apart the leadership of the local. In early 1951 shop steward and alleged Communist Party member Robert Wooley had a bitter falling out with Valentino over union tactics and personnel. He was approached by FBI agent Phillip Carroll, who had been closely monitoring Local 80 for some time. Carroll convinced Wooley to turn state's evidence against his former comrade. Gradually, and under severe FBI pressure, the long-festering strains between Local 80's leftists and unionists from the Maintenance Department, and personal antagonisms among its activists, broke apart the old group that had led the local since the organizing campaign of the late 1930s.

The Trials of Local 80

Two weeks before the UPWA-RWDSU affiliation vote, the leader of the Packinghouse Workers group was indicted by a grand jury on charges that he perjured himself by signing a Taft-Hartley affidavit when he was still a member of the Communist Party. Though the FBI suspected that hundreds of affidavits may have been signed by unionists still loyal to communist ideals, Local 80's Anthony Valentino was the first in the nation to be charged with violating Section 9(h). The timing of the indictment, as well as that of other attacks against Campbell's union and its leaders over the next couple years, suggests that there may have been some collusion among the various interests who would gain from a weakened Local 80. That, in any case, was the conclusion reached in an article titled "The Hand of the Government at Campbell's" in the New Jersey edition of the *Worker*, a Communist Party publication:

> "I pledge allegiance to Campbell Soup, and to the profits for which it stands..."
>
> That's what the Pledge of Allegiance looks like in Camden these days since the government started helping Campbell's smear and divide the workers at the giant cannery, and crush their union, Local 80 of the CIO United Packinghouse Workers.
>
> All branches of government—from the FBI to the U.S. Attorney to the Federal judge to the police magistrate, right down to the cop

assigned to the picketline—joined in a many-sided attack on the union and its leadership—all in the name of "loyalty."[33]

Such collusion—or coincidence—was most blatant during the contract battles of early 1952. On February 5, the union took a strike vote in anticipation of the contract expiration on March 1. On the same day, longtime Local 80 activist Sylvia Neff was arrested and charged with perjury in her testimony before the grand jury investigating Valentino. The turmoil of the ensuing contract negotiations, walkouts, and suspensions was paralleled by daily sensational news reports of Neff's trial. Seven hours after her conviction on May 28 the company and union reached a settlement. For the UPWA and Local 80's new leadership, composed primarily of the remaining core of old leftists along with many African American activists, the tough contract fight was a trial of their ability to continue the militant tradition of the local in the midst of internal strife and external attacks.[34]

Despite the obvious problems Local 80 faced, it still had a lot going for it as it confronted the soup company in 1952. Though the factional fights had taken their toll, the local still had a strong shop steward system. Some 203 stewards represented every part of the company; the Maintenance Department and the power house had thirty-five stewards, all white men, but production departments boasted 115 men and 53 women stewards from every ethnic and racial group at Campbell. Of the top officers, the president, the financial secretary, and the chief steward were all African American, and eleven of the twenty-six officers were women. The officers included the chairs of several committees that enhanced the influence of the union both on the shop floor and in the community, ranging from the Educational, Labor Standards, and Organizing Committees (all headed by women) to the Social, Sports, Civil Rights, and Unemployment Committees. To this local strength the new parent union, the UPWA, added its own experienced strategists, researchers, and organizers. The most important asset provided by the UPWA was the dynamic African American field organizer Don Smith. Standing above the fray that had compromised many local leaders, he kept the activists and members of Local 80 focused on the task at hand.[35]

The demands arrived at by the local with the UPWA's help and its response to the attacks on its leaders were a brilliant statement of the workers' position against each of the strategies Campbell had employed to maintain its dominance in the plants and keep production costs at a minimum: rationalization and control of production, segmentation of the workforce, and antiunionism/anticommunism. To deal with the issues of shop floor control, the union's demands took on the Bedaux labor standards plan from several angles, proposing a wholesale transformation of the system. Most significantly, these provisions would have taken the decision-making process out of the exclusive domain of management and made it subject to negotiation and arbitration. Further, they would have sharply limited the scope of standards in the plant and provided protections for workers against the most onerous aspects of the system. Most ambitiously, Local 80 demanded the complete elimination of the "Rights of Management" clause of the contract, which a union negotiator called "unnecessary and meaningless with a union shop." To carry on Local 80's efforts to combat the "divide and rule" tactics of the company, the union demanded the inclusion of an antidiscrimination contract clause. To lessen the divide between Campbell's permanent and contingent employees, the union proposal eliminated any wage differential between the two groups. It further included much strengthened seniority provisions that would substitute enforceable plantwide seniority for the existing system the company had used, especially in the large preparatory department, to segment workers in a labyrinthine system of gender, race, "effectiveness," and favoritism. Finally, though the union's main fight against attacks on its existence and its leaders took place outside of contract negotiations, the union did propose several amendments to eliminate existing antiunion language—such as Section II(d): "The Union agrees that neither it nor any of its officers or members will in any way intimidate or coerce employees into membership in the Union"—and to bolster its position in the plants (by, for example, requiring the company to pay for all time spent by stewards performing union duties).[36]

Both sides in the contract battle came prepared to fight. The national union was determined to help its important new local achieve a significant victory but, on the other side, both the federal government and the AFL came to the company's aid in crucial ways. The difficulties to come were evident from the first time that negotiators sat down together in mid-January. Ralph Helstein (national president of the UPWA) asked the company for financial information on its operations—information not available to the public because the Campbell Soup Company was privately held—but company representatives rejected any requests outright. An argument ensued and Helstein asked why "the people who helped make the money" were kept in the dark on financial data, and he threatened to take legal action. The company refused to budge on this point, and then listened to the union's demands with few comments. Talks were abruptly cancelled when reports filtered into the meeting about a dispute over a slowdown on the second floor. It was the beginning of a long four-and-a-half month struggle for the future of the Campbell Soup Company in Camden.[37]

While Local 80 was beginning talks with the company, a handful of its members were again trying to wreck it from within. A few of those who had backed the RWDSU now went to the AFL in an attempt to decertify the UPWA. President William Green of the AFL quickly obliged them by sending a letter to all Campbell employees—somehow the AFL supporters had obtained a list of their names and addresses—asking them to sign an enclosed authorization card in support of affiliation with his federation. The new "AF of L Committee" also tried to derail membership meetings of Local 80 at the critical period at the beginning of negotiations. It sent a telegram to all former "Clean Slaters" urging them to disrupt the next meeting: "Most important that you and your followers attend this meeting. Remember go early get seats get there before Valentino and his clique. . . . Turn down company offer. Make motion to take back strike fund. . . . Don't sign or agree to anything that will put you and the left wingers all in the same pot." However, even many previous RWDSU backers had resigned themselves to the fact that the UPWA was now their union, and the AFL raiding attempt quickly disintegrated.[38]

The federal government, on the other hand, had much greater power than the few rightist dissidents in Local 80, though its attempts to crush, or at least weaken, the union did not meet with much more success, at least in the short term. The initial focus of the government campaign was Tony Valentino. After his indictment in the middle of the affiliation campaign, he was scheduled to go to trial on January 28, 1952, just as contract negotiations were getting underway. Local 80's new parent union strongly backed Valentino, both because "his support of the UPWA was a substantial factor in the testimony that was given against him" by RWDSU backers, and because of the critical importance of this first Taft-Hartley case to the entire progressive union movement. Helstein urged all UPWA locals to send "substantial contribution[s]" to Valentino's defense fund and asked the CIO to raise funds from all its member unions. When the local leader's trial date was postponed to September, the focus of the U.S. attorney shifted to Sylvia Neff, longtime Campbell worker on the potato preparation line and now an office worker at the union local. She had notarized Valentino's Taft-Hartley affidavit and was charged on February 5 with lying to the grand jury investigating him about her own ties to the Communist Party. Local 80 immediately pounced on this charge as another step in the campaign of Campbell and its "Stool Pigeons" to destroy their union:

> They had Anthony Valentino indicted by going before the Grand Jury
> and telling a bunch of lies.

They thought that by this dirty move our members would get scared and vote for the R.W.D.S.U.

But our members were not fooled.

Now the same "Company Union Stool Pigeons" bring in the A.F.L., with the help of some one in the Company supplying the names and addresses of all employees in the plant.

So to scare our members into voting for their new union, the A.F.L., they have another one of our members, who worked hard to build Local 80, indicted on another phony issue, that she lied....

Why is it that this move again comes when we are asking for a wage increase.

Because the "Company Union Stool Pigeons" must do the dirty work of the company through the A.F.L.

Local 80's attention to the contract was clearly being distracted by the attacks on its leaders and its very existence. A special shop steward meeting on February 16, 1952, listed "Discussion of the A.F.L. and their committee" and "Indictment of Valentino and Sylvia Neff" before what would normally be the only agenda item at this point: "Contract negotiations." Talks with the company had resumed three days earlier, but with little progress. When the contract expired on March 1, both sides agreed to a sixty-day extension, but the union made a slightly veiled threat after receiving what it considered to be an insulting counterproposal to its demands: "If we accepted the company's proposals we really would have a Company Union....Our members instructed our officers to get them a good contract. We intend to, if it takes us until tomato season to do it." By hinting at a tomato season strike, Local 80 threatened to use its ultimate weapon in defiance of the attacks by government, right-wing unionists, or company.[39]

As negotiations moved toward the new expiration date of May 1, job actions by various departments escalated. The slowdown targeting the unsatisfactory resolution of grievances in the labeling department that had begun on January 16 lasted twenty-four days. Though the union scaled back its demands throughout talks in March and April, the company continued stonewalling Local 80 while Neff's trial got underway. The union responded by deciding at a membership meeting that workers would work at "100 percent effectiveness" as measured under the Bedaux system, but would refuse to work at a rate of 150 percent effectiveness, which, it claimed, the company was trying to enforce.

A virtual guerilla war ensued in the soup plants, with workers slowing down and bosses trying to push out more work and disciplining recalcitrant employees. Though the agreed-upon contract extension ran out on May 1, the language of the contract mandated that it would continue in force unless either side notified the other that it was pulling out. When workers escalated by engaging in "hit-and-run strikes" in which "several hundred... disappeared" from various departments, the company announced that the contract was cancelled. The rolling strikes had begun when a manager suspended a Can Filling Department worker for slowing down, followed immediately by some one hundred department workers leaving their posts to attend a "special meeting" to discuss the suspension. After those workers were similarly suspended, some 1,300 unionists throughout the plants left in groups large and small "to attend union meetings." When, as expected, the company imposed a similar punishment on those employees, all five thousand production employees halted work. Some three thousand "milled around the entrances to the main plant," and some, "singing songs," formed a spontaneous picket line. Campbell's Camden plants remained shut down in a "protest stoppage" that lasted seventeen days. Though unionists did not hesitate to take decisive actions, many suspected that the company was provoking a walkout by dealing harshly with any worker protests. By forcing an early strike, Campbell pushed the plant shutdown up by two months, before the critical tomato season; the simultaneous trial of Sylvia Neff in May was an added benefit for the company.[40]

Under the direction of the UPWA's Don Smith and the Local 80 executive board, the strikers used several creative tactics to pressure the company. Above all they stressed "Negro and White Unity," ensuring that all picket lines and strike activities were integrated. Union members visited local businesses, making their case that they had not received a raise since 1950 and collecting petition signatures from 180 business operators in support of the strikers. Local restaurant owner William Orland wrote to Campbell plant manager L. S. Potter that "the sentiment of the community... is overwhelmingly in support of the requests for wage and other adjustments." The union also sent a letter requesting cooperation to thousands of farmers who supplied the soup company. Though Local 80 had parted ways with its sister local in Chicago over the DPOWA merger, two local leaders visited Local 194 to ask support and, no doubt, frighten the company.

The rank and file's continued support for Tony Valentino was demonstrated when a policeman arrested him for disorderly conduct on the picket line; when police pushed Valentino into a patrol wagon, "six or eight pickets tried to get in" with him, and many more followed the vehicle to police headquarters and crowded outside and in the doorways. In the end, the company met the union halfway on the contract demands, granting wage and benefit improvements, improving language on work clauses, seniority, and grievances, and granting a modified union shop. Though Campbell still adamantly refused to accept an antidiscrimination clause in the contract, it agreed "to post copies of N. J. Anti-discrimination law in plant and to publicly state it does not discriminate." Despite the pressures of fighting the contract battles during the trial of Neff and the raids by the AFL, Local 80 held its own. The UPWA proclaimed, "Local 80's Unity Soup proved hotter than the company's own special concoction, 'Witch Hunt Stew.'" Shortly before the union's partial victory, however, Neff was found guilty of perjury. An apoplectic Judge Thomas Madden sentenced her to five years in prison, excoriating her as an "ingrate" and "atheist," and blaming her and her attorney for upsetting him so much that he needed to be hospitalized. Camden's *Courier-Post* the next day carried a banner headline announcing the end of the Campbell strike, but the rest of the front page was filled with stories depicting the growing perils of world communism: Neff's conviction for lying to protect Campbell's communist union leader, the invasion of Berlin by "6000 Reds," and a prison uprising by communists in Korea put down by American and British troops.[41]

Though Campbell's Camden union survived—and, even more surprising, further developed its tradition of militancy and unity—in the spring of 1952, its trials were not yet over. In the fall Valentino's case came before Judge Madden, and between Local 80's disgruntled right-wing members and severe pressures on others from the FBI, the local's leadership was further shaken.

Valentino had lived in South Camden most of his life, several blocks away from his old friend John Tisa and, like Tisa, he was the son of Italian immigrants. In 1926 he started working at Campbell. Though he was eighteen years old, he was hired as a "packing boy," and he soon became involved in the union organizing campaigns of 1934 and 1939–1940. Among those arrested during the militant but abortive strike in 1934 was Valentino's future wife, Rose Abiuso. When the UCAPAWA won its landslide victory to represent Campbell's production workers in 1940, he was elected its first business agent, a post the union members continued to reelect him to every year. Tisa had become involved in socialist politics in high school and moved closer to the Communist Party as he decided to join the antifascist volunteers in Spain. It is not clear when Valentino joined the party, but by the time of the UCAPAWA's victory he was supporting the party position on many issues; Joseph Gallo remembers that "we were wondering why [Valentino and others] were against Finland" when "everybody was against Russia" during the short Winter War of 1939–1940.

Of all Communist Party issues, Valentino seized upon its opposition to racism and segregation and made that crusade his own. He had experienced the castelike environment of Campbell himself, with Anglo-Saxon Protestants running the company and reaping the rewards, Italian immigrants like himself performing the back-breaking, mostly manual, production work, and African Americans relegated to a few of the dirtiest jobs. Though his unwavering support for equality won him the enmity of some of his coworkers, he stuck to his beliefs. As the proportion of African Americans in the Campbell workforce increased, he gained their strong support, a factor that became significant when the McCarthyite campaign against him intensified.[42]

The government's case consisted of attempting to prove that Valentino was still a member of the Communist Party when he signed the Taft-Hartley affidavit in October 1949; the defense made no attempt to claim that he had not earlier been a member. The way the U.S. attorney did this, however, went far beyond merely establishing the truth of this allegation. Instead, the prosecution built a sensational story of pervasive communist control of the labor movement in Camden, especially its "cannery cell" run by Valentino. In fact, very little evidence was presented that could have proven that he was still a member by late 1949. Those who testified were either members of the RWDSU faction or former communists who had decided for various reasons to side with the government. Jacob Carlin, former RCA worker, UE member, and ex-communist, started naming names as soon as he was sworn in and placed Valentino at the heart of the Camden branch of the Communist Party.

Much of the testimony that was intended to damn Valentino actually demonstrated that he was a good unionist concerned with advancing the cause of labor. Campbell shop steward and former communist Robert Wooley (earlier the main witness against Neff) testified that Valentino had recruited him: "He said it would make me a better steward and a better union man." Joseph Gallo related an incident that occurred when the union was short on funds. The executive board of the union had decided to cut expenses by eliminating the customary purchase of jackets for the champions of the intrashop baseball league. "The Digesters, who won, were burned up," according to Gallo. He told Valentino that the union should instead end the subscriptions to the *Daily Worker* that it provided for all stewards, but Valentino told him that the *Worker* was good for the education of the stewards and that if something had to go, it would be the jackets before the *Worker*. Many others called to testify refused to answer any questions that could incriminate Valentino. When Sylvia Neff, out on bail from her conviction the previous spring, was subpoenaed to testify, her refusal to answer questions again infuriated Madden and he held her in contempt of court. The prosecutor had no more success with other stewards and union officers like George Dance and Al Paglione, who each refused to answer over thirty questions. One former union officer, however, claimed that the defendant had said that the "Communist Party is collecting arms and ammunition to overthrow the government of the United States." Frank DiMaio testified that this statement was made in 1944—a time when Valentino was urging all-out support for the war effort. The defense attorney asked why he had waited seven years—until the FBI talked to him—before reporting the alleged statement to authorities; DiMaio had no answer. In the atmosphere of the times, a conviction was almost assured. Madden denounced Valentino and all godless communists and sentenced him to five years in prison.[43]

Still, the ordeal of Local 80's progressive leaders was not over. Joseph Ward, who had previously tried to destroy the CIO union by appealing to the AFL, announced in December that he would lead a slate—ironically named "Rank and File"—to challenge the Valentino leadership group in the local's annual elections in early January. Another founder of Local 80 from the Maintenance Department, John Juditz, also mounted a challenge as an independent. Ward first tried using a preemptive strike to knock out his main opponents before the vote. At a union membership meeting he proposed a resolution banning "Communists, Fascists, and KKK members" from holding office in Local 80, and demanded that UPWA regional director and communist sympathizer Meyer Stern be refused admittance to union meetings. When his proposals were roundly defeated, he went ahead with his campaign against Valentino. He was aided by a major public relations campaign conducted by the local media and the Association of Catholic Trade Unionists (ACTU). Anticommunist CIO regional director George Craig also weighed in with warnings about the potential loss of the local to the AFL if something was not done to change its leadership, for "this South Jersey area is pre-dominately [sic] Catholic." Even during the strike the previous spring, ACTU local chaplain Rev. George Sharkey had claimed the strike was illegal under Taft-Hartley provisions and publicly denounced Local 80. On the eve of the elections at the beginning of 1953, Sharkey, also director of the Catholic Institute of Industrial Relations, stepped up his rhetoric:

> The first object of the Communist is control of labor unions. . . . A typical example exists here in Camden County in the actions and purposes of Anthony Valentino. . . . Union members should not pass over these facts lightly. They should also remember that it is a known fact that Communist labor leaders are secretly enlisting union members into the Communist party. . . . In some cases, these followers of the Communist party line have even paraded as Catholics. It is well to point out that

the Holy Father in 1949 warned members of the Italian Labor Movement that any Catholic who followed the Communist party line is automatically excommunicated from the Catholic Church.

Local 80 president Benjamin Butler blasted Sharkey for trying to influence the election. The *Courier-Post* featured Sharkey's response ("Father Sharkey Defends Right of Priest To Counsel Union") on the front page and threw its full support into the campaign against Valentino's ticket. In a prominent editorial labeled "Fight on Reds in Unions Is Up to All Members," it warned that unionists were being duped by "wily Communist propaganda."[44]

Despite the barrage of anticommunist propaganda, Valentino and his whole team went on to soundly trounce both opposing tickets combined. Despite all attacks, both internal and external, Valentino and Local 80's leadership could feel with some justification that they had been vindicated. The members knew the job the local's leaders had done and the sacrifices they had made to maintain Local 80's tradition as a militant and democratic union, and they clearly were not interested in abandoning them in the interests of a "responsible" trade unionism that kowtowed to the company or even the government. Nonetheless, Valentino's presence was an undeniable burden in this dark period. NLRB certification was at stake, and the internal disruptions had not abated. Less than two weeks after Valentino's victory, some three hundred Maintenance Department workers—all white men—seceded from Local 80 to form an independent craft union. Led by former Local 80 leaders like Joseph Gallo and Daniel Harkins, they announced they were leaving to escape the "Communist infiltration and Communist thinking" of their old union. The focus of Local 80 on racial and gender equality, and its commitment to industrial unionism over craft interests—"these people don't favor any group," as Gallo said—no doubt played an important role in the secession as well. Valentino finally decided the cost to Local 80 of his continued presence was too great, and he resigned his position as business manager in early February 1953.[45]

How can this period, from the end of World War II through 1953, be summarized for the Campbell Soup Company, its workers, and their union? There is no simple answer. From the company's point of view, the McCarthy era demonstrated the usefulness of zealous anticommunism in fighting a progressive union. Throughout the next decade it made anticommunism a hallmark of its public relations. Campbell was also beginning to recognize the importance of a more sophisticated and "modern" approach to labor relations; for the first time it inserted into its contract with the union the requirement that its new Personnel Department be a participant in grievance resolutions.

Yet the resurrection of Local 80 from what appeared to be devastating blows must have given the company some concern. On the plus side for the union, it navigated the treacherous waters of the McCarthy period remarkably well compared to most other progressive unions. Another FTA union, the tobacco workers' Local 22 in Winston-Salem, had fought a tremendous battle for its members and had even given birth to the modern civil rights movement in that city before going down in defeat in the darkest days of the Red scare. Local 80 rejected—due perhaps as much to luck as to the political configuration of the local—what turned out to be the doomed merger its national union was pushing and reemerged in the only truly progressive union still in the CIO. The UPWA carried on and strengthened Local 80's fight for unity and equality and both national and local organizations continued to support their leftist members when they came under attack. On the other hand, the Camden union suffered some debilitating defeats. Most serious was the loss of unity with other Campbell workers. No longer would all workers strategize together and act together against the company. Chicago's Local 194 had followed its parent union into the short-lived DPOWA, and workers at the new plant in Sacramento were represented by the Teamsters. Further, even in the Camden plants another union represented the craft employees for the first time. Local 80's other enduring loss was in its leadership. Though the convictions of Valentino and Neff were later overturned, the goals of the prosecution had succeeded: neither would ever work for Local 80 or the Campbell Soup Company again. The union officers who remained had been through divisive internal struggles and the leadership team consisted of a mix of progressive unionists and a more "pragmatic" group close to the maintenance workers who had seceded. The lessons for Local 80's leftists were also complex. The dedication of the union's communists won them the undying support of the majority of the soup company workers. However, their secrecy concerning their ideological viewpoint confused many union members when their opponents "exposed" them. Some of Valentino's supporters maintained years later that "we don't believe he was a Communist." Others saw how anticommunism was used by the company: "If you were any way progressive, they called you a communist." As the events of McCarthyism made clear, the party's position on concealing the membership of many activists was not due entirely to paranoia, yet this policy had undeniable negative consequences.[46]

Though the union had survived and was unapologetically continuing Local 80's progressive tradition, it would be facing in the coming decades a management and a chief executive determined to take back full control of the company.

✹ CHAPTER 5

The UPWA's Social Unionism versus William Beverly Murphy

Less than a month after Tony Valentino relinquished his union post, another significant resignation took place at the Campbell Soup Company. The interim president of the company, James McGowan, announced his retirement and handed over the reigns of the company to W. B. Murphy on March 1, 1953. Murphy, who had been groomed for this role since he was hired in 1938, would transform Campbell into an even leaner company that was more profitable than ever, with plants spread across the United States and the world by the time he stepped down in 1972. Yet he maintained strict adherence to the goals and basic philosophy of the man who built the Campbell empire, John T. Dorrance. While Valentino's resignation marked a serious weakening of the union's unity and leadership, McGowan's retirement strengthened the company's position, for his successor had a clear vision of where he wanted to take the company. Toward the end of Murphy's reign, in 1968, came the apocalyptic battle between his iron rule and the social-justice unionism of the United Packinghouse Workers of America (UPWA). That contest will be the subject of the next chapter; the present chapter will examine the changes Murphy initiated in the day-to-day operations and structure of the Campbell Soup Company and, in particular, his skillful blending of all of the company's traditional strategies for keeping production costs at rock-bottom levels. While Murphy was certainly the protagonist in this period of Campbell's history, the company's rank-and-file workers and union activists did not slack in their own ongoing drive to have a say in how their company was run and how its profits were distributed.

The significance of the Murphy era consisted in his use of Campbell management's proven strategies of production redesign, labor segmentation, and steadfast antiunionism/anticommunism combined with another that had previously been only slightly tested: moving (or threatening to move) production to cheap labor areas. Murphy understood his company's philosophy well, and he likely authored the internal bulletin to supervisors issued during the contract negotiations less than a year before he assumed the top position at Campbell. In it, the company swore it would never accept three provisions in a contract: arbitration of labor standards, a nondiscrimination clause, and a union shop. Each of the proscribed clauses corresponded to one of the company's three core strategies.[1]

Murphy's primary approach to perfecting Dorrance's goal of producing quality food products cheaply centered on increasing labor productivity. He viewed the elimination of human labor through automation as the most important method in this campaign, but he also continued to pursue relentlessly the "scientific" redesign of the labor process and management of the labor force. In Murphy's implementation of the second strategy—fighting a united workforce through segmentation—he continued at first to adamantly refuse to accept the elimination of distinctions based on race or gender, as symbolized by management's rejection of an antidiscrimination clause in the union contract. As this policy fell to the tenacious opposition of Local 80, civil rights legislation, and the decreasing acceptance of overt discrimination in American society at large, he shifted his divisive tactics to building walls between workers in the different Campbell plants. By the time of the 1968 confrontation, union representation in the plants was spread among five international unions, and all had different contract termination dates. This strategy blended into the next, with Murphy outdoing all his predecessors in hostility to unions. Adopting the take-it-or-leave-it tactics that his friend and mentor Lemuel Boulware had pioneered at General Electric, Murphy sought to sideline union officials and render their organizations inconsequential. Further, he built on the usefulness that anticommunism had provided in weakening labor in the McCarthy era by becoming an intrepid foe of communism and even vaguely socialistic ideas. His role as the head of the Crusade for Freedom and the Radio Free Europe Fund also brought him closer to media and government leaders, from Henry Luce to Lyndon Johnson. Murphy went beyond the strategies initiated by Campbell's previous chief executives in his careful introduction of an approach used by RCA, Campbell's neighbor in Camden, New Jersey, decades earlier. Previously, the

Campbell Soup Company had sited its four plants—in Camden, Chicago, Sacramento, and Toronto—in consideration of markets to be served and transportation costs. Aided by changes in transportation and mechanized harvesting, Murphy pushed a bold plan to build a new plant every five years; his would be located in rural areas with cheap labor forces and no union traditions. His intentions in these expansion plans went beyond the mere flight of capital to cheap labor areas; no existing plants were shut down during his administration, and Camden remained the major production site at the conclusion of his term. Yet the incipient movement of production enhanced each of the long-standing company strategies. The latest automated techniques of production could be installed and tested at the new sites. With each additional plant, unity among all Campbell workers became increasingly more difficult to maintain. And workers in the new plants, most located in "right-to-work" states, became competitors to those in the original plants. Years of struggle had won for Camden and Chicago workers decent wages and a modicum of power, but now, if they demanded "too much," the company could say, it could move to places where people would be happy to have the jobs. Little or no production need actually be moved; the mere threat of moving had the desired effect.

William Beverly Murphy's sophistication and ruthlessness in carrying out his agenda at the helm of the Campbell Soup Company was met by an equally determined workforce in the Camden plants. Yet their organization and leadership during the Murphy period did not match their resolve. The forces arrayed against the workers, as outlined in the previous paragraph, made the workers' task a herculean effort. Perhaps the activists who had led the 1940 organization drive and kept Local 80 a body with unbreakable unity could have overcome the multifaceted tactics of management, but they had been divided and in some cases defeated during the anticommunist witch hunts that preceded Murphy's presidency. The fact that the workers and their surviving and new leaders were able to hold their own against Murphy and continue to make modest gains attests to the deep well of strength in Local 80, as well as the invaluable assistance provided by the new national union, the United Packinghouse Workers.

🥄 "Campbell Takes the Lid Off"

When John T. Dorrance died in 1930, his will ensured that the Campbell Soup empire that he had built would remain a Dorrance family possession. The administrators of his estate (the second largest in U.S. history to that time) paid large dividends to his heirs but kept tight control of the company. Initially, even the day-to-day management of the company remained under direct control of another Dorrance, John's brother Arthur. When W. B. Murphy became chief executive, Campbell was still a privately held company owned entirely by Dorrance's descendents. That was about to change. In 1954, the estate sold off 13 percent of its shares in a public offering. The reasons for this change were complex, but they marked the initial inklings of a gradual breakdown in the unitary voice of the Dorrance family with regard to its prize possession, the Campbell Soup Company. The stock offering was not required in order to obtain outside financing; the company had always been, and would continue to be, internally financed through earnings. Publicly, spokesmen explained that going public would allow the estate to diversify its holdings, grant top executives stock and stock options ("good for the morale of the Company"), and gain more public (stockholder) support in the event it needed "to have a few stockholders rooting in its corner." But it also established a market value for Campbell stock. An immediate need for such valuation resulted from the death in 1954 of one of John Dorrance's children, Margaret Dorrance Strawbridge; the stock sale set a value for her estate. Her death resurrected a nagging issue that contributed to bitter disputes decades later, due to the family patriarch's different attitudes toward his male and female offspring. His only son Jack received double the inheritance allocated to each of his daughters. The elder Dorrance had made clear his favoritism toward the family of his male heir in another, perhaps even more galling way; he stipulated that only descendents bearing the last name "Dorrance" would be permitted to be buried in the family mausoleum. When the first child of his daughter Ethel Colket died at age three in 1937, his widow had another mausoleum built next to his for the little girl.[2]

To assist with the company's first stock sale and to help build a more sophisticated public face for Campbell, Murphy engaged the prominent public relations firm of Earl Newsom and Company in late 1954. This was a first for the company. Though Campbell had long used an advertising firm to help it sell soup, it had had little interest in what various constituencies thought about the company. Murphy and other executives had interviewed several public relations firms, but were impressed with Newsom's nuanced approach to its task of promoting the company—"an evolutionary rather than a revolutionary process." Newsom and Company was perhaps the most prestigious public relations firm of the 1950s, representing corporate behemoths like the Ford Motor Company and Standard Oil of New Jersey.

At Campbell, Newsom consultants quickly brought company executives to see the importance of "creating a stronger and clearer impression of the company's personality...in terms of both the general public and...such special publics as the financial community, the trade, retailers, suppliers and the government." They promised to make Campbell "the kind of company...that the people of this country care for" so that "the company would not be an easy target for either political or mercantile attack." Campbell Soup thus was to become a leading player in the 1950s marketing of corporate America itself as a positive good for the American people. While its products had always enjoyed a good reputation, the company's management had often been perceived as cold and harsh toward its workers and suppliers and indifferent to the public good. In its campaign to remake the company's image, Newsom wanted to win the public to Campbell's side in any future disputes; if unions called a boycott, for instance, he wanted public sentiment to lie with the company, not the unions. Newsom and Company was able to demonstrate its worth immediately. When *Fortune* magazine decided in 1955, on the occasion of the public stock offering, to run "Campbell Takes the Lid Off," its second in-depth article on the Campbell Soup Company (the first had been in 1935), Newsom obtained an advance draft. Analysts from the public relations firm led Campbell executives in an intensive review of the draft. The magazine, while certainly supportive of business, had a reputation for independence and had occasionally riled the companies it wrote about. The new Campbell Soup Company, by way of Earl Newsom and Company, sent *Fortune* a detailed annotated copy of the draft. The magazine did not capitulate on all the suggested revisions, but a number of significant changes were made in the version of the article that made it into public view in the March 1955 issue. Thus a less than favorable section on labor relations gained three new sentences: one claimed major improvements since World War II, another pointed out that "the earnings of Campbell workers are about the highest in the industry," and the third claimed that "instead of shutting down entirely in off season, as many other canners do, Campbell can offer year-round employment to three-quarters of its employees." In regard to the company's efforts to cut down the wait times for the trucks delivering tomatoes from its suppliers, a line in the draft suggesting that "most tomato growers believe this effort was prompted only by a move in the New Jersey legislature" disappeared from the published version.[3]

Campbell's new public relations advisors also helped the company get past some of its earlier awkward approaches to the public. For example, Newsom consultants gently let company executives know that their latest *Lassie* television commercial, while not quite in poor taste, could be improved. In the commercial, "Tommy, the boy, asks the audience to help keep 'Lassie' on the air by buying 'just one more can of soup this month.'" Newsom pointed out that people realized that Campbell could continue to put on the show even if they did not buy more soup and that they "might feel that this approach has a touch of commercial charlantism [*sic*]."[4]

Campbell's new "modern" approach to public relations was but one of the changes that the trustees of the Dorrance estate expected when they selected the forty-five-year-old Murphy to be the company's new leader. Though his training, experience, and outlook prepared him to take full advantage of new techniques and approaches, his attitude toward running the business bore an uncanny resemblance to that of John T. Dorrance. Born and raised in Wisconsin, Bev Murphy (as he was known to almost everyone) graduated from the University of Wisconsin in 1928 with a degree in chemical engineering (Dr. Dorrance's academic field was chemistry, but he had become much more an engineer at Campbell). After working his way up to executive vice president at the market-research pioneer A. C. Nielsen Company in Chicago, Murphy took the apparently less prestigious position of assistant to the general manager at Campbell's Camden plant in 1938. After a few years working on special projects for Arthur Dorrance, he left for Washington to become Campbell's man on the War Production Board (WPB). There he learned the importance of close ties to the government, for he played the central role (according to company managers) in keeping the supply of tin rolling into Camden during the war. It was at the WPB that Murphy developed an important relationship with Lemuel Boulware. Boulware, a WPB vice chairman, had wide experience in management but was especially interested in market research and surveys, the specialty of Murphy's previous employer, A. C. Neilson. When the war ended, General Electric tapped Boulware to reinvigorate the company's damaged employee relations. Reversing a pattern of company failure in dealing with its union (the United Electrical Workers), Boulware initiated a novel approach of going past union leaders during contract negotiations and making a "final offer" directly to the workers. Though the practice that became known as "Boulwarism" became infamous, Murphy was fascinated by tactics that he believed could give Campbell the upper hand in its dealings with its own employees.[5]

On his return he continued his rapid rise in the company hierarchy, becoming executive vice president in 1949, a company director in 1950, and finally president in 1953. Murphy, a Presbyterian and a Republican, resided in the exclusive Main Line Philadelphia suburb of Gladwyne, not far from several of the Dorrance heirs. At work in decidedly unfashionable Camden "he struck some company veterans as another J. T. Dorrance." In fact, many of the descriptions of the two were similar. Though it was said of Murphy that he was "impatient with people who don't think as fast as he does, and the brusque, quasi-military charm of his own manner might well be lost on an erring subordinate," the remark could equally as well have been made of Dorrance. Despite the similarities, however, there was some resentment among the old guard over the young outsider's new power. An observer in 1954 noted that "there appeared to be a polite and restrained tension between Mr. Murphy, who is the new management for all practical effects, and [the] surviving retainers in the old Dorrance management, most of whom are considerably senior in years to Mr. Murphy."[6]

For all his "brusque charm" and market research experience, however, the Dorrance estate executors hired Murphy primarily for his ability to reach one overarching goal: to continue making Campbell's soups at a cost low enough to retain their towering position in the marketplace (80 percent to runner-up and competitor H. J. Heinz's 10 percent) while still generating the high and steady profits that the family had become accustomed to. Murphy would demonstrate that their faith in him had not been misplaced. He worked tirelessly to automate anything that could be automated, kept labor costs low by encouraging divisions among his workers and dealing harshly with unions, and began to move production to newer, cheaper locations.[7]

🦐 Automation and "the Will to Work"

W. B. Murphy had been at Campbell Soup through the tumultuous times of the 1940 union organization drive, the contract negotiations often accompanied by strikes, and, most troublesome of all, the daily skirmishes on the shop floor between management and workers. The lack of certainty that managers had about the output of each part of the manufacturing process, more so even than the vagaries of crop yields and deliveries, led Murphy to see automation as the holy grail of his mission as chief executive. Every time a machine replaced a human process, another uncertainty due to absenteeism and "poor work habits" through slowdowns, walkouts, and sabotage could be eliminated. For whatever could not be automated—at least not yet—there was the "Rule Book," the thick tome that dictated how every tiny detail was to be performed for every process in the plant, a document that was legendary at Campbell. The Rule Book (more formally known as the Manual of Procedures or "M-O-P") went back to the days of John T. Dorrance and had been supplemented by numerous studies by the Methods Engineering section of the Industrial Engineering Department and graded to Bedaux incentive rates by the Labor Standards group. Campbell's managers did their best to make machines of the men and women whose labor created the company's products, but individual differences and human failings—like the desire for better pay and working conditions—ensured that the workers would never be automatons. And, crucially, soup production depended on the workers' skills; vice president of operations George Crabtree admitted that, "When you come down to the blending and cooking, you need human skill." An ideal soup-making plant might be made up exclusively of machines, but in the real world engineers had failed to automate very many processes, and others were still done more cheaply by humans than by machines. *Fortune* portrayed the situation facing Murphy as he took over as president:

> There is still much handwork. Some is unavoidable in dealing with fragile and perishable ingredients of varying shapes and sizes. Even so, canning is a technologically backward industry, and Campbell is no exception. Spaghetti cans are filled by hand because no one has yet devised a machine that will put exactly the right amount of spaghetti in each can. Some soups... are stirred with paddles and ladled out by hand to keep the garnish—e.g., diced carrots—from settling.

The first target for production improvement was to be "Campbell's cluttered and unappetizing Camden plant," but even the newer plants had only a fraction of their operations automated. Murphy was convinced that most of the "unavoidable" handwork could succumb to imaginative solutions by motivated engineers. So one of his first actions in 1953 was to assign twenty engineers to tackle these difficult problems. One of their first successes was to replace the men who stirred the soup with mechanical agitators.[8]

Two unrelated factors in the history of the Campbell Soup Company gave an added impetus to the drive to lower production costs through automation. While Campbell was growing to become the behemoth of the canned soup industry earlier in the century, it was able to return an unusually high rate of profit (compared to other food products companies) by constantly increasing volume, thus progressively lowering overhead cost per unit. As the market became saturated, Murphy believed that only cost-cutting changes in production techniques would keep profits rising (though he also actively sought out new markets, as will be discussed later in this chapter). At the same time that Campbell was taking over its market, its labor costs were rising, due largely to the unionization of its production plants. Edward Cheeseman, then an industrial engineer at Campbell, maintains that rising labor costs "made it more justifiable to turn to more mechanical means." However, the solutions often combined both mechanization and redesign of the human component of the manufacturing process. Only part of the work that Cheeseman did on the blending operation, for example, involved automating a section of the process.[9]

Whether these reasons impelled Murphy to throw his full effort into automation and process redesign, or whether he was simply impatient with an outmoded industry that had once stood at the forefront of innovation in mass production techniques, he made the modernization of Campbell Soup production the hallmark of his regime. When Campbell executives, under the guidance of Earl Newsom's public relations consultants, responded to *Fortune's* first draft of its important 1955 article, Murphy chose to focus entirely on research and development for his part of the response. He discussed the plans for all-new plants in Ohio and in an undisclosed location. He described a five-million-dollar overhaul planned for the flagship plant in Camden. Murphy pointedly noted that the upgrade would not result in an increase in production capacity but would focus on elimination of "many of the hand operations long necessary in the production of soups" and "completely reverse Campbell Soup's longstanding emphasis on hand-labor." He sardonically added that these changes would parallel "the mechanized operations to which the American housewife has herself now become so accustomed in her own modern kitchen." He also argued that the company needed continued high profits if his ambitious plans were to come to fruition, noting that in the previous year his board of directors had divided profits equally between dividends and reinvestment in the business. Campbell would continue the uncommon practice of financing all expansion and modernization plans internally.[10]

The twin mantras of automation and increased worker productivity appeared constantly in company documents and officers' statements from the start of Murphy's term in 1953 through his retirement in 1972. Even before that period, automation and productivity had been increasing steadily. Since the canning industry was starting from a relatively low level of mechanization compared with other industries, its jump in productivity was sharp once several of its bottlenecks had been overcome. Thus, from 1947 through 1956, output per worker hour in canning and preserving rose 56.6 percent, compared with a 38.4 percent increase for all manufacturing. According to the Bureau of Labor Statistics, mechanization in canning led to both "(1) an increase in the production rate, and (2) a reduction in the number of workers required for a specific volume of output." In the years just before Murphy's tenure, the reductions in unit labor requirements came primarily from "increasing speeds of the closing machines and allied equipment, the development of continuous processing equipment, and the use of fork-lift trucks and palletizing in warehouse operations." When Murphy took over, the company had already reduced costs below those of its rivals in the food products industry. Despite the low price of Campbell's soup (still twelve cents in many markets), its profit rate bested all its main competitors. The only industry firms larger than Campbell, General Foods and Standard Brands, earned 8 percent and 5 percent, respectively, on sales before taxes, and Heinz returned 6 percent. Campbell's 15 percent outdistanced them all, and the company had performed equally well for decades. Yet the changes introduced during Murphy's reign would soon dwarf the earlier advances.[11]

For example, in a typical year during his administration, 1964, some three hundred changes were made in various aspects of production. In almost every annual report to stockholders the company emphasized its planned growth and the expenditures in research and development that would be made to assure that growth. One by one, processes in can making, rice sorting, vegetable preparation, and labeling, among many others, saw people replaced by machines, though even by the end of Murphy's term there were hundreds of processes still performed by actual workers. Nonetheless, in his first decade as president, production employment in Camden fell from just under five thousand to under three thousand year-round workers. Because the harder-to-automate, more skilled jobs were held predominantly by men, the job cuts hit women especially hard. As preparatory jobs in particular were automated, women fell from half the workforce to just over a quarter. By 1968, 1,941 men were members of Local 80; only 740 women were. As direct labor costs fell, indirect labor costs—for supervision, inspection, and research and development—rose sharply, reaching double the direct costs by the late 1950s. With the total for all wages and salaries accounting for about a quarter of total sales, Campbell had to push hard to squeeze any additional profits out of labor costs.[12]

The primary concern of W. B. Murphy soon became the top concern of Campbell workers as well. Though the company claimed it was a "warm vital organization working to raise productivity to create better jobs," layoffs and speedups were the outcome of the continuous drive to improve productivity that production employees experienced. These effects were the grievances at the heart of many wildcat walkouts and slowdowns during the period. Though the company argued that constant revolutionizing of the work process was in its employees' best interests, it did not conceal its expectations that they must work very hard. In the special issue of the company publication *Harvest* issued in 1970 to celebrate its hundredth anniversary, it boasted that "Campbell employees work hard. There are ex-employees who will attest to this, because they (or the Company) decided that their concept of hard work and the Company's did not agree." Many lost their jobs, however, not because they refused to work hard, but because machines replaced them. Luz Melendez worked in the preparatory department on rice and chickens, but machines were installed in 1956 that eliminated her position; though she had enjoyed her job and hoped to be called back, she never was. At a conference sponsored by their national union in 1958, Camden workers listed automation and speedup as their main concerns at Campbell. A few years later, Local 80 president Benjamin Butler blamed sharp job cuts on "increased automation of soup processing and packaging facilities," though Campbell's personnel director William E. Harwick referred to the changes as merely "an updating of equipment and a realignment of production schedules."[13]

For those workers who survived the job cuts, the frenetic pace of work at the soup company made the workday difficult and even hazardous. Though canning was not generally recognized as a dangerous industry, its accident rates were far higher than the average for manufacturing. Department of Labor statistics showed that the accident rate in canning was twice that of industry in general, and about five times as high as in steel mills. The medical dispensary at Campbell was kept busy, dealing mostly with minor injuries, but occasionally very serious accidents occurred. On October 13, 1959, fifty-one-year-old Willie Strand was crushed to death after getting caught between a large bucket and a conveyor belt.[14]

The drive to streamline production was given a further push by competition with Campbell's newer plants. Industrial engineers compared all manufacturing sites on a cost-per-case basis. Despite their old buildings and often outdated machinery, the Camden plants compared favorably with newer sites organized along much more efficient lines. Camden made up for what it lacked in its physical plant by demanding more of its workers. Though this often led to job actions by workers who felt they were being driven too hard, the net result for Campbell convinced top management that Camden should remain the crown jewel in its growing production empire. The detailed organization of work and the production process was extended to all Campbell plants.

When the company acquired the frozen-food company C. A. Swanson and Sons in 1955, its first actions were to bring the new subsidiary in line with Campbell's almost military organization of production. When the young food technologist Harry Nelson was vacationing in Chicago that summer, he was notified that he should go directly to Omaha, the location of Swanson's main plant, rather than return home to Camden. Nelson's job, over the next six years, was to bring Swanson in line with the Campbell way. His first task, before becoming plant supervisor, was to collect formulas and procedures for all Swanson products. He started by asking the production manager for the procedures and formula for chicken pies. The manager told him to go to the eighth floor and ask for a certain person, who turned out to be the cook on the blending platform. The cook knew how the pies were made, but, Nelson learned to his horror, nothing was written down. "I commenced to write procedures for one product at a time," Nelson reports. "It took me a little while, a couple months." Jack Dorrance (John T. Dorrance's son) was quite upset with this problem, and he backed Nelson in hiring an inspector for each operation for every Campbell plant.[15]

The documented production procedures delineated both the mechanical and human parts of each process. And, to ensure that the human component of the procedure would perform as reliably as the mechanical portions, the company used the Bedaux system. As earlier chapters have described, this system was adopted at Campbell in 1927, and it remained a core ingredient in Murphy's overall plan for manufacturing the increasing number of food products that Campbell sold. Though the name of the system was changed to the "Standard Hour System" during his administration, its basic premise remained the same: industrial engineers "scientifically" rated each job and assigned the number of *B* units (or standard hour units) that an ordinary "good" worker would be expected to earn for each operation. Any output in excess of the standard rating earned a bonus. The system did not always work as planned, and it was the cause of the majority of the shop floor battles between management and labor. Two years after Murphy became president, *Fortune* reported,

> The passion for high quality and low costs that distinguishes the Campbell executive has not always been shared by the cheese trimmers, diced-meat sorters, mutton boners, and onion slicers who actually make the soup.
>
> The most constant source of friction has been the company's incentive plan, a modification of the Bedaux system. . . . In many preparatory operations performance standards are hard to establish, enforce, and justify. Disputes over standards have precipitated countless slowdowns and walkouts.[16]

Though the union tried to end, weaken, or at least ameliorate the worst features of the plan, the best it achieved was a labor-management standards committee. This committee, however, never gained any real power and the company refused to relinquish its total authority over standard setting. The company viewed the committee, in fact, as simply a means to "educate" workers about labor standards. In the 1956 contract negotiations, the union had once again come in with an ambitious list of changes it wanted in the plan. What it got was a guarantee of six hours per week for committee members and a list of topics they would be trained in, including "the use of the slide rule." When the system worked the way Campbell's executives and industrial engineers wanted, the result was someone like "Onion Mary." Camden resident Mary Comanda had started working at Campbell in 1933. In 1964 she was still peeling onions, but peeling so many that she earned over two hundred dollars per week, more than double the average for the job. Though a newspaper reporter conceded that "Campbell's does have machines, of course," her report revealed the tight interconnection between workers and machines that "[kept] the soup pot bubbling in an attractive, tasty and by all means profitable way."[17]

The system did not always work as planned, however. In addition to the frequent wildcat job actions that resulted from workers' opposition to the Bedaux plan, "cheating" the system became widespread. Industrial engineer Edward Cheeseman found that "it was too easy to manipulate the numbers... there were too many ways to beat the system." Production worker Franklin Williams concurs: "You'd find ways to beat the system. They put a meter up to count cans, people would go back and change the meter. And supervisors could work the pencil if they liked you."

The problem, as top managers gradually came to see it, was that employees had not internalized the spirit of hard work needed to make quality products at low cost. True believers in scientific management had paid little attention to the personal character of workers—they believed they had found the correct measure of work and had simply to manipulate their formulas to generate the results they wanted. But workers resented being treated as part of the machinery and viewed the system as just another way that the company was using to squeeze more work and profits out of them. The company responded by attempting to instill in its employees the proper attitude toward work and toward the company's profits. Head of operations G. W. Crabtree led the charge in a 1964 address, reprinted in an internal management publication. In portraying the challenges the company would face in the 1970s, Crabtree argued that Campbell and all American industry would need "productivity beyond belief." And while much of this would come from further mechanization, a crucial factor would be "the will to work":

[The will to work] is affected not simply by the individual's economic needs, but to a large extent by the prevailing view or climate of society. One wonders whether our society today is not placing too little emphasis on the will to work, and too much emphasis on security, fringe benefits, leisure time, the coffee break, paid holidays, sick leaves, and the right to strike. Here we are talking about the all-important matter of proper attitudes.

Crabtree further complained that "it disturbs me that so many people... regard profits as something almost anti-social, something that deserves to be curbed." Other Campbell leaders, and especially William B. Murphy, repeated and expanded on the same theme. To keep Campbell profitable, especially as it continued to hold down prices, both automated procedures and a more dedicated workforce would be required.[18]

Regardless of the success the company could achieve in molding its employees' attitudes toward work, it never relented on its need and its right to control the production process. Its usual rival in the fight for control was the union and the workers they represented. But company executives began to feel that another group had too much power and was standing in the way of the strict execution of its plans. This group was the company's foremen (and a small number of "foreladies"). Foremen had held a powerful position at the company since early in the century. Many were feared by their subordinates and a few had reputations as "slave drivers." But they also had a measure of independence from upper management. Foremen were the ones most directly responsible for the quantity and quality of production, and many jealously guarded their power in their own little fiefdoms. Despite directives to carry out the company's "scientific" methods of management, foremen used favoritism and bullying to get their way, and they almost never let grievances go above the first step—that is, between the foreman and the worker alongside his or her steward. Though workers were subjected to the arbitrary rule of their supervisors, they also held some real power in the relationship; as Sylvester Akins comments, "We made them and we could break them." Even representatives from upper management were sometimes afraid to confront foremen. When industrial engineer Edward Cheeseman had to confront Charlie Goering—"a tough old bird"—with the news that a "loose" labor standard would need to be adjusted in his department, he feared that Goering would "sail into" him, because the adjustment would lower the bonus for the job and thus create problems with Goering's workers. He explained to Goering that a mistake had been made in calculating the standard, and apologized. Cheeseman was enormously relieved when Goering told the young engineer that "nobody's perfect" and made the change without further trouble.[19]

The anxiety that corporate leaders had about the power of foremen extended far beyond the Campbell Soup Company. In the late 1940s, about a hundred thousand foremen had joined foremen's unions, mostly in the automobile and defense industries. As historian Howell John Harris has portrayed in his *The Right to Manage,* top executives feared a nightmare scenario in which foremen and blue-collar workers respected each other's picket lines and upper management lost all control of their factories. While there were apparently no serious attempts to unionize by Campbell's foremen (just a company-sponsored Foremen's Club started in the 1930s), they still held enormous power in the plants, and when Murphy took the reins as president the company made a number of decisive moves to curtail that power. Joseph Morrison had worked his way up in the company, starting as a temporary worker during tomato season. After years of Morrison's doing a good job in shipping and receiving, a manager asked him to become a foreman. Morrison thought he was doing a good job in that role too, but, in 1964, just shy of his twenty-fifth anniversary with the company, he lost his job: "They had a purge—twenty-five foremen were laid off." In Morrison's case, the job cuts were apparently part of a company reorganization of management that decreased the number of foremen plantwide. But in other cases, Campbell fired foremen who ran their units as independent bosses, many of whom had bad reputations among workers and whose actions had precipitated walkouts in the past. According to Franklin Williams, "There were a lot of old foremen who thought they owned Campbell Soup. They fired them, the guys who were really nasty. I know one they let go, they were people you couldn't talk to... [he] thought he was God Almighty!" In place of the despotic rule of the foremen, the new Campbell Soup advanced the Personnel Department. There had been no such department before 1949, but with the introduction of more modern employee relations the reliance on the arbitrary rule of foremen ended—or at least lessened—as the firm moved away from reliance on the old "drive system." Those foremen still in the employ of the company after the purge were given "special training" to ensure that they carried out the company's plan and nothing more. W. B. Murphy had knocked down another potential threat to his control of the Campbell Soup Company.[20]

As the proportion of the sales dollar attributable to labor costs declined with the aggressive introduction of automation and more rigid labor control, Murphy realized he could use some of the same techniques to cut ingredient costs. Though Campbell did not directly employ the farm workers who picked the tomatoes and other vegetables that went into its soups, it in effect set a ceiling on their wages by offering a no-negotiation price to farmers. Farmers and their employees had not caused as much trouble as the company's unionized production employees, but they had tried to combine into cooperatives, and farmworkers had made some sporadic attempts at organization. Campbell dealt with the first problem by continuing to refuse outright to work with any cooperatives; it would sign contracts with individual farmers only. Despite the passage in 1967 of the Agricultural Fair Practices Act, nominally aimed at protecting the rights of growers to bargain as a group, Campbell refused to alter its long-standing policy. As to the vagaries of migrant farm workers, it sought to eliminate any potential problems by simply eliminating the workers. Campbell first experimented with mechanized harvesting of California tomatoes for its Sacramento plant. When that proved a success, Murphy ordered a full-scale effort to develop a tomato that would be rugged enough to withstand mechanical harvesting in New Jersey (for its Camden plants) and Ohio (for its new Napoleon plant). Soon the company was inserting into its contracts the requirement that tomatoes must be mechanically harvested. Continuing problems in the East, however, prevented the automation of its tomato supply system there, and the firm continued to suffer from the uncertainties and expense of employing human labor to harvest its tomatoes and other crops. Ultimately the sharply lower costs of mechanical harvesting in the West and the failure of attempts to adapt the technology to New Jersey farms would be a crucial factor in the company's future plant location decisions.[21]

About midway through his term as president, Murphy outlined his goals for the company for the coming years. In addition to points dealing with marketing and international operations, he reemphasized the importance of achieving ever greater control and continuing to lower costs:

> Make progress towards effective mechanical harvesting of tomatoes. . . .
> Hold the line on selling prices or lower them through improved ingredients and greater productivity.
> Reduce Camden and Chicago controllable expenses to enable them to hold their own. . . .
> Improve employee morale through good supervising.

The concern about employee morale rose with the deterioration of workers' enthusiasm about their jobs that became increasingly evident even as automation made some jobs easier but heightened fears of further layoffs. Rather than improving the "will to work," the further mechanization of their lives left many Campbell workers more dispirited than ever.[22]

Race and Geography: Labor Segmentation in the Murphy Era

If automation was William B. Murphy's primary method for transforming productivity at Campbell Soup, keeping its workers divided was his main strategy for forestalling any opposition to his plans. However, the nature of labor segmentation at Campbell changed over his time at the helm of the company. At the start, in 1953, Murphy continued the company's long practice of maintaining a rigid segmentation of jobs by race and gender, supplemented even by locker rooms divided by race. However, under the joint assaults on these practices by the social-justice unionists of UPWA Local 80 and by workers influenced by the rising nationwide civil rights movement of the 1950s and 1960s, these practices crumbled, to be replaced by a more sophisticated corporate approach to racial issues. In their place, Campbell actively worked against unity among its employees across its growing number of plants nationwide. It adamantly refused to bargain jointly with more than one plant at a time, made sure that no two plants had the same contract termination date, and actively sabotaged unity campaigns among the diverse unions that represented its workforce. Campbell did not entirely abandon the use of racial divisiveness in dealing with its workers, but by the late 1960s these tactics were supplementary to the new geographical focus of its divide-and-rule strategy.

In Murphy's first years as president, most of the old divisions on the shop floor were still in place. The union had successfully forced the company to hire African American women and to end the "boys" category of employees. It had also significantly narrowed the wage differential between men and women. But most jobs in the plants were still segregated by race and gender. Most glaring of all, there were no black supervisors. Campbell's reputation on race was so well known that some African Americans boycotted all Campbell products. According to Sadie Harris, "My doctor didn't buy Campbell's Soup because they didn't have any black foremen or foreladies."[23]

Perhaps most perplexing was Campbell's refusal to accept an antidiscrimination clause in its contract with the union. Though Local 80 had fought to get such a clause into every contract since the early 1940s, the company refused to give in. Even as late as 1954, the best that plant manager L. S. Potter would do was send the union a letter saying that, though the company would not agree to an antidiscrimination clause, it would abide by the New Jersey Anti-Discrimination Law of 1945. Finally, in 1956, a more formal letter on the subject was attached to the contract and section 2 of the contract declared that the letter was "to be considered a part of the current labor agreement"; however, this section was still not subject to arbitration. Only in the 1960s would a ban on discrimination make its way into the contract in the same form as all other sections of the agreement. This final victory in the formal contract merely recognized the de facto situation that the workers and their union had won after numerous skirmishes and a few major walkouts.[24]

Just months after Murphy became chief executive, Local 80 and UPWA organizer Don Smith launched a massive antidiscrimination campaign. It began after a wildcat sit-down strike on June 12, 1953, in which twelve hundred workers, primarily in the Preparation, Spaghetti, and Pork and Beans departments stopped work and sat down to protest management's assignment of black and white women to work on separate asparagus tables. When the company suspended two stewards and a rank-and-file union member for participation in the protest that Friday afternoon, the whole plant was on the brink of a shutdown. According to Smith:

> Management of Campbell soup will stand behind [their] foremen and Foreladies. I expect this to be [an] all out strike by Monday. Campbell soup claims that anybody who took part in the Stoppage will be disciplined with warning notices, Suspensions or discharges. In other words they will apply [their] book of rules. This also means Campbell soup will punish you for fighting against Jim Crow.

On Monday the women in the department went back to working on integrated tables on their own initiative and managers "made no effort to enforce segregated seating." In daily departmental meetings and special plantwide stewards' meetings, union leaders and members worked out a strategy. They wanted to avoid a full walkout just before the upcoming vacation (which always preceded tomato season); instead, they made demands on the company that all punishments be rescinded and that no reprisals be made, and initiated a "very effective in-plant campaign...with more and more depts. slowing down to 100 percent effectiveness." The slowdown was resumed when workers returned from vacation on July 13, and the company finally capitulated to the union demands. During the tomato season that summer, the union escalated the battle over discrimination in a many-pronged attack against the inferior treatment of African Americans and temporary employees. Between Local 80's traditional stand against racist practices and the UPWA's dedicated help on the issue, upper management came to realize that its efforts to divide the workers were backfiring.[25]

With the help of its new public relations consultants, Campbell gradually developed a new approach to issues of race and eventually made some efforts to be seen as progressive on this issue. The transition was hardly smooth, however. Besides the company's continued balking on the contract antidiscrimination clause, some of its supervisors continued to act in the old way. When Oliver Cunningham, an African American employee with eleven years at Campbell, came in late to his second-shift job one evening, his white foreman began cursing him and threatened to suspend him. The foreman then kicked Cunningham and refused to discuss the matter with the shop steward. Stewards managed to disperse an angry crowd that had gathered to "even the score," and union efforts eventually resulted in the lifting of Cunningham's suspension and the firing of the foreman. Murphy would not have an easy time changing Campbell's reputation.[26]

One prong of the new Campbell approach consisted of co-opting a few "responsible" African Americans into lower management positions. As early as 1953, the company gave James Murrell, an African American who had run for union president in the recent election, a job in the Standards Department. He joined only one other African American in the entire company in a white-collar job. After the purge of old-line foremen in the late 1950s and early 1960s, management promoted a handful of black shop stewards to the position of foreman. Many black union activists, however, refused to move up and out of the union. Franklin Williams had distinguished himself as both a good worker and a militant steward. When offered the job of leader, he took it because it was still a union job. But when asked to become a foreman, he declined. Many other African Americans had first been recognized as leaders for their roles in Local 80, and several held top elected positions. They were not about to abandon the union and go over to the other side.[27]

Very gradually and very carefully Murphy, along with Newsom and Company, began to reengineer Campbell's image to portray it as a company concerned with problems of race relations. Though top management always remained almost exclusively white and male, the company began making donations to Camden charities and supported a few small initiatives to improve education for African Americans. Some of Murphy's actions in this period appear awkward, and his public relations advisors spent much time coaching him and writing and revising speeches he was to deliver on the "race question." Still, Campbell was hardly a pioneer in such activities. As late as 1959, a detailed proposal to boost the company's "community relations" did not even mention African Americans inside or outside the company. In the section on community groups to be courted by the firm, the only groups mentioned were "Rotary, Women's Clubs, Chamber[s] of Commerce," and similar organizations. When, in 1963, Clarence Funnye of the Congress of Racial Equality (CORE) sent Murphy a letter demanding that the company send a representative to a meeting to discuss how Campbell and other companies could "change their policy of excluding negroes from television commercials," the Campbell president was taken by surprise. Murphy's flustered immediate dictated response was intercepted by consultants from Earl Newsom and Company, and they completely revised the tone and content of his reply. The letter pointed out that 26.6 percent of Campbell employees were

"Negroes," as were about eighty "members of [the] management team," and that the company did use "Negro" performers in its advertising. After the shock of the CORE letter, Murphy, with the urging of Newsom and Company, began to seek a more proactive approach to the issue of race relations. What they came up with was a rather small program of assistance to elementary and high schools in economically depressed areas and several speeches by Murphy on corporate aid to education and the war on poverty. Even then, his arguments focused on how such aid would eventually help business by providing better-prepared workers and opportunities for increased sales for the food industry "in the promotion of low-cost, balanced diets in such places as (a) Appalachia and (b) city slums." A Newsom advisor also suggested that "Mr. Murphy could, of course, rephrase 'war on poverty' if he wants to avoid being Johnsonian."[28]

Despite generally cordial relations with the Lyndon Johnson administration, Campbell became a poster child for the "Nixon technique" of promoting black-owned small businesses as the solution to poverty a few years later. Through fairly small contributions to Camden's ill-fated revitalization efforts and the encouragement of minority-run small business enterprise, Murphy attempted to place the company on the side of uplifting black America without changing very much at all. By the early 1970s, the majority of production workers and Local 80 members were African Americans, though their overall population in the company remained at about 27 percent. The close identification with and strong support for Local 80 among African Americans at Campbell threatened to make the company's future labor relations problematic, especially if it was seen as hostile to the growing aspirations of black Americans. In the larger society at this period, cities had erupted in flames and the civil rights movement was taking a more militant turn. Over the course of the 1960s Campbell had contributed some six million dollars to causes in Camden, but the embattled city needed far more than that to reverse its decline. In particular, it needed good jobs for its residents, something that Campbell could not provide; efficiencies due to automation and process improvement had in fact reduced production employment in the Camden plants to about twenty-five hundred by 1971. Instead, the company made small loans to some start-ups owned by African Americans in the city. During the important nationwide strike in 1968 (see chapter 6) "Campbell... quietly [began] cosigning business loans for Negro businessmen." It guaranteed loans for forty-six thousand dollars for "a printing plant operated by two Vietnam veterans, a modeling and charm school and a sewing factory run by black militants that turn[ed] out African garments." Nonetheless the city continued its slide downward economically to become one of the poorest in the country. In the 1970s, however, Campbell was still its one bright spot, providing decent blue-collar jobs for some residents. The company was rewarded with laudatory business articles and thanks from politicians, and *Business Week* chose Campbell—the "rehabilitator of its hometown"—to receive its Award for Business Citizenship for 1970.[29]

For the burgeoning Puerto Rican population in Camden, Campbell Soup did not remain the stalwart employer that it had appeared to be for a short time during World War II. The chain migration set in motion by the wartime recruiting continued to bring Puerto Ricans to Camden, but relatively few were employed by the soup company. By 1955, about 150 Puerto Ricans worked there year-round, and more were temporarily employed during tomato season. But Campbell no longer was a partner with the federal government in its efforts to find mainland industrial work for unemployed islanders. Though a glossy government brochure advertised that "Capable Hands can be flown to your Plant from Puerto Rico U.S.A.," most Puerto Ricans in South Jersey worked in agriculture in the 1950s. The severe unemployment suffered by this group by the early 1970s led to a number of social problems and, according to a reporter, "Camden was on the brink of exploding." When police beat a Puerto Rican man to death on July 31, 1971, the city did explode. Starting with protests by several hundred angry city residents on the steps of the city hall, Puerto Rican sections of the city erupted in rioting, and a state of emergency was declared in the city. Of all the urban rebellions of the late 1960s and early 1970s, only a small number involved mainly Puerto Ricans, and Camden's was perhaps the most significant. Racial antagonisms exacerbated the city's problems, and residents who could leave—most of them white—did. The city's population declined from 124,555 in 1950 to 102,551 in 1970, then plummeted to 84,910 by 1980. Despite the troubles, the Campbell Soup Company continued to maintain both its corporate headquarters and its largest plant in Camden, for that location had provided the workers, the raw materials, and the access to markets that had made it one of the premier food companies in the United States.[30]

Though the Camden plants remained the largest in the Campbell chain, they accounted for a shrinking portion of total company employment as new plants were built in rural Ohio, Texas, and elsewhere. As the old distinctions among racial, ethnic, and gender groups in the allocation of jobs fell and as Campbell reworked its approach to racial issues, the division of company employees along geographic lines rose to become the primary basis of management's strategy to prevent unity among its workers. By the late 1950s, workers in the four major plants in the United States were represented by four different unions: the UPWA in Camden; the Retail, Wholesale, and Department Store Union in Chicago; the Teamsters in Sacramento, and the Amalgamated Meat Cutters (AMC) in Napoleon, Ohio. Further, Camden's mechanics were now in the International Association of Machinists. To make the possibility of working together even more difficult, each contract ran out on a different date, so Campbell could simply increase production in its other plants if workers in one location chose to strike. The Teamsters (who were not affiliated with the AFL-CIO, as were the other unions) had declared that they intended to rectify this situation by raiding all the non-Teamster sites and uniting the Campbell chain under their banner. The raids never amounted to much, but even a UPWA analysis in 1957 conceded that "Teamster raids on the Campbell Soup Camden plant, while unethical, are based on a certain logic of bringing together a related group." Though the threatened raids directly concerned union members, Murphy took them as striking at the heart of a central Campbell strategy for continued profitability. He announced at a management staff meeting in early 1964 that one of his goals for the year was to "continue labor relations policies and practices that will stave off the Teamsters' drive to combine all unions into one, since this will be injurious to employees, the consumers and the Company."[31]

Union tradition and continued member activism in Camden and Chicago had resulted in stronger contracts in those cities than in the Teamster and AMC plants. So, when organizers from both the UPWA and AMC tried to sign up workers at the new Paris, Texas, plant in 1965, the company tried to stop both unions but reserved its harshest attacks for the UPWA. The plant manager sent a letter to all Paris employees warning them of the consequences of union affiliation. He claimed that in UPWA-affiliated Camden, there had been over sixty-eight work stoppages in the past six years, costing the employees over two million dollars in lost wages. Meanwhile, AMC representatives used "viciously anti-Negro verbal propaganda," according to a UPWA organizer, in their campaign to win the vote at the majority-white plant. The racial climate in the rural Texas community continued to be hostile toward African Americans; the year before the Campbell plant opened, an African American man had been lynched near there. As a result, African Americans were hesitant to be seen as open union supporters. However, UPWA organizers reported that gradually "even the Negro workers [began] to sign cards," and, when the representation election was held, the UPWA won. Now two major plants were represented by the most militant of the Campbell unions; Murphy was determined to put a stop to any further unity among workers in his far-flung plants. The occasion to do so was the fast-approaching contract negotiations in 1968.[32]

✺ W. B. Murphy's Crusade for Freedom

Campbell's practice of segmenting its workers by race, ethnicity, and gender had shifted to a conscious strategy of dividing them by geography, and that dovetailed nicely with the company's ongoing antiunionism. An important element in the corporate attack against unions in postwar America was a virulent anticommunism, and Local 80 had been dealt a very serious blow by assaults on its leftist leaders. The Campbell Soup Company's public part in this campaign had been subdued, but W. B. Murphy was to elevate anticommunism to a core value of his company. He attacked communist states and communist influence in other countries because they could threaten the business interests of Campbell (which under his leadership began serious expansion into international markets). He opposed communism at home because of its alleged threats to the values and hegemony of business. And he even warned against the illusory dreams of utopian cooperative communities for their rejection of the moral foundations of capitalism. Just as the anticommunist witch hunts of the late 1940s had been a joint project of business organizations like the National Association of Manufacturers, the media, and government "Cold Warriors" like Harry S. Truman, Murphy's ascendance into the top echelons of official anticommunism was accompanied by increasingly close ties with top government and media leaders, including presidents Dwight D. Eisenhower and Lyndon Johnson and Time-Life publisher Henry Luce. Luce, who coined the phrase "American Century" in 1941, was the keynote speaker at a 1964 conference, "Food and Civilization," sponsored by the Campbell Soup Company. He was introduced by W. B. Murphy. Despite the lofty circles he traveled in, however, Murphy never lost sight of his first priority as president of Campbell—to continue the company's profitability—and he never abandoned Campbell's antipathy toward unions who were trying to impede him from reaching his goal.[33]

Right from the beginning of his presidency, Murphy set the tone for dealing with the union, and it looked just like the company's earlier stance. UPWA field organizer Don Smith reported, in early 1953, "Company really trying to do a job on Packinghouse Local 80A." *Fortune* claimed in 1955 that "Campbell appears to have made up its mind to live with the unions," but, if so, it intended to live with them on its terms. Throughout Murphy's presidency, the company continued its hard line in contract negotiations and in day-to-day dealings with the union. In the 1956 negotiations, Campbell began a new tactic that it would repeat often in the future. Following the lead of his War Production Board mentor Lemuel Boulware, Murphy started by making a "final" offer to the union and refused to meet to discuss any changes. Then the company sent all employees a letter with the details of its offer and blamed the union for the lack of a settlement. Next, after a work stoppage, it cancelled the old contract outright. It then concocted a fake ballot that it mailed to employees, asking them either to vote for the company's final offer or to indicate that they "want[ed] a prolonged strike." Finally, it unilaterally put its proposal into effect, including a wage increase retroactive to the previous contract termination date. Such tactics raise questions about Campbell's willingness to "live with the unions." In any case, more powerful unions were out of the question: when faced with the threat of coordinated bargaining in 1968, Campbell declared it would take a twenty-five-million-dollar loss rather than concede.[34]

On the issue of communist influence in its plants, it took an even more uncompromising position under Murphy than under earlier chief executives. When Tony Valentino tried to get his job back in the plant after resigning his union position, the company refused to take him. The UPWA's Don Smith became concerned about what Local 80's members would do, for hundreds at a union meeting demanded the union back him. Faced with the company's intransigence, he warned international headquarters, "This means trouble." Still the company refused to budge. By that time U.S. president Dwight D. Eisenhower had asked him to take over as head of the Crusade for Freedom, and Murphy was not about to let an ex-communist agitator work in his plant.[35]

The Crusade for Freedom and its successor, the Radio Free Europe Fund (RFEF), were the supposed sources of funds for Radio Free Europe (RFE), the U.S. propaganda effort targeted at the "captive nations" of Eastern Europe. In fact, the Central Intelligence Agency supplied most of the funds for the project, but RFE's government backers believed it would look better if it was funded by ordinary Americans concerned about the spread of communism. Murphy eagerly took on the leadership of the puppet organization and even campaigned hard to actually raise money from sympathetic Americans, especially businessmen. He spoke before a number of groups on the subject and wrote letters to business leaders asking their support. His main selling point to this audience was that they must "keep the Commies from gaining," for otherwise they would hurt American business abroad. Murphy warned of the dire consequences that would befall the world if Radio Free Europe— the "only offensive weapon we have"—did not do its part to destabilize the countries of Eastern Europe: "If the Commies can show success in the five captive countries, this will help snowball their prestige elsewhere." The RFEF did not confine its propaganda to Eastern Europe; its newsletter targeted

Americans, warning of "Reds on the Rampage" and other horrors. The post of RFEF head eventually proved too time-consuming for Murphy, but he continued railing against communism in a number of forums. In *Country Beautiful* he penned an article on the importance of food as a weapon, under the heading "Better Fed Than Red." A company publication even took on the innocuous Amana Colonies, a religious utopian community near Iowa City, making the point that "Communism Doesn't Work," for its residents had voted to abandon their near-century-old communalism in 1931.[36]

The anticommunist theme was so pervasive at Campbell during Murphy's term that it penetrated the company's decision making on charitable donations and marketing plans. In addition to support for Radio Free Europe, the company made a point of donating its products to Cuban refugees "escaping Communist tyranny" in their homeland. The Cold War also provided new opportunities for selling Campbell products. A memo circulated in 1961 urged increased company attention to the rising popularity of fallout shelters, for they all should be stocked with Campbell's soups and pork and beans.[37]

Murphy's anticommunism was consistent with his views on government. He strongly supported the Cold War and the role of the United States in the Vietnam conflict, but he opposed government meddling in the affairs of business. In a 1963 address to a *Harvard Business Review* seminar, he blasted the inefficiency of government in the economic field and called the government's intervention in the U.S. Steel price rise the previous year "frightening." He decried Americans' "growing tendency to turn to government to solve all our problems" and their inability to understand the "vital role [of profits] in our democratic society." Yet Murphy also nurtured his relationships with top government officials. As far back as World War II he had used his position as a "dollar-a-year man" at the War Production Board to help smooth Campbell's access to tin plate. His friend Dwight D. Eisenhower later asked him to lead the Crusade for Freedom, but Murphy's contacts in government were bipartisan. During Lyndon Johnson's presidency Murphy was a guest at the White House, and the two held many phone conversations. Murphy advised the president on matters of concern to business, and Johnson used the relationship to improve his administration's image in the business community. After a series of discussions between the two in the summer of 1966, Murphy announced to the press that relations between business and the administration were cordial and that Johnson carefully listened to the views of business leaders. He added, "I have never heard a businessman who did not support the President on Vietnam."[38]

Murphy's association with government leaders and his interest in world affairs, however natural for one of his stature, were also tied to another of his plans to boost Campbell's sales and profits. He came to believe that the U.S. market for the company's traditional products was near saturation. His approach to this problem was multifaceted: he relentlessly worked to drive down production costs, but he also moved the company into new product lines, mostly through acquisitions, and he vastly increased Campbell's presence in other countries. Archrival H. J. Heinz had become a household name in Europe early in the twentieth century, but Campbell only ventured beyond its small foreign operations in Canada and Britain in 1959. As a latecomer the company took heavy losses in its international operations for many years, but Murphy pursued his new course anyway, confident that his gamble would pay off in the long run. The new global perspective included opening manufacturing plants in other countries, acquiring interests in foreign companies, greatly expanding marketing efforts overseas, and importing raw and semiprocessed materials for U.S.-made products. The latter effort led to some marketing problems at home. When the United States cut the tariff on beef in half in 1958, Campbell rushed to replace expensive domestic beef and its processing by Campbell butchers with precut and cheaper Argentinian beef. When American farmers began complaining about falling prices and advertised the fact that Campbell and other companies were using foreign beef, alarmed Campbell executives phoned their public relations firm for help. The solution was to claim that the reason for the change went back to Campbell's prime objective: quality. Argentinian beef, they said, was leaner, and therefore better for the soups the company made. The scare did not deter Campbell from exploring even deeper moves into Argentina. Two years after they outsourced their beef supply another call from Campbell to Earl Newsom and Company requested detailed information on Argentina in relation to the possible establishment of manufacturing operations there. Newsom's report reassured Campbell that Argentine leader Arturo Frondizi was "an extreme free-marketer" and friendly to foreign investment. Of all the freedoms W. B. Murphy crusaded for, free trade was near the top of his list.[39]

✹ Local 80 in the Murphy Era

While Campbell president W. B. Murphy was driving the company to new levels of productivity and expanding into new areas at home and abroad, the union at the home plants in Camden, Local 80 of the UPWA, was struggling to overcome a number of challenges. Structural changes in the prepared foods industry, and especially at the Campbell Soup Company's Camden plants, resulted in a decrease in the number of production jobs needed to turn out ever greater quantities of food products. The reasons for these changes fell into two categories: first was the rapid introduction of automation and the continuous redesign of the work process, and second was the transfer of some production to Campbell's growing network of plants and the outsourcing of some production processes. Local 80 confronted these changes from a weakened state. Many of the strongest leaders on the left had been driven out in the early 1950s, and the politically conservative but militant mechanics had left to form their own craft union. Of those who remained, several proven shop stewards, mostly African Americans, rose to take over positions of leadership. These new leaders had learned to be trade unionists under the guidance of militant leftists like Tony Valentino, and many were also influenced by the growing civil rights movement in America. However, they also suffered a number of handicaps. Prime among these was a destructive factionalism; as different individuals jockeyed for power, more energy often went into union election battles than into confronting the company. Also, among the survivors from an earlier period of the union were two groups that had never previously had much impact. One was the small handful of right-wingers who continued to badger the local's officers. The other was to have a more significant impact in the long term. Since the early days of the local a few unionists had associated with neither of the dominant groups (the leftists or the mechanics) but saw union office as an easy job with few requirements other than minimum servicing of members and winning small improvements in wages and benefits through periodic discussions with management. These business unionists allied with whatever group of stewards and activists appeared most likely to win the next election. While this group never held more than a minority of union offices, their influence sapped the old Local 80 traditions of militancy. In sum, Local 80 moved through the Murphy years in less than top form. When the titanic confrontation of 1968 pitted Campbell's unions against the company, the dedicated activists who led the struggle would face a difficult test.

Of the two groups that contributed most to the founding and early success of Local 80—the communists and the mechanics of the Maintenance Department—neither remained by the time of the early Murphy era. The two leftist leaders convicted during the McCarthyite hysteria saw their convictions overturned, but neither played any role at Campbell again. Tony Valentino's life after he resigned his union post was tragic. He felt forsaken by his old friends and coworkers when neither the company nor the union would offer him a job. He attended Local 80 meetings for a year—he was granted a "voice, but no vote"—to plead his case, and scores of union members urged their local to demand his old job back, but the union refused to back up the issue with action, and the company rebuffed the request. Increasingly dispirited and bitter at his abandonment by the union he had played a crucial role in founding, he went to the Federal Bureau of Investigation "to make a complete statement of everything." He indicated that he wanted to do anything he could "to put Local 80 out of business."[40] He next made a hopeless effort in 1955 to start a new union to challenge Local 80. Ironically, he chose the same name—Local 1, United Cannery, Maintenance, and Allied Workers—that the mechanics had temporarily used when they seceded from Valentino's Local 80 in early 1953. Even more surprisingly, the organizers of his new union included Frank DiMaio, an ex-communist who had testified against Valentino and who had even sued Valentino and Sylvia Neff for slander. By this time the Camden branch of the Communist Party was in disarray after the attacks of the McCarthy era, and Valentino claimed he had no further interest in "un-American" causes. Though his new cause was hopeless, he made a plaintive plea, in "An Open Letter To My Negro Brothers and Sisters," that hearkened back to the glory days of Local 80:

> But regardless of whether you help me or not, there is no hard feelings, I will continue to fight for all the things I believe in.... Workers are joining our Union every day. We cannot lose. With me, we will be fighting like we did in the old days, and with all of us in the new Union we will have a strong united Union that the Company cannot smash.

Though several hundred workers signed cards for the new union, Valentino's quixotic campaign went nowhere, and he spent the remainder of his working days in a nursery and garden store in nearby Pennsauken.[41]

The mechanics of the Maintenance Department fared much better in their post–Local 80 reincarnation. After a short time as the independent Local 1, they affiliated with the International Association of Machinists (IAM), an AFL union. The maintenance men had always smarted under the egalitarian ethos of the old industrial union, and now they could focus on getting the rewards they felt they deserved as skilled workers. Local 2031-IAM members retained their old militancy on trade union issues and they continued to keep their department Bedaux-free. When founding president Daniel Harkins became "too soft" on the company, he was ousted by financial secretary Joseph Gallo, who promised to keep Local 2031 strong. Of course, the new local's activism did not extend to fighting discrimination; only after agitation by Camden civil rights activists did the local (and Campbell) agree to initiate an integrated apprenticeship program with five slots for black workers.[42]

For the overwhelming majority of Campbell workers in Camden, however, Local 80 would remain their union to the end. Its greatest strength continued to be its strong shop steward system. Those most committed to standing up for the interests of all workers volunteered to run for steward, and union members usually elected those most able to put their ideals into practice. Virtually the entire new batch of top union officers got their start as stewards, and this background of fighting in the trenches in the day-to-day skirmishes with the company prepared them well for continuing Local 80's tradition as a strong union. Another quality bequeathed from the union's early days was its democratic culture and practices. All union posts, from president to steward, were contested annually. A notice sent to all members in 1954 by chief steward Joseph Speight and his four assistant chief stewards reminded them of the importance of choosing good stewards and then backing them up:

> You are the only ones who can decide what kind of steward will represent you in battles with the company. AND—it is your duty to back that steward when he or she goes to bat for you. . . .
> We'll get what we fight for. A weak-kneed steward who's afraid of the boss, adds up to a weak department. . . . A fighting, progressive, fearless steward—backed up 100% by his department—adds up to a strong department. . . .
> It is your responsibility to come out and elect your department steward! You get what you vote for![43]

Though the annual contested elections kept Local 80 democratic and close to its members, they also provided the occasion for divisiveness. Often this was due to honest disagreements over the best way forward for the union, but occasionally elections deteriorated into factionalism. Until 1957 the slate led by Benjamin Butler, the union's first African American president, easily won every election. Usually the only organized opposition was led by perennial right-wing candidate Joseph Ward, whose campaign harped on "getting rid of the Reds" and charges of financial mismanagement. Butler's ticket countered with promises of future fights against discrimination and denounced the "crew of little McCarthys in the plant who operate on the idea that it's un-American to fight for your rights." But a simmering dispute over how the union should be run between Butler and another black union officer, chief steward Joseph Speight, finally came to a head in 1957. That year Speight, charging that the incumbents had accepted a poor contract and did not deal with grievances aggressively enough, defeated Butler for president and his slate swept all fourteen offices. His chief running mate was Joseph

Colangelo, who won the position of business agent. Though Colangelo's campaign literature stressed his support of the fight against discrimination and his history as a steward in the early years, he had largely remained in the background. One of his more noticeable earlier roles was in the unlikely crew backing Tony Valentino's abortive new union in 1955. His approach to his new job in union leadership soon marked him as a classic business unionist who maneuvered through local politics to retain his increasingly powerful position no matter who occupied the president's office.[44]

Speight's victory was due in no small part to widespread dissatisfaction with the way Local 80 was being run. The local's parent union, the UPWA, was so concerned that it was on the verge of appointing an administrator to take over the local. The reasons the UPWA's regional director gave for the proposed move centered on "a complete breakdown in local authority" and financial irregularities. Though wildcat job actions were a hallowed tradition in Local 80, they were usually actually a part of a larger coordinated plan. But in recent months workers had simply taken things into their own hands and stopped work without regard for how their actions affected the rest of the plant and without a strategy for victory. Members also stopped attending meetings, and several members of Butler's team, including Speight and recording secretary Clarence Morris (who led a third slate in 1957) broke with Local 80's president. The change in leadership was probably good for everyone in Local 80, including Butler, for he reformed his ways and returned as an active leader. Over the next decade the presidency revolved among Speight, Butler, and Morris, and, in 1959, when four slates split the vote, even Joseph Ward held the office for a year. And throughout most of the next two decades Joseph Colangelo held onto and consolidated his role as business agent.[45]

Despite the turmoil at the top of Local 80, Campbell workers, shop stewards, and even union officials (when they were not bogged down in election battles) continued the independent and militant style of unionism that the soup company had become known for. In fact, the need to adhere to this tradition even forced competing slates to try to outdo each other in campaign promises to stand up to the company. Their national union aided this tendency by helping to coordinate antidiscrimination campaigns and organizing an industry-wide canning conference. Thus spontaneous walkouts against company moves to segregate workers were followed up by a national-organizer-coordinated yearlong battle to send African Americans to apply for off-limits jobs at Campbell as guards and secretaries. And when the first UPWA Canning Conference was held in New York City, the delegates recognized Local 80 for the "spirit of its members"; Joseph Speight was elected chairman of the new Canning Council and Joseph Colangelo was elected vice chairman.

In addition to discrimination, the cause of most job actions in the 1950s and 1960s was the threatened job losses due to automation and job redesign. This was true for both Local 80 and the mechanics' local. Forty-five loaders at Warehouse 20 stopped work when they feared a planned experimental change in the loading operation would lead to a loss in jobs. And 320 IAM members did the same when two of their members were given warnings for taking too long to repair peeling machines. But grievances that led to job actions still ran the gamut. After a fight between a foreman and a labeling department worker in which two other foremen allegedly held the worker while the first struck him, thirty-five department workers sat down at their machines and refused to work; by the next day, fifty had joined the sit-down. To readers of Camden and Philadelphia newspapers during this period, stories of walkouts and sit-downs at Campbell Soup were as common as they had ever been. Local 80's spirit, while battered, was undiminished.[46]

A standard contract battle in 1958, however, led to a strike that left a bitter taste for Local 80 members. The new leadership of the union under Joseph Speight was not about to be pushed around like the last group in charge, when Campbell tested its new tactic of take-it-or-leave-it and the union eventually took a settlement that its members were not pleased with in 1956. This time the union called the company's bluff and embarked on a long and difficult strike. But after eight weeks of walking the picket line, union members were unable to budge Murphy and his team. Campbell had built up enough inventory and had enough other plants still turning out its products that it seemed to be able to wait out the workers indefinitely. The dispirited membership eventually accepted an offer that included an increase of only one cent per hour and a one-time bonus of thirty dollars over the offer the company had made two months earlier. Almost fifty years later former union members still resentfully recalled the "one-cent strike."[47]

By the late 1960s Campbell workers and their union leaders realized that they were in a life-or-death struggle to save their jobs and the gains they had won over three decades that provided them a decent living. Automation was cutting hundreds of jobs out from under the workers with every new advance in technology. The new plants that were springing up in cheap labor areas threatened to steal even more work—perhaps all work—from Camden. In this situation, Campbell's Camden workers were faced with two choices: accept the cuts due to automation and join the "race to the bottom" by accepting whatever wage scales the company demanded, or join with workers in all other Campbell plants to face the company with unbreakable unity, the unity they had learned was their only source of strength in the past. In 1968 the unions representing Campbell workers in Sacramento, California; Napoleon, Ohio; Chestertown, Maryland, and many other places were coming to the same realization. William Beverly Murphy's crusade for the freedom to run his business as he saw fit was about to run directly into a wall of eight thousand united workers.

CHAPTER 6

1968

The Strike for Unity

Nineteen sixty-eight is remembered as the year the world was almost turned upside down. From the uprisings in America's cities following the assassination of Martin Luther King Jr. to the rebellions in Prague and Mexico City, people seemingly everywhere had decided that they had had enough. In the streets of Paris and the streets outside the Democratic convention in Chicago, angry citizens broke through the confines of society's rules and took direct action to redress their many grievances. Less well remembered is the upsurge in labor militancy in the United States throughout the 1960s and the growing disaffection of America's workers toward their jobs and their employers. While there had been some two hundred major strikes per year in the United States in the early years of the decade, the number jumped to 381 in 1967, 392 in 1968, and 412 in 1969. The number of workers taking part in these strikes grew similarly, and the stoppages threatened to cause serious dislocations in the economy if the trend continued. About ten million work days per year had been lost to strikes from 1961 through 1963; the figure reached over thirty-five million in 1968 and almost fifty-three million by 1970. Further, employers increasingly reported that their employees had "bad attitudes" toward their work; disaffection appeared rampant.[1]

The Campbell Soup Company did not escape the surging wave of working-class unrest. Its personnel department searched in vain for ways to improve employee morale, reported to be at its lowest point ever. And in the summer of 1968, New Jersey's governor Richard Hughes, the harried chairman of the credentials committee at the tumultuous Democratic convention, received a telegram at his Chicago hotel that he wished he hadn't. Employees at Camden, New Jersey's leading employer, the Campbell Soup Company, who had walked off the job along with employees from almost every other major Campbell plant across the country, were in no mood to return to work. The impact on his state was extensive, for they had chosen the beginning of tomato season for their action. Thousands of idled migrant workers waited at hundreds of farms to begin picking tomatoes, and farmers warned that they would soon begin plowing under tons of South Jersey's "Red Gold." Governor Hughes had no solution to offer beyond a call to all parties to resolve their differences quickly.[2]

For Local 80 and for William Beverly Murphy, Campbell's president, this was the final test. The union had been engaged in a rearguard action to counter Murphy's tactics of rapid automation and antiunionism ever since he took over in 1953. Most of all, labor activists hoped to beat back the company's divide-and-rule strategy that had allowed Campbell to defeat workers on strike at one of its facilities by transferring work to other plants in its growing chain of operations. By using the novel strategy of coordinated bargaining, five international unions put aside their differences and delayed agreeing to new contracts in 1968 until all contracts had expired; they then demanded joint bargaining for all plants and a common expiration date. With a solid mandate from his board of directors never to concede to such a demand, W. B. Murphy pulled out all the stops in an equally coordinated campaign to defeat the unions. By the turbulent spring of 1968, it was not clear who would emerge the victor from the battle looming on the horizon.

✄ The Copper Strike and Coordinated Bargaining

The union movement in the United States has periodically been plagued by interunion rivalry. Raiding by one union of another's members became especially bitter in the late 1930s between American Federation of Labor–affiliated unions and the new industrial unions that made up the Congress of Industrial Organizations (CIO). A further intense round of raiding followed the expulsion of several left-led unions from the CIO in the late 1940s by other new or existing CIO affiliates. And some internationals, notably the Teamsters, regularly raided other organizations' members. These self-inflicted injuries greatly weakened the labor movement in the United States, as both raiding and raided unions often spent more time fighting each other than uniting against their corporate employers. Beyond the issue of raiding, unions in different federations, and sometimes even in the same federation, had spotty records of solidarity. In particular, a union representing workers in one plant typically told its members to continue working while their brothers and sisters in other plants of the same company went on strike; in many cases workers even put in overtime at their company's behest in such situations. As company mergers and acquisitions increased through the 1960s, the problem—for unions—of dealing on a local level with each plant separately became more severe. And the reuniting of the two major labor federations into the AFL-CIO in 1955 made the issue of cross-union solidarity more relevant than ever.

In the early 1960s, the AFL-CIO's Industrial Union Department (IUD) took on this problem by proposing that unions representing different plants of a single employer unite in "coalition bargaining" or "coordinated bargaining." The IUD formally adopted this strategy at its 1965 convention, and it proceeded to take the lead in upcoming negotiations with a number of companies. Because of strong employer opposition and, in some cases, unfriendly court decisions, most early attempts at coordinated bargaining were at best only partially successful. The real test of the unions' new strategy came in 1967, when twenty-five unions representing workers of four major copper producers united to demand joint bargaining.[3]

The Western mines and processing facilities of the copper industry had a turbulent record of labor relations. Early in the twentieth century they were the home of some of the strongest elements of the radical Industrial Workers of the World. Later most copper workers joined the Mine, Mill, and Smelter Workers, a militant, communist-led union. Even when Mine-Mill was expelled from the CIO (along with the Food and Tobacco Workers, Campbell Soup's union), its members stuck with it. Only a relative handful of locals in the West went over to the United Steelworkers (USW), the CIO leadership's hand-chosen replacement for Mine-Mill. Across the country, however, workers in the industry were spread among Mine-Mill, the USW, the Machinists, and almost two-dozen other unions, though the great majority belonged to Mine-Mill. Though the leftist union retained the loyalty of its members, it had been distracted and weakened financially by endless fights to ward off raiding attacks by the USW and others, and its numbers had also been in decline because of automation in the industry. In the decade before 1967 Mine-Mill had been in sporadic merger negotiations with the USW, and it was again in that year. When the AFL-CIO's IUD proposed coordinated bargaining to Mine-Mill, it readily accepted the offer, despite the fact that it was not a federation member (the Teamsters, also independent, joined as well). The IUD set up a coordinating council for negotiations with representatives from twenty-five unions as well as IUD staffers. They drew up a common set of negotiating demands, and prime among them were a master contract for all locals and common contract expiration dates. As contracts with Anaconda, Kennecott, and the other companies began expiring in the first half of 1967, each union presented the full package of joint demands to its employer. When the companies rejected the union proposal out of hand, the unions declined to negotiate further. By July 1, the overwhelming majority of contracts had expired, and the coordinating council finally began serious negotiations with the employers as over fifty thousand workers went on strike. The companies, to varying degrees, resisted the demands for combined contracts and dates, and the strike dragged on for nine months. Because the federal government—a major customer, especially during the conflict in Vietnam—had accumulated a huge stockpile of copper, it took no serious action initially to resolve the strike. And industry in general did not suffer greatly due to a large increase in copper imports (from Anaconda's operations in Chile and elsewhere). Old Mine-Mill unionists were accustomed to hard-fought struggles, but a momentous event at the start of the strike swept the foundation of their union out from under them. July 1, 1967, marked not only the start of the strike but was also the date Mine-Mill ceased to exist, submerged into its erstwhile archrival, the USW. Though the steelworkers union now represented an even larger proportion of the strikers than Mine-Mill had, it also had an uneven record of wins and concessions. By the end of March 1968, worn down by their inability to enforce their will on the copper companies, USW leaders agreed to accept far less than their original demands. The settlements did include some limited sectoral agreements, as well as sizable wage increases, but the initial goals would have to wait for another day.[4]

Though the IUD's new strategy was taking some bruising, department activists like Richard T. Leonard and Stephen Harris rededicated themselves to what they believed was critical to labor's future. Even before the copper strike started, Harris was already pulling together meetings of union leaders from Campbell Soup plants across the country. The most profitable food manufacturer in the United States would be the next target for labor's coordinated bargaining strategy.

Overcoming Divisions among Campbell's Unions

Even as late as the post–World War II strike wave, Campbell's production workers were solidly united in one union. The Food and Tobacco Workers

(FTA) locals in Camden and Chicago both had leftists in leadership positions, and both fought hard against racism and for unity among all workers. In preparation for negotiations they always consulted with each other, and unionists from the two locals often visited one another. But all that began to unravel in the hostile climate of Cold War America. Local 194 in Chicago followed the expelled national FTA into the ill-fated Distributive, Processing, and Office Workers (DPOWA) and eventually found itself in the conservative Retail, Wholesale, and Department Store Union (RWDSU). Camden's Local 80 did not follow the same course but joined the progressive United Packinghouse Workers of America (UPWA) after a year as an independent. Its mechanics, however, seceded shortly thereafter to form another local in the International Association of Machinists (IAM). Meanwhile, Campbell's new plants in Sacramento, California, and Napoleon, Ohio, were organized (some said with company collusion) by the Teamsters and the Amalgamated Meat Cutters (AMC), respectively. Neither of these unions presented anywhere near the challenge to the company that the FTA (and later the UPWA) did. In both of their plants they accepted far weaker contracts than those in Camden or Chicago, and they made virtually no effort to overcome divisions within the workforce.

Though the UPWA (a CIO union) and the AMC (an AFL affiliate) were, after 1955, nominally members of the same federation—the AFL-CIO—their antipathy toward each other was undiminished. The AMC, the old craft union of the butchers, had failed, earlier in the century, to organize the industrial workers of the packinghouses of Chicago and the Midwest. When leftist radicals, African Americans, and old-time trade unionists united in the Packinghouse Workers Organizing Committee (PWOC) in the late 1930s, all the major meatpackers fell to their organizing campaigns. Yet even after PWOC activists received their CIO charter as UPWA, their rivals in the AMC tried to raid their locals whenever possible. Thus the likelihood of the two unions cooperating in the Campbell campaign was as problematic as the situation that had faced Mine-Mill and the Steelworkers.[5]

The rivalry between the UPWA and the AMC in the Campbell chain, in fact, intensified in the years immediately before the proposed coordinated bargaining campaign. As described in chapter 5, the UPWA won a bitterly contested representation election over the AMC to represent the workers at Campbell's new Paris, Texas, plant in 1965. And when Campbell opened another new plant in Sumter, South Carolina, in 1967, both unions sent organizers to face off against each other just as the IUD's Harris was calling their leaders together. Once again, the biggest difference to emerge between the unions was their diametrically opposite stands on racism and unity.

Conditions in the Sumter plant certainly made an organizer's job easier. One reported that working conditions were "well-nigh unbearable, despite the new plant set-up" and that workers complained of heavy job loads: "efficiency, no matter how high, is never satisfactory for the supervisors." But the racial environment in the small town made unity difficult. UPWA organizer Irene Baldwin tried to set up meetings near workers' homes in surrounding towns, but often could find no place in which to hold integrated meetings. AMC organizers, meanwhile, were pointing out to white workers that the UPWA, unlike the AMC, was employing both black and white organizers. Leaflets from the competing groups also were as different as night and day. The AMC just listed some wage and benefit improvements they promised would come if they were chosen, while the UPWA's leaflets blasted the company and explained how capitalism stole the wealth produced by workers in stories such as "The Fable of the Pump." When the company granted a ten-cent wage increase to fend off the unionization campaign, the UPWA berated the AMC for thanking the company, then derided their opponents as the "Amalgamated Wage Cutters" and the "Amalgamated Race-Baiters." When the National Labor Relations Board postponed the election indefinitely, hostilities drew back slightly from the brink, but the two unions were hardly on good terms.[6]

The other unions in the Campbell plants were not on much better terms. Chicago's unionists never entirely overcame what they considered their betrayal by their former brothers and sisters in Camden when Local 80 rejected the FTA's call for their locals to join the DPOWA. Further, their contract expiration date at the end of 1968 meant that they would have difficulty joining all the other plants, whose contracts all expired before tomato season that year. Local 80 was patching up relations with its former Maintenance Department members now in the IAM, but the reconciliation, led by Local 80 business unionists like Joseph Colangelo, never went very far among the union's growing African American leadership. Finally, the Teamsters had made a number of attempts over the years to raid almost every other Campbell site. Despite all their differences, the five unions had strong reasons to overcome their past problems and work together. Management at Campbell Soup's local plants, after all, enjoyed no autonomy when negotiating with their unions; all decisions came down from W. B. Murphy and his team in Camden. By making the attempt at coordinated bargaining, labor hoped to once again confront the company as its equal.

Union efforts at coordination at Campbell had, in fact, begun over a decade before the 1968 confrontation. Years before the IUD began experimenting with coalition bargaining in 1961, canning locals in the UPWA had begun discussing the possibilities of coordination throughout the Campbell chain. They were encouraged in this by UPWA national leaders, who had had great success in organizing "chains" in each of the large meatpacking companies. The first step was a Canning Caucus in late 1957 followed by a Canning Worker Conference held in New York City in 1958. Twenty-five representatives from UPWA canning locals (including nine from Local 80) met with a few staff members from the international union to compare contracts and discuss how they could work together in the future. Around the same time, the AMC began researching agreements between various unions and canners and made some tentative contacts with other canning unions about sharing information. Despite these promising beginnings, however, cross-union cooperation made little headway until the revival of the concept of coordinated bargaining by the IUD in the mid-1960s.[7]

As the IUD surveyed the industries and corporations that would make the best targets for a coordinated strategy, the Campbell Soup Company quickly came into focus as a prime candidate. It was one of the largest food companies in the country and the most profitable, and its projected growth and continued profitability meant that it could well afford to negotiate a more generous deal with its workers. It also consisted of plants covered by a variety of CIO, AFL, and independent unions, and so would be a good test case for the IUD's new coordinated bargaining strategy. And the flagship Campbell plant at Camden had a proud history of united workers standing up to the company and, often, winning in difficult struggles. Campbell had another attraction for IUD strategists: unlike the distant copper companies, Campbell was a household word across America. The power of public opinion might be brought against the company if it was perceived as a rich corporation dealing unfairly with its underpaid soup makers. When representatives of Campbell's locals across the country enthusiastically embraced the idea, the IUD's collective bargaining director Richard T. Leonard appointed his assistant Stephen Harris to pull together a Campbell Soup coordinated bargaining council.

IUD researchers presented delegates to the first council meeting in February 1967 with a detailed financial analysis of the company and a comprehensive side-by-side comparison of the union contracts at every Campbell plant. The union representatives unanimously voted to participate in a coordinated bargaining campaign with the company between December 1967 and May 1968, during which time nine contracts covering almost all of the large plants would expire. The presidents of the international unions involved formally endorsed the decision, and the campaign was underway. After Campbell's W. B. Murphy—as expected—rejected their request for a joint meeting, the planning began in earnest. An October conference drew up a list of common demands; the final demand stated, "There shall be a common expiration date for all agreements expiring during this period." By December a "traveling committee" with representatives from each union—the UPWA, the AMC, the IAM, the RWDSU, and the Teamsters—and IUD staff members was prepared to begin the negotiation process as the first contracts began to expire.[8]

✍ Campbell Prepares for Battle

W. B. Murphy and his executive team in Camden, meanwhile, were not idly waiting to see what their unions would do. Since the 1930s the Campbell Soup Company had a reputation of hostility toward organized labor. Though its obstinacy in dealing with the unions its workers chose varied over the years depending on union strength and external conditions, it at times reverted to its hard-boiled, no-negotiation stance, and 1968 was one of those times. W. B. Murphy had been a rising executive at Campbell when the FTA overpowered the company in a series of postwar strikes. He well knew the power workers held when united; he would not permit such a situation to arise again under his watch. And, though Murphy was chief executive, not all the credit (or blame) for such a policy was his. Campbell's board of directors was equally determined that it, and not its employees, would decide how things were run.

In the run-up to the strike Murphy reiterated that the company would deal with no united adversaries, and this included the farmers who supplied Campbell with its raw materials. For decades farmers had tried to negotiate with Campbell through a number of associations and cooperatives. Though the company did occasionally meet with grower committees to discuss grading techniques and "labor problems," it refused to deal with them at all when it came to advance contracting for crops. President of the American Farm Bureau Federation Charles B. Shuman warned that "continued refusal of plant management to confer with growers is causing widespread resentment and misunderstanding." Yet once again, nothing came of the growers' request to negotiate as a group. Despite continuing dissatisfaction with Campbell's take-it-or-leave-it approach, farmers grudgingly resumed doing business—individually—with the soup company.[9]

Though Campbell pushed aside its farmers' attempts at joint bargaining with little trouble other than some bad publicity, it faced a far more organized and determined foe in the unions that represented its production workers. Consequently, it treated the threat from labor's planned coordinated bargaining with far more seriousness. Murphy took a multipronged approach to preparation for a potential strike. First, Campbell and its public relations firm began an unprecedented campaign to reach workers, their families, government officials, and the general public with the company's version of the conflict (as will be discussed later in this chapter). Next, to enable the company to hold out in the event of a strike, it arranged for all its major customers to build up substantial inventories of Campbell products in the spring. And, most important, Murphy and the company's board of directors committed themselves to a no-negotiation strategy on the issues of joint bargaining and a common expiration date. They combined this with a commitment to sweeten the rest of the deal that they would offer the various locals: heftier-than-usual wage increases and improvements in pensions and other benefits. As was their practice since the late 1950s, they put the company-determined pay increases into effect as soon as the locals rejected the company offer, in order to weaken the resolve of workers to endorse a strike. No matter what concessions the unions made on joint bargaining—such as their offer to accept an expiration date in the winter instead of the original demand of a date at the start of tomato season—the company did not budge an inch. Instead, Murphy made belligerent comments about his willingness to shut down plants in noncooperative areas or even see the entire business go under before he would agree to coordinated bargaining.

Both Murphy and the unions believed that coordination would tip the balance of power between the two toward labor. In the case of a single-plant company, like Campbell in the early years, employees' workplace bargaining power consisted in their ability to withhold their labor. But with the spread of production among multiple, and divided, locations, the company had clearly gained the upper hand. Companies with many production sites had the enormous strategic advantage of being able to use one group of their workers against another. This advantage was recognized by all corporate leaders, and they regularly discussed among themselves the best way to safeguard their position. Campbell's Murphy bragged to union negotiators that he had conferred with "personal friend[s]" at the top of other corporations that had faced coordinated bargaining challenges. The president of Union Carbide had faced this problem in his company in 1966 and 1967. He and Murphy agreed on the necessity of holding out, no matter what happened, and Union Carbide succeeded in fending off common expiration dates in the contracts it finally signed. Similarly, another friend who led one of the copper companies told Murphy that the industry could hold out "forever" in the copper strike. All these men saw their roles as protecting not only their individual companies but also the interests of the owners of corporate America as a class. Thus, by the summer of 1967 Campbell had decided how it would respond to the new challenge from its unions. In late July the presidents of each of the international unions representing workers at Campbell sent letters to Murphy indicating that they intended to bargain jointly in the next round of contracts. Murphy did not deign to answer these letters himself, but had his personnel director, William Harwick, reply to the union leaders. The request to bargain with a joint committee was rebuffed outright. "We have watched with dismay," Harwick wrote, "the efforts to usurp the responsibility of the local unions and concentrate power in the hands of a few international officials." This theme would be repeated relentlessly over the next year, as company management sought to portray the coordinated bargaining campaign as a grab for power by international officials rather than as an attempt to redress the power imbalance brought on by the spread of production across several sites separated by different unions as well as geography.[10]

🍅 Tomatoes in Ghettos and the Campbell Kids on Strike: Public Relations in the 1968 Campaign

When the IUD targeted a quintessential consumer-focused corporation— the Campbell Soup Company—its president W. B. Murphy realized that a skillfully manipulated public relations campaign would be crucial if he was to prevail. The unions recognized that they needed to do the same, and they hoped that favorable public opinion might improve their chances over the less-than-stellar results of earlier IUD-led campaigns, which had mostly gone after basic industry. The audiences for both company and union public relations campaigns were many: workers, whose allegiance to the union effort was critical, especially in right-to-work states like Texas where only a small majority were union members; employees' families, whose attitudes toward the strike could influence the workers; government officials, who could aid either side if they received enough pressure; shareholders, whose solid support the company relied on; and consumers, who had the potential to significantly impact the company's bottom line.

In the company's efforts to win the hearts and minds of its employees and the public, it made maximum use of the premier public relations firm of Earl Newsom and Company. Newsom and Company went beyond the normal responsibilities for such firms, becoming deeply involved in employee relations, as well, though Campbell's personnel department played the leading role in trying to dissuade workers from supporting the coordinated bargaining endeavor. In the past, cultivating close ties with employees had been a minor concern for Campbell; the primary method for getting workers to do what the company wanted was direct supervision by foremen utilizing the stick of the threat of dismissal and the carrot of incentive system bonuses. The personnel department did publish plant newsletters and irregularly put up posters around the plants encouraging greater productivity and less waste, but the only consistently utilized employee recognition tool—and one also highly regarded by workers—was the Wall of Honor, on which was inscribed the names of twenty-five-year employees. Newsom encouraged that the use of posters be expanded but in a more sophisticated way. They could be used to remind the employees of the "high labor costs" at unionized plants, carrying the unsubtle threat that the company could decide to move work to cheaper locations. Posters could also warn of the severe losses workers suffer during strikes: "Dollar figures on lost wages in the 8½ month copper strike, and other long strikes, can be cited with the objective of making the Campbell employee nervous about the danger of getting sucked into a strike that might last a long time." Newsom's advice went far beyond the use of posters, however. As the consultants pointed out, posters never reached workers' families, who could potentially be a conservative force against strikes: "To get a company's point of view across to wives, we have never found anything better than letters from the plant manager addressed to the employee at his home." The gender bias of the consultants apparently blinded them to the fact that from one-quarter to over one-half of the production workers at the various plants were women.[11]

The attention to employee communications moved into high gear in April of 1968, three months before tomato season and the threatened joint strike. The manager of employee relations initiated an intensive project to use first-line supervisors—"our most effective means of communications"—as advocates for the company's position. Managers instructed foremen in the details of the status of negotiations and why the company was unalterably opposed to coordinated bargaining. They warned supervisors about "What May Happen Here," ranging from sabotage and slowdowns to boycotts and strikes. They reminded foremen to treat their subordinates with dignity and respect (apparently something that required repeated prodding) and to convince them that they had nothing to gain from coordinated bargaining. The Personnel Department stepped up the production of posters, including one attempting to appeal to workers' patriotism by reminding them that soldiers in Vietnam were eating Campbell's Soup. Plant and company bulletins appeared with increasing frequency, and the company paid special attention to recognizing workers, from the "cook of the month" and the "labeling operator of the month" to the distinguished employees newly elevated to the Wall of Honor. The company also pointed out to minority employees that its recently started aid to groups like the Urban League and the Opportunities Industrialization Center would be jeopardized by a strike. The employee relations manager followed up these initiatives with an effort to gauge their effectiveness. He encouraged personnel managers in each plant to conduct "employee audits," in which first-line supervisors filled out a questionnaire for each employee they supervised, covering such areas as the worker's attitude to the company, his or her job, and level of satisfaction with wages, benefits, and opportunities for advancement. A common theme of all communications with employees during this period was the portrayal of the IUD and the joint bargaining committees as "outsiders." The company kept repeating that coordinated bargaining would rob workers of their right to have their locally elected officials conduct negotiations. Why, management argued, should Camden (or Sacramento or Paris) workers lose pay for the sake of workers in distant plants or for some questionable goal such as coordinated bargaining that would only help outsiders in the IUD? As the weeks moved irreversibly toward the peak season and the strike, the drumbeat against the trouble caused by the "outsiders" grew ever louder.[12]

Campbell and Newsom had other audiences in mind, of course, beyond the company's employees. W. B. Murphy wrote letters to shareholders to keep them updated on the status of negotiations. An overwhelming majority of the company stock was still held by a handful of members of the Dorrance family, but as *Fortune* magazine noted in 1955 when the company went public, "They also felt it wouldn't hurt Campbell, in the event it has to go to Washington... to have a few shareholders rooting in its corner." As was noted in chapter 5, Murphy was a confidante of U.S. presidents of both parties, and federal intervention could be of crucial importance in the event of a strike. For example, the Taft-Hartley Act gave the president the authority in an emergency to request the courts to halt strikes for an eighty-day cooling-off period—just about the length of the tomato season. Newsom and Company further advised Campbell to pay visits to governors, mayors, and other officials to apprise them of the situation and warn them of the dire consequences of a strike. While all these efforts were vigorously taken up by Campbell's top management and public relations staff, they expended an even greater effort in appealing to the public for understanding of their side of the dispute. The first intended effect of such an undertaking was to keep tens of millions of Americans as loyal customers of Campbell's Soup, both during and after any labor dispute. This loyalty might be put to the test most severely in the event of a consumer boycott called by the unions. But a publicity campaign aimed at the broadest public could also help in reaching the other audiences the company was concerned with. Workers and their families were exposed to the mass media as much as anyone else, and company spokespeople might speak to them more directly through television or newspaper articles than they could through the unreliable medium of foremen on the shop floor. Constituents frightened by the same articles about the potential consequences of a strike could also apply pressure on government officials from a different angle. Though stories about Campbell had long been featured in Camden and Philadelphia area newspapers, these were not necessarily written in the way management might always have wished, and there had been only minor interest in the company in media markets outside its home region. In this arena Newsom and Company was quickly to prove its worth.[13]

By the mid-1960s Newsom had already succeeded in getting Murphy's face on the covers of *Forbes* and *Business Week,* along with favorable articles in a host of other business and general-interest publications. Often these were unabashed celebrations of Murphy and the company. A feature article in Philadelphia's *Sunday Bulletin Magazine* gushed in 1964 that "electronic computers have some way to go before they compete with the natural machinery located inside William Beverly Murphy that pops up right answers," then went on to marvel at his leadership and the company's progress. But in 1968 the articles Newsom got published in the hometown papers of every Campbell plant were far more to the point. The *Northwest Signal* in rural Napoleon, Ohio, warned that if Campbell were forced to shut down due to a demand for common expiration dates, area farmers and small businesses would be hard hit. The *Paris News* in Paris, Texas, editorialized ("Nobody Wins In a Strike") that the union's goals were "purely national, not local." It fully supported the company stand against coordinated bargaining. The farm editor of the *Woodbury Daily Times* in South Jersey reiterated the company line and described the havoc a strike would cause in the area and called for invocation of a Taft-Hartley injunction. Each of these (and other) articles repeated the claim that the company was willing to negotiate a decent settlement with each local plant; only the fact that "the shots are being called from the top level of the ... unions involved" prevented a reasonable settlement. The company tried to win growers to its side by offering to cover the losses tomato farmers would suffer during a strike and attempted to diffuse support for the workers in Camden's African American community by buying off local black businessmen with loan guarantees. All in all, Campbell rolled out a comprehensive and sophisticated public information campaign to bolster its side in the struggle with its unions.[14]

Perhaps the most bizarre public relations scheme to emerge from the active minds of Newsom and Company and Campbell's Public Information Department was a plan, apparently never executed, to use "the ghetto" as a marketing site to demonstrate the company's good intentions. The idea was sold as an opportunity for Campbell to "project itself into history and win for itself new business strengths." The action would be

> So warm or human that people everywhere feel closer to the company and hopefully to its products....
>
> And so dramatic and timely that the action is favorably reported in a large way in most all of the nations newspapers and news magazines, and on the network news programs of both radio and television.

In the event that a massive strike prevented Campbell from processing its tomatoes, some "70 truckloads of fresh Campbell tomatoes [would roll] into Harlem, or South Philadelphia or some other ghetto area."

> Each of these trucks could take stations at exactly four block intervals in these ghetto areas and begin dispensing free fresh Campbell tomatoes to any and all people on a first come first serve basis provided they brought their own containers—bags, boxes, pots, pans, tubs, dresser drawers, what have you. The mass of people and their assorted containers would be photographically interesting to the media.

Though the action would be presented as emanating from the highest motives, Campbell's bottom line would benefit directly. It would "certainly...help us with negro leadership around the country" and "could even win us some customers in the ghetto." It would demoralize strikers when they saw that the company was "living through the strike with equanimity and [was] *prepared to last it out.*" Their unions would be put in a bad light while the company shined. Workers would even feel great pride that their company took such a step and start pressuring their leaders to settle. The proposal was significant in that it revealed a company that had not moved much in its attitude toward people who lived in the inner cities. They could be used for a photo opportunity or to drum up more business, but when the city residents who worked for Campbell tried to deal with the company on an equal footing, Campbell dismissed their attempt outright.[15]

While the company was reaching out to workers, growers, and the general public giving its side of the conflict, the unions and the IUD were mounting an equally comprehensive campaign. Though labor's communications with its rank and file were decentralized and uneven, the IUD coordinated a sophisticated national media campaign that centered on a boycott of the company's products. With its democratic grassroots traditions, Local 80 in Camden probably did a better job than the other locals involved of keeping its members informed and involved, though perhaps not as thoroughly as it had in the early days of the union. Workers, stewards, and union officials were angry with W. B. Murphy's tough-guy stance toward the unions, and they were physically closer to him day in and day out than unionists in other regions. Local 80 activists prepared their members to take up picket duty in the event of a strike and encouraged all workers to come out to union meetings to learn about the issues and the status of negotiations. Former Local 80 mechanics now in their own Machinists' local also maintained close attention to developments and were equally ready to strike. Other locals, especially those in the AMC and the Teamsters, did not have the same strong shop steward tradition that acted as a transmission belt for ideas between the rank and file and union leaders, but all locals made extra efforts to prepare their members for a potential strike.[16]

To reach other constituencies, local unions made some efforts to plead their case with farmers and the general public, such as letters and leaflets to tomato growers generated by Local 80. But most of the publicity for the coordinated bargaining battle was handled by the IUD and, to a lesser degree, by the national offices of the unions involved. Stephen Harris and other IUD staffers prepared press releases and planned advertisements in publications like the *Supermarket News,* but their most concentrated public relations activities focused on planning and carrying out a consumer boycott. Because of Campbell's direct contact with consumers—unlike most previous coordinated bargaining targets—IUD activists began early to discuss a boycott of the company. Such an undertaking required legal consultation, preparation of imaginative publicity materials, recruitment of support from the umbrella union federation (AFL-CIO) and others, and planning for informational picketing at grocery stores. All of these came together during the months leading up to the summer of 1968, but the most ingenious component was the selection of the celebrated Campbell Kids as the mascots for the boycott. These cherubic icons of Campbell Soup had adorned company advertising since the beginning of the century, and the unions' iconoclastic use of these symbols was as brilliant as it was blasphemous. Mocking the Campbell advertising style, the UPWA's own public relations and advertising firm (Maurer, Fleisher, Zon and Associates) drew up boycott leaflets showing chubby Campbell Kids holding balloons or stirring pots all emblazoned with

"Don't Buy Campbell's Products." Even the company's signature limericks were present:

Our friends are in trouble
And that makes us cry
'Til they get a good contract
We say "Please Don't Buy"

and

If our "Don't Buy"
Should sound unpleasin'
Believe us, there's a
Very good reason

The first draft of the latter verse (changed before it was used) started "If our 'Don't Buy'/Should sound like treason…" The thought of their cherished Campbell Kids being used by their enemies no doubt did appear as treason to W. B. Murphy and Jack Dorrance.[17]

As both sides approached the brink of a strike, each had done all it could to enlist as many allies as possible. However, it was an internal change within the union configuration that was to have an even greater impact on the ultimate outcome of the struggle.

🍎 A Bad Time to Go: The Demise of the United Packinghouse Workers

At the height of McCarthyism, Local 80 had engineered what appeared an almost phoenix-like resurrection. Leaving the doomed FTA just as it collapsed, it emerged a year later in the one CIO union that could carry on Local 80's proud traditions of unity and militancy: the United Packinghouse Workers of America. Throughout the 1950s and 1960s UPWA regional organizers and national officials backed the Camden union's struggles against racism, anticommunism, and the effects of automation. And as Campbell opened new plants, UPWA organizers battled company propaganda and AMC business unionists to organize workers in Paris, Texas and Chestertown, Maryland. But throughout this period the UPWA was suffering its own long decline. The canning industry was growing, but the UPWA's base was in the packinghouses of Chicago and the Midwest. There the UPWA was losing members as packinghouses automated and the old "Big Four" packing companies lost ground to new unorganized competitors. Paralleling

Local 80's fights with Leon Schachter's AMC local in South Jersey since the early 1940s, the UPWA had constantly fought off AMC attempts to raid its locals, but by 1968 it could no longer stand alone as an independent national union. In the midst of the coordinated bargaining campaign and just before the projected strike date at the beginning of tomato season, the UPWA went out of business. Its locals now became AMC locals (prefaced with a *P*, as in the new Local P-80) and a few of its national leaders got jobs in the new Packinghouse Division of the AMC. Activists throughout the old UPWA locals were unhappy with the merger, and there was bitter resentment at accepting their old foes as their new leaders. In Camden that summer, Local 80 continued publishing its bulletin under the proud name and seal (black and white hands clasped) of the United Packinghouse Workers, though that symbolic act did nothing to forestall the changes that would soon come in their current conflict with Campbell.[18]

Nominally, the merger strengthened the coordinated bargaining campaign, for now over three-quarters of the affected workers were represented by one union, the AMC. But several national leaders of the AMC were reluctant participants in the coordinated campaign and did not believe that the unions could prevail against Murphy. When the earliest Campbell contracts had expired in late 1967 in several poultry plants represented by the AMC, the union had quickly negotiated settlements with the company, thus removing them from participation in the joint campaign. By the time the confrontation came, only one plant originally represented by the AMC (in Napoleon, Ohio) was in the coalition. After the merger, of course, several former UPWA plants now inflated the AMC portion of the coalition. As a result, the leadership of the coordinated campaign itself shifted from the IUD-led joint union council to the headquarters of the AMC, for the joint council was now a majority-AMC council, and that union's leaders had serious differences with IUD activists. Though some AMC leaders like Patrick Gorman had episodically led strikes, their whole outlook on union-management relations was far more conciliatory and cooperative than the confrontational approach of the UPWA. The AMC was also far less interested in addressing issues outside its narrow wages-and-benefits perspective. In dealing with the companies who employed their members, AMC officials felt a certain camaraderie with their corporate counterparts, with whom they were often on a first-name basis. They might engage in weighty negotiations (in the best hotels) with company executives, but afterward they would smile, shake hands, and resume their old attitude of goodwill. The AMC was not, in other words, the best candidate to lead the fight to the death with Campbell that summer of 1968. The year before, the old leftist Mine-Mill union had been assimilated into the more mainstream Steelworkers just as the copper strike for coordinated bargaining began. Though the Steelworkers had a more militant tradition than the AMC, they eventually settled for a far weaker agreement than the original coalition demands called for. In the Campbell campaign, rank-and-file workers in most plants were more than ready for a strike, and Stephen Harris and the IUD were working night and day to build a solid front against the company. As the critical tomato season approached, the unity and militancy of the Campbell workers—and the AMC—was about to be tested.[19]

✿ Showdown: The Summer of 1968

After a few bumps in the road in late 1967, the coalition bargaining train rolled inexorably toward a nationwide confrontation with Campbell in the hot summer of 1968. Though all five international unions representing Campbell workers had agreed to joint bargaining early in 1967, the contract expiration date of the sole RWDSU plant in Chicago fell at the end of 1968, effectively removing the RWDSU from participation in the campaign. Further, national AMC and Teamster leaders were, at best, lukewarm in their support for the joint effort. When four AMC and one Teamster poultry plants' contracts expired at the end of September 1967, all quickly signed agreements with Campbell. The same thing happened later in the year with other AMC plants in Salisbury, Maryland, and Modesto, California. But after these early defections, every plant joined the campaign, including all the soup plants (except Chicago), the core of the Campbell business. The company tried every tactic it could to derail the strengthening unity of its workers, but with no further success after the early settlements.[20]

The UPWA-organized plant in Paris, Texas, was the first to get on board. Just before its contract expired on Christmas Day, 1967, the company offered the local a 10-percent wage increase. Union members overwhelmingly rejected the offer. Instead they demanded not only a heftier wage increase but also, in true UPWA fashion, an arbitrable antidiscrimination clause, plantwide seniority, and the sharp curtailment of the "rights of management." The flustered company representative "was quite mad about his 'prize' offer being turned down by the membership," and the company put its offer into effect anyway. Next came another poultry plant—the only one represented by the UPWA—in Chestertown, Maryland. Workers there followed the lead of their union brothers and sisters in Texas and rejected a sixteen-and-one-half-cent offer, which the company again unilaterally implemented. The contract of the AMC soup plant in Napoleon, Ohio, did not expire in 1968, but it did include a "wage reopener" on February 1, under which workers could strike on the single issue of wages. This time the company came up with an offer of eighteen cents (or higher for some jobs) for the notoriously underpaid rural plant. Again it was rejected; again the company put its decision into effect.[21]

Campbell vice president William Harwick began contacting the leaders of each of the unions involved in early January and reiterated the company's refusal to bargain collectively. As the first few contracts expired, the IUD and the Campbell union committee made no special efforts to insist on participation by members of the national "traveling committee" in local negotiations, largely because there essentially were no negotiations. In each case, the union presented demands, the company made a nonnegotiable offer, the union membership rejected it, and the company put its version into effect. In essence, Campbell began acting as if the unions did not exist or at least did not matter very much. In a letter to Chestertown's UPWA members, plant manager E. A. Kavanagh informed the employees that the company cared more about them than their union did, and so was putting a "substantial increase" into their next paychecks. He explained that the plant was operating without a union contract, and that they should feel free to discuss any problems directly with their supervisors or any member of management.[22]

When the Camden contracts were about to expire (on March 3 for UPWA Local 80 and March 13 for IAM Local 2031), the rhetoric and maneuvering escalated on both sides. Local 80's president Clarence Clark urged all members of the traveling committee to attend negotiating sessions in Camden as well as the local's membership meeting on March 10. Though management tolerated the presence of traveling committee members, no more negotiating was done in Camden than at any of the earlier plants. Predictably, the company offers were rejected by both Local 80's production workers and the IAM mechanics. In response, plant manager W. S. Crowley blasted the instigators of the coordinated campaign:

> Unfortunately, it is now apparent that nothing we could have done would have been acceptable to the Union negotiating committee. "Outsiders" were successful in convincing the union negotiating committee that a settlement should be delayed. The "outsiders" would have you and your committee believe that something can be gained by delaying agreement on a new contract. The "outsiders" are wrong. The Company's offer is final.

The presence of "outsiders" at your negotiations is under the direction of the Industrial Union Department of the AFL-CIO in Washington. Their objective is to gain centralized control of everything to do with working people. The "outsiders" will deny this, but in fact it is true.

Then, as expected, management installed its new wage scale "to prevent employees from losing money," even though the "outsiders" would want the workers "to give up your entire income by striking for some purpose that has nothing to do with you or your job."[23] The coordinated union council made one more attempt to break the deadlock in Camden and pressure the company into accepting joint bargaining that spring. At the end of April, UPWA international president Ralph Helstein called Campbell's P. S. Holbrook about reopening negotiations. Helstein indicated that the presidents of all five unions and other officers would be present to participate in the talks. The union committee planned to break the news of their secret weapon at the session: the consumer boycott of Campbell products (starring the Campbell Kids) then on the drawing board. Holbrook rejected the chance to resume negotiations under those conditions, saying that only the local plant manager would be present to handle Camden issues exclusively.[24]

The final stop in the growing coordinated campaign took place in Sacramento in May. When the Teamster contract there expired on May 12, all the unions participating in the campaign would be without contracts and ready to strike. The traveling committee planned to attend Sacramento negotiations starting May 6. At its sole Teamster soup plant Campbell hoped to split the independent union from the AFL-CIO unions. Its plan was to finally allow the Sacramento plant to join the California Produce Institute (a joint union-company master agreement for Northern California) and raise its wage rates substantially to match the area contracts that the Teamsters had with other canneries in the area. Though this was a goal the Sacramento Teamsters had long coveted, they resisted the bait and stuck with the IUD–Campbell committee. They, too, rejected the "final" company offer. At the beginning of June, all the plants held strike votes, and the vote at every one was overwhelmingly in favor of striking. Even at this late date, however, Campbell was still trying to divide its workers. Two days before the Paris union members took their strike vote the company requested a meeting with local leaders only. There company representatives made an unofficial offer to the local president of a twenty-one-cent raise in the second year of the contract, an offer that had not been made before, on the condition that Paris withdraw from coordinated bargaining. None of the locals were budging at all, however, and the Paris UPWA local voted 419 to 12 to strike.

Murphy's team was undeterred, however. The Campbell president declared that the company had already spent over one million dollars in strike preparation and was prepared to lose twenty-five million more if necessary. Though attempts at breaking off Teamster and UPWA locals from the campaign proved futile, company executives began working on the weak link, the AMC. Its leaders had never been very enthusiastic about the ambitious campaign, and they were becoming increasingly nervous about facing Murphy in a final battle. The company began its own campaign to seduce the AMC leaders into a "responsible" settlement that would sidestep the hotheads in the UPWA and the IUD. Campbell vice president William Harwick had begun this tactic the previous summer. He tempered a letter to AMC president Thomas J. Lloyd unequivocally rejecting the first proposal of joint bargaining with personal touches. Harwick crossed out the formal salutation "Dear Mr. Lloyd" and wrote in "Jack" (Lloyd's nickname). He also signed the letter "Bill" in his own hand. The company turned up the charm offensive in late June. The Campbell company plane (with Harwick and Holbrook on board) landed in Chicago to pick up Lloyd and his assistant Stephen V. Coyle. Those four and Murphy then met in Philadelphia for a heart-to-heart talk. Lloyd presented the union position, but Murphy was immovable and clearly dominated the meeting. A cowered Coyle summed up the meeting by indicating that Campbell would take a strike though it did not want to. He suggested the first concession even though the strike was still a month away: rather than insisting on coordinated bargaining, perhaps "the possibility of obtaining uniformity of conditions at the local level" might be "a possible alternative to the strike situation which seems to be developing." On the eve of the strike, the company again met with AMC leaders only, including Local 80's perennial rival Leon Schachter. This time the gathering took place at a breakfast meeting at the Bellevue Stratford Hotel in Philadelphia (the same hotel John T. Dorrance had selected for the opulent coming-out parties for his daughters in the 1920s and 1930s). AMC leaders almost begged Campbell to put an improved economic package that Harwick had hinted at on the table, so that they could convince their members to accept a better bread-and-butter agreement, with or without coordinated bargaining. For some reason the company failed to do this, and it appeared that a strike would be inevitable.[25]

Not only was the strike deadline approaching but on July 12 another seminal event took place—the dissolution of the UPWA into the AMC. The old UPWA locals in Camden, Paris, and Chestertown continued, for a while, to act like Packinghouse locals. Union members were ready for a confrontation, and they believed they finally had the unity to win that had escaped them since the demise of the FTA in 1950. On a national level, the IUD continued to prod both the AMC—which by late July represented about three-quarters of the potential strikers—and the top leadership of the AFL-CIO to give the coordinated campaign their full backing. The federation's executive council decided at its May 14 meeting to give the Campbell campaign its full support and pledged to promote a consumer boycott if a strike was called. The final negotiations between Campbell and its unions took place on July 25 in the offices of the federal mediation service in Philadelphia. William Harwick, representing the company, simply repeated management's position that "negotiations must take place in each locality with local plant management." His instructions from Campbell president Murphy, Harwick said, were that there could be "absolutely no changes in [expiration] dates." Faced with this company intransigence, the union leaders caucused and expressed their commitments to coordinated dates. Local 80's Clarence Clark "accused Campbell of bad faith and expressed [the] strike sentiment of [his] people." The IUD's Stephen Harris informed the federal mediator that the company's position made it necessary for the unions to recess the negotiations. That Thursday evening the union presidents made a momentous decision: all union members in the Campbell Soup council would strike by the following Monday, July 29.[26]

Paris and Sacramento were the first to walk out. Then, following a mass membership meeting in Camden on Sunday, the largest soup plant in the country shut down at 12:01 a.m. on Monday. Pickets ringed the many entrances to the Campbell plants and warehouses in Camden, and the battle quickly escalated. After three days of mass picketing, the company obtained an injunction to limit pickets to four per plant entrance. But large-scale picketing was not required to keep the plant shut down tight; no nonsupervisory workers attempted to cross the picket lines, and the company did not even consider trying to restart any production. The same solidarity held at the other plants, with the exception of under a hundred nonunion members in right-to-work Texas who went to work in the Paris plant but could do little with a thousand of their coworkers on strike.[27]

Just as the unions had planned, the strike hit Campbell at the worst possible moment for the company. Vast fields of tomatoes across South Jersey and Ohio were just ripening, and if they were not picked within a few days they would be lost. The source of the greatest part of Dorrance family wealth was the South Jersey tomato. For decades, Camden had turned out over ten million cans of tomato soup every day during tomato season, a time

when "the streets ran red" in the city and everything revolved around turning the redolent tomato into the famous—and profitable—soup in the red-
and-white cans. The economic impact of the season cut across all sectors of
South Jersey's population. Employees of Campbell worked twelve-hour days,
six days a week. Farmers hired thousands of Puerto Ricans, African American migrant laborers from the South, and local residents of South Jersey and
South Philadelphia to pick their crops. For hundreds of farmers on contract
to the soup company, this was the short period in which they made almost
all their profit for the year. Even restaurants, bars, and other small businesses
in Camden relied on this period for a boost in their trade.

But, in 1968, all this hectic activity came to a halt, replaced by a different kind of restless action on the picket lines and behind the closed doors
of business leaders and politicians. Though the strike shut down all tomato
processing at Campbell, its effects on different groups varied widely. Union
members had expected a work stoppage for some time, and many had tried
to save a little money to help them through the hard strike times. Each
also received a small strike benefit from the international unions coordinating the action. Most migrant farm workers from Puerto Rico—those on
contract—did not suffer greatly due to the strike, for they were guaranteed a
minimum number of hours of pay for the tomato season at an agreed-upon
rate. Those who came as individuals, and the—mostly African American—
mainland migrants, however, had no such guarantees, and their plight quickly
became desperate. The New Jersey branch of the National Association for
the Advancement of Colored People appealed to Governor Richard Hughes
for emergency aid for these migrants, though it was quick to note that it
strongly supported the workers on strike.[28]

The situation of the farmers was less clear. For many, their entire liveli-
hood depended on this season. But for those under contract with Campbell, their legal agreements with the company appeared to indicate that the
company was required to accept their produce at an agreed price. Though
company attorneys had inserted escape clauses into contracts in the event of
emergencies, it was questionable whether courts would enforce these. The
contracts included a provision that excused the company from performance
of its side of the contract in the event that "war, strikes or labor disputes, or
any act of God" prevented Campbell from using the tomatoes at its Camden
plant. The company decided to sidestep any legal challenges to this provision
and gain some positive publicity by offering to cover contracted growers'
losses plus a "reasonable profit," to be determined by the company. Newspapers praised Campbell for its action, but some farmers grumbled that the
amount actually offered was far less than they would have earned in a normal

FIGURE 10. The "strike for unity." The 1968 strike shut down Campbell Soup plants across the country. Here pickets in Camden allow a truck carrying seed tomatoes into the plant.
Temple University Libraries, Urban Archives, Philadelphia, Pennsylvania.

year; one farmer, who claimed a crop worth one hundred thousand dollars, said Campbell offered him only eighteen thousand dollars.[29]

Both the company and the union coalition appealed to the growers for support, and in the resulting standoff most farmers' organizations appealed to both sides and the government to end the strike. Local 80 reminded growers that both the farmers and the production workers were victims of Campbell's low-cost mission. "We don't want this strike," a leaflet addressed to the growers contended. "It would be a hardship for us and a hardship for you, especially when Campbell uses the escape clause in its tomato contract to stop the purchase of your tomatoes." The company responded with its own letters to growers, but it again relied on its public information department and its public relations consultants to plead its case with growers and the general public through the media. A typical antistrike article appeared in Philadelphia's *Evening Bulletin* some three weeks into the strike. Under the headline "'Red Gold' Rots on Vine In Campbell Soup Strike," the reporters painted a heartrending picture of the victims of the strike while ignoring the reasons that led the workers to take this step. They told the story of

Sam Patane, a hardworking South Jersey farmer, and his "honey-tressed wife," five daughters, and widowed mother. "The bulk of the six million tomatoes in his field were beginning to spoil. Sour flies zeroed in on the rotting fruit.... [Patane and his wife] had hoped to put money away toward their daughters' education—and, eventually, their weddings. Now that's out." Also victims were the migrant workers: "Wilfredo Lopez, 20, oldest of eight children, works for Patane. But he's flying back to Puerto Rico this weekend" since there was no work for him in South Jersey and "living costs less in Puerto Rico." Even the unwitting strikers were victims: "Many have children in high school. One or two have sons in college. They hope their children will have better jobs than the parents have." One striker said, "This should be our golden time. For five weeks at this time of year we work overtime every day, plus Saturdays.... But not now while we're on strike." Articles like these had their intended effect. A Mrs. Ascough from Paoli in Philadelphia's elite Main Line suburbs "saw red" and denounced the strikers in a letter to the paper's editor.[30]

Counting on such public support to bolster the company's side in the conflict, Murphy continued his inflexible stand in negotiations. While the unions offered on August 6 to move the common expiration date they wanted outside of tomato season and do "anything reasonable" to achieve a quick settlement, the company hunkered down and refused to budge at all, instead seeking injunctions against picketers. A mediation session that all sides attended at the Department of Labor in Washington, D.C., on August 9 was, therefore, almost pointless. After company representatives just repeated the same line, the best chief mediator William Simkin could offer was that "this kind of discussion is healthy." Then the following exchange took place between Campbell president Murphy and IUD representative Stephen Harris (as recorded in a handwritten transcription of the meeting minutes):

> MURPHY: I would resign before I would go before the Stockholders and say I have transferred the power to shut down our operations to a group of unions. This is an impossible situation.
> HARRIS: Mr. Murphy—
> MURPHY: You shut up. You are the "N____" in the woodpile.

The union's Don Smith immediately called for the unionists to go into caucus. Murphy later returned and apologized for his comments but made no movement from his earlier position.[31]

According to a Local 80 leaflet, Murphy made another racially tinged statement before federal mediators. He allegedly said that 60 percent of Camden plant employees were from minority groups because Campbell "was forced to hire Negroes and other minority citizens" during World War II when "whites could get better jobs in other industries." The union blasted the company for "deliberately trying to provoke a situation in the City of Camden in an effort to embarrass the Union by creating a situation between the police and the workers whom they, by their stubborn action, have forced out on the street." The company escalated the rhetoric, again reviving its favored epithet of "outsiders," but this time applying it to African American city residents. In the tense atmosphere of the hot summer of 1968 the company was playing with fire. In a Camden *Courier-Post* article headlined "Racial Trouble Feared in Soup Strike," company officials charged that "outsiders" provoked violence when they prevented trucks from entering a plant gate. The reporter stoked fears further when he quoted an observer that "there's lots of guys with necklaces hanging around here.... They act like they're looking for a reason to start something. And this could give them an excuse. They could start to burn." A company official added, "The strike has reached the nasty stage. Racism is rearing its head." In earlier years Campbell had bluntly relied on racial, ethnic, and gender divisions to segment its workforce. In the 1940s it had fought the hiring of African Americans and in the 1950s it had refused to accept an antidiscrimination clause in its contracts. By the 1960s geographic divisions replaced the earlier ones, but during the strike the company appeared to be toying with a bid to rekindle racial animosities. That, in any case, was the belief of union activists. To prevent a conflagration that could wreck the unity of the strike, the union called on "all responsible Camden citizens" to "protest the provocative acts of the Campbell Soup Company and demand that they live up to their moral responsibility to the Camden Community."[32]

Procompany publicity even resurrected old gender stereotypes. Company supporters at a newspaper near the rural Napoleon plant bemoaned the effects a strike would have on local housewives. Ignoring the fact that many women had to work at the soup plant year round to support their families, the paper warned that "hundreds of housewives who count on this seasonal work for vacation and spending money will have to forgo a good many luxuries this summer." And in Camden, company public information officials drew up letters to send to workers' homes in order to reach workers' wives. They seemed to be unaware of the 740 Camden workers who were women.[33]

If the company was trying to divide its workers in order to beat them, the unions were responding by emphasizing unity and solidarity. They began by pointing out the logic of their core demand of common expiration dates. Joseph Colangelo, Local 80's business manager, contended that the roots of the demand went back to the 1958 strike in Camden. In that conflict workers returned to work after a long strike for only a penny more than the company's original offer. Workers at other plants had equally unfavorable outcomes during strikes over the next several years. "The results were always the same," according to Colangelo. "The company shifted its production to another plant. While one group of workers struck, the others worked overtime and weekends. While we were on strike in 1958, employees in Ohio were making double-time."[34] Striker C. T. Sheppard's wife (apparently one not convinced by company letters) made the same point in a rebuttal to the letter to the editor of the Main Line's Mrs. Ascough:

> If the union didn't time the strike for the crop harvesting season, there would be no bargaining as in past years. The company tells the union what it is giving them in their contract, and that is the end of it. Without coordinated bargaining, one plant strikes and the other plants are put to work around the clock. The company hardly notices the strike, and doesn't care if they "walk" or not.[35]

Along with explaining the rationale of unity to the public, the strike leaders made efforts to build solidarity beyond the ranks of the strikers. Their attempts to reach farmers paid off in Ohio, where supportive growers and farm workers planned a parade through town to back the strikers. The IUD secured the endorsement of George Meany, head of the AFL-CIO, and the federation's newspaper ran a large article calling on unionists to back their brothers and sisters. Exploratory contacts were made with various transportation unions that could potentially have a serious impact on Campbell's business, starting with the Teamsters (one of the unions on strike) but extending to railroad workers, airline pilots, and the West Coast longshoremen led by Harry Bridges. The IUD's Stephen Harris even made pathbreaking moves to go beyond national borders and enlist the support of food workers internationally. Juul Poulsen, general secretary of the International Union of Food and Allied Workers' Associations in Geneva, Switzerland, promised Harris his organization's full support, and he provided detailed information on Campbell's operations in Europe and the unions representing that sector. While most union activists counted on growing national and international solidarity to tip the struggle in their favor, a few unknown people tried to ratchet up the stakes by taking things into their own hands. There had been minor incidents of violence since the beginning of the strike when, for example, the company tried to bring in tomatoes and strikers angrily toppled dozens of bushels onto the ground. But, on August 15, an arsonist set a three-block-long warehouse on fire, destroying eight freight cars and three hundred thousand pounds of tin plate.[36]

Campbell workers' strongest weapon was not the damage that a few individuals could cause but their ability to shut down production. But their second most powerful tool was the solidarity of millions of other unionists and sympathizers as expressed in a consumer boycott. The IUD and the unions had prepared for a boycott for months, and, after the fruitless Washington negotiations went nowhere, the AFL-CIO declared a nationwide boycott of all Campbell products. Starting on August 12, union leaders asked their fifteen million members to spearhead the campaign. Millions of the innovative Campbell Kids boycott leaflets were printed and distributed to union locals across the country. Detailed plans for picketing retail outlets were activated; shoppers were not requested to boycott the retail establishments (which would be an illegal secondary boycott) but simply to avoid buying Campbell, Swanson, and Pepperidge Farm products. Earl Newsom and Company conferred with Campbell executives to map a strategy to deal with the new front in their war with the unions. Initially company spokesmen were to say that the boycott was having no effect. Only if it seemed to be growing would the company move to the next stage, in which they would portray the union leaders as heartless demagogues unconcerned with their innocent victims. By August 20, Murphy confided to William Lydgate (of Newsom and Company) that "[the unions] are now roughing us up just a little bit here and there," and suggested a new approach. Campbell should go to the public with dire predictions about what could happen if there were one national food union, the ultimate goal, according to Murphy, of coordinated bargaining: "Presented properly I should think this would be a very scary thing for the general public." The day before Murphy had received notice that the Giant Eagle Markets of Pittsburgh had signed an agreement with their truckers "that they will not order or receive shipments of Campbell products during the duration of our present strike." It was beginning to appear that Murphy's hard-line stance had about reached the end of its effectiveness. A prolonged consumer boycott threatened to do what decades of trying had failed to achieve for Campbell's competitors: strike-induced shortages and boycott supporters might finally provide an opening for H. J. Heinz and others in the heretofore impenetrable market for canned soup.[37]

✺ Escalation or Surrender

By mid-August 1968 the leaders of the Campbell strike were at a crucial point in their battle with the company. The nationwide boycott was just getting underway and the IUD had made important initial contacts with other unions in the United States, Canada, and Europe to enlist their aid. The potential support of transport unions, including one of the striking unions, the Teamsters, threatened to shut down trade in Campbell products. No previous coordinated bargaining campaign had been able to wield the power of a boycott of the second most recognized brand in America. About one-quarter to one-third of the tomato crop had been lost by that point, and in the next month all of it would be lost if no settlement was reached. With the crop would go probably all of Campbell's profits for the year, as well as its stranglehold on the canned soup market. If the coordinated bargaining council were to raise the stakes and put everything into the boycott and solidarity campaigns, they would be in a very good position to call Murphy's bluff and force the company to accede to their basic demand. Murphy claimed that he would hold out forever, but it is unlikely that Jack Dorrance and the board of directors would let him run the source of their wealth into the ground in order to make a point, no matter how noble or important to their class. Such a daring plan, however, would require union leadership of the caliber and dedication of the founders of the UCAPAWA or the UPWA. The IUD's Stephen Harris, the UPWA's Don Smith, Jesse Prosten, and Ralph Helstein, and several activists in Camden's Local 80 and the machinists' Local 2031 appeared likely candidates to lead such a crusade. Yet at this turning point in the history of the Campbell Soup Company and its workers, power shifted to a very different kind of union. With the takeover of the UPWA by the AMC, the AMC's leaders T. J. Lloyd and Patrick Gorman, their compliant underlings like Stephen Coyle, and long-time South Jersey AMC leader Leon Schachter took center stage. They had always been, at best, reluctant converts to the coordinated cause. Even more important, they had little faith in their members' ability to beat the intransigent W. B. Murphy. Just when their cause demanded a rededication to the hardships and possibilities of the struggle, they faltered.

Just a week into the strike the new leadership gave up one of its strongest bargaining chips. The demand for a common expiration date at the beginning of tomato season was modified to accept a date even in mid-winter, when it would have not nearly the clout that a summer date would. Murphy, of course, conceded nothing in return. Ten days later the AMC's leaders appeared just about ready to give up. Patrick Gorman gloomily reported to Lloyd about a telephone conversation he had just had with the federal government's chief mediator, Joseph Kirkham: "Kirkham talked to me for I'd say ten minutes, and there is no solution and it is useless to talk to Murphy again. Murphy is determined to operate the plants and not turn the keys to close them. He feels that Campbell soup will lick the union." Even getting back into negotiations would be "a near impossibility," Gorman reported. Most surprisingly, he repeated the latest revival of Campbell's favorite propaganda line: the resistance to a settlement, which was especially strong in Camden, was due to the agitation of "outsiders." This time, however, the "outsider" charge was leveled at the most consistent proponent of the Campbell coordinated campaign:

> The Camden, New Jersey, group [Kirkham] said has been fed up all year with how bad Murphy is and how he can break the union at any time without a common expiration date. Even if something half real would come out, at present Camden would not accept it. They are boisterous and Murphy knows it. . . .
>
> The surprising thing Kirkham told me, which was supposed to be confidential too, was that UPWA used outsiders to get the Campbell people in the present frame of mind of hating the company, and the principal outsider was Steve Harris.

Though Harris had come to the IUD from his earlier job as a researcher and pension expert for the AMC, he enthusiastically adopted the industrial division's militant approach and distanced himself from the AMC's conciliatory brand of business unionism. With the shift of the membership of UPWA into the AMC, however, the direction of the coordinated campaign likewise shifted from the IUD and the union council to the national office of the AMC.[38]

While the union campaign seemed to founder at the top just as the boycott was getting under way, the company propaganda machine continued in high gear. Campbell spokesmen relentlessly hammered at the alleged dictatorial role of "outsiders." They asked Camden plant workers why they should be concerned with abstract concepts like coordinated bargaining when the company was ready to sign a good wage deal with them. With little upbeat counterpromotion from their top union leadership, the Campbell tactics began to have their effect. Some Local 80 members began to ask their officers why they needed to continue the strike for nonlocal issues, and the AMC's Leon Schachter and the local's leading business unionist, Joseph Colangelo, began sounding the same call.

By the time all parties agreed to meet again at the federal mediation office in Philadelphia on August 26, it was all over but the details. The company still insisted that those negotiations apply to Local 80 only. In a union caucus those still believing in the coordinated campaign, especially former UPWA leader Jesse Prosten and Sacramento Teamster Arthur Rose, bitterly confronted AMC leaders who were advocating a concession on the major demand of a common expiration date. Schachter and Colangelo joined the call for abandoning joint bargaining. AMC vice president Harry Poole tried to put the best face on the failure to adhere to the initial goals: "Coordinated bargaining means many things. If great strides are made on issues nationally we have achieved success...if we can get [the] gain applied to all the plants." Mediators then called company representatives in and an agreement was reached after several hours of negotiations—but for Local 80 only. The company had been prepared to offer a better wage and benefit package, but, when they saw how eager the union leaders were to settle the strike, they merely added a few cents to the second year of the contract over and above their earlier "final offer." Workers ratified the new contract two days later.

Separate negotiations with Camden's machinists lasted a couple days more. Local 2031's leaders were outraged when they found that their phone lines were wiretapped just after a nationwide conference call with the other unions to discuss strategy before the mediation meeting. The local's leaders recommended a vote against the contract proposal, but their members voted to accept it. The Camden plant resumed operations in time to save perhaps half of the 1968 tomato crop.[39]

Similar separate agreements were negotiated in Paris, Napoleon, and Chestertown. In Sacramento, however, members of Teamsters Local 228 rejected a contract recommended by their leadership. After several more negotiating sessions, the final plant in the Campbell chain returned to work about a month after Camden had. All contracts had distinctly different expiration dates. W. B. Murphy gloated in a letter to shareholders that "employees returned to work without any concession from the company on the matter of coordinated bargaining and under wage and benefits conditions...that the company was prepared to offer prior to the strike." Though the AMC was obligated to continue the boycott until the Sacramento plant settled, it quickly reverted to its preferred businesslike relations with the company once they had settled. Gorman and Schachter congratulated each other on ending the strike "not...one day too soon." The national AMC leaders then informed all local unions that "Campbell Soup Company Products Should Be Highly Recommended!" and "This company should now have our full cooperation and their fine products recommended wholeheartedly to the public."[40]

❧ The Legacy of the Strike

Though coordinated bargaining was defeated in 1968, the various local contracts that were ratified did include a greater improvement in wages and benefits than was usually achieved in new contracts. This result marked a new trend in labor relations at the Campbell Soup Company. From the first strike in 1934 through the initial heady days of the 1968 strike, workers and their unions at Campbell had fought for something more than just a slightly better economic deal. They had struggled for a say in how they did their jobs. They battled discrimination against blacks and women. Perhaps most of all, they had fought for respect for the people who were looked down upon because they were soup makers. But that type of social-justice unionism had been eclipsed by a number of factors both external and internal. McCarthyism had destroyed much of their early leadership and Campbell continued to manipulate divisions among its workers. On a national level, structural changes in the meatpacking industry led to the untimely demise of the United Packinghouse Workers, the organization Local 80 had embraced after its first leftist national union was destroyed. The militant heritage of the Campbell union did not entirely evaporate, and shop stewards and some officials continued to press for larger goals. For the most part, however, the union was disconnected from broader social issues; future battles would be over the straightforward and limited economic issues understood by business unionists.

Beyond the short-lived interunion solidarity and consumer boycott, there were other possibilities unrealized in 1968. In several of the hot spots of the worldwide upheaval of that year—notably France and Italy—workers turned protests initiated by students into rebellions that for a time seemed to threaten the foundations of capitalism. This was not the case in the United States, where the popular image of construction workers attacking antiwar protestors is the dominant memory. Yet as described at the beginning of this chapter, the late 1960s was also a period of rapidly rising labor unrest in the United States, but an unrest largely cut off from the movements in the streets challenging "the establishment" and demanding civil rights and an end to the war in Vietnam. There were some tenuous connections, however, between these parallel challenges to the status quo. The UPWA and the IUD had been early supporters of the Students for a Democratic Society and the Student Nonviolent Coordinating Committee, and many unionists were active in the civil rights movement. Indeed, Martin Luther King Jr.'s last battle had been in support of the unionization struggle of Memphis, Tennessee's sanitation workers. The collapse of the UPWA, following on the destruction of other leftist unions in the early 1950s, removed a vital link at a critical moment in the history of the labor, civil rights, and other progressive movements.[41]

But the legacy of the 1968 Campbell coordinated campaign can be more than one of defeat of a broader vision of progressive unionism. It can also provide lessons for a union movement in the early twenty-first century searching for its bearings. To engage in a bit of counterfactual history, what might have been the results in 1968 if a few things had gone differently? If the UPWA had survived for a few more years and the IUD had maintained leadership of the strike, they may have chosen to escalate rather than concede in late August 1968. If the incipient boycott had been allowed to develop, if the novel approaches to national and international solidarity bore fruit, if the unions' struggle had become part of the general societal tumult of that year, it is entirely possible that the outcome could have been very different. Corporations like Campbell already had extensive experience by 1968 in shifting production to defeat unions. This trend has only increased in the succeeding decades, and now usually involves transnational transfer of production. Coordinated bargaining across disparate unions was a remarkable response to this strategy, one that was given only a few years of testing in the 1960s. If that coordination were to be extended across borders—as the IUD began experimenting with—global capital would face far more obstacles than it has become accustomed to. The experiences of the Campbell unions and the other unions that attempted to implement coordinated bargaining deserve to be examined far more closely than they have been.

CHAPTER 7

Waiting for the End

William Beverly Murphy came away from the 1968 strike quite self-satisfied. He had beaten the one force potentially capable of challenging his plans for the company's future. Yet the early 1970s were a bad time for the Campbell Soup Company and a worse time for Camden, New Jersey, the city of its birth. From the time John T. Dorrance started producing condensed soup at the beginning of the century through the 1960s, the company had been an outstanding profit generator. As described in earlier chapters, Dorrance and his successors built their success by producing vast quantities of high-quality convenience foods cheaply. By the early 1970s, however, Wall Street analysts began to question Campbell's performance. Unlike earlier decades, in which Campbell's profit margin topped the food industry, by early 1971 the *New York Times* was complaining that its sluggish sales and profit growth—both about 6 percent—were now lagging the industry. Murphy had gambled on diversifying the company's products and entering the international market (beyond Canada and the United Kingdom); both had mixed results. He launched the "Red Kettle" brand of dry soups in 1961, only to fold it five years later. Campbell's initial forays into foreign markets drained millions of dollars from company profits for years while it tried to catch up with rival H. J. Heinz, which had a long-standing global presence. Though Campbell's experiments beyond condensed soup often failed, analysts faulted its management for being too conservative and not taking advantage of its ability to finance itself to expand more aggressively. Critics also pointed to the aging Camden and Chicago plants as drags on profitability.[1]

While Murphy moved energetically to respond to investor criticisms once he had contained the challenge from his unions, an unexpected event later in 1971 threw all his calculations off balance. In late August that year a company spokesman announced that Campbell was recalling all chicken vegetable soup produced in one of its newest plants in Paris, Texas. Botulism had been discovered in some cans of that variety, and Campbell moved rapidly to reassure the public and remove any possibly tainted products from store shelves. Still, Campbell stock plunged sharply on Wall Street, driving even more brokers to advise investors to sell their shares in the company. Though Campbell's efforts to recover its tarnished image eventually succeeded, some unease remained due to the fact that company and government inspectors were never able to locate the cause of the contamination.[2]

If Campbell was going through a troublesome period, its home—the city of Camden—appeared to be sinking fast. In April 1970, the *Philadelphia Inquirer* ran a five-part series, "Camden: City in Trouble." The paper portrayed Camden as "a glaring example of every negative aspect of urban life," with mounting poverty and racial problems combined with the flight of white residents, stores, and factories from the city. The rapid decline in jobs for city residents was at the core of many of the city's other problems. The first signs that things were getting worse for the once bustling industrial city began appearing as early as the 1940s and 1950s. RCA shipped radio and television assembly to Bloomington, Indiana starting in 1940, and by the mid-1950s several midsize employers had left, including Armstrong Cork and the C. Howard Hunt Pen Company. The opening of one of the nation's first shopping malls in nearby Cherry Hill in 1961 attracted shoppers away from the downtown area, and the once grand Stanley Theatre was leveled to make a parking lot. By the 1960s the loss of jobs escalated. Both the Esterbrook Pen Company and New York Shipbuilding shut down, and by 1970 Camden had twenty-two thousand fewer manufacturing jobs than it had two decades earlier.

Several scholars have traced the decline of manufacturing in the United States and the creation of a "postindustrial" America. Historians such as Thomas Sugrue and Judith Stein ascribe the glaring poverty and racial strife especially evident in the old rust-belt cities to structural changes in the economy, but they lay the blame for the specific contours of the "urban crisis" on the actions of corporate executives, political leaders, and others. Sugrue sees decisions made by the "Big Three" automakers to escape Detroit's powerful union movement traditions as the core of that city's problems, exacerbated by the "white resistance" of working-class homeowners that sparked racial violence. Stein, on the other hand, charges federal government policies that privileged Cold War foreign policy goals over domestic industrial policy with the decline in the U.S. steel industry and its consequent devastating impacts on working-class jobs. Both scholars conclude that federal programs to outlaw discrimination and provide job training were doomed to failure without the massive creation of new jobs, and, according to Stein, such policies led almost inevitably to racial conflict. The evidence from late-twentieth-century Camden similarly indicts political and corporate elites for that city's crushing problems.[3]

The effects of deindustrialization on Camden and its residents were predictable. Just as African Americans and Puerto Ricans broke through the barriers to get jobs in industry, the industries were disappearing. Frustrated city residents like Charles "Poppy" Sharp were fed up with politicians' promises versus the reality of their daily lives. After hearing a speech by Student Nonviolent Coordinating Committee president H. Rap Brown at Camden's convention center, Sharp organized a group that would become an important vehicle for advocating the goals of the city's black residents, the Black People's Unity Movement (BPUM). The BPUM and other activists had a contentious relationship with city government and the police in the late 1960s. In May 1968, the BPUM and supporters confronted heavily armed police at the luxury Northgate apartment building next to the Benjamin Franklin Bridge. One of the BPUM supporters was John Tisa, the leftist organizer who had helped Campbell workers form a union in 1940; as a result, Camden mayor Alfred Pierce charged that the BPUM actions were communist-inspired. Tensions continued to rise in the city, and a confrontation between police and residents of a black neighborhood in South Camden in 1969 resulted in the deaths of a policeman and a black teenage girl. Two years later an even more violent conflagration erupted in the city's Puerto Rican community. After police beat a Puerto Rican man to death, five days of rioting ensued. Through it all, Campbell Soup stayed in Camden. Not only did Plants No. 1 and No. 2 continue making the company's products; by the summer of 1970, a new corporate headquarters and research center opened in the city as well. Though politicians regularly promised a comeback for the beleaguered city, the best news they could come up with was the expansion of two public institutions, Cooper Hospital and the Camden campus of Rutgers University. The taxpaying private sector that had provided relatively good jobs for the city's blue-collar workers was fast disappearing. It was no wonder that Mayor Joseph Nardi called Campbell Soup "the best citizen we have." By the end of the decade another *Inquirer* profile of the city, while almost as pessimistic as its earlier series, at least had a defiant edge in its title: "Camden, the Worst City in New Jersey, Fights Back."[4]

Beyond falling profits, product recalls, and a deteriorating city, Campbell management continued to encounter problems with its workforce in the early 1970s. To be sure, it had defeated the unions in the 1968 strike and Local 80 and its members were less confrontational than in the past. Yet these defeats contributed to a growing malaise that spread through the Campbell plants despite moderately good wage and benefit improvements in the preceding years. Part of the problem continued to stem from the mind-numbing repetitive work. Automation had relieved workers of some of the heavier tasks, but the continually increasing production rate gave them no relief. Paradoxically, the decline in worker solidarity and belief in the union, which might have been expected to work in the company's favor, also led to a more dispirited workforce. Dissatisfaction with local and national Amalgamated Meat Cutters (AMC) leaders, petty squabbles, and racial animosities replaced the vigorous and united spirit that had built Local 80's proud traditions. In response to what the personnel department perceived as a growing threat to a productive workforce, management launched a number of initiatives to study the problem and find solutions. The company engaged former U.S. Labor Secretary William J. Usery to conduct an in-depth study of morale problems at the Sacramento, California, plant, and Camden personnel director J. J. Sosiak polled all his managers for suggestions on how "to ensure that employees have favorable attitudes." One of the less favorable responses he received bitterly complained that employee morale was at its lowest point in twenty-five years. The respondent also grumbled that he had no hopes of moving into a community-relations post he coveted solely because he was a Caucasian.[5]

Campbell management's worries about employee morale, just as with product recalls or any other problems, were ultimately tied to its concern for the bottom line. In this, things had not changed much in a hundred years. But in the 1970s and 1980s, many of the old techniques of cheap production seemed to be faltering. New methods that managers implemented sometimes introduced real changes in how things were done at the soup plants, but often were no more than fads. In most cases only the surface of management style changed. The net result, however, was once again a profitable company, at least until the late 1980s. William Beverly Murphy, however, would not be a part of most of these changes. In 1972 he retired as Campbell's president, replaced by Harold B. Shaub.

ℳ Lean Production in the Age of Toyota

For its one hundredth anniversary, the Campbell Soup Company published a glossy special issue of its publication *Harvest,* with the title "Century II." In the magazine the editors devoted a section to each part of the company. Though dwelling on management, the Personnel Department, and advertising, it conceded that "Production" was the "keystone in the food distribution arch": "Anyone who knows how a modern food company operates cannot deny it is among the most basic of corporate functions." It then gave a remarkable description of how a can of vegetable soup was made:

> As each of the ingredients is received at the plant, it is inspected. Any which do not meet Campbell's high standards of quality are rejected. Vegetable ingredients which pass the receiving inspection are washed by high-pressure jets of water and conveyed to "preparatory rooms."....
>
> At the blending kettles, all of the ingredients are brought together, weighed, and blended....
>
> Blended ingredients are fed into can-filling machines. Cans, each tested for air leaks and thoroughly washed, are filled and hermetically sealed. Moving on conveyors, the filled cans are cooked much as they would be in a home pressure cooker....
>
> After cooking, the containers are cooled and then conveyed on tracks to machines which put labels on the cans.

What is striking about this account is the almost total invisibility of the people involved in performing each step in the process. By using the passive voice almost exclusively, the authors create an image of a totally automated factory that no longer relies on the inconveniences of human labor. The single reference to (female) human workers in the piece equates human and mechanical labor and hints that they too will soon be gone: "There [where ingredients enter the preparatory room] trained women or electronic machines inspect each item of food which is to be used as an ingredient."[6]

As should be clear from earlier chapters, Campbell's presidents from John T. Dorrance through W. B. Murphy worked as hard as possible toward the dream of a workerless factory. Both certainly recognized that this dream would never be realized, but they constantly pushed toward their goal by automating every step of every process that could be automated, then scientifically managing the human component to fit in where needed. The mantras of productivity and low cost continued to be the guiding lights of all changes in production in this period, though the specific manifestations varied among the latest management fads from "quality circles" to expert systems to robotics. One of the most significant changes was the final abandonment of the Bedaux system of "scientific management"—the "incentive plan"—over a several-year period in the 1970s and early 1980s. Workers had long ago learned how to beat or at least circumvent the plan. Eventually even the Industrial Engineering Department gave up trying to make it work, and arrangements were made in later union contracts to supplement the pay of workers who had previously been eligible for bonuses. To take the place of the plan, according to industrial engineer Edward Cheeseman, the company relied on both "mechanical methods to replace labor" and outsourcing. The cumulative effect of decades of automation was that significantly fewer workers produced far greater quantities of food products. The five thousand year-round workers in Camden in the 1930s and 1940s had dwindled to only three thousand by 1969 and less than two thousand by 1979. This trend was intensified by the company's ever-greater use of outsourcing to reduce costs. As early as the 1950s the company had begun using precut beef from Argentina. The imported beef was not only cheaper but also allowed the company to eliminate the jobs of many skilled butchers. Later they outsourced the preparation of other ingredients such as onions. Previously, workers had flame-peeled the outer skin of onions, then women in the preparatory department prepared them by hand. By the 1980s the Campbell employees who had done these jobs were gone; an outsourcer now provided prepared onions much more cheaply.[7]

If outsourcing was one well-known tool of late twentieth-century capitalism, there were many others that competed for the attention of managers. Perhaps the most famous is known as "lean production." In the narrowest definition (as discussed in chapter 1), lean production is the set of practices associated with the Toyota Production System (TPS), created by the Japanese automobile manufacturer after World War II. These practices, according to its proponents, include just-in-time manufacturing, flexible production, and the empowerment of workers who ostensibly take ownership of their jobs and work at high rates of productivity and quality. At the core of the TPS is the philosophy of *kaizen,* or "continuous improvement." No matter how well a work team is performing, engineers and the workers themselves must constantly search for ways to improve the work process, eliminate waste (especially wasted time), and improve quality, often through the mechanism of quality circles. Though breathless early accounts of the TPS in American management literature praised the system as a win–win solution for companies and workers in the next stage of global capitalism, a substantial body of criticism has challenged many of its basic tenets and claims. Labor activists and writers Mike Parker and Jane Slaughter have proposed a different term for lean production: "management by stress." They and other analysts have convincingly argued that TPS, rather than being empowering for workers, in fact continually stresses them to, and beyond, their physical and mental limits. Thus, through kaizen, speedup never ends. The net result is not a superior replacement for Fordist mass production and Taylorism but an extension of both: "Jobs are still subdivided into narrowly defined tasks...; work is still regimented by the assembly line and by strict adherence to standardized procedures...; mass production at high volumes still characterizes the system's output...; and management retains fundamental control of the overall production process." In the words of a leading American advocate of the TPS, lean production is "original Fordism with a Japanese flavor." Parker and Slaughter, and others, contend that workers need unions more than ever in a lean environment.[8]

The Campbell Soup Company toyed with several popular management techniques in the 1970s and 1980s, most of them based on Japanese innovations. Despite strong support from the top of the company, these were all short-lived. As Edward Cheeseman has noted, Campbell still relied on automation as its primary tool for productivity improvement. Throughout this period, the company's annual reports were filled with stories of extensive modernization programs and the opening of the unprecedented Maxton, North Carolina, plant in the mid-1980s, "a pace-setting example of cost-efficient production." Nevertheless, this did not stop Campbell from joining a large part of corporate America in their introduction of Japanese management techniques. Quality circles—worker-management discussion groups whose purpose was to devise and suggest to management workplace improvements—swept through the company. Between 1981 and 1986 there was scarcely an article published about Campbell that did not tout its 450 quality circles. Sounding like a page out of Frederick Taylor, a trade journal described how the Campbell program "recognizes that employees who do the work in the plant are the 'experts' in their...areas of specialization." Though they may have been the experts, they rarely led the circles; supervisors guided members in their search for continuous improvement. A circle named the Night Owls (a trade journal noted that Campbell's circles "have names, like bowling teams") was led by supervisor Lee Paulikas. The Night Owls proposed to management that a project be initiated to label all electrical equipment and power panels. The purpose, in true win-win style, would ostensibly help both the company and the workers; it would "reduce downtime, smooth production, [and] improve safety." By the late 1980s, however, barely a mention was made of Campbell's quality circles. Industrial engineer Cheeseman has called them "a fad that faded fast" and that had no lasting positive results. He had a better impression of the company's experimentation with "expert systems." A briefly popular branch of computer artificial intelligence, expert systems were also pioneered by Japanese researchers. These systems sought to tap the knowledge—both formal practices and heuristic "rules of thumb"—of "experts" in any field. In one case, Campbell hired consultants from Texas Instruments to "capture the knowledge" of Aldo Cimino before he retired. Cimino repaired the giant hydrostatic sterilizers that cooked the soup, and his skill was legendary. Eventually the consultants created an expert system with 175 rules from their interviews with Cimino, and it was installed in eight plants to aid less experienced repair personnel.[9]

Perhaps more fascinating than Campbell's partial adoption of 1980s' popular management trends, however, were the similarities between the company's practices earlier in the twentieth century and the latest pronouncements of self-proclaimed management experts. Most clearly of all, "continuous improvement"—the concept at the heart of Japanese lean production—was also the core philosophy of John T. Dorrance and his successors. In addition, the company employed contingent (seasonal) workers in order to grow or shrink the labor force to meet the just-in-time requirements dictated by the constantly varying inputs of raw materials. Though management earlier in the century did not go through the pretense of "empowering" workers by extracting their knowledge in quality circles, it sought to achieve the same goal through careful study of workers by International Bedaux Company engineers. Though allegedly recent developments in management strategies may have a Japanese pedigree in their latest incarnation, many similar techniques have enabled companies like Campbell to successfully engage in cheap production for decades. Paradoxically, the final decades of the Camden plants were probably the weakest period for the dominance of lean techniques there. This was due to two factors. First, so much had been automated by then that the proportion of production costs due to direct labor was at an all-time low; thus, relatively little could still be gained by squeezing more work out of every second of labor. Second, the many hard-fought struggles between union Local 80 and Campbell had secured for workers a modicum of security and at least adequate pay and benefits. Though Campbell had won the battle over unified bargaining, it finally came to the realization that it would be easier to live with a "responsible" union than continue to fight a more confrontational one. As a result, it was just "biding its time" until the next significant qualitative change in cheap production, the move of all Camden work to Maxton.

By the 1970s and 1980s then, Campbell had at least the appearance of a "kinder, gentler" company. It engaged consultants to study ways of improving morale, it sought worker input in quality circles, and it chose to collude with business unions rather than fight militant ones. Yet just below the surface not much had really changed. A survey of Sacramento employee attitudes conducted in 1977 revealed the continued existence of deep-seated hostility between many workers and the company. The statements gathered from employees depict a world of harsh discipline not very different from the "slave house" descriptions of the 1930's Camden plants, a place where only production matters:

> "They try to control by fear and intimidation."
> "They think you are a machine. My foreman never says thank you."
> "Supervisors shouldn't have the right to cuss at you and treat you like dogs."
> "Keep the machines running, even if your safety is at stake."

Even some foremen made similar complaints:

> "The company always wants more. Run it 'til it breaks."
> "We are afraid to stop the line for repair or adjustment that might take an hour. We must push the product."
> "If we have a super day, there is no thanks. It is expected to be the norm from then on."
> "The company concept seems to be. 'Don't tell the workers. Demand it.'"[10]

As many American corporations began "offshoring" production as their preferred method of lowering costs and increasing profit margins, Campbell's history demonstrates that the same goal could often be achieved in American factories using other strategies. And the strategies that the soup company continued to use looked, in many cases, very much like ones it had perfected much earlier in the twentieth century.

🐟 Persistent Divisions

The Campbell Soup Company proudly advertised its latest advances in automation and lean production techniques. News of the ultramodern Maxton plant, company research and development efforts, and the widespread use of quality circles at Campbell filled trade, business, and even popular media. But the company did not publicize other components of its cheap production scheme. Foremost among these was the continuing persistence of workforce segmentation, the division of its employees along geographical, racial, and gender lines and into a multitiered system of permanent, temporary, and outsourced and subcontracted workers. Not only were these divisions hidden but Campbell used its accommodation to the formal legal rights gained by minorities and women in the 1960s to present itself as a model corporate citizen while maintaining or heightening tensions among its workers. Campbell continued to reap extra profits from the lower wages it could pay disadvantaged segments of its workforce while at the same time some managers told white, male, permanent employees that they must sacrifice because of the new rights won by African Americans and women. Without a progressive union like the United Cannery, Agricultural, Packing, and Allied Workers of America (UCAPAWA) or the United Packinghouse Workers of America (UPWA) to lead Campbell workers in a fight for unity, little was done to counter the company strategy. The one exception was a brilliant campaign by subcontracted farmworkers in Ohio, under the banner of the Farm Labor Organizing Committee (FLOC), to carry their grievances to the corporate headquarters under the spotlight of the national media.

Rarely after 1968 did workers at various company sites unite for any reason. The defeat of unity in that year was to have lasting effects for all Campbell workers. While the AMC now represented a majority of unionized Campbell production workers, the union did not use its potential power of solidarity; each local faced Campbell alone. Geographical division was the bedrock category separating Campbell workers after 1968. Yet the older segmentations that had characterized the company since its earliest days demonstrated a remarkable tenacity, despite the company's belated acceptance of antidiscrimination clauses in its contracts in the 1960s. Though the UCAPAWA and UPWA had campaigned to end discrimination in the plants they represented, managers in the AMC, Teamster, and nonunion plants continued to assign women and minorities to lower-paying jobs. The contrasts within these plants were stark. When W. J. Usery studied the Sacramento plant in 1977, he found nonwhite men occupying lower-paying jobs, on average, than those held by white men and, even more markedly, women of every racial and ethnic group clustered in the lowest range (see table 2).

While similar data is not available for Camden, the distribution there was likely comparable though not as pronounced. Whether the relatively egalitarian distribution of jobs and pay (excluding maintenance) reverted to a more unequal pattern after the ascendance of the AMC in 1968 is unclear. The Sacramento data, however, show that blatant discrimination existed in Campbell facilities more than a dozen years after the passage of the 1964 Civil Rights Act presumably barred such practices.[11]

Despite the overwhelming evidence of the subordinate position of minority and female workers in the Sacramento plant, many supervisors and white

Table 2. Hourly Pay by Race and Gender, Campbell Soup Company, Sacramento, California, Plant, 1978

HOURLY PAY ($)	WHITE		BLACK		HISPANIC		ASIAN	
	MEN	WOMEN	MEN	WOMEN	MEN	WOMEN	MEN	WOMEN
7.00–8.00	147	1	4	0	15	0	7	0
6.00–7.00	106	1	17	0	82	0	20	0
5.51–6.00	124	25	36	13	135	20	57	6
5.00–5.50	87	120	27	56	74	103	63	21

Source: Compiled from data in W. J. Usery Papers, Sacramento Plant Study, 1978.

male workers believed that women and minorities were receiving special favors at the expense of white men, thus further exacerbating disunity. One worker claimed that "supervisors are so darned afraid of the NAACP and the EEO people, they're unfair to the rest of us." But another worker argued that "management *causes* friction among the employees just to keep them from uniting." He may have had in mind the supervisor who gave his opinion of recent changes at the plant: "There has been a definite down trend here since we started give-away programs like EEOC and Women's Lib. They hire too many unqualified people.... Personnel should have a little more balls in dealing with these people."[12]

One way that Sacramento managers dealt with women's demands for an end to discrimination was by assigning female workers to jobs that required heavy physical labor. Ignoring the fact that women were paid far less than men when they performed jobs that required just as much skill and experience, managers in effect said, If you want the same rights as men, we'll assign you to heavy manual work. An Asian American woman who had worked in production at Campbell for twenty-six years collected six pages of comments from her coworkers to use in responding to the consultants studying employee morale. The very first topic on her list was labeled "I. Women's Liberation—Misinterpretation":

A. Women at Campbell Soup feel that they should not be forced to do a man's job if they don't want to and especially if they did not request for it.

B. Women who qualify mentally on the same level as men...should have equal jobs and pay as men. However, women physically are no match to men's physical superiority when it comes to hard manual labor and should not be expected to perform as the men do.[13]

The complaints this worker gathered indicate that many women supported demands for equal rights but resented the distortion and misuse of this issue by the company. Campbell's practices in handling demands for equal rights evolved from, and in turn fed, the resentment that grew among some sectors of the American public in the 1970s against the limited gains made by women and minorities in the previous decade. Thus the segmentation within the Campbell Soup Company again reflected divisions within the larger society of which it was a part.

In earlier days in Camden, union activists had united with women and, especially, African American workers to break down the barriers of discrimination. African American production worker Sadie Harris noted that in the Camden plants women could choose whether or not they wanted to take jobs previously limited to men. She said she decided to stay with her old job, though some of her friends took jobs as jitney drivers, formerly a "male" occupation.[14] Those occupying the lower rungs in the Sacramento plant did not have a strong and socially conscious union to coordinate the struggle. It just was not an issue their Teamsters local concerned itself with.

There was, however, a groundswell of protest by one group and its allies in Sacramento. This alliance took place, however, not within the union but with people in the community and other cannery workers in northern California. Mexican American employees had witnessed the recent success of the United Farm Workers under the leadership of César Chávez. A former Libby employee, Rubén Reyes, attempted to build a similar campaign among all Chicano cannery workers in northern California. With no leadership from their union to address their grievances, Mexican American workers at Campbell thronged to Reyes's crusade. Campbell's Sacramento plant manager became extremely concerned with this development. "The Mexicans feel that it is now time that they become recognized and are far more militant and—the larger part of this group—very radical." He was even more afraid of Reyes, "the most radical of them all, really revolutionary" who "had a pretty strong following in the first shift Labeling Department. . . . This bunch is 'trouble.'" The manager felt that the company's attempt to co-opt Chicano leadership by promoting some to supervisory positions had backfired. "The workers seem to look on them as 'Uncle Toms' and instead of the employees relating well to a Mexican supervisor, which we had hoped to be the case, it has been the opposite."[15]

Mexican workers in another part of the country proved to be an even bigger headache for Campbell and achieved one of the few victories for labor in the 1980s. Also inspired by the example of Chávez, Baldemar Velásquez founded the Farm Labor Organizing Committee in the late 1960s to organize workers in the fields around Campbell's Napoleon, Ohio, plant in the north-western section of that state. After patient and tenacious organizing over the next decade and the refusal of the soup company to meet with them, FLOC members voted in 1978 to strike all Campbell tomato operations in Ohio. Campbell management maintained that it had nothing to do with the farmworkers; it merely contracted with growers to provide tomatoes at an agreed price, and it was the growers' concern to decide what to pay their workers. As Velásquez related, the farm workers "soon discerned that it was the agricultural corporations, rather than the growers, who controlled the conditions. . . . Most farmers were contracted in the crops we harvested and paid an amount per ton or other unit. The company pressed the farmer and the farmer pressed us for productivity. . . . I wondered if the company ever had an appreciation for those of us at the bottom of the supply chain."[16] Just as giant retailers in the 1990s washed their hands of any responsibility for the child labor and sweatshop conditions of their subcontractors in Latin America and Asia, Campbell steadfastly refused to acknowledge any obligation to the workers who picked the crops that went into its food products.

In its response to the FLOC, Campbell was continuing a long and unbroken tradition. In 1956 and 1962 the company even refused to allow a union representation election for its direct agricultural employees at its mushroom plant in Prince Crossing, Illinois. The company claimed that under National Labor Relations Act rules, agricultural workers were not entitled to union protection. When 113 of 120 workers at Prince Crossing signed union cards in 1962 and went out on strike for union recognition, Campbell went on the offensive in a propaganda campaign to demonstrate the excellent conditions that it claimed its mushroom workers labored under. Ignoring the fact that almost 95 percent of the workers had signed union cards, the company blamed a Chicago priest (who had "developed a jaundiced view on American exploitation of Mexican labor") for "calling the tune." When workers in Campbell plants around the country failed to recognize picket lines set up by the striking union, a company leaflet informed the workers, "all employees are passing through the picket line. . . . You are acting alone." Predictably, in the absence of solidarity, the union campaign failed.[17]

The movement that grew into the FLOC had a far more positive outcome. Unlike the Prince Crossing campaign, which was initiated from the outside by a Teamsters union local, the FLOC grew organically from within the immigrant farm laborer community itself. In the 1950s, Baldemar Velásquez, though only a small child, had worked the fields with his family along the migrant routes extending out of his native Texas. Only after his family settled in north-western Ohio was he able to go to school. He overcame discrimination and language barriers and eventually excelled in his studies. With the help of a supportive priest he obtained a scholarship and attended college, where he learned the history of his people and came in contact with the civil rights movement. After working as a volunteer with the Congress of Racial Equality (CORE) and inspired by the example of César Chávez, he returned home committed to organizing the Mexican farmworkers in the communities around the Campbell plant in Napoleon. Such a goal was close to insurmountable. The UCAPAWA had made several heroic attempts to organize farmworkers in various parts of the country in the late 1930s, but most efforts were eventually defeated, leading the union to change its focus from the fields to the canneries. Agricultural workers were excluded from the coverage of the National Labor Relations Act, and vigilantes and growers' organizations dealt ruthlessly with any laborers who dared to challenge their authority. Further, many farmworkers were migrants, making the job of building stable unions all the more difficult. At least this last obstacle was a little easier to overcome for FLOC organizers, for many people who worked the fields of northwestern Ohio lived there year round. However, many did not, instead following the seasons to Texas and Florida every winter. In dealing with this issue, Velásquez and the FLOC demonstrated their creative approach. Since the organizers came from within the community, they were intimately aware of when and where migrant workers were traveling, and so they too moved south to continue organizing efforts in the off-season.[18]

When FLOC workers on tomato farms voted to strike Campbell in 1978, however, they soon realized that they were at a serious disadvantage in any competition with the mammoth food-processing company. A standard union-recognition campaign would have almost no chance of success. But at this point the FLOC again displayed its creative approach, one that grew out of the fact that the FLOC was as much a movement as a union. Without a government labor board to turn to, the farmworkers took their cause to the general public, calling for a citizens' boycott of all Campbell products. Opening a second front in their struggle with the company, the FLOC called on religious, labor, and student groups to set up committees across the country to build the boycott and pressure Campbell to settle with the people who picked its tomatoes. In a campaign reminiscent of the earlier United Farm Worker boycotts of grapes and lettuce, supporters eagerly took up the cause. Students at the University of Notre Dame voted 2,012 to 1,321 to make their campus Campbell-free, and the Sisters of Providence submitted a shareholder resolution calling on the company to study the social impact of its practices on the agricultural workers in Ohio. Campbell responded with its own two-pronged defense. First, it claimed it had no responsibility in the matter, for the farmworkers were not its direct employees. Second, it moved to eliminate the problem by using Campbell's favored method for dealing with labor problems, by eliminating the workers. It ramped up its program to require that growers harvest all Campbell tomatoes mechanically, and its success rate rose from 30 percent of Ohio tomatoes picked by machine in 1978 to a remarkable 80 percent the following year. Automation had a devastating effect on the numbers required to work the harvest, though hundreds of workers were still needed. The number of Campbell FLOC members revived again in 1983 when workers in the company's Vlasic pickle division joined the movement in Michigan. In that year, FLOC organized its most visible and dramatic action against Campbell. Farmworkers marched in a 550-mile trek from Ohio to company headquarters in Camden, all along the way publicizing their issue and gaining support. When they arrived in the city, a special mass was held in the Catholic Cathedral of the Immaculate Conception for them, and, in a ritual deep with religious symbolism, fifteen priests washed the feet of the marchers. The next day the farmworkers marched to company headquarters and presented a petition listing their grievances. Finally the company began talks with the FLOC and the growers, and in February 1986 all parties signed a unique three-way labor contract that covered eight hundred workers. Among the features of the agreement was the creation of a commission that had the legal power to arbitrate and resolve differences, in the absence of National Labor Relations Board jurisdiction. By the 1980s most of the unions in Campbell's plants had settled into a comfortable business unionism and had forgotten much of their history of progressive social unionism. The immigrants who worked at the bottom of the Campbell supply chain, however, resurrected that tradition and again demonstrated its relevance and power.[19]

Campbell's treatment of Mexican migrants in the fields and women and minorities in its plants made clear the continued centrality of labor segmentation to the company and also hinted at the difficulty it would have in adjusting to its new public role as corporate good citizen. John T. Dorrance had not contributed even a dollar to charity and, at least until the company went public in 1954, executives cared little about how various publics perceived Campbell Soup beyond its role as producer of reliable low-cost food products. Least of all did it concern itself with criticisms from African Americans, women, or migrant workers. Yet a combination of new legal restraints, lessening public acceptance of overt discriminatory practices, and long-term pressure from some of its unions pushed the company into the realization that it would be better to make some modest gestures in the direction of corporate responsibility. As described in chapter 6, this change began in the 1960s and, by the late 1970s, was the established company line. Still, as employment practices in Sacramento and the FLOC boycott showed, it never challenged core company policies. By the early 1970s over half of the production workers in Camden were African American or Puerto Rican, earning the company praise from the *New York Times* for its "progressive hiring practices."[20] Still, in 1974 the New Jersey Division on Civil Rights filed a complaint against Campbell resulting from the low number of female and minority supervisors. Of 140 first-line supervisors, 126 were men and 119 were white, though 54 percent of production workers were from minority groups. The company reached an agreement with the state agency two months later, promising to increase the numbers of female supervisors to 15 percent of the total, and minority supervisors to 30 percent.[21] In contrast to Campbell's earlier hostility to even an antidiscrimination clause in its union contracts, the company readily conceded to Local 80's demands for the addition of Martin Luther King Jr.'s birthday as a company holiday in 1976 and the addition of "age" as a new category covered by the contract's antidiscrimination clause in 1978. In that year Campbell also agreed to print copies of the contract in Spanish, at company expense.[22] In belated reaction to the second-class status it had long assigned to its women employees, the company organized a "Leadership Opportunities for Women" conference in 1982. The next year, just a few years before the plants would close, Cheryl Evans began training as the company's first and only female powerhouse worker. Hired in 1968, her longtime interest in machines had led her to attend evening courses and become certified as a boiler operator by the state, but only in 1983 was she able to begin to put her knowledge to work as a powerhouse trainee.[23] Opportunities for a handful of individuals—in the power house or as first-line supervisors—were a welcome change, but they could not replace the collective victories that had uplifted thousands through the unity forged on the shop floor and the picket lines in earlier years.

From Conflict to Collusion

Campbell management's modification of its approach toward its segmented labor force was superficial; a public image of corporate responsibility covered continuing deep fissures in its treatment of its workforce. But it made a substantive change in its strategy for dealing with unions. Following the defeat of the coordinated bargaining strike in 1968 and aided by the collaborationist stance of the AMC leadership, company management worked to support "responsible" union leadership that could help it finally gain control of the shop floor and prevent strikes. As it concurrently ramped up the automation of many work processes, the company in return accepted contract demands for moderate wage increases for its declining workforce. Thus its earlier three-pronged strategy of production speedup, labor segmentation, and antiunionism was replaced by more production speedup and continued labor segmentation, but now made possible with the collusion of "responsible" union leaders. The new approach was only partially successful with Local 80, where many dedicated union activists remained. Other Local 80 officers, however, willingly went along with the new regime, along with national AMC leaders and, to an uneven degree, Teamster officials. Many labor historians have characterized the period between the late 1940s and the early 1970s as an era of a grand labor-management accord, in which unions shed radical activists, demands beyond bread-and-butter issues, and rank-and-file democracy in return for security and steadily rising wages and benefits. Though that characterization is an oversimplification, it describes fairly accurately what happened in Camden in a much later period. Due to a combination of persistent rank-and-file activism and militant and supportive national unions between 1940 and 1968, a progressive social unionism held sway in Campbell's Camden plants until much later than was the case for the dominant industries in the United States. Only after the decline of activism in Local 80 and the UPWA's merger into the AMC did the Camden plants belatedly follow the earlier trend. The looming crisis for the American labor movement, of course, was not limited to the AMC. The Faustian deal that Cold War–era leaders of the AFL–CIO made with corporations and the Democratic party began to unravel as early as the 1970s, and union members were left with little to protect themselves against the ravages of late-twentieth-century capitalism.[24]

The leaders of the AMC were uncomfortable with their new packinghouse locals from the day the agreement was signed merging all UPWA locals into the AMC. The old American Federation of Labor union got its start representing butchers and related craft workers, while the UPWA always focused on the industrial organization of all workers in the packinghouses. And except during a few strikes, the AMC's relations with employers were far more cordial than the UPWA's confrontational stance. Thus, once AMC leadership put an end to the unpleasant 1968 coordinated bargaining strike, it lost no time in making overtures to Campbell's president W. B. Murphy regarding their future relationship. Less than six months after the end of the strike, AMC executive vice president Harry Poole sent a special-delivery letter to Campbell's vice president for personnel, W. E. Harwick. He related the results of a meeting attended by AMC president Thomas J. Lloyd, secretary-treasurer Patrick Gorman, vice president and long-time South Jersey AMC leader Leon Schachter, and himself, at which they discussed their relationship with Campbell Soup:

> I thought you would be interested to know that we reviewed the relationship that existed prior to our last contract negotiations for the Soup plants, as well as our last negotiations. We were unanimous in our opinion that our International Union would prefer to have our relationship with your Company continue the same as it was prior to our last negotiations.[25]

In other words, the AMC officials wanted to return to the amicable status that had existed between Campbell and the old AMC locals in Napoleon and several poultry plants, and now they wanted to extend it to the former UPWA plants as well. Campbell executives reciprocated, though they scolded the unionists for their earlier foolish behavior. Campbell chief executive Murphy told AMC officials that he did not hold them primarily responsible for the events of 1968: "We never felt that the relationship between our Company and the locals of the Meat Cutters had reached a low point. It was our feeling that the Meat Cutters had let the Washington coordinated bargaining specialists take over the responsibility of the Meat Cutters." The deterioration in the union leadership's relations with its members after the AMC takeover of the UPWA was demonstrated most starkly in one of the original packinghouse locals. In May 1971, management at Armour, one of the "Big Four" meatpackers, complained to AMC president Thomas J. Lloyd that Local P-4 was violating the contract. Without any investigation, Lloyd telegrammed local officials ordering them to stop their contract violations. P-4 president John Dettwiler wrote Lloyd in disbelief that the international president would take the word of the company over his members,' and told Lloyd that "we're disgusted" with the AMC "leadership." Former UPWA leader Jesse Prosten also sent an angry memo to Lloyd, blasting him for his disruptiveness and for undermining bargaining.[26]

The renewed friendly relationship between AMC International officials and Campbell management soon paid off for both parties. During a grassroots revolt in the summer of 1970 to decertify the AMC local at Campbell's Salisbury, Maryland, frozen food plant, company and union officials had frequent meetings—unbeknownst to plant employees—and exchanged materials obtained from the decertification campaign. The campaign was led by activist shop stewards "not to rid themselves of a Union, but to get, in their opinion, a better or stronger Union." Under the direction of company management, the local AMC officials defeated the insurgency and maintained their posts, and Campbell retained a docile union in its Salisbury plant.[27]

The mending of relations at the top between Campbell and the AMC continued in the following years. During the botulism scare in 1971, AMC secretary-treasurer Patrick Gorman sent his condolences to Campbell president Murphy, expressing the satisfaction of his membership with the "fine relationship we have had with the Campbell Soup Company" and bemoaning the fact that "the world in which we live is more prone to criticize than to give praise."[28]

The shift in Campbell's strategy from conflict to collusion was not limited to its relations with the Amalgamated Meat Cutters. Though the AMC represented most of its production workers, one very important site, the soup plant in Sacramento, was represented by the Teamsters. There, as in Salisbury, the union membership gradually lost faith in their local, while the company worked to prop up the union for its own reasons. Between 1966 and 1977, a majority of Sacramento union members had voted down every contract but one. However, because of the Teamsters' constitutional requirement for a two-thirds vote to strike, the will of the majority had always been stifled. The weak and ineffective leadership of the local became a more serious concern to the company as insurgent movements began challenging the Teamster-company regime, increasingly allied with the growing militant Chicano movement (discussed earlier in this chapter). The plant manager complained that the international union "allows [Campbell Local 228 officers] to fall on their faces and then comes in after negotiations are completed and ratification has failed to 'pull them out of the fire'—*and this is at our behest.*" Campbell's vice president of personnel argued that the company must do more to strengthen the union: "We started a program last winter designed to work with Union Leadership to strengthen their relations with the membership. We must continue this effort."[29] This program bore little fruit by the time he made this statement in 1977. Workers looked at the union as almost an extension of the company, as demonstrated by some of the comments collected in the Usery survey:

> This union is hopelessly ineffective and of no use to anyone but the company.
> In reference to [the] union, we might as well give the company our $12.00 a month.
> What union? We don't have one here.[30]

Though Campbell's new approach to its unions was most obvious in its outlying plants, the company moved to modify its former antagonistic stance even in Camden. Former steward Franklin Williams has commented that "the company got along with the union more as time went on," and industrial engineer Edward Cheeseman has made the same point, adding that union problems declined by the 1970s after its radical leaders "departed," though he recalls that some radical stewards remained. By 1971, a *New York Times* reporter observed that relations between Local 80 and plant management were improved over the 1968 low, and Joseph Gallo, president of the International Association of Machinists (IAM) mechanics, boasted of a "very good relationship with the company." Relations between the Camden unions and Campbell became even more cooperative over the next several years. The union contract, formerly a document that recorded the relative strengths of the two parties and the tentative truce reached in their ongoing class war, began to look more like just another publication of the personnel department. Starting with Local 80's 1978 contract, company "General Information" was printed inside the front cover. In addition to providing company phone numbers, the information page instructed employees to inform the company of any personal changes, accidents, and, especially, unexpected absences from work. In the negotiations leading to the contract, union recording secretary Sylvester Akins made the point that the company could include this kind of information in paychecks. However, after the union committee demanded (and won) the removal of the most egregious of the proposed company statements (such as "Be familiar with all of the Rules for Personal Conduct"), it accepted the inclusion of the company information page. By 1988 the back cover of the contract was adorned by a smiling and pudgy "Campbell Kid" surrounded by large letters proclaiming "THINK SAFETY."[31]

If a "labor-management accord" came belatedly to the Campbell Soup Company, it shared much with the reputed social contract that labor historians retroactively applied in their analyses of the 1950s and 1960s. Nelson Lichtenstein has shown that, beyond "a certain industrial relations stability" in core industries, many of the tenets of such an accord are questionable. He makes the important point, however, that, to whatever degree such a compact existed, it was the result not of labor's strength but of its weakness. By the late 1940s labor was in political retreat, as resurgent business elites challenged the New Deal and pushed the Taft-Hartley Act through Congress. Further, the Congress of Industrial Organizations (CIO) had sharply weakened itself by expelling its most militant unions. Thus, the accord "was less a mutually satisfactory concordat than a dictate imposed upon [the]...labor movement.... It was a product of defeat, not victory."[32]

In the same way, the new, more cooperative relationship between Campbell and its unions did not mark an acceptance by the company of an equal partnership between the two. Rather than emerging from the strength of its unions, the new order was imposed by management on a set of divided and severely weakened unions. When workers' organizations at Campbell's plants had been united, and when militant unions like the UCAPAWA/FTA and the UPWA led them, they were often able to fight the company to a draw. Sometimes they even prevailed, as in two post–World War II confrontations (see chapter 4). Yet that period can hardly be characterized as one of a labor-management accord. It was instead the heyday of the company's fiercest antiunionism. Only after the destruction of FTA, the splitting of Campbell's locals into different international unions, the decimation of Local 80's leftist leadership, and finally the defeat of the 1968 unity strike and the dissolution of the UPWA was Campbell willing to change its approach to its unions. During the ensuing post-1968 "accord," the company personnel department and union negotiating committees worked out moderate pay and benefit improvements in collective bargaining sessions. But—except for minor irritations from some remaining combative shop stewards—the company moved forward unhindered in its implementation of automation and lean production methods. Such a change for Local 80 required that its surviving progressive social unionists—by this point, mostly African Americans—be sidelined or at least pacified. Just as the CIO leadership had disciplined its own unruly members to the benefit of capital at the start of the "labor-management accord," national AMC leaders and Local 80's business unionists collaborated in attempting to turn the once-militant local into a more well-behaved organization.

🍃 The Marginalization of Local 80

By the early 1970s, Local 80's business unionists—especially in the person of business manager Joseph Colangelo—had become entrenched in the local. Colangelo had been a steward, recording secretary, and labor standards specialist in earlier years, but he had always kept his distance from the leftist leadership of the local. A few years after former communist Tony Valentino resigned as business agent, Colangelo ran for the position of business manager on a slate challenging the incumbents. He and his running mate for president, Joseph Speight, swept the election. From that point in 1957 until his retirement in 1983, and through a series of various presidents, he held the powerful business manager position (reclassified as "secretary-treasurer" for part of that period). In keeping with the Local 80 tradition of splitting the top two union positions between white and black candidates, all of the presidents he served with (with a one-year exception) were African Americans. As the proportion of African Americans in the Camden plants passed the 50 percent point, Colangelo always made a point of reiterating his support for black workers and against discrimination. However, Joseph Gallo, a leader of the secession movement of the all-white Maintenance Department in the early 1950s, counted Colangelo as a "good friend": "After [Tony] Valentino, [John] Tisa, and [Sylvia] Neff went to jail, people on our side got in.... Joe Colangelo... was the bigwig of the union after we got Valentino out." Though relations between Local 80 and the new IAM local were strained at the beginning, "our relationship got good around 1960 with Colangelo."[33]

If the major development in Campbell's Camden plants during the 1970s and 1980s was the gradual but continuous and unchallenged decline in the size of the workforce due to automation, work process redesign, outsourcing, and transfer of work to new plants, it is also true that Local 80 did a fairly good job of maintaining and even increasing pay levels in a time of high inflation and improving benefits for the workers who still had jobs. For example, wage rates rose 16 to 23 cents per hour (depending on labor grade) in the first year of the 1972 contract, 42 to 60 cents in 1978, and 26 to 36 cents in 1988. As a result, starting rates of just over $2.00 an hour before the 1968 strike rose to $4.40 ten years later and $9.17 in the final year of operations (1989). To keep level with inflation (as measured by the Consumer Price Index), the starting rate would have needed to rise to $3.84 and $7.87 in each of these later years. Thus, despite the fact that American workers on average lost ground to the cost of living between the early 1970s and the late 1980s, Campbell production workers continued to improve their relative position, albeit for an ever shrinking workforce. Campbell management was willing to make such concessions for the very reason that it was able to take whatever steps it wished to improve productivity without the kinds of union objections or guerilla actions by workers on the plant floor that had been a part of everyday life at the Camden plants during the UCAPAWA/FTA and UPWA era. This earlier opposition to job-cutting productivity measures had not stopped the attrition of employees, but it did certainly make the task more troublesome for Campbell. Though the effects are difficult to quantify, the decline in the size of the workforce in the pre-AMC era (1940–1968) averaged about 1.4 percent annually. In the AMC period (1968–79) the rate rose to 3.5 percent, and in the first seven years (1979–1986) of Local 80's final union, the United Food and Commercial Workers (UFCW—see below) to 4.6 percent per year. In the following four years the number of workers dropped to zero, as Campbell took the ultimate step in its quest for low-cost production by moving work to its new Maxton plant. While there was no guarantee that the union strategies of earlier years would have stopped or slowed the decline, earlier struggles suggest that the possibility was real. The history of the early years of Local 80 abounds with examples of how intraplant solidarity stopped speedups and reductions in the number of workers assigned to various processes. And in 1946 the interplant solidarity of Camden and Chicago stopped the company plan to bypass the union and hire lower-paid workers in the seasonal Salisbury plant. The abortive 1968 strike may have provided a similar lesson had it been allowed to develop. In any case, the benefits for the employees that resulted from the "labor-management accord" of the post-1968 era were temporary, at best.[34]

The focus on limited bread-and-butter issues set the tone not only for the Local 80 leadership but also increasingly for the range of debate within the membership as well. Challengers for union office attacked incumbents for mishandling a vacation pay dispute with the company and for raising dues, yet ignored critical issues concerning job-cutting productivity changes. On one non-bread-and-butter issue, however, there was repeated protest: the loss of internal union democracy. Yet ultimately the fragmented and weak opposition within Local 80 after the early 1970s failed to revive the local's democratic traditions.

Nine months after the bitter defeat in 1968 there was an equally bitter union election. Though incumbent Joseph Colangelo ran unopposed for business manager, his running mate for president, incumbent Clarence Clark, ran against Joseph Speight. Colangelo and Speight had both won office together in 1957 when they challenged and crushed the old-line leadership. The sad state of Local 80 politics by 1969 resulted in name-calling and even a reversion to "red-baiting." Clark and Colangelo's Administration ticket promised union members that it would "Keep all Communists Out of Your Union" and charged that its challengers' leaflets were being written by union founder and Communist John Tisa. Speight's Concerned Members ticket blasted back that "If the two present 'conniving' 'sell-out' 'red-baiting' 'Company Minded' Uncle 'Tom Turkeys' are reelected, kiss your Union Hall Bye Bye." Clark and Colangelo easily held on to their positions in this and the next election in 1971, in which two other Concerned opponents—Fred Redd and Louis Vitarelli—charged that the union officials were mishandling their jobs.[35]

In the intervening year between these two elections, the Clark and Colangelo team pushed through constitutional changes that drastically reduced rank-and-file democracy. The shop steward system had always been the backbone of Local 80's activism and the means by which workers and union officials were connected. For thirty years workers in each department had elected their stewards by secret ballot. With the new constitution, the union leadership appointed all stewards. The new rules also abolished departmental meetings, which had been the primary place where workers raised concerns and grievances to their stewards. Though opponents of the changes claimed that the new constitution was voted down in a raucous voice vote, the international union backed Local 80's officers.[36] The national AMC, in fact, was working to suppress the untidy democratic traditions of the former UPWA locals now in its fold. AMC leader Patrick Gorman expressed his exasperation with members who refused to follow the directions of their leaders in a memo to his loyal subordinate Stephen Coyle:

> In every situation where there are a few loud voices raised there is a human inclination for the others to join in the chorus. It hasn't been too long ago when things were not as they are now and if someone got up in the local union meeting making rash statements, someone would shout, "Sit down!", then two or three more would join in and the chairman would bang the gavel and everybody would be shouting, "Sit down!" It's funny what a few years will do. Now the fellow who talks rashly is usually joined by the hammer and anvil chorus.

Yet he had faith that reason would prevail: "This has been proven when a good proposal is submitted to a referendum vote and it's always 'Yes'...instead of giving in to the hooligans shouts of vote 'No.'"[37] Still, there were even fewer problems if the members did not vote at all. In 1978, Local 80's leaders informed its members that the international union had decreed that dues would be raised and that, due to a recent national convention decision, no vote to approve the increase would be required.[38] Campbell's Camden workers, nonetheless, continued to press their grievances as best they could, and many worked hard to keep their union as democratic as possible. Still, South Jersey's longtime AMC leader Leon Schachter reassured Gorman that "[Local 80] is one of the Local Unions which has been more 'Amalgamated' than any of the other packinghouse locals"—a statement that earlier Local 80 activists would have considered slanderous.[39]

One of the most troubling periods in Local 80 history surrounded the election of 1975 and its aftermath. After their handy defeats of all previous opponents, all seemed to be going well for Clarence Clark and Joseph Colangelo. In 1973 the New Jersey Labor Press Council presented its Martin Luther King Award to Clark, and he was further honored at the annual A. Phillip Randolph Dinner that year. Colangelo and AMC's Gorman exchanged letters promising to get together for a songfest. But then, shockingly, Clark was defeated for the office of president by a young upstart, Ronald Redd, whose father had run against Clark four years earlier. The rest of the incumbent team remained, including the two other paid union officials, secretary-treasurer Colangelo and vice president Samuel "Jack" Williams. Leon Schachter quickly moved to get the defeated Clark a position with the international union. Just four months after the election, Colangelo made a strange request to AMC's international president. In order to stem a shortfall in funds, he suggested that the three paid officials be cut back to two, with the third returning to the plant. The two who should remain, according to Colangelo, were the vice president and the secretary-treasurer: Williams, who had held his position for ten years, and himself, who had held office for eighteen years; the new president should be canned. He complained that president Redd would not accept the petition to hold a vote on Colangelo's motion—which would send Redd back to the plant. Because of Redd's resistance, the plan went no further. The next year Colangelo and Gorman made good on their promise to get together; at the AMC national convention, Colangelo gave a rendition of a song he had composed, "A Tribute to Patrick Gorman."[40]

In July 1976, Local 80 president Ronald Redd left for a vacation to Montreal with his wife. On their return to South Jersey, they checked in to a motel in Bordentown, several miles north of Camden. The next morning a motel maid heard several shots. Police found Redd and his wife Brenda shot to death. Though no suicide note was found and police were unable to discover a motive, they ruled the deaths "an apparent murder-suicide." They claimed that Redd had shot his wife with a .32 caliber rifle, then used his toe to trigger the final shot. Four weeks later Mother Teresa, who was visiting Camden, comforted the victims' eight-year-old daughter Dana. A week before her visit Joseph Colangelo informed AMC's president that the local had abolished the office of vice president, and that Jack Williams would be moved to the office of president. To make the changes official, Colangelo scheduled three meetings—one per shift—in place of the traditional weekend membership meeting. Some workers protested, but again the AMC upheld the revised plan. The deterioration in members' interest was evident in the numbers voting. In the 1957 election that brought Colangelo and Joseph Speight to office for the first time, 2,176 members had voted. Though Local 80 still counted about two thousand workers on its rolls, only 159 voted in all three 1976 meetings combined. The constitutional amendment and the confirmation of Jack Williams as president both passed overwhelmingly.[41]

Over the next decade Williams proved himself a dedicated and concerned union leader, but he was able to do little about the company's unstoppable program to lower labor costs. When a layoff of three hundred workers was announced in 1979, Williams told a reporter, "I'm concerned with my members and this community," and he warned of the consequences for Camden, in which, he said, almost half of the minority workers were already unemployed. Two years later the company gave the union only a few days notice of another layoff of 230 of its 1,670 production employees. There was no longer any real contest between the company and the union. The old Local 80 was no more, and the company called all the shots.[42]

When the UPWA merged with the AMC in 1968 as a very junior partner, at least its old locals made up a significant minority in the union, and several of its leaders moved to posts in the packinghouse division of the merged union. But in 1979 its clout was further diminished when the AMC joined with the Retail Clerks International Union to form the United Food and Commercial Workers (UFCW). Some of the old "P" locals tried to keep alive the militant spirit of the UPWA, but no longer with any support from their international union. In the most notorious case, the UFCW national leadership even actively worked against a strike by one of its locals. In 1985, when Local P-9 in Austin, Minnesota struck Hormel, the UFCW initially followed common practice and endorsed the strike. Yet after the old packinghouse local began building a broad social movement in support of the strike and initiated an imaginative corporate campaign against Hormel, the international union withdrew support and then worked to undermine the movement and the strike. The UFCW was interested in maintaining cooperative relationships with its employers, not returning to class-struggle unionism. Thus, Local P-80's gradual slide into ineffective business unionism would hardly be challenged by its parent union. Most Camden workers were, in fact, only vaguely aware at best that their new International had changed from the AMC to the UFCW.[43]

✄ Leaving Camden

Campbell management had tamed its labor problem and had settled into a comfortable truce, if not quite a social compact, with its unions. It was moving ahead unhindered in implementing new cost-saving programs that included more automation and outsourcing. Yet by the 1980s it was becoming clear that all of its low-cost production strategies, which had allowed the company to keep its flagship plant in Camden for over a century, would not be enough for it to resist the lure anymore of a different strategy that promised higher profits: moving all production out of Camden. Every other large or midsize firm in the city that had not gone out of business had already moved to greener pastures. For Campbell, however, Camden had always provided many advantages. Most important, the city was surrounded by the South Jersey and Pennsylvania farms that supplied its prize ingredient, the tomato, and most of the other vegetables it needed. After its workers had turned these ingredients into soup and other food products, Camden was ideally situated for distribution to its largest market along the eastern seaboard and beyond, with excellent rail and marine connections. The city was also ideally located for the kind of close supervision that its majority owners, the Dorrance family, preferred. John T. Dorrance and his brother Arthur had micromanaged virtually every operation in the company until Arthur's death in 1946. Though the Dorrances brought in nonfamily chief executives after World War II, John Dorrance Jr. (known to everyone as Jack) kept a close watch on the company as chairman of the board until his retirement in 1984 (though even then he remained chairman of the board's executive committee). Over many decades the company had invested heavily in plant and equipment at its two Camden plants and a large warehouse on the city's border. Tens of thousands of the area's residents had worked for the company, acquiring the experience, developing the skills, and providing the labor without which no soup and no profits could have been made. Thus, the proximity to raw materials, the excellent transportation facilities, the millions of dollars sunk in investments, and the pool of experienced employees made the Dorrances reluctant to move their home plant anywhere else. A constellation of factors centering on changes in the Dorrance family and the increasing difficulty of keeping the aging Camden plants as profitable as newer plants, however, made such a move a real possibility, though by no means a certainty, by the mid-1980s. And, though the company had reached an accommodation with its unions, its management always preferred not to deal with unions at all.

As Jack Dorrance approached retirement in the mid-1980s, the third generation of Dorrances—Jack's children and his sisters' children—were becoming increasingly restless with their patrimony. None had worked at Campbell (beyond a short stint after college), and none really understood the family business. Even more troubling to Jack Dorrance was the rising animosity between his children, who were bequeathed the major share of their grandfather's estate, and their cousins. Those heirs who did not bear the Dorrance name began to look at their Campbell stock as an investment, not a family heirloom, and some advanced the idea of selling their shares when the company's profit rate lagged sporadically through the 1970s and 1980s.[44]

As a consequence, Gordon McGovern, who assumed the company presidency in 1980, was under intense pressure to turn Campbell once again into a profit-making powerhouse. McGovern reorganized the management structure to encourage innovation and entrepreneurship, and he embarked on an ambitious expansion and acquisition program. To finance his plans, he did something no one had ever dared at Campbell: he borrowed one hundred million dollars in the company's first public debt offering. Unfortunately for McGovern, some of his new ideas did not work out as planned, and many of his investments would pay off only after his departure. He snapped to a *Forbes* reporter in 1988, "We're not running the company for the stock price"—not what the younger Dorrances wanted to hear.[45]

Throughout the 1980s company executives and business reporters spoke disparagingly of the continuing existence of the anachronistic plants in Camden and Chicago. In the same *Forbes* article in which he ridiculed the chase for short-term profits, McGovern joined the chorus lamenting the inefficiencies of the old plants. "We make [soup] in big kettles like they did in 1910," with the reporter's rejoinder: "Nostalgic, yes. Efficient, no." McGovern added, "Anything 50, 60, 70 years old is out of date."[46] Company executives had threatened to move operations out of Camden throughout the twentieth century. In 1915 John T. Dorrance was about to move the entire company to a new model town south of Camden; during the 1934 strike Arthur Dorrance warned he might leave the city; and again similar threats were made in the early 1950s, during the 1968 strike, and in the late 1970s. But this time things were different; almost everyone knew they were "biding their time." The first and most ominous warning came in 1979, when the Campbell Soup Company announced it would no longer use South Jersey tomatoes for its soups. The vegetable that had been synonymous with the rise of the company, that John T. Dorrance had lavished with care and attention, fell to cheaper alternatives from the Midwest and California that could be harvested mechanically. The announcement, upsetting to South Jersey residents who had always taken pride in their region's famous tomatoes, was even more disconcerting to Campbell employees.[47] Suddenly South Jersey began to lose its special place in company tradition. Advances in breeding tomato varieties and growing techniques had doubled crop yields in South Jersey to twenty tons per acre by 1962. But the plant varieties best suited to the region and the fact that South Jersey was often subject to fall rains prevented the profitable use of harvesting machinery there. In areas where mechanical harvesters could be employed, notably California, their use exploded in the 1950s and 1960s, for they reduced harvesting costs by two-thirds. As a result the proportion of tomatoes in the U.S. grown in California grew from 20 percent before World War II to 50 percent by 1953. The development of the interstate highway system in the 1950s and the deregulation of the trucking industry later reduced costs of shipping ingredients as well as finished products. California's share of the tomato crop reached 90 percent by the 1990s. The efficiencies of West Coast tomato cultivation were so significant, in fact, that Campbell even discontinued using fresh tomatoes at its Napoleon plant, preferring to ship in concentrate produced in Sacramento.[48]

Increasingly, company spokesmen began denigrating the older plants, referring to the six-story jumble of buildings that made up Plant No. 1 as hopelessly behind the times (they no doubt felt the same about its unionized workforce). One needed only to compare the company's original plant with Campbell's newest facility in Maxton. When the first can of soup rolled off the line in Maxton in 1982, the trade journal *Food Engineering* gushed that it marked a "new era in food manufacturing" and presented the plant the journal's first annual award as "New Plant of the Year." Maxton's spacious design and red, white, and blue colors ostensibly made it look more like a shopping mall than a factory. The essence of its attractiveness, however, was its high-volume efficiency. Like all newer Campbell plants, all primary operations were on one floor, with ingredients entering at one end and finished products going out the other. The system was still a batch one rather than a continuous one because of the large variety of soups, but now automation was built into the very design of ever more segments of the production process. Engineers planned that eventually, "microprocessors [would] ... control everything." Though that hope was a bit overblown, new methods did eliminate much manual work and greatly increased line speeds. Equally as important as automation, significantly, was the carefully selected and trained workforce. Campbell's first consideration in planning its new plant was to select a location with low taxes and a plentiful and pliable labor supply. Maxton, on the rural southern edge of the state, fit the bill perfectly. Campbell reasonably expected that residents of Robeson County, where Maxton was situated, would be eager to work in the new plant. There were few opportunities in the largely agricultural county, and about a quarter of the population lived below the poverty line. About two-thirds of Maxton's population and a quarter of the county's was African American, while 38 percent of county residents were Native Americans of the Lumbee tribe. It had also been the site of Ku Klux Klan activity in the 1950s until five hundred armed Lumbee attacked a Klan rally and shot four Klansmen. No further Klan activity occurred in the county. Campbell made a heavy investment in training and set up many quality circles because, according to company vice president Andy Whitelaw, "We can't go back to the policeman's mode of using a sledgehammer." Plant manager Don Lanning was "most pleased by the attitude of the employees." Maxton appeared to have it all—superefficient production facilities and apparently happy workers. Camden's days were numbered.[49]

Though almost everyone expected that Campbell would soon shut down its oldest plants, there apparently was some disagreement about this at the highest levels of the company. Jack Dorrance and the wing of the Dorrance family that supported him were ambivalent about whether to abandon the city in which Jack's father began making condensed soup almost a century earlier. Company directors decided in any case to keep corporate headquarters in Camden. In 1957 the company had separated the corporate offices and production operations. Until then, the offices occupied the sixth floor of Plant No. 1. The new General Office Building, about a mile from the plants, was joined in 1971 by a pilot plant where new products and processes were tested. The company's commitment to Camden, at least as the continuing home for its corporate offices, seemed assured in April 1985 when Campbell announced that it would build a 120-million-dollar world headquarters building on the city's Delaware River waterfront. The proposed complex would also include a "world visitors' center" and be adjacent to a new aquarium that was announced the same day by New Jersey governor Thomas Kean. Together, the new waterfront construction was a significant step in the "redevelopment" of Camden as envisioned by corporate and government leaders. With no input from the residents of the city, the new plan divided Camden into a valuable waterfront section facing Philadelphia and the increasingly desperate postindustrial remainder. Campbell's commitment—though many of the specifics were still unclear—made the new plan a reality and reassured its white-collar employees that their jobs would not leave the area.[50]

More surprisingly, company spokesmen announced the same day that Campbell would embark on a complete modernization of the Camden plant to make it competitive with other company sites. Herbert Baum, head of the company's U.S. division, revealed the details of the thirty-seven-million-dollar project the following January. The company had considered moving production, he said. "But in the end, we decided that Camden offered an impressive array of advantages, especially its nearness to the major Northeast market and the fine transportation system which surrounds it, and we made the decision to modernize and keep our plant in Camden." Though the news was welcome, the road to modernization curiously appeared to consist mostly of cuts to various parts of the Camden operations and would result in the loss of another 450 jobs. "Highlights" included:

Discontinuing the in-house manufacture of metal cans in favor of purchasing them from outside vendors.
Eliminating the preparation... of fresh root vegetables.

Reducing the number of varieties of products produced at Camden and eliminating low-volume and more costly production runs. Consolidating warehousing... and selling an off-site warehouse. Demolishing unneeded or unused buildings totaling 690,000 square feet.[51]

Despite promises to keep the old manufacturing plant open, other changes portended a less positive future. After it stopped using fresh tomatoes in Camden in 1979, the company discontinued food processing at Plant No. 2 (where tomato pulp processing took place) in 1980. Though it continued canning operations there for several more years, it closed Plant No. 2 entirely in 1987.[52] The next year it shut down the Chicago plant. The second-oldest facility in the Campbell empire (opened in 1929), it had much in common with Camden's Plant No. 1. The plant had grown into a rambling conglomeration of six-story buildings, and a company spokesman said that it would not be worth the cost of turning it into a state-of-the-art facility. Even Chicago Local 194's president, Jewel Frierson, acknowledged the hopelessness of expecting the company to keep the old factory open. The union official described the thirteen freight elevators that, "even when they are working... can tie production up while ingredients on one floor are waiting to go to another floor. There's a lot of lost time with that vertical setup." Company spokesman David Hackney boasted that in the newer Napoleon, Ohio, and Paris, Texas, plants, "Production flows smoothly... in one door and out the other, Japanese-style."[53] Ominously, Campbell president McGovern, distressed over continuing declines in soup sales and under increasing pressures from disgruntled members of the Dorrance family, believed, according to a *Forbes* reporter, that the company's "plant paring was only half done" and that the old plants were doomed.[54]

Through 1987 and 1988 Campbell's profit margin continued to lag its competitors. Still, Jack Dorrance was able to keep discontent within the family from spilling over into the management of the company. In April 1989, however, the family patriarch died, and family members quickly broke into warring camps, some advocating a merger or sale of the company. Campbell stock rose sharply on speculation that the company was a good target for a takeover bid. In response, company directors decided to implement the decision almost everyone had been waiting for: on August 24, Campbell announced it would close its flagship plant in Camden. Along with cuts in smaller plants elsewhere, 2,800 employees would lose their jobs. Stock analysts applauded the move and the stock price rose again.[55]

CHAPTER 8

Legacies

"It was difficult to believe that so much of Camden's history could disappear in almost a whisper." Thus did a reporter record the reactions of witnesses to the implosion of Campbell Soup Company's Plant No. 1 on a crisp Sunday morning in November 1991: "As quickly and almost as quietly as an autumn leaf pulled from its branch by a gust of wind, a piece of Camden's history crumbled to the ground...in a vivid display of the city's daily tug of war between the old and new." Of course, Campbell had been too integral to Camden for too long for its history to suddenly disappear. But the apocalyptic three-second annihilation sent observers in search of hyperbolic metaphor. Even visitors who came for the spectacle were moved: "You just had a feeling something unbelievable was happening." But most of those who had spent their lives in the soup plant realized they could not truly express their feelings in words. Harry Nelson just remarked, "I really thought it would last forever." Dan McHenry, after noting that he had spent half his life in the plant, simply said, "It's sad."[1]

Perhaps part of the reason many former employees seemed numbed that day was that the plant demolition was just one in a series of devastating events—and not the last. The August 1989 announcement of the plant closing was followed less than three months later by the forced resignation of Gordon McGovern as Campbell's president. His efforts had not turned the company's fortunes around quickly enough for the demanding (or greedy, according to some Campbell workers) Dorrance clan that had profited from the company for so long. McGovern's successor, a corporate hatchet man named David W. Johnson who was adored by Wall Street, lost no time in setting the new tone at the company. On his first day on the job in January 1990, Johnson, accompanied by four trumpeters playing a fanfare of Campbell's "Mmm, Mmm, Good" advertising theme, presented himself to office workers at the general office a mile from the plant. He then announced that he was canceling plans for the new corporate headquarters building on the Camden waterfront. He followed this, on May 1, with a 19 percent cut in headquarters staff. Johnson's swaggering bravado and self-deprecating stunts were undergirded by actions like these that eliminated thousands of jobs and intimidated the survivors. Corporate units and manufacturing plants were forced to bid against each other for work; the losers were pushed out of the company and into unemployment. On March 1, 1991, the last can of beans rolled off the line in Plant No. 1. The Maxton, North Carolina, plant successfully bid for the work from Camden and struggled to become the first plant to drive total manufacturing costs below 50 percent of the retail price of its products. Johnson bragged to shareholders, as profits rose, that he had created "a more disciplined Campbell Soup Company": "We eliminated jobs. The result is a new mood." In a direct cut at his predecessor's claim not to be running the company for the stock price, Johnson declared, "Our purpose is to make money.... I am the servant of the shareowners."[2]

Meanwhile, Camden, with an official unemployment rate of 13 percent, suffered the loss of its final large manufacturing plant and 940 jobs. Joseph and Jennie Morrison, who had raised their family on the wages both had received from working at the plant, recall the day it closed down in early 1990. "It was a shame, a sorrowful day," remembers Joseph. Leona Laird was the last woman working in the plant. Though she had put forty-seven years into the company, she had been hoping to make it to fifty, a milestone reached by only a very few in Campbell's history. Many, however, had persevered twenty-five years and achieved a coveted spot on the Wall of Honor. When workers realized that the Wall of Honor was about to be destroyed in the implosion of the plant, several implored the company to save this monument to the employees who had dedicated their lives to the plant. Company officials just brushed them aside, saying nothing could be done, in stark contrast to their earlier apparent reverence for the wall.[3]

Fate saved, if just for a while, an even better known Campbell relic and created a minor headache for the company's new leadership. Despite the dynamite that leveled the six buildings, one of the Campbell's Soup-can-painted water towers atop the plant miraculously survived almost intact after crashing to the ground. Workers upset about the loss of the Wall of Honor, Camden residents accustomed to the sight of the famous red-and-white water towers, and a few amateur historic preservationists rallied to the cause of turning the giant soup can into a memorial to all who had worked there. The company at first adamantly refused to consider saving the water tower, but, after considerable agitation from the Yes We Can Save the Can Committee and much unwelcome publicity, it agreed to pay the demolition company ten thousand dollars for the tower. A local trucking company donated its services to carry the rusting tank to the South Jersey Port Corporation's Beckett Street Terminal to await refurbishment. The committee raised funds for the project and petitioned Governor Jim Florio to set aside a plot of waterfront land near Wiggins Park and the new aquarium as the Campbell Soup Company Employees Memorial Park. However, when Campbell's Johnson reneged on his promise to support the plan and fundraising efforts dwindled, the project died. The giant can rusted into oblivion.[4]

Remembrance of the past was no longer in vogue at Campbell. Anything that would not contribute to enhanced corporate earnings was eliminated, and reminders of the decrepit plant where the company had begun making soup were unwelcome. CEO David Johnson even discontinued the company's sponsorship of retired pilot plant manager Harry Nelson's trips to conventions of the Institute of Food Technology. Instead, when Johnson met Nelson at a gathering of a retirees' group that Nelson headed, the company president told the former manager, "I want to see what you can do to help Campbell Soup's bottom line." Nelson recalled, "I wanted to hit him." The company's neglect of its former workers affected many in even more serious ways. Pensions were not adjusted for inflation, and after a decade or more of retirement, many former employees were having a hard time making ends meet, though many others benefited from the rising share prices of company stock that they had received as a fringe benefit. In the most significant assault on the living standards of ex-employees, Campbell downgraded their medical insurance. After a series of cuts in benefits, many could no longer afford to get adequate medical care. Jorge Melendez, for example, who had numerous heart problems, had an implanted pacemaker. Though his doctor prescribed that he take a heart medication twice a day, Melendez took it only once a day because he could not afford the prescribed dosage: "The medical plan for retirees used to be great, but they cut it down." In response, some employees (including several who had been active unionists) contacted an attorney and pursued a suit against Campbell challenging changes in postemployment medical benefits. Although the union's Local 80 had gone out of existence with the plant closing, the original Amalgamated Meat

Cutters local in South Jersey, Leon Schachter's Local 56 (now affiliated with the United Food and Commercial Workers, or UFCW) filed a class-action suit on behalf of the former Campbell workers. The agreement they reached with the company, however, infuriated members of the Campbell Retirees Class Action Committee, who continued to use the old United Packinghouse Workers of America (UPWA) emblem of clasped black and white hands over the slogan "An Injury to One Is an Injury to All." Former union activist Armand Meccariello blasted the judge who brokered the agreement as well as the "corrupt unions who have helped Campbell Soup to divide Campbell Retirees." Promising that they would not "allow Campbell Soup to compromise one penny of what was unjustly stolen from us," the committee attempted to enlist the support of Camden's congressman Robert Andrews. The congressman, who liked to portray himself as a friend of labor, in reply merely sent them a booklet describing their legal rights. The medical benefits were never restored.[5]

If many former employees felt abandoned by the new leadership at the helm of the Campbell Soup Company, many of those still living in Camden, the city of its birth, were fighting the nightmare of the virtually total deindustrialization of the city. In its heyday, vigorous working-class neighborhoods filled the city. Residents walked or rode buses to jobs at Campbell, RCA, New York Shipbuiding, Esterbrook Pen, and many other industrial establishments. By the 1990s none of these factories remained. Campbell's headquarters (still located in the general office complex after plans for a new waterfront building were scuttled) and RCA's surviving offshoot, the military contractor L-3 Communications, employed almost exclusively white-collar suburbanites. A relative handful of jobs for Camden residents existed at the Camden campus of Rutgers University and at Cooper Hospital, but again suburban commuters filled most of the jobs. Without jobs, the future for Camden's residents was bleak. "You see all the empty factories.... Used to be so many people worked between RCA, Campbell Soup, Esterbrook," recalls former Campbell employee Franklin Williams. "When people talk about drugs, a job is the one thing that eliminates drugs.... When jobs go...." His voice drifts off wistfully, the meaning of his sentence clear enough not to require completion.[6]

The contrast between the ways that Campbell ex-employees and Camden residents experienced the hollowing out of the industrial core of their city, on the one hand, and what the owners of capital view simply as investment decisions, on the other, puts a human face on a conundrum pointed out by Jefferson Cowie and Joseph Heathcott. In introducing a collection of essays that begins to evaluate deindustrialization "beyond the ruins," they argue that this period is just "one episode in a long series of transformations within capitalism," following an earlier, also ephemeral, phase of industrial culture. Yet people living through these transformations experience them as devastating to their lives and communities, for "the aura of permanence that surrounded the industrial culture of Europe and the United States throughout the twentieth century has made the experience of deindustrialization seem more like the end of a historical epoch." As they and others have also made clear, these changes are not solely the result of impersonal economic forces.[7]

The lack of investment in Camden was exacerbated by the cynical plundering of the city for the benefit of a political machine, real estate developers, and suburban governments. This process did not begin after Campbell closed its soup factory; as Howard Gillette relates in *Camden after the Fall*, disinvestment and political missteps went hand-in-hand in the city for decades. Camden County, which includes well-off suburbs like Cherry Hill and Haddonfield as well as the city of Camden, used the city as a dumping ground for all of its unwanted waste. Assuming that the city was too desperate to refuse anything, the county sited its sewage treatment plant and a trash-to-steam plant there, complete with hundreds of trash trucks rumbling through its narrow streets daily. The county jail was located in downtown Camden, and the State of New Jersey built a state-of-the-art prison on the waterfront in North Camden. The county Democratic Party machine tightly controlled politics in the city and rewarded banks, developers, and construction unions that supported it with lucrative contracts.

The citizens of Camden, meanwhile, were virtually disenfranchised. Politicians and developers drew up plans to split the potentially profitable waterfront section facing Philadelphia from the devastated remainder of the city. A few perfunctory public hearings provided the only participation in redevelopment planning granted to city residents. Even more egregiously, the state coupled a sizable aid plan to a state-administered takeover of city government that removed the right of city residents to elect those who governed them. Not unexpectedly, almost all the aid money went to waterfront development and to well-connected developers. The economically and politically powerful assumed they could benefit at the city's expense because no one cared about the poor and mostly minority residents of the city.[8]

They neglected, however, to consider the opposition to their plans that the allegedly powerless city residents would organize themselves. In surprising eruptions of grassroots democracy in neighborhoods throughout the city, some involving former Campbell workers, Camden's citizens joined together to take charge of redeveloping their own communities and to oppose plans that would destroy those communities. Concerned Citizens of North Camden organized a land trust to rehabilitate abandoned houses, and Sacred Heart Church in South Camden did the same through its affiliate, the Heart of Camden (which also tapped into support from suburban parishioners). South Camden Citizens in Action organized rallies against the siting of another polluter in their midst—St. Lawrence Cement. A lawsuit initiated by the group even stopped operation of the cement plant for several months, until the company won an appeal in a higher court. In one of the biggest—though by no means permanent—victories against the city redevelopment plan and Cherokee Developers, residents of the Cramer Hill section used imaginative tactics that scuttled a plan that would have displaced 1,200 families to make room for upscale housing and a golf course. In an attempt to draw together neighborhood organizations fighting the political establishment across the city, activists formed Camden United in 2006.[9]

Though Camden residents were struggling for survival in the deindustrialized city, by the 1990s the Dorrance heirs were reveling in a level of wealth unknown even to John T. Dorrance. The policies of Campbell's new chief executive officer, David Johnson, were devastating to the cities that housed the old plants and were driving workers to higher levels of productivity at newer highly automated sites, and they were also succeeding in raising Campbell's profit margin. Return on sales skyrocketed from 0.1 percent in 1990 to 9.6 percent in 1996, moving it well above the average for food-products companies. Johnson's mantra that every action of the company must raise share value meant that the family, which still held 58 percent of the stock in 1995, gained enormously from the 14.2 percent compound annual growth rate for the Campbell stock price over five years. Still, some of the Dorrances were unhappy that they were constrained in their investments by having so much money tied up in Campbell stock. Yet if they sold the stock, an unacceptable portion would be lost in taxes on capital gains. John Dorrance III, the grandson of the "inventor" of Campbell's condensed soups, devised a novel way to avoid the taxes. He renounced his American citizenship and became an official resident of Dublin, Ireland. Though he now ranked as that country's richest resident, he continued to own property around the world, including a ranch in Wyoming (where he had earlier failed in a bid to establish an exotic game hunting preserve). Former Campbell manager Harry Nelson articulates the views of many former employees about the new generation of Dorrances: "They wanted more, more, more!"[10]

Despite their disgust at the greed of the younger generation of Dorrances, most former Campbell production workers retained a remarkable pride in their work at the soup plant. In the kitchens and living rooms of the ex-workers where the interviews for this study were conducted, Campbell Soup memorabilia were a common fixture. Many retirees spoke proudly of the hard work they had done and declared that the soup and other food products they had made were of the highest quality. They undertook efforts like the doomed campaign to "save the can" because, as Leona Laird comments, "we put our lives into those buildings." She considers Campbell "the backbone of Camden....RCA came second....I'll never regret one day of it." Joseph Gallo cuts to the heart of Campbell workers' pride: "Who made the soup?"[11]

Years after the implosion of Plant No. 1, former workers still maintain the camaraderie that had developed in the plants through regular meetings of two retiree organizations, which also sponsor outings like casino trips. The larger retiree group, the Campbell Kids, meets monthly in a diner in Cherry Hill, and local and national human-interest news stories about the group have appeared every year or so. Club 80 similarly meets monthly, but in the old headquarters of Local 80 in Camden; no reporters, however, have written about their activities. Both groups carry on vestiges of the solidarity that went back to the first time Campbell workers united to advance their interests in 1934. Yet the existence of two groups rather than one testifies to the lasting effects of the segmentation that was at the heart of Campbell's labor policies and that the UCAPAWA/FTA and the UPWA had long fought to defeat. At recent meetings of the two groups, most of those who attended the Campbell Kids meeting were white, while most at the Club 80 meeting were black.[12]

In many ways David Johnson's "new" approach to running the Campbell Soup Company in the 1990s hearkened back to the managerial style of the company patriarch, John T. Dorrance, in the 1920s. Both focused single-mindedly on the bottom line and ruthlessly and continuously revolutionized the production process to that end. Neither let considerations about Camden or the company's employees impact their decision making. They were able to do essentially whatever they wanted because neither faced any force that could get in their way. Public controls, in the form of government regulations, were at most a minor nuisance. And challenges to their control of the company from its workers were minimal or nonexistent during these periods. The first serious attempt at unionization came four years after Dorrance's death, and, with the shutdown of the Camden plant at the start of Johnson's term, Campbell's CEO once again had free rein on charting the company's course (at least for the time being).

Despite his success in Camden, John T. Dorrance had threatened to move the company lock, stock, and barrel out of the city to a new superefficient site in 1915. David Johnson carried through the plans that moved all Camden production to just such a plant in Maxton in 1990. This strategy—moving production to wherever costs, and especially labor costs, are cheapest—is the most visible one, but not the only tool that companies have used in the drive to lower costs and maximize profits. As labor activist and author Kim Moody reminds us, global sourcing is only one facet of today's "lean" world. Lean production (or "management by stress"), flexible and contingent labor force practices, and strong resistance to sharing decision-making power with unions or others are equally important components of the apparatus of corporate success. In fact, in many cases companies may have great difficulty in moving work to cheap labor sites. Many service occupations by their very nature, such as nurses and hotel workers, must remain at the same location as the customers. In the case of many consumer-oriented manufacturing jobs, big retailers and their suppliers have moved much work to the lowest bidders in a global supply chain. Yet production facilities that require a large capital investment (such as automobile manufacturing) or that must be near sources of raw materials (like tomato processing) have greater difficulty in quickly moving factories around the globe. And, as crucial as minimizing labor costs is to global corporations, there is a large constellation of factors that go into plant location decisions, and other advantages of a site may outweigh labor-cost considerations. Rising fuel costs could well temper the attraction of global sourcing in the future. When firms do move the site of production, as Jefferson Cowie has shown in the case of RCA, the same problems corporations are running away from often reappear in the new locations. Even in the most extreme cases of global sourcing—in fact, *especially* in these cases—all the features of work intensification, labor market segmentation, and antiunionism are typically employed. Small manufacturers need to take every avenue available to them to be able to sell their products to distributors at extremely low prices and still make a profit in the hypercompetitive world in which they operate. When capital draws on all these strategies within the context of globalization, the plight of workers might seem hopeless. Yet this conclusion would hardly be justified. In difficult-to-move industries, workers still possess much of the power they have always had, and job actions from strikes to varied forms of day-to-day resistance complicate the job of managers. Even in more mobile industries, workers' organizations have experimented with novel forms of cross-border solidarity, and this trend is likely to grow.

In coming to grips with the complexities of today's economy, then, we can profit from the study of how firms and their employees dealt with many similar factors in earlier periods. Because the Campbell Soup Company, for a variety of reasons, kept its flagship plant in Camden for most of the twentieth century, its operations there served as a veritable incubator for low-cost-production strategies. To keep millions of dollars in profits rolling in from the sale of ten-cent cans of soup, company managers relentlessly pushed for continuous improvement in production, from automation to scientific management and process redesign. When workers rebelled against job loss, speedup, and low pay, the company responded with harsh antiunionism and reinforced its segmentation of the workforce to discourage a unified opposition. The reactions and tactics of a wide array of unions—from the UCAPAWA to the UFCW—demonstrated the strengths and weaknesses of various approaches. When unions fostered internal democracy and fought for unity and an expansive social program, they made their greatest gains. When there was no organized workers' voice, before 1934 and after 1990, the company put its plans into effect with little trouble.

Those on both sides of the production divide—owners of capital, and workers—should be interested in the lessons of history. Corporate executives, their advisors, and the business schools that prepare new generations to perpetuate their power clearly have studied these lessons closely. Those who make the soup—and everything else—need to do likewise.

✹ Notes

Introduction

1. Douglas Collins, *America's Favorite Food: The Story of Campbell Soup Company* (New York: Harry N. Abrams, 1994).

2. Andrew F. Smith, *Souper Tomatoes: The Story of America's Favorite Food* (New Brunswick, NJ: Rutgers University Press, 2000), 126; Jim Terry, "Campbell Soup in Hot Water with Organized Labor," *Business and Society Review* 46 (Summer 1983): 37.

3. Jefferson Cowie, *Capital Moves: RCA's Seventy-Year Quest for Cheap Labor* (Ithaca, NY: Cornell University Press, 1999). For another industry that pursued a similar solution to its labor problems, see Philip Scranton, *Figured Tapestry: Production, Markets, and Power in Philadelphia Textiles, 1885–1941* (Cambridge: Cambridge University Press, 1989).

4. See Daniel T. Campbell, "New York Shipbuilding Corporation: The First Two Decades" (PhD diss., Temple University, 2001).

5. Sylvester Akins, interview with the author, Philadelphia, November 20, 2003.

6. "Campbell Takes the Lid Off," *Fortune*, March 1955, 124.

7. Cindy Hahamovitch, *The Fruits of Their Labor: Atlantic Coast Farmworkers and the Making of Migrant Poverty, 1870–1945* (Chapel Hill: University of North Carolina Press, 1997).

8. "Campbell Soup Co. announced today it will spend $37 million over the next three years to modernize its Camden canned food plant to keep it competitive with other plants in the company and in the food industry," *PR Newswire*, January 27, 1986. Retrieved August 10, 2008, from Lexis-Nexis.

9. For a small sample of the vast scholarly and popular literatures that have arisen on the topic of globalization, see Kenichi Ohmae, *The Evolving Global Economy: Making Sense of the New World Order* (Boston: Harvard Business Review Books, 1995); "Robert Reich Speaks," *Dollars and Sense*, September–October 1995, 24–26; William Greider, *One World, Ready or Not: The Manic Logic of Global Capitalism* (New York: Simon and Schuster, 1997); and Thomas L. Friedman, *The Lexus and the Olive Tree: Understanding Globalization* (New York: Farrar, Straus and Giroux, 1999). An important recent work that challenges the inevitability of labor's collapse in the wake of capital mobility is Bill Dunn, *Global Restructuring and the Power of Labour* (New York: Palgrave, 2004); see also "Symposium: Bill Dunn, *Global Restructuring and the Power of Labour*," *Labor History* 47 (February 2006): 95–126. A book that skillfully ties together the various strands of capital's strategies and workers' responses (but gives only limited attention to historical precedents) is Kim Moody, *Workers*

in a Lean World: Unions in the International Economy (London: Verso, 1997). James Womack, Daniel Jones, and Daniel Roos, *The Machine that Changed the World* (New York: Rawson Associates, 1990) and Steve Babson, ed., *Lean Work: Empowerment and Exploitation in the Global Auto Industry* (Detroit: Wayne State University Press, 1995) discuss, from opposing points of view, the rise of "lean production." Saskia Sassen describes how immigrants fill niches in advanced economies in *The Global City: New York, London, Tokyo* (Princeton, NJ: Princeton University Press, 1991). The rise of temporary and other forms of contingent work is documented in Kathleen Barker and Kathleen Christensen, *Contingent Work: American Employment Relations in Transition* (Ithaca, NY: Cornell University Press, 1998), and Françoise Carré, Marianne A. Ferber, Lonnie Golden, and Stephen A. Herzenberg, eds., *Nonstandard Work: The Nature and Challenges of Changing Employment Relations* (Ithaca, NY: ILR Press, 2000).

10. On the power of global capital, see Greider, *One World, Ready or Not;* for an alternative view, see Dunn, *Global Restructuring and the Power of Labour.*

11. Howard Gillette Jr., *Camden after the Fall: Decline and Renewal in a Post-Industrial City* (Philadelphia: University of Pennsylvania Press, 2005).

Chapter 1

1. "Campbelltown: A Foretaste of Industrial Utopia," *North American* (Philadelphia), magazine section, April 11, 1915.

2. "Campbell's Soup," *Fortune,* November 1935, 130. For more on Port Sunlight and the transnational movement of Progressive ideas, see Daniel T. Rodgers, *Atlantic Crossings: Social Politics in a Progressive Age* (Cambridge, MA: Belknap Press of Harvard University Press, 1998).

3. "Campbelltown." The site for Campbelltown became available when Washington Park, then one of the largest amusement parks in the country, burned to the ground in a disastrous fire in 1913. After Campbelltown was abandoned, the location had a less illustrious career as a bag loading plant that packaged powder for the army during World War I. Today it is the site of Texaco's Eagle Point refinery.

4. Ibid.; "New Plant of the Year," *Food Engineering,* March 1983, 75–85.

5. Paul F. Cranston, *Camden County 1681–1931: The Story of an Industrial Empire* (Camden, NJ: Camden County Chamber of Commerce, 1931), 60.

6. John M. Connor, Richard T. Rogers, Bruce W. Marion, and Willard F. Mueller, *The Food Manufacturing Industries: Structure, Strategies, Performance, and Policies* (Lexington, MA: D. C. Heath, 1985), 42, 45–52.

7. Andrew F. Smith, *Souper Tomatoes: The Story of America's Favorite Food* (New Brunswick, NJ: Rutgers University Press, 2000), 39–53.

8. Mary B. Sim, *History of Commercial Canning in New Jersey* (Trenton: New Jersey Agricultural Society, 1951), 152–63; "Campbell's Soup," 72–73; Smith, *Souper Tomatoes,* 87.

9. National Park Service, "Dorrance Mansion," ParkNet, http://www.cr.nps.gov/nr/travel/delaware/dor.htm; accessed August 5, 2006.

10. "Campbell's Soup," 72.

11. Douglas Collins, *America's Favorite Food: The Story of Campbell Soup Company* (New York: Harry N. Abrams, 1994), 46.

12. "Campbell's Soup," 124–28; Susan Strasser, *Satisfaction Guaranteed: The Making of the American Mass Market* (New York: Pantheon, 1989), chapter 1; Connor et al., *Food Manufacturing Industries,* 46–47. For a fascinating analysis of Campbell's exploitation of anxieties about traditional gender roles through its magazine advertising, see Katharine Parkin, "Campbell's Soup and the Long Shelf Life of Traditional Gender Roles," in *Kitchen Culture in America: Popular Representations of Food, Gender, and Race,* ed. Sherrie A. Inness, chapter 2 (Philadelphia: University of Pennsylvania Press, 2001).

13. Collins, *America's Favorite Food,* 29–32.

14. Patricia Condell, "Campbell Soup Company—Plant No. 1, Camden, New Jersey" (Camden, NJ: Historic Conservation and Interpretation, 1991), 46–47. See also Edward S. Rutsch and Robert A. Fischer, Jr., "Campbell Soup Company—Plant No. 2, Camden, New Jersey" (Camden, NJ: Historic Conservation and Interpretation, 1987).

15. Condell, "Plant No. 1," 49.

16. "Campbell's Soup," 128.

17. Ibid., 128–29.

18. David A. Hounshell, *From the American System to Mass Production, 1800–1932: The Development of Manufacturing Technology in the United States* (Baltimore: Johns Hopkins University Press, 1984), 241–43.

19. Sigfried Giedion, *Mechanization Takes Command: A Contribution to Anonymous History* (New York: Oxford University Press, 1948), 77.

20. "Campbell's Soup," 73.

21. *Employment and Housing Problems of Migratory Workers in New York and New Jersey Canning Industries, 1943,* Women's Bureau Bulletin No. 198 (Washington, DC: GPO, 1944), 18. The other alleged cause of Camden's decline in this view was the Benjamin Franklin Bridge, opened in 1926, which, among other things, allowed Philadelphians easy access to Camden and its jobs.

22. Cranston, *Camden County 1681–1931.*

23. Martha Gellhorn to Harry Hopkins, April 25, 1935; box 66, Harry Hopkins Papers.

24. Joseph Gallo, interview with the author, Pennsauken, NJ, September 4, 2003.

25. United States Bureau of the Census, Manuscript Census, Camden, NJ, 1920, 1930.

26. Rutsch and Fischer, "Plant No. 2," 58. Actually, at this earlier period most RCA employees were also women; Jefferson Cowie, *Capital Moves: RCA's Seventy-Year Search for Cheap Labor* (Ithaca, NY: Cornell University Press, 1999), chapter 1.

27. Harry Nelson, interview with the author, Mount Laurel, NJ, August 12, 2003; Leona Laird, interview with the author, Pennsauken, NJ, August 27, 2003; Joseph Morrison and Jenny Morrison, interviews with the author, Maple Shade, NJ, September 29, 2003; Sim, *Canning in New Jersey;* "Campbell's Soup," 132.

28. Nelson interview.

29. Laird interview; Joseph Morrison interview; Gallo interview.

30. "Campbell's Soup," 130.

31. *Samuel Calabro v. Campbell Soup Co.,* Superior Court of New Jersey, 244 N.J. Super. 149, 581 A.2d 1318, 1990 N.J. Super. LEXIS 362. Calabro was awarded

$2,538, or $47 per week for fifty-four weeks. In similar cases two other workers were awarded $5,292 and $8,938.

32. *Anna Lloyd v. Campbell Soup Co.*, 4 N.J. Misc. 553, 1926 N.J. Misc. LEXIS 10; *Louis Spiewak v. Campbell Soup Co.*, 6 N.J. Misc. 869, 1928 N.J. Misc. LEXIS 26; *Aubray Claborn v. Campbell Soup Co.*, 6 N.J. Misc. 864, 1928 N.J. Misc LEXIS 29; *Alos Dapas v. Campbell Soup Co.*, 8 N.J. Misc 767, 1930 N.J. Misc LEXIS 43. In most cases, suits brought by workers or their survivors were either resolved in favor of the company or with small amounts awarded to the petitioners. Judges dismissed the cases of Spiewak and Lloyd because, in the courts' opinion, the culpability of the company could not be established. The court awarded Dapas $1,650 for the disability resulting from his injury. Claborn's estate was awarded $600.

33. For a description of the "drive system," see Sanford M. Jacoby, *Employing Bureaucracy: Managers, Unions, and the Transformation of Work in American industry, 1900–1945* (New York: Columbia University Press, 1985), chapter 1.

34. "Campbell's Soup," 72.

35. Ibid., 71, 132.

36. Nelson interview; Collins, *America's Favorite Food*, 86.

37. W. F. Watson, *The Worker and Wage Incentives: The Bedaux and Other Systems* (London: Leonard and Virginia Woolf, 1934).

38. "Campbell's Soup," 73, 130.

39. International Bedaux Company, *Bedaux Measures Labor* (New York: Chas. E. Bedaux, 1928), 3–4.

40. Case minutes, War Labor Board Records, June 16, 1944, 39, 52, 71.

41. Watson, *Worker and Wage Incentives*, 29–30.

42. Unidentified investigator of the Bedaux system, quoted in Watson, *Worker and Wage Incentives*, 30–31.

43. Steven Kreis, "The Diffusion of Scientific Management: The Bedaux Company in America and Britain, 1926–1945," in *A Mental Revolution: Scientific Management since Taylor*, ed. Daniel Nelson (Columbus: Ohio State University Press, 1992), 168.

44. Dan Clawson, *Bureaucracy and the Labor Process* (New York: Monthly Review Press, 1982), chapter 6.

45. Kreis, "Diffusion of Scientific Management," 156.

46. International Bedaux Company, *Bedaux Measures Labor*, 10; International Bedaux Company, *General Considerations Pertaining to the Bedaux Plan* (New York: International Bedaux Company, 1937), 10; Charles E. Bedaux, *Bedaux Efficiency Course* (Grand Rapids, MI: Bedaux Industrial Institute, 1917), 405.

47. Gallo interview; "'Incentive-Wage' System Spurs Campbell Workers to More Work and Pay," *Evening Bulletin* (Philadelphia), August 25, 1932.

48. Laird interview; Franklin Williams [pseud.], interview with the author, Cherry Hill, NJ, May 30, 2004.

49. Edward Cheeseman, interview with the author, Southampton, NJ, June 7, 2004.

50. Kreis, "Diffusion of Scientific Management," 168.

51. Taiichi Ohno, *Toyota Production System: Beyond Large-Scale Production* (Cambridge: Productivity Press, 1988), 4, 95; "Campbell Takes the Lid Off," *Fortune*, March 1955, 82.

52. Ohno, *Toyota Production System,* 18–20; "Campbell Takes the Lid Off," 79.

53. Ohno, *Toyota Production System,* 4; Nelson interview; "Campbell's Soup," 126.

54. Ohno, *Toyota Production System,* 4; James Womack, Daniel Jones, and Daniel Roos, *The Machine that Changed the World* (New York: Rawson, 1990), 57, 99; Mike Parker and Jane Slaughter, "Unions and Management by Stress," in *Lean Work: Empowerment and Exploitation in the Global Auto Industry,* ed. Steve Babson (Detroit: Wayne State University Press, 1995), 44.

55. "Campbell Takes the Lid Off," 79.

56. Womack et al., *The Machine That Changed the World,* 57; W. B. Murphy, address to National War College, September 5, 1969, box 9, Earl Newsom Papers.

57. "Campbell Takes the Lid Off," 82; "Campbell's Soup," 128.

58. Victor DeStefano [pseud.], interview with the author, Cherry Hill, NJ, September 24, 2003; "A Report Concerning Second Floor Labeling," n.d. [April 1959], N131, Cotton, Watts, Jones and King Records; handwritten interview notes in arbitration file, case no. 60–199, n.d. [1960], N130, Cotton, Watts, Jones and King Records.

59. Womack et al., *The Machine That Changed the World,* chapter 6; "Campbell's Soup," 130, 132; Sim, *History of Commercial Canning,* 165.

60. Womack et al., *The Machine That Changed the World,* 14. Toyota's docile union, the Confederation of Japanese Automobile Workers, found in a 1992 survey of members that "the level of workers' exhaustion... [has] almost reached a critical point"; see Steve Babson, "Lean Production and Labor: Empowerment and Exploitation," in Babson, ed., *Lean Work,* 16. See also the other essays in Babson's edited volume and Darius Mehri, *Notes from Toyota-Land: An American Engineer in Japan* (Ithaca, NY: Cornell University Press, 2005).

61. DeStefano interview; Gallo interview; Laurie Graham, "Subaru-Isuzu: Worker Response in a Nonunion Japanese Transplant," in Babson, ed., *Lean Work,* chapter 10; Parker and Slaughter, "Unions and Management by Stress," 16.

62. Ohno, *Toyota Production System,* 19, 53, 114, 124.

63. "Campbell's Soup," 124.

64. Ibid., 69, 134, 136; Tom Huntington, "The Park Hyatt Philadelphia at the Bellevue," Historic Traveler website, http://away.com/primedia/park_hyatt_bellevue. html; accessed July 31, 2008.

65. "Campbell's Soup," 135.

66. Cranston, *Camden County 1681–1931;* "Recovery Is Now General," *Evening Bulletin* (Philadelphia), August 20, 1930; "Campbell's Soup," 69.

67. Gellhorn to Hopkins, April 25, 1935; John F. Bauman and Thomas H. Coode, *In the Eye of the Great Depression: New Deal Reporters and the Agony of the American People* (DeKalb: Northern Illinois University Press, 1988), 1.

68. Gellhorn to Hopkins, April 25, 1935.

69. Ibid.

70. Ibid.

71. Richard C. D. Lyon, "Soup, Ships and Strikers," *Union Labor Record* (Philadelphia), April 6, 1934.

72. Writers' Program (U.S.), *Housing in Camden. Housing Authority of the City of Camden* (Camden: Huntzinger Co., printers, 1942).

Chapter 2

1. Franklin Williams [pseud.], interview with the author, Cherry Hill, NJ, May 30, 2004; "Mmm...good! Retirees Recall Years at Soup Plant," Camden *Courier-Post,* April 6, 1999.

2. Writers' Program (U.S.), *Housing in Camden. Housing Authority of the City of Camden* (Camden: Huntzinger Co., printers, 1942); Stuart Jamieson, *Labor Unionism in American Agriculture* (New York: Arno Press, 1975; reprint of the 1946 ed. published by the U.S. GPO, Washington, DC, and issued as Bulletin no. 836 of U.S. Bureau of Labor Statistics), chap. XIX.

3. Giovanni Arrighi, "The Labor Movement in Twentieth-Century Western Europe," in *Labor in the World Social Structure,* ed. Immanuel Wallerstein (Beverly Hills, CA: Sage, 1983), 55. See also Melvyn Dubofsky, "Technological Change and American Worker Movements, 1870–1970," in *Technology, the Economy, and Society: The American Experience,* ed. Joel Colton and Stuart Bruchey (New York: Columbia University Press, 1987), 165.

4. "Campbell's Soup," *Fortune,* November 1935, 124.

5. *1938 Labor Standards Bulletins,* vol. 1, RG1, Campbell Soup Company Archives ["A. C. Dorrance" imprinted on book cover].

6. Edward Cheeseman, interview with the author, Southampton, NJ, June 7, 2004.

7. Minutes of Proceedings, 3rd Regional War Labor Board, June 16, 1944, 70–71, box 2118, War Labor Board Records. In Labor Board testimony, union witnesses claimed "one to two hundred people a week" were laid off in Chicago for failure to meet Bedaux standards, as were two hundred workers at the Camden River Plant No. 2. Company witnesses did not contest the claim.

8. Leona Laird, interview with the author, Pennsauken, NJ, August 27, 2003; Campbell Soup Company, *Soup Tureen,* March 1937, RG3, Campbell Soup Company Archives.

9. Frederick Winslow Taylor, *The Principles of Scientific Management* (New York: Harper and Brothers, 1911); Harry Braverman, *Labor and Monopoly Capital* (New York: Monthly Review Press, 1974); Craig Littler, "Deskilling and Changing Structures of Control," in *The Degradation of Work? Skill, Deskilling, and the Labour Process,* ed. Stephen Wood (London: Hutchinson, 1982), 141.

10. Campbell Soup Company, *Campbell News Roundup,* May 15, 1961, 1; Harry Nelson, interview with the author, Mount Laurel, NJ, August 12, 2003.

11. Williams interview; Laird interview; Veronica Kryzan, Testimony at CIO Hearings on FTA, John Tisa Papers.

12. "Campbell's Soup," 130.

13. Martha Gellhorn to Harry Hopkins, April 25, 1935; box 66, Harry Hopkins Papers; emphasis in the original.

14. "Hints Soup Firm May Quit Camden," *Evening Bulletin* (Philadelphia), April 18, 1934.

15. Howell John Harris, *The Right to Manage: The Industrial Relations Policies of American Business in the 1940s* (Madison: University of Wisconsin Press, 1982), 17.

16. NLRB Inter-Office Memorandum, November 4, 1940, "Investigation by Daniel House, Case IV-R-533," box 1854, National Labor Relations Board Records.

17. "Camden Strikers Stick to Demands," *Evening Bulletin* (Philadelphia), March 31, 1934.

18. P. W. Chappell to H. L. Kerwin, April 8, 1934. File 176-1402, Federal Mediation and Conciliation Service Records; "Strike Started on Wage Demands at Soup Factory," *Public Ledger* (Philadelphia), April 2, 1934.

19. "Soup Co. Plans 'Armed Defense,'" *Evening Bulletin* (Philadelphia), April 4, 1934; "Labor Board Acts in Soup Co. Strike," *Evening Bulletin* (Philadelphia), April 21, 1934; "500 Soup Plant Strikers Storm Camden City Hall," *Evening Bulletin* (Philadelphia), May 2, 1934; "Women Strikers Maul Two Men," *Public Ledger,* April 3, 1934.

20. "Women Strikers Maul Two Men," *Public Ledger* (Philadelphia), April 3, 1934; "Pepper Throwing Picketer Is Fined," *Evening Bulletin* (Philadelphia), April 23, 1934.

21. J. McGowen to Fred Keightly, August 13, 1934. File 176-1402, Federal Mediation and Conciliation Service Records. Thompson and Rollins were each sentenced to thirty days in the county prison. Most of those convicted were required to pay fines, although several were sentenced to prison terms ranging from a few days to a month.

22. "Women Strikers Maul Two Men," *Evening Bulletin* (Philadelphia), April 3, 1934; "Pepper Throwing Picketer Is Fined," *Evening Bulletin* (Philadelphia), April 23, 1934; "500 Soup Plant Strikers Storm Camden City Hall," *Evening Bulletin* (Philadelphia), May 2, 1934; Jeffrey M. Dorwart, *Camden County, New Jersey: The Making of a Metropolitan Community, 1626–2000* (New Brunswick, NJ: Rutgers University Press, 2001), 138.

23. "Principals in Writ Suit by Campbell Soup Co.," *Evening Bulletin* (Philadelphia), April 9, 1934.

24. P. W. Chappell to H. L. Kerwin, April 8, 1934, and April 17, 1934; P. W. Chappell to Mr. Wolff, April 27, 1934. File 176-1402, Federal Mediation and Conciliation Service Records.

25. Chappell to Wolff, April 27, 1934.

26. Frank Manning to Fred Keightley, August 17, 1934; Fred Keightley to H. L. Kerwin, August 21, 1934. File 176-1402, Federal Mediation and Conciliation Service Records.

27. Frank Manning to H. L. Kerwin, August 22, 1934. File 176-1402, Federal Mediation and Conciliation Service Records.

28. Gellhorn to Hopkins; Jamieson, *Labor Unionism in American Agriculture,* 350.

29. Manning to Keightly, August 17, 1934; NLRB Inter-Office Memorandum, November 4, 1940, "Investigation by Daniel House, Case IV-R-533," box 1854, National Labor Relations Board Records.

30. Minutes of Proceedings, 3rd Regional War Labor Board, July 7, 1944, box 2118, War Labor Board Records.

31. "Campbell's Soup," 130; "Camden Labor Spreads Revolt," *Union Labor Record* (Philadelphia), April 6, 1934.

32. "Jobless Demand Changes in Relief," *Courier-Post,* February 1, 1933. For the definitive discussion of how workers in another city "made a new deal," see Lizabeth Cohen, *Making a New Deal: Industrial Workers in Chicago, 1919–1939* (Cambridge: Cambridge University Press, 1990).

33. "Soup Firm Seeks Court Aid on Strike," *Public Ledger,* April 5, 1934; Jamieson, *Labor Unionism in American Agriculture,* 351–55.

34. Vicki L. Ruiz, *Cannery Women, Cannery Lives: Mexican Women, Unionization, and the California Food Processing Industry, 1930–1950* (Albuquerque: University of New Mexico Press, 1987), xvii, 90–91.

35. Robert Korstad, *Civil Rights Unionism: Tobacco Workers and the Struggle for Democracy in the Mid-Twentieth-Century South* (Chapel Hill: University of North Carolina Press, 2003), 3–4; Michael Honey, *Southern Labor and Black Civil Rights: Organizing Memphis Workers* (Urbana: University of Illinois Press, 1993), 124. See also Devra Weber, *Dark Sweat, White Gold: California Farm Workers, Cotton, and the New Deal* (Berkeley and Los Angeles: University of California Press, 1994).

36. Steve Rosswurm, "Introduction," in *The CIO's Left-Led Unions,* ed. Steve Rosswurm, 1–17 (New Brunswick, NJ: Rutgers University Press, 1992).

37. *Employment and Housing Problems of Migratory Workers in New York and New Jersey Canning Industries, 1943,* Women's Bureau Bulletin No. 198 (Washington, DC: GPO, 1944), 7–8.

38. "Labor Groups Mass against Vigilantes in Bridgeton Area," *Record* (Philadelphia), August 13, 1934, reported in Jamieson, *Labor Unions in American Agriculture;* UCAPAWA, First National Convention Proceedings, July 9–12, 1937, microfilm P94-644, State Historical Society of Wisconsin.

39. UCAPAWA, Third National Convention Proceedings, Dec. 3–7, 1940, microfilm N94-529, State Historical Society of Wisconsin.

40. Gallo interview; John Tisa, *Recalling the Good Fight: An Autobiography of the Spanish Civil War* (South Hadley, MA: Bergin and Garvey, 1985).

41. Gallo interview.

42. Ronald W. Schatz, *The Electrical Workers: A History of Labor at General Electric and Westinghouse, 1923–1960* (Urbana: University of Illinois Press, 1983), chapter 4. See also Peter Friedlander, *The Emergence of a UAW Local, 1936–1939: A Study in Class and Culture* (Pittsburgh: University of Pittsburgh Press, 1975).

43. Union members referred to national headquarters or the central body of the union as "the International."

44. "Directory, District No. 7," *Cannery and Field Union News,* November, 1937; "6 UCAPAWA Leaders Win Court Case," *CIO News, Cannery Edition,* September 17, 1938.

45. NLRB, "Investigation by Daniel House"; Gallo interview.

46. Gallo interview; Edward E. Thompson, "Campbell's Soup Peppers Up," *UCAPAWA News,* October, 1939; "Who Is Who in Our Union," *UCAPAWA News,* September–October, 1940; Tisa, *Recalling the Good Fight,* 16.

47. "Union Wins NLRB Poll at Campbell's Soup," *UCAPAWA News,* September–October, 1940.

48. Thompson, "Campbell's Soup Peppers Up," *UCAPAWA News,* October, 1939.

49. Amended Charge, February 12, 1940, box 1854, National Labor Relations Board Records; Gallo interview; "The CIO in Campbells," *UCAPAWA News,* July–August 1940.

50. "'Organize Campbell Soup' Aim of Camden CIO," *UCAPAWA News,* May–June, 1940.

51. NLRB, "Investigation by Daniel House."

52. NLRB, "Investigation by Daniel House."

53. "Certification of Representatives, Case No. R-2161," January 23, 1941, box 1854, National Labor Relations Board Records.

54. "Wage Increase for Campbell Soup Workers," *UCAPAWA News,* September, 1941; "Local 80's Fighting Shop Steward Guns for A. Hitler's Scalp," *UCAPAWA News,* May 12, 1942.

Chapter 3

1. Andrew F. Smith, *Souper Tomatoes: The Story of America's Favorite Food* (New Brunswick, NJ: Rutgers University Press, 2000), 127–31; John M. Connor, Richard T. Rogers, Bruce W. Marion, and Willard F. Mueller, *The Food Manufacturing Industries: Structure, Strategies, Performance, and Policies* (Lexington, MA: D. C. Heath, 1985), 42; Harry Nelson, interview with the author, Mount Laurel, NJ, August 12, 2003.

2. U.S. Department of Labor, Mediation and Conciliation Service Records, file 209–129, n.d. [1942]; Nelson interview; C. M. Hardwick, *Time Study in Treason: Charles E. Bedaux, Patriot or Collaborator* (Chelmsford, UK: Peter Horsnell, 1989), 78; see also Jim Christy, *The Price of Power: A Biography of Charles Eugene Bedaux* (Toronto: Doubleday Canada, 1984).

3. Smith, *America's Favorite Food,* 127–28.

4. "Campbell Lifts the Lid on Assets and Earnings—and They're Big," *New York Times,* October 28, 1954.

5. For discussion of the contentious issue of the no-strike pledge and labor's place in the war effort, see Nelson Lichtenstein, *Labor's War at Home: The CIO in World War II* (Cambridge: Cambridge University Press, 1982); Martin Glaberman, *Wartime Strikes: The Struggle against the No-Strike Pledge in the UAW during World War II* (Detroit: Bewick, 1980); and Robert Zieger, *The C.I.O., 1935–1955* (Chapel Hill: University of North Carolina Press, 1995), chapter 7.

6. "Campbell Soup Plan Spurs Bond Buying," *UCAPAWA News,* January 15, 1942; "Joint Effort Brings First Camden Award," *UCAPAWA News,* June 10, 1942; "80," *UCAPAWA News,* July 1, 1942.

7. "Joint Body to Speed Army Food Production," *UCAPAWA News,* July 1, 1942; "Campbell Soup Workers Hail Winning of WFA 'A' Award," *UCAPAWA News,* April 1, 1944.

8. "Local 80's Fighting Shop Steward Guns for A. Hitler's Scalp," *UCAPAWA News,* May 12, 1942; "80," *UCAPAWA News,* July 1, 1942; "The Honor Roll," *UCAPAWA News,* August 1, 1942.

9. Joseph Gallo, interview with the author, Pennsauken, NJ, September 4, 2003; "Tisa's 'Goodbye' Plea Is for 2nd Front Now," *UCAPAWA News,* October 15, 1942.

10. Tisa, *Recalling the Good Fight,* 223–24; "A Yank from the Ranks," *UCAPAWA News,* November 15, 1943.

11. Steve Rosswurm, ed. *The CIO's Left-Led Unions* (New Brunswick, NJ: Rutgers University Press, 1992), 10.

12. For evidence of the hard-hitting approach to negotiations by both sides, see testimony to the War Labor Board, case 111–7619-D, June 16, 1944, and case 111–8085-D, July 7, 1944, box 2118, War Labor Board Records.

13. U.S. Department of Labor, Mediation and Conciliation Service Records, file 209–129, March 5–May 12, 1942; "Campbell Soup Co. Signs Wage Pact," *Evening Bulletin* (Philadelphia), February 24, 1941; "Soup Workers Sign Pact," *Evening Bulletin* (Philadelphia), May 14, 1942.

14. War Labor Board, case 111–7619-D, June 16, 1944, 72, and case 111–8085-D, July 7, 1944, 208–211, 253, box 2118, War Labor Board Records; *Local 80 News*, February, 1943, Sylvester Akins Papers; Joseph Califf to Lyle Cooper, June 4, 1952, UPWA Papers; International Bedaux Company, *Bedaux Measures Labor* (New York: Chas. E. Bedaux, 1928), 10.

15. U.S. Department of Labor, Mediation and Conciliation Service Records, file 300–2799, March 22, 1943.

16. "Swift Action Wins Wage Increase at Campbell's," *FTA News*, September 1, 1945. The UCAPAWA was renamed the Food, Tobacco, Agricultural, and Allied Workers at the end of 1944 to reflect the increased importance of tobacco workers in the union; see Robert Korstad, *Civil Rights Unionism: Tobacco Workers and the Struggle for Democracy in the Mid-Twentieth-Century South* (Chapel Hill: University of North Carolina Press, 2003).

17. "Picket Line at Campbell's Wins Grievance Case," *FTA News*, July 15, 1945; Veronica Kryzan, letter to the editor, *FTA News*, November 1, 1945; FTA, "Proceedings of the Fifth National Convention," December 4–9, 1944, microfilm N94-529, State Historical Society of Wisconsin.

18. Sylvester Akins, interview with the author, Philadelphia, PA, November 20, 2003.

19. U.S. Department of Labor, Mediation and Conciliation Service Records, file 209–7118, October 13, 1942.

20. U.S. Department of Labor, Mediation and Conciliation Service Records, file 301–6154, October 18, 1943; also see file 301–8645, December 9, 1943; "Campbell Soup Co. Suspends Group," *Evening Bulletin* (Philadelphia), October 14, 1945; Gallo interview; FBI report, July 19, 1955, file 100–18191, Freedom of Information Act request 1034900–000.

21. "How 2 Locals Plan for Union Consolidation," *UCAPAWA News*, August 1, 1945.

22. War Labor Board, case 111–8085-D, July 7, 1944, 252, box 2118, War Labor Board Records; "Local 80 Heaps Praise on Stewards, at Banquet," *UCAPAWA News*, December 15, 1943; "We Wanted to Strengthen Union," *UCAPAWA News*, February 1, 1944; "School's in Again," UCAPAWA News, March 1, 1944; "Union-Builder Number-One," *UCAPAWA News*, August 1, 1944.

23. Agreement, Campbell Soup Company and UCAPAWA Local No. 80, March 15, 1943, War Labor Board Records file 300–2799.

24. United States Patent Office, patent 2,166,528, July 18, 1939; Nelson interview; Camden Manpower Priorities Committee, minutes, April 11 and May 9, 1945, War Manpower Commission Records, regional central files.

25. Victor DeStefano [pseud.], interview with the author, Cherry Hill, NJ, September 24, 2003; Leona Laird, interview with the author, Pennsauken, NJ, August 27, 2003.

26. "N.J. Governor Asks Tomato Crop Aid," *Evening Bulletin* (Philadelphia), August 19, 1943.

27. "Facts We Face," manuscript, n.d. [1944], box 2299, War Manpower Commission Records. In fact, most labeling line and filling line jobs were filled by regular Campbell employees, while the inexperienced volunteers performed unskilled labor such as unloading baskets of tomatoes.

28. Rudolf Vogeler, memo, July 31, 1943, box 2340, War Manpower Commission Records.

29. "Recruitment of Workers" packet, box 2340, War Manpower Commission Records.

30. "Recruitment of Workers" packet, box 2340, War Manpower Commission Records; "Fla. Workers Start Tomato Pack Rolling at Campbells Soup," *UCAPAWA News*, August 15, 1943; "438 Florida Laborers Due in Camden Today," *Evening Bulletin* (Philadelphia), August 1, 1943.

31. "Fla. Workers Start Tomato Pack"; "Pickers End Strike As Union Goes to Bat," *UCAPAWA News*, December 15, 1943.

32. "KKK Rides again in Orange County" and "$400 Raised for Nation's Defense," *UCAPAWA News*, October 1, 1943.

33. Leon Schachter, *The Migrant Worker in New Jersey* (Camden, NJ: 1945).

34. R. E. Worden to F. L. McNamee, March 2, 1944, box 2299, War Manpower Commission Records.

35. R. E. Worden to F. L. McNamee, March 13, 1944, box 2299, War Manpower Commission Records.

36. Frank McNamee, "Interstate Recruitment for Food-Processing Labor," April 6, 1944, box 2299, War Manpower Commission Records.

37. Joan Koss, "Puerto Ricans in Philadelphia: Migration and Accommodation," (PhD diss., University of Pennsylvania, 1965), 64; Victor Vázquez-Hernández, "Puerto Ricans in Philadelphia: Origins of a Community, 1910–1945," (Ph.D. diss., Temple University, 2002), 116, note 79.

38. R. J. Eldridge to R. E. Worden, March 27, 1944, box 2299, War Manpower Commission Records; "Employment Contract for Puerto Rican Workers," n.d. [1944], box 2299, War Manpower Commission Records; George W. Cross, "Immigration of Puerto Rican Workers," June 30, 1944, box 2330, War Manpower Commission Records.

39. "Employment Contract"; Cross, "Immigration"; Edwin Maldonado, "Contract Labor and the Origins of Puerto Rican Communities in the United States," *International Migration Review* 13 (Spring 1979): 111.

40. Koos, "Puerto Ricans," 64; Vázquez-Hernández, "Puerto Ricans," 105; Julio A. Ruiz, *Batienda La Olla,* Oral History Project (Philadelphia: Taller Puertorriqueño, 1979), 43.

41. Jorge Melendez and Luz Melendez, interviews with the author, Pennsauken, NJ, July 3, 2003.

42. "300 Quarantined for Meningitis," *Evening Bulletin* (Philadelphia), September 11, 1944; see also Cindy Hahamovitch, *The Fruits of Their Labor: Atlantic Coast Farmworkers and the Making of Migrant Poverty, 1870–1945* (Chapel Hill: University of North Carolina Press, 1997), 190–193.

43. President's Commission on Migratory Labor, *Migratory Labor in American Agriculture* (Washington, DC: GPO, 1951).

44. Albert L. Nickerson, "Retention of Jamaican Workers in New Jersey Canning and Food Processing Plants," September 4, 1943, box 2334, War Manpower Commission Records; "Consolidated Report of Jamaican Workers Assigned to Industrial Companies 10–15 to 12–15–44," n.d., box 2334, War Manpower Commission Records; J. E. Heap to Anthony Conway, August 14, 1945, box 2329, War Manpower Commission Records.

45. J. L. Meagher to Edward Webb, May 26, 1945, box 2331, War Manpower Commission Records; Jorge Melendez interview.

46. Handwritten notes (4 pp.), n.d., box 2334, War Manpower Commission Records; J. E. Heap to Ashley Burrows, February 10, 1945, box 2331, War Manpower Commission Records.

47. J. E. Heap to Anthony Conway, August 14, 1945, box 2329, War Manpower Commission Records; "Jobs Open for 1500 at Campbell Soup," *Evening Bulletin* (Philadelphia), August 25, 1945.

48. Thomas F. Costello, "Certification of Need for Employment of Prisoners of War—Campbell Soup Company," March 7, 1945, box 2328, War Manpower Commission Records; Camden Manpower Priorities Committee, "Minutes of Meeting," March 14, 1945, box 2303, War Manpower Commission Records.

49. "Union Campaign Wins Jobs for Negro Women," *UCAPAWA News,* December 1, 1942; "Hitler's Pal, Jim Crow, Kayoed at Campbell's," *UCAPAWA News,* November 15, 1943; Thomas Smith, "Stopped Jim Crow Hiring at Campbell Soup Plant," *FTA News,* September 15, 1945; Veronica Kryzan, testimony at CIO Hearings Before the Committee to Investigate Charges Against the Food, Tobacco, Agricultural & Allied Workers of America, January 6, 1950, 311–13, box 6, John Tisa Papers, Camden County Historical Society.

50. Campbell Soup Company, *Soup Tureen,* July 1936, RG3, Campbell Soup Company Archives.

51. "New Amos-Andy Sponsor," *Evening Bulletin* (Philadelphia), July 9, 1937; Akins interview; Rev. David Burgess, quoted in Hahamovitch, *The Fruits of Their Labor,* 191; R. E. Worden to Frank McNamee, September 16, 1943, box 2331, War Manpower Commission Records.

52. "Campbell Chorus Sings," *Evening Bulletin* (Philadelphia), June 6, 1945.

53. "Campbell's Soup," *Fortune,* November 1935, 130; War Labor Board, cases 111–7619-D and 111–8085-D, June 16, 1944, 37, 55–65, box 2118, War Labor Board Records.

54. *Employment and Housing Problems of Migratory Workers in New York and New Jersey Canning Industries, 1943,* Women's Bureau Bulletin no. 198 (Washington, DC: GPO, 1944), 7; Laird interview; Ruth Milkman, *Gender at Work: The Dynamics of Job Segregation by Sex during World War II* (Urbana: University of Illinois Press, 1987), 99–127.

55. U.S. Conciliation Service, Submission and Decision, March 15, 1946, 5, file 46A-188, U.S. Department of Labor, Mediation and Conciliation Service Records.

56. War Labor Board, cases 111–7619-D and 111–8085-D, June 16, 1944, 32–55, box 2118, War Labor Board Records.

57. Nelson interview; Hahamovitch, *The Fruits of Their Labor,* 11.

58. UCAPAWA, Proceedings, First National Convention, July 9–12, 1937, 59–60, microfilm P94-644, State Historical Society of Wisconsin; Harold J. Lane, "Local

Officers Have New Responsibilities," *UCAPAWA News,* July 1, 1943; "Condemn Strike on Philadelphia Transit Lines," *UCAPAWA News,* September 1, 1944.

59. Sadie Harris, interview with the author, Philadelphia, November 20, 2003; Franklin Williams [pseud.], interview with the author, Cherry Hill, NJ, May 30, 2004; Akins interview.

60. Harris interview; Laird interview; Joseph Morrison and Jenny Morrison, interviews with the author, Maple Shade, NJ, September 29, 2003; Victor DeStefano [pseud.], interview with the author, Cherry Hill, NJ, September 24, 2003; Jorge and Luz Melendez interviews.

61. Ernest Kornfeld to George Weaver, February 26, 1944, box 199, CIO Secretary-Treasurer Papers; Campbell Soup Company and UCAPAWA Local 80 Agreement, March 15, 1943, file 300-2799, War Labor Board Records; Campbell Soup Company and FTA Local 80 Agreement, March 22, 1950, box 228, United Packinghouse Workers of America Papers; Harris interview; Akins interview.

62. Akins interview; DeStefano interview.

63. Gallo interview.

64. See Howell John Harris, *The Right to Manage: Industrial Relations Policies of American Business in the 1940s* (Madison: University of Wisconsin Press, 1982) for an excellent discussion of management efforts to hold on to and strengthen control in this period.

Chapter 4

1. James P. Nolan, "Valentino Gets 5 Yrs.," *Courier-Post* (Camden, NJ), November 7, 1952; collection of Joseph Gallo.

2. Nolan, "Valentino Gets 5 Yrs."; "300 Bolt Union at Campbell's," *Courier-Post* (Camden, NJ), January 19, 1953.

3. For the effects of McCarthyism on the union movement, see Ellen Schrecker, "McCarthyism and the Labor Movement: The Role of the State," in *The CIO's Left-Led Unions,* ed. Steve Rosswurm, 139–57 (New Brunswick, NJ: Rutgers University Press, 1992).

4. "Campbell Takes the Lid Off," *Fortune,* March 1955, 83, 124; "Campbell Lifts the Lid on Assets And Earnings—and They're Big," *New York Times,* October 28, 1954.

5. Howell John Harris, *The Right to Manage* (Madison: University of Wisconsin Press, 1982), 91–95; "Campbell Takes the Lid Off," 83.

6. "Campbell Takes the Lid Off," 126.

7. "Farmers Ask to Join Talks at Campbell's," *Philadelphia Inquirer,* August 10, 1946; "Campbell Takes the Lid Off," 126.

8. *Campbell Soup Co. v. Wentz et al.,* No. 9648, United States Court of Appeals, Third Circuit, December 23, 1948; "Campbell Loses Carrot Fight," *Evening Bulletin* (Philadelphia), December 23, 1948; "Campbell Soup Loses Test Case," *Evening Bulletin* (Philadelphia), December 18, 1951; "Court Orders Man to Sell Tomatoes Only to Campbell," *Evening Bulletin* (Philadelphia), September 5, 1952; "4 Tomato Growers Sued by Campbell," *Evening Bulletin* (Philadelphia), September 9, 1952; "Tomato Contract Appears to Be Legal, Judge Says," *Evening Bulletin* (Philadelphia), September 18, 1952; "Court Upholds Tomato Contract of Campbell Co.," *Evening Bulletin* (Philadelphia), September 27, 1952.

9. See the discussion of labor-marketplace and workplace bargaining power in chapter 2.

10. "Swift Action Wins Wage Increase at Campbells," *FTA News,* September 1, 1945; "Stoppage Halts Speed-up Plans at Campbell's," *FTA News,* April 1, 1946; "Win $4,000,000 at Campbell Soup," "'United We Won' Say Leaders," and Harold Lane, "United Strategy Wins," *FTA News,* May 15, 1946. For the 1968 strike, see chapter 6.

11. "Bare Campbell's Soup, AFL Plot to Bust CIO by Terror," *Daily Worker,* July 1, 1946; "Charge Conspiracy to Campbell's, AFL," *Courier-Post* (Camden, NJ), July 1, 1946; "Campbell Strike Threatened at Peak of Tomato Season," *Philadelphia Inquirer,* July 1, 1946; "$500,000 in Back Pay Withheld by Campbell," *Philadelphia Inquirer,* July 3, 1946; "Campbell Soup Holds Back Pay as Strike Looms," *Record* (Philadelphia), July 2, 1946; Donald Henderson, telegram, July 1, 1946, file 462-2089, U.S. Department of Labor, Mediation and Conciliation Service Records.

12. Advertisement, *Evening Bulletin* (Philadelphia), August 9, 1946; "Farmers Ask to Join Talks at Campbell's," *Philadelphia Inquirer,* August 10, 1946; New Jersey-Pennsylvania Tomato Growers' Association to President Harry S. Truman, August 10, 1946, file 462-2089, U.S. Department of Labor, Mediation and Conciliation Service Records.

13. "Campbell Strike Plan 'Red Plot,' Union Says," *Sun* (Baltimore), July 5, 1946; H. L. Mitchell to Lewis Schwellenbach, July 11, 1946, file 462-2089, U.S. Department of Labor, Mediation and Conciliation Service Records.

14. Final Report, August 12, 1946, file 462-2089, U.S. Department of Labor, Mediation and Conciliation Service Records; "Campbell Strike Settled a Minute before Deadline," *Evening Bulletin* (Philadelphia), August 13, 1946; "Campbell Locals Celebrate," *FTA News,* September 1, 1946; "Soup Workers Give Quick OK to Settlement," *Courier-Post* (Camden, NJ), August 15, 1946.

15. Editorial, *Courier-Post* (Camden, NJ), August 14, 1946; Earl Mazo, "FTA Officers Admit Reds among Local 80 Leaders" and "Commies Out in the Open in Campbell Soup Union," *Courier-Post* (Camden, NJ), August 23, 1946. Local 80 made full use of the opportunity to pay the *Courier-Post* back a few months later when Newspaper Guild workers went on strike against the newspaper; four thousand Campbell workers joined a mass picket line around *Courier-Post* headquarters, and Local 80 provided food and the use of its building to the strikers; "Local 80 Helps Guild Strikers," *FTA News,* December 1, 1946.

16. On the 1934 strike, see chapter 2; "Campbell's Soup," *Fortune,* November 1935, 130; "Campbell's Soup Peppers Up," *UCAPAWA News,* October 1939.

17. "Soup Workers Give Quick OK"; Sylvester Akins, interview with the author, Philadelphia, November 20, 2003; "FTA 80 Wins on Shop Steward, Speedup Beef," *FTA News,* October 1949.

18. "Campbell Co. Stalls as Congress Hits Unions," *FTA News,* March 1, 1947; "Campbell Pact Extended; US in," *FTA News,* March 15, 1947; "'Continuous Session' in Campbell Talks," *FTA News,* April 1, 1947; "Campbell Pay Is Highest in U.S.A. in FTA Contract," *FTA News,* July 15, 1947; "Campbell Strike Is Averted," *Evening Bulletin* (Philadelphia), June 6, 1947; Harris, *The Right to Manage,* 130.

19. Unsigned report on meeting of FTA Communists, January 10, 1947, box 109, CIO Secretary-Treasurer Papers; Tim Flynn to Philip Murray, July 23, 1948, box 109,

CIO Secretary-Treasurer Papers; Steve Rosswurm, "Introduction," in Rosswurm, ed., *The CIO's Left-Led Unions,* 205 note 6; see also Robert Korstad, *Civil Rights Unionism: Tobacco Workers and the Struggle for Democracy in the Mid-Twentieth-Century South* (Chapel Hill: University of North Carolina Press, 2003), especially chapter 12.

20. Schrecker, "McCarthyism and the Labor Movement," 147.

21. Rosswurm, "Introduction," 1–17; Judith Stepan-Norris and Maurice Zeitlin, *Left Out: Reds and America's Industrial Unions* (Cambridge: Cambridge University Press, 2003), especially chapter 1; Robert H. Zieger, *The CIO, 1935–1955* (Chapel Hill: University of North Carolina Press, 1995), 286.

22. Report on FTA communists; newspaper clippings, 1949; and resolutions from CIO locals, May 1949, box 52, CIO Secretary-Treasurer Papers.

23. CIO meeting transcript, February 15, 1950, box 239, and FTA Statement in FTA Hearings, box 109, CIO Secretary-Treasurer Papers.

24. Akins interview.

25. CIO FTA trial testimony, John Tisa Papers, Camden County Historical Society.

26. *Local 80 Bulletin,* December 8, 13, 15, and 22, 1949 and January 12, 1950, John Tisa papers, in possession of Vicki L. Ruiz.

27. *Local 80 Bulletin,* June 1950, John Tisa papers, in possession of Vicki L. Ruiz.

28. Stepan-Norris and Zeitlin, *Left Out,* 299–327; *Local 80 Bulletin,* October 31, 1950, John Tisa papers, in possession of Vicki L. Ruiz.

29. *Local 80 Bulletin,* October 19, 1950; leaflets dated October 23 and 27, 1950; and brochure, "We've Just *Begun* To Fight," n.d., John Tisa papers, in possession of Vicki L. Ruiz.

30. "10,000 Still Idle at Two Plants," *Evening Bulletin* (Philadelphia), November 2, 1950; "Walkout Ends at Campbell's," *Evening Bulletin* (Philadelphia), November 8, 1950.

31. Rick Halpern, *Down on the Killing Floor: Black and White Workers in Chicago's Packinghouses, 1904–54* (Urbana: University of Illinois Press, 1997), especially chapters 4, 5, and 7; Roger Horowitz, *"Negro and White, Unite and Fight!": A Social History of Industrial Unionism in Meatpacking, 1930–90* (Urbana: University of Illinois Press, 1997). According to an FBI report in 1947, "Leading Communists in FTA" explored the possibility of a merger among the FTA, the UPWA, and the Fishermen, all leftist unions; Report on FTA Communists, CIO Secretary-Treasurer Papers. Local 194's Veronica Kryzan testified that officers of her local received phone calls from CIO and UPWA officials suggesting that they leave the FTA for the UPWA. However, Les Orear, one of those officials, does not recall any such actions. CIO FTA trial testimony, John Tisa Papers, Camden County Historical Society; Les Orear, e-mail communication to the author, June 23, 2005.

32. "Questions and Answers," October 2, 1951, box 483, UPWA Papers; Joseph Gallo, interview with the author, Pennsauken, NJ, September 4, 2003; "Clean Slate" leaflet, n.d., in possession of Joseph Gallo; documents on steward suspension case, March 13, April 9, and May 2, box 85, UPWA Papers; "Packing Union Wins in Camden," *Evening Bulletin* (Philadelphia), October 25, 1951.

33. "Agent for Union Arrested as Red," *Evening Bulletin* (Philadelphia), October 11, 1951; *Worker,* New Jersey ed., n.d. [1952], in possession of Joseph Gallo.

Valentino was charged under his "true name," Anthony Valenti. Government prosecutors made a big issue of the alleged use of "aliases" by their targets, neglecting the fact that many immigrants changed their names (or had them butchered by Anglo-Saxon immigration officials); thus they implied nefarious motives to the fact that Sylvia Neff had been known as Cile Konefsky at the time of her naturalization and that John Tisa's name had once been misspelled as Tisso.

34. "Soup Union Aid Arrested by U.S." and "Campbell Soup Union Members Vote Strike," *Evening Bulletin* (Philadelphia), February 5, 1952; "Soup Workers Ratify New Pact," *Evening Bulletin* (Philadelphia), May 30, 1952; "Campbell Soup Goes Cold, Win Strike," *Packinghouse Worker,* n.d. [1952], John Tisa Papers, in possession of Vicki L. Ruiz.

35. "Local 80 Shop Stewards" and "Officers of Local 80," November 29, 1951, box 320, UPWA Papers.

36. Eugene Cotton to Ralph Helstein "Re: Campbell Soup Contract," January 11, 1952, box 79, UPWA Papers; "Agreement, Campbell Soup Company and FTA Local 80," March 22, 1950, box 228, UPWA Papers.

37. "Campbell Soup Company Negotiations," January 15–16, 1952, box 79, UPWA Papers.

38. William Green to "The Employees of the Campbell Soup Company," January 24, 1952; telegram from "AF of L Committee" to Elsie Bonner, n.d.; box 85, UPWA Papers.

39. Ralph Helstein to "All Local Unions," January 4, 1952; Helstein to Allan Haywood, January 4, 1952; leaflet "The Time Table Is Working on Schedule," February 6, 1952; "Special Shop Steward Meeting Agenda," n.d. [February 1952]; and *Local 80 Bulletin,* February 14, 1952; box 85, UPWA Papers.

40. "Bulletin for Supervisors," March 14, 1952, box 79, UPWA Papers; "Campbell Voids Union Contract in 'Hit-Run Strike,'" *Evening Bulletin* (Philadelphia), May 3, 1952; "Campbell Shuts Out 100 in Labor Dispute," *Evening Bulletin* (Philadelphia), May 7, 1952; "Dispute Closes Campbell Soup," *Evening Bulletin* (Philadelphia), May 13, 1952; "Campbell Soup Strike Settled after 16 Days," *Evening Bulletin* (Philadelphia), May 29, 1952.

41. "Campbell Soup Goes Cold, Win Strike"; "Leader of Pickets Arrested in Front of Campbell Soup," *Evening Bulletin* (Philadelphia), May 16, 1952; "Mrs. Neff Found Guilty in Red Perjury," *Philadelphia Inquirer,* May 29, 1952.

42. Minutes of Proceedings, 3rd Regional War Labor Board, cases 111-7619-D and 111-8085-D, June 16, 1944, box 2118, War Labor Board Papers; Gallo interview.

43. James P. Nolan, "Ex-Red Tells Recruiting by Valentino," *Courier-Post* (Camden, NJ), October 20, 1952; James P. Nolan, "Red Cells in City Plants," *Courier-Post* (Camden, NJ), October 21, 1952; James P. Nolan, "Valentino Plans Fight for Freedom Pending Appeal," *Courier-Post* (Camden, NJ), October 25, 1952; James P. Nolan, "Valentino Gets 5 Yrs.," *Courier-Post* (Camden, NJ), November 7, 1952; collection of Joseph Gallo.

44. George Craig to Ralph Helstein, June 16, 1952, box 85, UPWA Papers; "Camden ACTU Asks Inquiry," *Labor Leader,* May 31, 1952; "2 Slates Challenge Valentino Control of Campbell Union," *Courier-Post* (Camden, NJ), December 29, 1952; "Balloting Starts for Officers of Campbell Union," *Courier-Post* (Camden, NJ), January 5, 1953; "Butler Says Priest Seeks to Influence Campbell Union,"

Courier-Post (Camden, NJ), January 6, 1953; "Father Sharkey Answers Butler on Union Vote," *Courier-Post* (Camden, NJ), January 7, 1953; "Fight on Reds in Unions Is up to All Members," *Courier-Post* (Camden, NJ), January 8, 1953; collection of Joseph Gallo.

45. "385 Secede from Union at Campbells," *Courier-Post* (Camden, NJ), January 19, 1953; James P. Nolan, "Valentino Quits Business Post of Campbell Union," *Courier-Post* (Camden, NJ), February 4, 1953; collection of Joseph Gallo; Gallo interview.

46. Akins interview; Franklin Williams [pseud.], interview with the author, Cherry Hill, NJ, May 30, 2004; for the history of Local 22, see Korstad, *Civil Rights Unionism.*

Chapter 5

1. "Bulletin for Supervisors," March 6, 1952, box 79, UPWA Papers; the bulletin also listed "retroactive pay" as a demand it would never agree to.

2. "Campbell Takes the Lid Off," *Fortune,* March 1955, 124; Jennifer Lin, Carol Horner, and Terry Bivens, "The Dorrance Legacy of Control: How a Patriarch Kept a Grip on His Company," *Philadelphia Inquirer,* March 18, 1991; Carol Horner, Terry Bivens, and Jennifer Lin, "Without a Natural Leader, the 3d Generation Splinters," *Philadelphia Inquirer,* March 19, 1991; J. Newsom to Mr. Tourtellot, November 11, 1954, box 8, Earl Newsom Papers.

3. J. Newsom to Mr. Tourtellot, November 11, 1954; "Campbell Soup (1st draft)," January 5, 1955, and "Aide Memoire on Discussion...on Questionable Areas in the Fortune Story Rough Draft," January 6, 1954 [1955], box 7, Earl Newsom Papers.

4. Mr. Olney to Mr. Lydgate, February 7, 1955, box 8, Earl Newsom Papers.

5. Herbert W. Northrup, *Boulwarism: The Labor Relations Policies of the General Electric Company* (Ann Arbor: University of Michigan Press, 1964), 25–31.

6. William Beverly Murphy, résumé, April 16, 1958; Harry Nelson, interview with the author, Mount Laurel, NJ, August 12, 2003; Arthur Tourtellot to J. Newsom, December 22, 1954, box 8, Earl Newsom Papers; "Campbell Takes the Lid Off," 80, 83, 126.

7. "Campbell Takes the Lid Off," 78.

8. "Soup Kitchen of the Nation," *Forbes,* April 15, 1961, 19–23; "Campbell Takes the Lid Off," 83, 120. For an example of the exceedingly minute level of detail typical of production procedures, see the forty-two-step "Tentative Operating Instructions: Two New Horizontal Digesters," February 12, 1957, box 210, UPWA Papers.

9. "Campbell Takes the Lid Off," 83; Edward Cheeseman, interview with the author, Southampton, NJ, June 7, 2004.

10. William Beverly Murphy, "Campbell Soup's New Expansion Plan," January 3, 1955, box 7, Earl Newsom Papers.

11. "BLS Surveys Productivity in Canning and Preserving Industry," n.d., box 79, UPWA Papers; "Wage Increase," n.d., box 31, UPWA Papers; "Campbell Takes the Lid Off," 79.

12. "In the Soup and Happy to Be There," *Business Week,* February 15, 1964, 133; J. R. Newsom to Mr. Lydgate, June 10, 1955, box 8, Earl Newsom Papers; wage and

hour information, January 17, 1968, UPWA Papers; Douglas Bedell, "Camden: A Case Study in Urban Economic Problems," *Evening Bulletin* (Philadelphia), July 8, 1962.

13. Luz Melendez, interview with the author, Pennsauken, NJ, July 3, 2004; Minutes from Canning Conference, May 18, 1958, box 482, UPWA Papers; Bedell, "Camden: A Case Study."

14. Victor DeStefano [pseud.], interview with the author, Cherry Hill, NJ, September 24, 2003; Leona Laird, interview with the author, Pennsauken, NJ, August 27, 2003; "Facts and Analysis," March 1, 1957, box 482, UPWA Papers; "Campbell Worker Crushed to Death," October 13, 1959, unidentified newspaper clipping, Employees folder, Campbell Soup clippings collection, Urban Archives, Temple University.

15. Cheeseman interview; Nelson interview.

16. Cheeseman interview; "Campbell Takes the Lid Off," 124.

17. "Collective Bargaining Agreement, Campbell Soup Company and Local 80-A," July 25, 1956, box 423, UPWA Papers; Rose DeWolf, "Champ Onion Peeler Soups up Production at Campbell Plant," *Philadelphia Inquirer,* April 5, 1964.

18. Cheeseman interview; Franklin Williams [pseud.], interview with the author, Cherry Hill, NJ, May 30, 2004; G. W. Crabtree, "The Challenge of the 1970s," *Campbell Management,* November–December 1964, 3–4, collection of Harry Nelson.

19. Sylvester Akins, interview with the author, Philadelphia, November 20, 2003; Cheeseman interview.

20. Howell John Harris, *The Right to Manage: Industrial Relations Policies of American Business in the 1940s* (Madison: University of Wisconsin Press, 1982), 74–87; Joseph Morrison, interview with the author, Maple Shade, NJ, September 29, 2003; Williams interview; "Campbell Takes the Lid Off," 124.

21. A. B. Winters to W. C. Handwerk, et al., October 20, 1966, box 9, Earl Newsom Papers; Hoy F. Carman and Ben C. French, "Economics of Fruit and Vegetable Processing in the United States," in *Economics of Food Processing in the United States,* ed. Chester O. McCorkle Jr. (San Diego: Academic Press, 1988), 236.

22. "Campbell Soup," memo, W. A. Lydgate to E. Newsom, January 30, 1964, box 8, Earl Newsom Papers; for an example of the decline in morale, see the exchange in memos, March 1–15, 1973, RG1, Campbell Soup Company Archives.

23. Williams interview; Sadie Harris, interview with the author, Philadelphia, PA, November 20, 2003.

24. Local 80 contracts with Campbell Soup Company, 1954, 1956, 1958, box 228, UPWA Papers.

25. "Sit-down by 1200 Shuts Campbell Soup Plant," *Philadelphia Inquirer,* June 13, 1953; Field Staff Weekly Reports, 1953, box 420, UPWA Papers.

26. "Report on Foreman Kicking Employee, Friday, Oct. 5, 1956," box 423, UPWA Papers.

27. Williams interview; Field Staff Weekly Reports, 1953, box 420, UPWA Papers.

28. W. A. Lydgate to K. N. Jolly, "Campbell's Community Relations," September 3, 1959, box 7, Earl Newsom Papers; Clarence Funnye to W. B. Murphy, September 10, 1963, and "Mr. Murphy's proposed reply," annotated, September 10,

1963, box 8, Earl Newsom Papers; "Murphy's Speech," April 6, 1964, box 8, Earl Newsom Papers.

29. "Enterprise in Camden," *Evening Bulletin* (Philadelphia), November 26, 1968; Michael C. Jensen, "Mm, Mm, Good—and Conservative," *New York Times,* April 11, 1971; "Campbell Stays with Camden," *Business Week,* February 6, 1971; "Business Fights the Social Ills—In a Recession," *Business Week,* March 6, 1971.

30. Isham Jones, *The Puerto Rican in New Jersey: His Present Status* (Newark: New Jersey State Department of Education, Division against Discrimination, 1955), 13; "Capable Hands Can Be Flown to Your Plant," n.d. [1952], box 154, Workers' Defense League Papers; David L. Kirp, *Our Town: Race, Housing, and the Soul of Suburbia* (New Brunswick, NJ: Rutgers University Press, 1995), 31, 198–204; Gregg Lee Carter, "Hispanic Rioting during the Civil Rights Era," *Sociological Forum* 7, no. 2 (June 1992): 301–22.

31. H. H. Gray, "Canning Offers Greatest Organizing Potential," March 14, 1957, box 482, UPWA Papers; "Campbell Soup," memo, W. A. Lydgate to E. Newsom, January 30, 1964, box 8, Earl Newsom Papers.

32. J. Rex to Paris Plant Employees, February 22, 1965, UPWA Papers; Edward Beltrame, "Weekly Organizational Report," March 8, 1965, UPWA Papers.

33. W. Lydgate to E. Newsom, "Our Visit to Campbell on June 10," June 8, 1964, Earl Newsom Papers.

34. Field Staff Weekly Reports, 1953, box 420, UPWA Papers; "Campbell Takes the Lid Off," 124; material on 1956 negotiations, May 23 and 25, June 9, 15, and 25, box 423, UPWA Papers.

35. Field Staff Weekly Reports, 1953, box 420, UPWA Papers; underlining in the original.

36. Cissie Dore Hill, "Voices of Hope: The Story of Radio Free Europe and Radio Liberty," *Hoover Digest* 2001, no. 4, http://www.hoover.org/publications/digest/3475896.html, accessed June 21, 2008; "Main Talking Points for RFE," November 25, 1959, Radio Free Europe Fund newsletter, July 1960, "Better Fed Than Red," *Country Beautiful,* n.d., all in Earl Newsom Papers; "Communism Doesn't Work," *Harvest,* September–October 1963, RG3, Campbell Soup Company Archives.

37. "Campbell Soup Donates 8000 Cases of Food to Cuban Refugees," *Evening Bulletin* (Philadelphia), November 25, 1965; "Food and Defense," memo, August 16, 1961, Earl Newsom Papers.

38. W. B. Murphy, speech to *Harvard Business Review* seminar, May 27, 1963, Earl Newsom Papers; Pete Martin, "I Call on Bev Murphy," *Sunday Bulletin Magazine* (Philadelphia) August 30, 1964; Recordings of telephone conversations between Lyndon B. Johnson and William Beverly Murphy, September 23, 1965, December 1, 1965, January 17 and 18, 1966, July 27, 1966, Citations 8901, 9304, 9514, 9515, 10436, 10437, White House Series, Lyndon Baines Johnson Library and Museum; "Comment by W. B. Murphy for *Saturday Review,*" July 25, 1966, Earl Newsom Papers.

39. "Campbell Soup and Imported Beef," April 22, 1964, Earl Newsom Papers; "Inquiry from Campbell Soup," September 23, 1960, Earl Newsom Papers; "Argentina (for Campbell)," October 19, 1960, Earl Newsom Papers.

40. FBI report, October 21, 1954, file 100–18191, Freedom of Information Act request 1034900–000.

41. Four leaflets from Local 1 campaign, August 23, September 8–9, September 28, and n.d., box 429, UPWA Papers.

42. Joseph Gallo, interview with the author, Pennsauken, NJ, September 4, 2003.

43. "Special Notice to All Members of Local 80-A UPWA-CIO," n.d. [1954], box 106, UPWA Papers.

44. Local 80 union election campaign leaflets, December 1953–January 1954, box 106, and December 1956–January 1957, box 429, UPWA Papers.

45. A. T. Stephens to Ralph Helstein, January 11, 1956 and Ralph Helstein to R. Lasley et al., October 12, 1956, box 423, UPWA Papers.

46. Field Staff Weekly Reports, 1953, box 420, UPWA Papers; Minutes of Canning Conference, May 18, 1958, box 482, UPWA Papers; "Loaders Return at Soup Plant," *Evening Bulletin* (Philadelphia), date illegible, "Peeling Machine Dispute Idles 320," *Evening Bulletin* (Philadelphia), date illegible [1956], and "35 Strike after Fist Fight at Campbell Soup Plant," *Evening Bulletin* (Philadelphia), September 6, 1957, Campbell Soup clippings collection, Urban Archives, Temple University.

47. "Campbell Strike Roots Go Back Decade," *Courier-Post* (Camden, NJ), July 30, 1968.

Chapter 6

1. Fehmida Sleemi, "Work Stoppages in 1999," *Compensation and Working Conditions,* Fall 2000, 44, table 1. For numerous personal stories of worker disaffection in this period, see Studs Terkel, *Working* (New York: Pantheon, 1974).

2. J. J. Sosiak and E. W. Zellery letters, March 1 and 15, 1973, RG1, Campbell Soup Company Archives; "NAACP Asks State Aid for Strike-Hit Migrants," *Evening Bulletin* (Philadelphia), August 21, 1968.

3. Philip J. Schwarz, *Coalition Bargaining* (Ithaca, NY: New York State School of Industrial and Labor Relations, 1970), 4–7.

4. William N. Chernish, *Coalition Bargaining: A Study of Union Tactics and Public Policy* (Philadelphia: University of Pennsylvania Press, 1969), 167–201; Janet L. Finn, *Tracing the Veins: Of Copper, Culture, and Community from Butte to Chuquicamata* (Berkeley and Los Angeles: University of California Press, 1998), 61–63.

5. Rick Halpern, *Down on the Killing Floor: Black and White Workers in Chicago's Packinghouses, 1904–54* (Urbana: University of Illinois Press, 1997).

6. UPWA leaflets, May 23, September 8, October 4 and 11, 1967 and n.d.; AMC leaflet, November 1, 1967; Irene Baldwin, Field Staff Weekly Report, September 24, 1967; all in box 466, UPWA Papers.

7. "Report from Meetings of UPWA Canning Caucus," October 3, 1957, and "News from Canning and Allied Plants—Bulletin No. 1," October 18, 1957, box 376, UPWA Papers; "Minutes of Canning and Related Plant Worker Conference," May 18, 1958, box 482, UPWA Papers; Steve Harris to Thomas Lane, January 3, 1958 and "1957 Settlements—Canning—BNA," n.d., box 31, AMC Papers.

8. "Campbell Soup Company," February 6–7, 1967; "1967–1968 Economic Bargaining Program—Campbell Soup-IUD Committee," October 16–17, 1967; Stephen J. Harris, memorandum, October 19, 1967; all in box 18, AMC Papers.

9. W. C. Parker to W. A. Lydgate, October 28, 1966, and A. B. Winters, "Advanced Crop Contracting," October 20, 1966, box 9, Earl Newsom Papers; UPI dispatch, "Tomato Soup," March 18, 1966, box 8, Earl Newsom Papers.

10. W. B. Murphy to Campbell shareholders, September 9, 1968; Harry R. Poole, memorandum, July 29, 1968; William E. Harwick to Thomas J. Lloyd, August 23, 1967, microfilm AP95–0088; all in AMC Papers; Chernish, *Coalition Bargaining,* 109–31.

11. "Campbell—Labor Communications," April 10, 1968, box 8, Earl Newsom Papers. During the interviews for this book, former employees Leona Laird, Joseph and Jenny Morrison, Harry Nelson, and others all expressed high regard for the "Wall of Honor."

12. A. C. MacLennan to Personnel Managers, Inter-Dept. Correspondence on Employee Communications, April 26 and May 3, 1968 and W. E. Harwick to D. L. Dole, et al., "Labor Relations," April 10, 1968, box 8, Earl Newsom Papers.

13. "Campbell—Labor Communications," April 10, 1968, box 8, Earl Newsom Papers.

14. "Soup Kitchen of the Nation," *Forbes,* April 15, 1961; "In the Soup and Happy to Be There," *Business Week,* February 15, 1964; Pete Martin, "I Call on Bev Murphy," *Sunday Bulletin Magazine* (Philadelphia), August 30, 1964; "Campbell Soup Strike Will Affect Area's Economy," *Northwest Signal* (Napoleon, OH), July 11, 1968; "Nobody Wins in a Strike," *Paris News* (Paris, TX), July 21, 1968; Amos Kirby, "County Farm News," *Woodbury Daily Times* (Woodbury, NJ), July 27, 1968; all in box 8, Earl Newsom Papers. The Newsom company evidently collected the media stories it placed or influenced to prove its value to Campbell.

15. J. R. Morris to E. M. Newsom, Jr., "Idea," August 8, 1968, box 8, Earl Newsom Papers; underlining in the original.

16. Patrick E. Gorman to Thomas J. Lloyd and Harry R. Poole, August 16, 1968, microfilm AP95–0088, AMC Papers; *Local 80-A Messenger,* July 24, 1968, box 18, UPWA Papers.

17. "To Campbell Soup Tomato Growers," July 24, 1968; "Advertisement in Supermarket News," July 30, 1968; Henry C. Fleisher to Ralph Helstein, February 16, 1968; box 18, UPWA Papers. A typical verse from an actual Campbell advertisement was this jingle, quoted in "Campbell's Soup," *Fortune* (November, 1935), 128: "We blend the best with careful pains/In skillful combination,/And every single can contains/Our business reputation."

18. Halpern, *Down on the Killing Floor,* 247–250; *Local 80-A Messenger,* July 24 and August 15, 1968.

19. Stephen J. Harris, "Draft Summary, Campbell Soup Negotiations," July 26, 1968, microfilm AP95–0088, AMC Papers.

20. Harris, "Draft Summary, Campbell Soup Negotiations," July 26, 1968.

21. Harris, "Draft Summary, Campbell Soup Negotiations," July 26, 1968; IUD to T. J. Lloyd, May 22, 1967; Stephen J. Harris letters to IUD-Campbell Soup Committee, December 14, 1967, January 10 and 19, 1968, box 18, UPWA Papers.

22. Harris to IUD, January 10, 1968; E. A. Kavanagh to Chestertown Employees, January 29, 1968, microfilm AP95–0088, AMC Papers.

23. Stephen J. Harris to IUD-Campbell Soup Committee, February 20, 1968; W. S. Crawley to Camden Plant Employees, March 20, 1968, box 18, UPWA Papers.

24. Stephen J. Harris to IUD-Campbell Soup Committee, April 22 and 29, 1968, box 18, UPWA Papers.

25. William E. Harwick to Thomas J. Lloyd, August 23, 1967, microfilm AP95–0088, AMC Papers; Stephen V. Coyle to T. J. Lloyd, June 27, 1968, and Harry Poole, "Campbell Soup Company Meeting," July 29, 1968, box 18, UPWA Papers.

26. Harris, "Draft Summary, Campbell Soup Negotiations," July 26, 1968; "Campbells," handwritten minutes, July 25, 1968, box 18, UPWA Papers.

27. "Campbell Soup Strike Is Expected to Spread Today," *Wall Street Journal,* July 29, 1968; "3000 Walk Out at Campbell's Camden Plant," *Philadelphia Inquirer,* July 29, 1968; "Curb on Campbell Pickets Is Extended," *Courier-Post* (Camden, NJ), August 5, 1968.

28. Freddie Boyle, "Campbell Strike Affects Businesses near Plant," *Evening Bulletin* (Philadelphia), August 25, 1968; "NAACP Asks State Aid for Strike-Hit Migrants," *Evening Bulletin* (Philadelphia), August 21, 1968; "Curb on Campbell Pickets."

29. "1968 Tomato Contract," microfilm AP95–0088, AMC Papers; "Conference Call Report," August 2, 1968, box 18, UPWA Papers.

30. "To Campbell Soup Tomato Growers," July 24, 1968 and R. A. Jones to Growers, July 25, 1968, box 18, UPWA Papers; Rowland T. Moriarity and Fred R. Zepp, "'Red Gold' Rots on Vine in Campbell Soup Strike," *Evening Bulletin* (Philadelphia), August 18, 1968; Mrs. C. T. Sheppard, "Soup Striker's Wife Replies," *Evening Bulletin* (Philadelphia), August 20, 1968.

31. Union Press Release, August 7, 1968, box 18, UPWA Papers; handwritten meeting minutes, Washington, D.C., August 9, 1968, microfilm AP95–0088, AMC Papers.

32. "Campbell Soup Company Attempts to Provoke Its Workers," August 15, 1968, box 19, UPWA Papers; "Racial Trouble Feared in Soup Strike," *Courier-Post* (Camden, NJ), August 21, 1968.

33. "Campbell Soup Strike Will Affect Area's Economy"; "Campbell—Labor Communications," April 10, 1968, box 8, Earl Newsom Papers.

34. "'No Winners' Seen in Soup Co. Strike," *Courier-Post* (Camden, NJ), July 30, 1968.

35. "Soup Striker's Wife Replies."

36. "Nine Months of Frustrating Talks End in Four-Plant Campbell Strike," *AFL-CIO News,* August 3, 1968; Harry Poole, "Things To Do in the Campbell Soup Strike," n.d., box 18, UPWA Papers; Juul Poulsen to Stephen J. Harris, August 9, 1968, microfilm AP95–0088, AMC Papers.

37. "Union to Boycott Campbell," *Philadelphia Inquirer,* August 9, 1968; William Lydgate to K. Jolly and W. Parker, August 14, 1968; C. J. McNutt to R. G. Colder, August 19, 1968; W. B. Murphy to William Lydgate, August 20, 1968; all in box 8, Earl Newsom Papers.

38. Union Press Release, August 7, 1968, box 18, UPWA Papers; Patrick Gorman to Thomas J. Lloyd and Harry R. Poole, "Confidential Memorandum," August 16, 1968, microfilm AP95–0088, AMC Papers.

39. Handwritten mediation session minutes, August 26, 1968, microfilm AP95–0088, AMC Papers; "Tentative Pact OK'd in Strike at Campbell's," *Evening Bulletin* (Philadelphia), August 27, 1968; "Work Resumes in Camden as Campbell's Strike

Ends,"August 29, 1968; Press Associates, Inc., "Union Phones Wiretapped in Campbell Soup Strike," August 26, 1968, microfilm A P95–0086, AMC Papers.

40. W. B. Murphy to Shareholders, September 9, 1968; Leon Schachter to Patrick Gorman, September 3, 1968; Patrick Gorman to Leon Schachter, September 5, 1968; T. J. Lloyd and Patrick Gorman to Local Union Secretaries, October 14, 1968; all on microfilm A P95–0088, AMC Papers.

41. On the 1968 workers' movements and their connections to the other protests of the period, see Gerd-Rainer Horn, "The Changing Nature of the European Working Class: The Rise and Fall of the 'New Working Class' (France, Italy, Spain, Czechoslovakia)," in *1968: The World Transformed*, ed. Carole Fink, Philipp Gassert, and Detlef Junker, 351–72 (Cambridge: Cambridge University Press, 1998); Peter B. Levy, *The New Left and Labor in the 1960s* (Urbana: University of Illinois Press, 1994); and Michael K. Honey, *Going down Jericho Road: The Memphis Strike, Martin Luther King's Last Campaign* (New York: W. W. Norton, 2007).

Chapter 7

1. Michael C. Jensen, "Mm, Mm, Good—and Conservative," *New York Times*, April 11, 1971.

2. "Heard on the Street," *Wall Street Journal*, August 24, 1971.

3. Thomas J. Sugrue, *The Origins of the Urban Crisis: Race and Inequality in Postwar Detroit* (Princeton, NJ: Princeton University Press, 1996); Judith Stein, *Running Steel, Running America: Race, Economic Policy, and the Decline of Liberalism* (Chapel Hill: University of North Carolina Press, 1998).

4. "Camden: City in Trouble," *Philadelphia Inquirer*, series, April 13–17, 1970; David L. Kirp, John P. Dwyer, and Larry A. Rosenthal, *Our Town: Race, Housing, and the Soul of Suburbia* (New Brunswick, NJ: Rutgers University Press, 1995), 26–31; Howard Gillette Jr., *Camden after the Fall: Decline and Renewal in a Post-Industrial City* (Philadelphia: University of Pennsylvania Press, 2005), 77–89; "Camden, the Worst City in New Jersey, Fights Back," *Philadelphia Inquirer*, September 9, 1979.

5. Sacramento Plant Study, 1978, W. J. Usery Papers; memos, March 1 and 15, 1973, RG1, Campbell Soup Company Archives.

6. "Century II," *Harvest*, 1970, 26.

7. Edward Cheeseman, interview with the author, Southampton, NJ, June 7, 2004.

8. Steve Babson, "Lean Production and Labor: Empowerment and Exploitation," 1–37, and Mike Parker and Jane Slaughter, "Unions and Management by Stress," 41–53, in *Lean Work: Empowerment and Exploitation in the Global Auto Industry*, ed. Steve Babson (Detroit: Wayne State University Press, 1995). The most well-known book advocating TPS in America is James Womack, Daniel Jones, and Daniel Roos, *The Machine that Changed the World* (New York: Rawson, 1990). Other works that take a critical view are Kim Moody, *Workers in a Lean World: Unions in the International Economy* (London: Verso, 1997); and William C. Green and Ernest J. Yanarella, eds., *North American Auto Unions in Crisis: Lean Production as Contested Terrain* (Albany: State University of New York Press, 1996). Darius Mehri has written a fascinating first-person account of working in a Toyota factory and his accompanying

disillusionment; see Mehri, *Notes from Toyota-Land: An American Engineer in Japan* (Ithaca, NY: Cornell University Press, 2005).

9. Cheeseman interview; "Quality Circles Require Employee Participation," *Processed Prepared Foods,* October 1981, 48–54; "How Quality Circles Can Work to Improve 'Quality of Life,'" *Food Engineering,* October 1984, 128; "Expert Systems in Use: Campbell Soup Company," *Plant Engineering,* June 18, 1987, 55.

10. "Employer–Employee Relations at the Campbell Soup Company Sacramento Plant," March 15, 1978, box 306, W. J. Usery Papers.

11. "Employer–Employee Relations"; "Campbell's Soup," *Fortune,* November 1935, 130; Local 80 contract with Campbell Soup Company, 1954, box 228, UPWA Papers.

12. "Employer–Employee Relations"; emphasis in the original.

13. "Employer–Employee Relations."

14. Sadie Harris, interview with the author, Philadelphia, PA, November 20, 2003.

15. "Employer–Employee Relations."

16. Jack Palmer, "'Liberty and Justice for All': Velasquez Remains a Shining Light for Farmworkers," *Crescent-News* (Defiance, OH), April 8, 2008.

17. "Campbell Walkout," October 16, 1962; "To All Campbell Employees," n.d.; "Facts About the Campbell Mushroom Farm Situation," October 19, 1962; "Letter to Mushroom Workers," October 18, 1962; all in box 8, Earl Newsom Papers. Fifteen years later not much had changed; Campbell denied a migrant worker council access to the "company town," according to newspaper columnist Dorothy Collin, "Close-up with Dorothy Collin," *Chicago Tribune,* October 2, 1977.

18. W. K. Barger and Ernesto M. Reza, *The Farm Labor Movement in the Midwest: Social Change and Adaptation among Migrant Farmworkers* (Austin: University of Texas Press, 1994), 54–60.

19. Ibid., 60–83; "A Short History of the Farm Labor Organizing Committee," http://www.iupui.edu/~floc/histfloc.htm, accessed April 9, 2006.

20. Jensen, "Mm, Mm, Good."

21. "Top Posts Open to Minorities," *Evening Bulletin* (Philadelphia), February 7, 1975.

22. *Local 80 Messenger,* March 3, 1976, reel 377, AMC Papers; Sylvester Akins, notes from 1978 contract negotiations, collection of Sylvester Akins.

23. *Campbell Update* 1, no. 6 (July 1982); *Campbell Update* 3, no. 3 (1984), collection of Harry Nelson.

24. On the alleged labor-management accord, see Nelson Lichtenstein, *State of the Union: A Century of American Labor* (Princeton, NJ: Princeton University Press, 2002), chapter 3. For the bankruptcy of the strategy of AFL-CIO leaders, see Paul Buhle, *Taking Care of Business: Samuel Gompers, George Meany, Lane Kirkland, and the Tragedy of American Labor* (New York: Monthly Review Press, 1999).

25. Harry R. Poole to W. E. Harwick, February 11, 1969, microfilm AP95-0088, AMC Papers.

26. W. B. Murphy to Thomas J. Lloyd, February 18, 1970, microfilm, AP95-0088, AMC Papers; John Dettwiler to Thomas J. Lloyd, May 24, 1971, and Jesse Prosten to Thomas J. Lloyd, May 19, 1971, microfilm reel 249, AMC Papers.

27. Leon B. Schachter, meeting minutes, July 17, 1970; NLRB Decertification Petition, case No. 5-RD-367, September 16, 1970; Local 199 Negotiating

Committee to "All Maintenance Members," n.d.; Herbert A. Simon to Frank S. Astroth, September 30, 1970, all on microfilm A P95-0088, AMC Papers.

28. Patrick E. Gorman to W. B. Murphy, October 21, 1971, M80-118, microfilm reel 249, AMC Papers.

29. W. W. Dreyer, "Sacramento Plant Labor Relations," June 9, 1977, emphasis added, and M. A. Zimmerman, "Sacramento Plant—Labor Relations," June 28, 1977, Usery Papers.

30. "Employer-Employee Relations."

31. Franklin Williams [pseud.], interview with the author, Cherry Hill, NJ, May 30, 2004; Cheeseman interview; Michael C. Jensen, "Mm, Mm, Good; "Company Proposals, 1978 Negotiations" with handwritten notes by Sylvester Akins, n.d. [1978], collection of Sylvester Akins; Collective Bargaining Agreements, Campbell Soup Company and Local 80, February 27, 1978, and February 29, 1988, collection of Sylvester Akins.

32. Lichtenstein, *State of the Union,* 99.

33. Joseph Gallo, interview with the author, Pennsauken, NJ, September 4, 2003.

34. Analysis of wage increases from "Schedule of Hourly Base Rates," n.d. [1972], microfilm reel 377, AMC Papers, and Collective Bargaining Agreements, Campbell Soup Company and Local 80, February 27, 1978, and February 29, 1988, collection of Sylvester Akins; for number of employees, see table I, introduction.

35. Election leaflets, n.d. [May 1969 and May 1971]; tabulated election results, May 7, 1971, microfilm reel 378, AMC Papers.

36. "Concerned Members" to Patrick Gorman, July 8, 1970, microfilm reel 378, AMC Papers.

37. Patrick Gorman to Stephen V. Coyle, October 8, 1970, microfilm A P95-0088, AMC Papers.

38. *Local 80 Messenger,* August 8, 1978, collection of Sylvester Akins.

39. Leon Schachter to Patrick Gorman, November 10, 1971, microfilm reel 378, AMC Papers.

40. "Labor Press Group to Honor 2 Leaders," *Newark Star-Ledger,* January 30, 1973; Collie Hairston to Patrick Gorman, February 7, 1973; Patrick Gorman to Joseph Colangelo, March 21, 1974; Joseph Colangelo to Joseph Belsky, September 4, 1975, all on microfilm, reel 377, AMC Papers.

41. Joseph Colangelo to Patrick Gorman, July 29, 1976, and attached newspaper clippings, n.d.; Joseph Colangelo to Harry Poole, August 11, 1976; William Wilson to Samuel J. Talarico, October 16, 1976; Colangelo to Harry R. Poole, October 28, 1976, all on microfilm reel 377, AMC Papers.

42. Eileen Stillwell, "Campbell Cans 300 Employees," *Evening Bulletin* (Philadelphia), April 21, 1979; James A. Walsh and James C. Lawson, "Campbell's Furloughs 230," *Courier-Post* (Camden, NJ), March 28, 1981.

43. Rick Halpern, *Down on the Killing Floor: Black and White Workers in Chicago's Packinghouses, 1904–54* (Urbana: University of Illinois Press, 1997), 249; Roger Horowitz, *"Negro and White, Unite and Fight!": A Social History of Industrial Unionism in Meatpacking, 1930–90* (Urbana: University of Illinois Press, 1997), 268–75, 284–85; Harris and Akins interviews. For a sample of the large literature on the P-9 strike, see Peter Rachleff, *Hard-Pressed in the Heartland: The Hormel Strike and*

the Future of the Labor Movement (Boston: South End Press, 1993); Dave Hage and Paul Klauda, *No Retreat, No Surrender: Labor's War at Hormel* (New York: William Morrow, 1989); and Hardy S. Green, *On Strike at Hormel: The Struggle for a Democratic Labor Movement* (Philadelphia: Temple University Press, 1990). See also Barbara Kopple's film *The American Dream* (1990).

44. Terry Bivens, Jennifer Lin, and Carol Horner, "The Dorrance Dynasty Battles Itself: A Bitter Feud over Whether to Sell Campbell Soup Is Pitting Cousin against Cousin in a Fight over the Family's Fortune and Its Future," *Philadelphia Inquirer,* March 17, 1991; Jennifer Lin, Carol Horner, and Terry Bivens, "The Dorrance Legacy of Control: How a Patriarch Kept a Grip on His Company," *Philadelphia Inquirer,* March 18, 1991; Carol Horner, Terry Bivens, and Jennifer Lin, "Without a Natural Leader, the 3d Generation Splinters," *Philadelphia Inquirer,* March 19, 1991.

45. Janet Novack, "We're Not Running the Company for the Stock Price," *Forbes,* September 19, 1988, 41–52.

46. Ibid., 41.

47. "Out of the Soup: After 100 Years, Campbell Says No to NJ Tomatoes," *Evening Bulletin* (Philadelphia), October 12, 1979.

48. Andrew F. Smith, *Souper Tomatoes: The Story of America's Favorite Food* (New Brunswick, NJ: Rutgers University Press, 2000), 111–13.

49. "New Plant of the Year," *Food Engineering,* March 1983, 75–85; "Raid by 500 Indians Balks North Carolina Klan rally," *New York Times,* January 19, 1958.

50. "State, City, Industry to Launch Waterfront Renewal," *News '85* (Campbell Soup Company General Office newsletter), April 24, 1985, collection of Harry Nelson; Eric Harrison, "Campbell Plans Big Camden Project," *Philadelphia Inquirer,* April 24, 1985.

51. "Campbell Soup Co. announced today it will spend $37 million over the next three years to modernize its Camden canned food plant to keep it competitive with other plants in the company and in the food industry," January 27, 1986, *PR Newswire.* Retrieved August 10, 2008, from Lexis-Nexis.

52. Edward S. Rutsch and Robert A. Fischer Jr., *Campbell Soup Company—Plant No. 2, Camden, New Jersey* (Camden, NJ: Historic Conservation and Interpretation, 1987), 36, 61.

53. Title illegible, *Chicago Tribune,* March 6, 1988, clipping in collection of Harry Nelson.

54. Novack, "We're Not Running the Company for the Stock Price," 48.

55. Michael Freitag, "Company News: Closings Set, 2,800 Jobs Cut at Campbell," *New York Times,* August 25, 1989.

Chapter 8

1. Maureen Graham, "A Camden Landmark No Longer," *Philadelphia Inquirer,* November 4, 1991; Kevin Riordan, "Campbell Demolition Saddens 5 Retirees," *Courier-Post* (Camden, NJ), November 3, 1991.

2. David Diamond, "Campbell's New Kid: After Some Tough Decisions, Aussie CEO David Johnson Has the Food Giant Cooking Again," *Business Journal of New Jersey,* April 1991, 30–36; Amy Barrett, "Hail to the Chef: CEO David Johnson Has Cut the Fat at Campbell Soup. Now What?" *Financial World,* June 11, 1991,

52–54; Bill Saporito, "Campbell Soup Gets Piping Hot," *Fortune,* September 9, 1991, 142–48; Anthony Ramirez, "Campbell Cutting 364 from Staff," *New York Times,* May 2, 1990; Campbell Soup Company, Annual Meeting Report, "The Campbell Share Owner," First Quarter Fiscal 1991.

3. Joseph Morrison and Jenny Morrison, interviews with the author, Maple Shade, NJ, September 29, 2003; Leona Laird, interview with the author, Pennsauken, NJ, August 27, 2003; and Harry Nelson, interview with the author, Mount Laurel, NJ, August 12, 2003.

4. Melanie Burney, "Saving a Relic of Old Camden: Campbell's Icon Bound for Place of Honor," *Philadelphia Inquirer,* n.d., and Sandee Vogelson to Governor James J. Florio, February 1, 1993, both in collection of Harry Nelson; Nelson interview.

5. Nelson interview; Jorge Melendez, interview with the author, Pennsauken, NJ, July 3, 2004; Campbell Retirees Class Action Committee to Congressman Rob Andrews, March 5, 2000, William W. Taylor to Robert Andrews, October 18, 2000, Robert Andrews to Armand L. Meccariello, October 25, 2000, Campbell Retiree Committee to Campbell Retirees, n.d. [2000], all in collection of Joseph Gallo.

6. Franklin Williams [pseud.], interview with the author, Cherry Hill, NJ, May 30, 2004.

7. Jefferson Cowie and Joseph Heathcott, eds., *Beyond the Ruins: The Meanings of Deindustrialization* (Ithaca, NY: ILR Press, 2003), 3–4.

8. David L. Kirp, John P. Dwyer, and Larry A. Rosenthal, *Our Town: Race, Housing and the Soul of Suburbia* (New Brunswick, NJ: Rutgers University Press, 1995), 176–86; Howard Gillette Jr., *Camden after the Fall: Decline and Renewal in a Post-Industrial City* (Philadelphia: University of Pennsylvania Press, 2005), 123–215; Thomas Knoche, *Common Sense for Camden* (Camden, NJ: Thomas Knoche, 2005).

9. Gillette, *Camden after the Fall;* Knoche, *Common Sense.*

10. Linda Grant, "Stirring It Up at Campbell," *Fortune,* May 13, 1996, 80–86; Nelson interview.

11. Leona Laird, interview; Joseph Gallo, interview with the author, Pennsauken, NJ, September 4, 2003.

12. Kevin Riordan, "Campbell Stirs Warm Memories: Former Workers Sustain Old Ties," *Courier-Post* (Camden, NJ), n.d., collection of Harry Nelson; Kevin Riordan, "Mmm…Good! Retirees Recall Years at Soup Plant," *Courier-Post* (Camden, NJ), April 6, 2000. A Campbell Kids meeting was held at the Silver Diner in Cherry Hill on August 12, 2003; Club 80 met at the old Local 80 headquarters in Camden on October 20, 2003.

Note on Sources

Those who write non-company-sponsored histories of businesses, especially of firms still in existence, are well aware of the difficulties in obtaining access to internal company records that could be essential for a full understanding of the subject. This problem certainly exists with companies, like Campbell Soup, that are extremely protective of their public image. The small company archives at Campbell accessible to the public have some interesting material, especially in the areas of marketing and advertising, but, understandably, little that is germane to the central theme of this book. Fortunately, other archival sources came to the rescue, helped immeasurably by interviews with former Campbell employees. Another problem presented itself on the union side. All records of the UCAPAWA/FTA, Campbell's first union, were lost decades ago to a flood. A full run of the union's newspaper, supplemented by records of the U.S. Department of Labor's Mediation and Conciliation Service and other materials, filled in many of the gaps.

🎔 BIBLIOGRAPHY

Manuscripts

Amalgamated Meat Cutters (AMC) and Butcher Workmen of North America Papers. State Historical Society of Wisconsin, Madison.

Campbell Soup Company Archives. Camden, NJ.

Campbell Soup Company. Miscellaneous papers. Camden County Historical Society, Camden, NJ.

Congress of Industrial Organizations (CIO). Secretary-treasurer Papers. Reuther Archives, Wayne State University, Detroit, MI.

Cotton, Watts, Jones and King Records. State Historical Society of Wisconsin, Madison.

Federal Bureau of Investigation (FBI). Classified reports, file 100–18191. Freedom of Information Act request 1034900–000.

Harry Hopkins Papers. Franklin Delano Roosevelt Library and Museum, Hyde Park, NY.

National Labor Relations Board (NLRB) Records. RG 25, National Archives, College Park, MD.

Earl Newsom Papers. State Historical Society of Wisconsin, Madison.

John Tisa Papers. Camden County Historical Society, Camden, NJ.

John Tisa Papers. In possession of Vicki L. Ruiz.

United Food and Commercial Workers (UFCW) Papers. State Historical Society of Wisconsin, Madison.

United Packinghouse Workers of America (UPWA) Papers. State Historical Society of Wisconsin, Madison.

Urban Archives. Newspaper clipping files and miscellaneous files. Temple University, Philadelphia.

U.S. Department of Commerce, Bureau of the Census. Population Manuscript Census, 1920, 1930.

U.S. Department of Labor, Mediation and Conciliation Service Records. RG 280, National Archives, College Park, MD.

W. J. Usery Papers, Sacramento Plant Study, 1978. Southern Labor Archives, Special Collections and Archives, Georgia State University.

War Labor Board (WLB) Records. RG 202, National Archives, Mid-Atlantic Region, Philadelphia.

War Manpower Commission (WMC) Records. RG 211, National Archives, Mid-Atlantic Region, Philadelphia.

White House Series, Recordings and Transcripts of Conversations and Meetings. Lyndon Baines Johnson Library and Museum, Austin, TX.

Workers' Defense League Papers. Reuther Archives, Wayne State University, Detroit, MI.

Interviews

All interviews were conducted by the author.

Akins, Sylvester. Philadelphia, PA, November 20, 2003.

Cheeseman, Edward. Southampton, NJ, June 7, 2004.

DeStefano, Victor [pseud.]. Cherry Hill, NJ, September 24, 2003.

Gallo, Joseph. Pennsauken, NJ, September 4, 2003.

Harris, Sadie. Philadelphia, PA, November 20, 2003.

Laird, Leona. Pennsauken, NJ, August 27, 2003.

Melendez, Jorge. Pennsauken, NJ, July 3, 2004.

Melendez, Luz. Pennsauken, NJ, July 3, 2004.

Morrison, Jenny. Maple Shade, NJ, September 29, 2003.

Morrison, Joseph. Maple Shade, NJ, September 29, 2003.

Nelson, Harry. Mount Laurel, NJ, August 12, 2003.

Williams, Franklin [pseud.]. Cherry Hill, NJ, May 30, 2004.

Books, Reports, and Articles

Adams, Carolyn T., David Bartelt, David Elesh, Ira Goldstein, Nancy Kleniewski, and William Yancey. *Philadelphia: Neighborhoods, Division, and Conflict in a Post-industrial City.* Philadelphia: Temple University Press, 1991.

Arrighi, Giovanni. "The Labor Movement in Twentieth-Century Western Europe." In *Labor in the World Social Structure,* edited by Immanuel Wallerstein. Beverly Hills: Sage, 1983.

Babson, Steve. "Lean Production and Labor: Empowerment and Exploitation." In *Lean Work: Empowerment and Exploitation in the Global Auto Industry,* edited by Steve Babson. Detroit: Wayne State University Press, 1995.

Baldoz, Rick, Charles Koeber, and Philip Kraft, eds. *The Critical Study of Work: Labor, Technology, and Global Production.* Philadelphia: Temple University Press, 2001.

Barger, W. K., and Ernesto M. Reza. *The Farm Labor Movement in the Midwest: Social Change and Adaptation among Migrant Farmworkers.* Austin: University of Texas Press, 1993.

Barker, Kathleen, and Kathleen Christensen. *Contingent Work: American Employment Relations in Transition.* Ithaca, NY: Cornell University Press, 1998.

Bauman, John F., and Thomas H. Coode. *In the Eye of the Great Depression: New Deal Reporters and the Agony of the American People.* DeKalb: Northern Illinois University Press, 1988.

Bensman, David, and Roberta Lynch. *Rusted Dreams: Hard Times in a Steel Community.* Berkeley and Los Angeles: University of California Press, 1987.

Bluestone, Barry, and Bennett Harrison. *The De-Industrialization of America.* New York: Basic Books, 1982.

Braverman, Harry. *Labor and Monopoly Capitalism: The Degradation of Work in the Twentieth Century.* New York: Monthly Review Press, 1974.

Buhle, Paul. *Taking Care of Business: Samuel Gompers, George Meany, Lane Kirkland, and the Tragedy of American Labor.* New York: Monthly Review Press, 1999.

"Business Fights the Social Ills—In a Recession." *Business Week.* March 6, 1971.

Campbell, Daniel T. "New York Shipbuilding Corporation: The First Two Decades." PhD diss., Temple University, 2001.

"Campbell Stays with Camden." *Business Week,* February 6, 1971.

"Campbell Takes the Lid Off." *Fortune,* March 1955.

"Campbell's Soup." *Fortune,* November 1935.

Carman, Hoy F., and Ben C. French. "Economics of Fruit and Vegetable Processing in the United States," in *Economics of Food Processing in the United States,* ed. Chester O. McCorkle, Jr. San Diego: Academic Press, 1988.

Carré, Françoise, Marianne A. Ferber, Lonnie Golden, and Stephen A. Herzenberg, eds. *Nonstandard Work: The Nature and Challenges of Changing Employment Relations.* Ithaca, NY: ILR Press, 2000.

Chernish, William N. *Coalition Bargaining: A Study of Union Tactics and Public Policy.* Philadelphia: University of Pennsylvania Press, 1969.

Christy, Jim. *The Price of Power: A Biography of Charles Eugene Bedaux.* Toronto: Doubleday Canada, 1984.

Clawson, Dan. *Bureaucracy and the Labor Process.* New York: Monthly Review Press, 1982.

Cohen, Lizabeth. *Making a New Deal: Industrial Workers in Chicago, 1919–1939.* Cambridge: Cambridge University Press, 1990.

Collins, Douglas. *America's Favorite Food: The Story of Campbell Soup Company.* New York: Harry N. Abrams, 1994.

Condell, Patricia. "Campbell Soup Company—Plant No. 1, Camden, New Jersey." Camden, NJ: Historic Conservation and Interpretation, 1991.

Connor, John M., Richard T. Rogers, Bruce W. Marion, and Willard F. Mueller. *The Food Manufacturing Industries: Structure, Strategies, Performance, and Policies.* Lexington, MA: D. C. Heath, 1985.

Cowie, Jefferson. *Capital Moves: RCA's Seventy-Year Quest for Cheap Labor.* Ithaca, NY: Cornell University Press, 1999.

Cowie, Jefferson, and Joseph Heathcott, eds. *Beyond the Ruins: The Meanings of Deindustrialization.* Ithaca, NY: ILR Press, 2003.

Cranston, Paul F. *Camden County 1681–1931: The Story of an Industrial Empire.* Camden, NJ: Camden County Chamber of Commerce, 1931.

Dicken, Peter. *Global Shift: Transforming the World Economy.* 3rd ed. New York: Guilford Press, 1998.

Dorwart, Jeffrey M. *Camden County, New Jersey: The Making of a Metropolitan Community, 1626–2000.* New Brunswick, NJ: Rutgers University Press, 2001.

Dorwart, Jeffery M., and Philip English Mackey. *Camden County, New Jersey 1616–1976: A Narrative History.* Camden, NJ: Camden County Cultural and Heritage Commission, 1976.

Dubofsky, Melvyn. "Technological Change and American Worker Movements, 1870–1970." In *Technology, the Economy, and Society: The American Experience,* edited by Joel Colton and Stuart Bruchey. New York: Columbia University Press, 1987.

Dunn, Bill. *Global Restructuring and the Power of Labour.* New York: Palgrave, 2004.

Employment and Housing Problems of Migratory Workers in New York and New Jersey Canning Industries, 1943. Women's Bureau. Bulletin no. 198. Washington, DC: GPO, 1944.

"Expert Systems in Use: Campbell Soup Company." *Plant Engineering*, June 18, 1987.

Finn, Janet L. *Tracing the Veins: Of Copper, Culture, and Community from Butte to Chuquicamata*. Berkeley and Los Angeles: University of California Press, 1998.

Friedlander, Peter. *The Emergence of a UAW Local, 1936–1939: A Study in Class and Culture*. Pittsburgh: University of Pittsburgh Press, 1975.

Friedman, Thomas L. *The Lexus and the Olive Tree: Understanding Globalization*. New York: Farrar, Straus and Giroux, 1999.

Giedion, Sigfried. *Mechanization Takes Command: A Contribution to Anonymous History*. New York: Oxford University Press, 1948.

Gillette, Howard, Jr., *Camden after the Fall: Decline and Renewal in a Post-Industrial City*. Philadelphia: University of Pennsylvania Press, 2005.

Glaberman, Martin. *Wartime Strikes: The Struggle Against the No-Strike Pledge in the UAW during World War II*. Detroit: Bewick, 1980.

Gordon, David M., Richard Edwards, and Michael Reich. *Segmented Work, Divided Workers: The Historical Transformation of Labor in the United States*. Cambridge: Cambridge University Press, 1982.

Green, Hardy S. *On Strike at Hormel: The Struggle for a Democratic Labor Movement*. Philadelphia: Temple University Press, 1990.

Green, William C., and Ernest J. Yanarella, eds. *North American Auto Unions in Crisis: Lean Production as Contested Terrain*. Albany: State University of New York Press, 1996.

Greider, William. *One World, Ready or Not: The Manic Logic of Global Capitalism*. New York: Simon and Schuster, 1997.

Hage, Dave, and Paul Klauda. *No Retreat, No Surrender: Labor's War at Hormel*. New York: William Morrow, 1989.

Hahamovitch, Cindy. *The Fruits of Their Labor: Atlantic Coast Farmworkers and the Making of Migrant Poverty, 1870–1945*. Chapel Hill: University of North Carolina Press, 1997.

Halpern, Rick. *Down on the Killing Floor: Black and White Workers in Chicago's Packinghouses, 1904–54*. Urbana: University of Illinois Press, 1997.

———. "Oral History and Labor History: A Historiographic Assessment after Twenty-Five Years." *Journal of American History* 85 (September 1998).

Hardwick, C. M. *Time Study in Treason: Charles E. Bedaux, Patriot or Collaborator?* Chelmsford, UK: Peter Horsnell, 1989.

Harris, Howell John. *The Right to Manage: The Industrial Relations Policies of American Business in the 1940s*. Madison: University of Wisconsin Press, 1982.

Honey, Michael. *Going Down Jericho Road: The Memphis Strike, Martin Luther King's Last Campaign*. New York: W.W. Norton and Co., 2007.

———. *Southern Labor and Black Civil Rights: Organizing Memphis Workers*. Urbana: University of Illinois Press, 1993.

Horn, Gerd-Rainer. "The Changing Nature of the European Working Class: The Rise and Fall of the 'New Working Class' (France, Italy, Spain, Czechoslovakia)." In *1968: The World Transformed*, edited by Carole Fink, Philipp Gassert, and Detlef Junker. Cambridge: Cambridge University Press, 1998.

Horowitz, Roger. *Negro and White, Unite and Fight! A Social History of Industrial Unionism in Meatpacking, 1930–90*. Urbana: University of Illinois Press, 1997.

Hounshell, David A. *From the American System to Mass Production, 1800–1932: The Development of Manufacturing Technology in the United States.* Baltimore: Johns Hopkins University Press, 1984.

"How Quality Circles Can Work to Improve 'Quality of Life.'" *Food Engineering,* October 1984.

"In the Soup and Happy to Be There." *Business Week,* February 15, 1964.

International Bedaux Company. *Bedaux Measures Labor.* New York: Chas. E. Bedaux, 1928.

——. *General Considerations Pertaining to the Bedaux Plan.* New York: International Bedaux Company, 1937.

Jacoby, Sanford M. *Employing Bureaucracy: Managers, Unions, and the Transformation of Work in American Industry, 1900–1945.* New York: Columbia University Press, 1985.

Jamieson, Stuart M. *Labor Unionism in American Agriculture.* 1945.

Jones, Isham. *The Puerto Rican in New Jersey: His Present Status.* Newark: New Jersey State Department of Education, Division against Discrimination, 1955.

Kirp, David L., John P. Dwyer, and Larry A. Rosenthal. *Our Town: Race, Housing, and the Soul of Suburbia.* New Brunswick, NJ: Rutgers University Press, 1995.

Knoche, Thomas. *Common Sense for Camden.* Camden, NJ: Thomas Knoche, 2005.

Korstad, Robert. *Civil Rights Unionism: Tobacco Workers and the Struggle for Democracy in the Mid-Twentieth-Century South.* Chapel Hill: University of North Carolina Press, 2003.

Koss, Joan. "Puerto Ricans in Philadelphia: Migration and Accommodation." PhD diss., University of Pennsylvania, 1965.

Kreis, Steven. "The Diffusion of Scientific Management: The Bedaux Company in America and Britain, 1926–1945." In *A Mental Revolution: Scientific Management since Taylor,* edited by Daniel Nelson. Columbus: Ohio State University Press, 1992.

Levy, Peter B. *The New Left and Labor in the 1960s.* Urbana: University of Illinois Press, 1994.

Lichtenstein, Nelson. *Labor's War at Home: The CIO in World War II.* Cambridge: Cambridge University Press, 1982.

——. *State of the Union: A Century of American Labor.* Princeton, NJ: Princeton University Press, 2002.

Littler, Craig. "Deskilling and Changing Structures of Control." In *The Degradation of Work? Skill, Deskilling, and the Labour Process,* edited by Stephen Wood. London: Hutchinson, 1982.

Maldonado, Edwin. "Contract Labor and the Origins of Puerto Rican Communities in the United States," *International Migration Review* 13 (Spring 1979).

Mehri, Darius. *Notes from Toyota-Land: An American Engineer in Japan.* Ithaca, NY: Cornell University Press, 2005.

Milkman, Ruth. *Gender at Work: The Dynamics of Job Segregation by Sex during World War II.* Urbana: University of Illinois Press, 1987.

Moody, Kim. *Workers in a Lean World: Unions in the International Economy.* London: Verso, 1997.

Morse, Dean. *The Peripheral Worker.* New York: Columbia University Press, 1969.

"New Plant of the Year." *Food Engineering,* March 1983.

Northrup, Herbert W. *Boulwarism: The Labor Relations Policies of the General Electric Company.* Ann Arbor: University of Michigan Press, 1964.

Novack, Janet. "We're Not Running the Company for the Stock Price." *Forbes,* September 19, 1988.

Ohmae, Kenichi. *The Evolving Global Economy: Making Sense of the New World Order.* Boston: Harvard Business Review Books, 1995.

Parker, Mike, and Jane Slaughter, "Unions and Management by Stress." In *Lean Work: Empowerment and Exploitation in the Global Auto Industry,* edited by Steve Babson. Detroit: Wayne State University Press, 1995.

Parkin, Katharine. "Campbell's Soup and the Long Shelf Life of Traditional Gender Roles." In *Kitchen Culture in America: Popular Representations of Food, Gender, and Race,* edited by Sherrie A. Inness. Philadelphia: University of Pennsylvania Press, 2001.

Rachleff, Peter. *Hard-Pressed in the Heartland: The Hormel Strike and the Future of the Labor Movement.* Boston: South End Press, 1993.

Rogers, Jackie Krasas. *Temps: The Many Faces of the Changing Workplace.* Ithaca, NY: Cornell University Press, 2000.

Rosswurm, Steve, ed. *The CIO's Left-Led Unions.* New Brunswick, NJ: Rutgers University Press, 1992.

Ruiz, Vicki L. *Cannery Women/Cannery Lives: Mexican Women, Unionization, and the California Food Processing Industry.* Albuquerque: University of New Mexico Press, 1987.

Rutsch, Edward S., and Robert A. Fischer Jr. "Campbell Soup Company—Plant No. 2, Camden, New Jersey." Camden, NJ: Historic Conservation and Interpretation, 1987.

Saporito, Bill. "Campbell Soup Gets Piping Hot." *Fortune,* September 9, 1991.

Sassen, Saskia. *The Global City: New York, London, Tokyo.* Princeton, NJ: Princeton University Press, 1991.

Schatz, Ronald W. *The Electrical Workers: A History of Labor at General Electric and Westinghouse, 1923–1960.* Urbana: University of Illinois Press, 1983.

Schrecker, Ellen. "McCarthyism and the Labor Movement: The Role of the State." In *The CIO's Left-Led Unions,* edited by Steve Rosswurm. New Brunswick, NJ: Rutgers University Press, 1992.

Schwarz, Philip J. *Coalition Bargaining.* Ithaca: New York State School of Industrial and Labor Relations, 1970.

Scranton, Philip. *Figured Tapestry: Production, Markets, and Power in Philadelphia Textiles, 1885–1941.* Cambridge: Cambridge University Press, 1989.

——. *Proprietary Capitalism: The Textile Manufacture at Philadelphia, 1800–1885.* Cambridge: Cambridge University Press, 1983.

Sim, Mary B. *History of Commercial Canning in New Jersey.* Trenton: New Jersey Agricultural Society, 1951.

Smith, Andrew F. *Souper Tomatoes: The Story of America's Favorite Food.* New Brunswick, NJ: Rutgers University Press, 2000.

"Soup Kitchen of the Nation." *Forbes,* April 15, 1961.

Stein, Judith. *Running Steel, Running America: Race, Economic Policy and the Decline of Liberalism.* Chapel Hill: University of North Carolina Press, 1998.

Stepan-Norris, Judith and Maurice Zeitlin. *Left Out: Reds and America's Industrial Unions.* Cambridge: Cambridge University Press, 2003.

Strasser, Susan. *Satisfaction Guaranteed: The Making of the American Mass Market.* New York: Pantheon, 1989.

Stull, William J., and Janice Fanning Madden. *Post-Industrial Philadelphia: Structural Changes in the Metropolitan Economy.* Philadelphia: University of Pennsylvania, 1990.

Sugrue, Thomas. *The Origins of the Urban Crisis: Race and Inequality in Postwar Detroit.* Princeton, NJ: Princeton University Press, 1996.

Summers, Anita A., and Thomas F. Luce. *Economic Development Within the Philadelphia Metropolitan Area.* Philadelphia: University of Pennsylvania Press, 1987.

———. *Economic Report on the Philadelphia Metropolitan Area.* Philadelphia: University of Pennsylvania Press, 1985.

"Symposium: Bill Dunn, *Global Restructuring and the Power of Labour.*" *Labor History* 47 (February 2006).

Taylor, Frederick Winslow. *The Principles of Scientific Management.* New York: Harper and Brothers, 1911.

Terkel, Studs. *Working.* New York: Pantheon, 1974.

Tisa, John. *Recalling the Good Fight: An Autobiography of the Spanish Civil War.* South Hadley, MA: Bergin and Garvey, 1985.

Vázquez-Hernández, Victor. "Puerto Ricans in Philadelphia: Origins of a Community, 1910–1945." PhD diss., Temple University, 2002.

Watson, W. F. *The Worker and Wage Incentives: The Bedaux and Other Systems.* London: Leonard and Virginia Woolf, 1934.

Weber, Devra. *Dark Sweat, White Gold: California Farm Workers, Cotton, and the New Deal.* Berkeley: University of California Press, 1994.

Whalen, Carmen Teresa. *From Puerto Rico to Philadelphia: Puerto Rican Workers and Postwar Economies.* Philadelphia: Temple University Press, 2001.

Womack, James, Daniel Jones, and Daniel Roos. *The Machine that Changed the World.* New York: Rawson, 1990.

Writers' Program (U.S.). *Housing in Camden. Housing Authority of the City of Camden.* Camden: Huntzinger Co., printers, 1942.

Zieger, Robert. *The C.I.O., 1935–1955.* Chapel Hill: University of North Carolina Press, 1995.

❧ ACKNOWLEDGMENTS

The operation of a soup factory is clearly a collective endeavor. Though it may not be as obvious, the process of researching, writing, and producing a book also depends heavily on the interactions and contributions of many people. Among the many who have been a part of this project in one way or another, I want to specifically thank those without whom there would be no book.

This book is, above all, the story of those who worked at the Camden, New Jersey, Campbell Soup plants over the last century, and I am indebted to all of them. I especially want to thank the former employees who shared their stories with me in their kitchens and living rooms: Sylvester Akins, Edward Cheeseman, Victor DeStefano, Joseph Gallo, Sadie Harris, Leona Laird, Jorge Melendez, Luz Melendez, Jenny Morrison, Joseph Morrison, Harry Nelson, and Franklin Williams. In particular I want to express my appreciation to Harry Nelson, president of the Campbell Kids, and Sadie Harris, president of Club 80, for letting me speak to their organizations and for putting me in touch with many of their members. Sylvester Akins, Joseph Gallo, and Harry Nelson also shared with me materials from their personal collections.

To a lesser degree this is also a part of the story of Camden in the twentieth century. I have learned much from and been inspired by the residents of Camden, including members of Leavenhouse, Camden United, and other organizations, who refuse to accept the raw deal handed them by corporate and government officials. Their victories in the face of apparently insurmountable odds prove that human agency is still a powerful force in determining the course of history. Thanks also to everyone in the Greater Camden Unity Coalition for fighting to make this a better world.

The other pillar of this work, in addition to the experiences of those who lived through the events described, is the edifice of knowledge built by historians and other scholars who provided me the foundation and the analytical tools necessary for this project. To be sure, that "edifice" is constantly shifting and subject to internal and external conflicts, but it would not be a living and growing organism otherwise. Kenneth Kusmer, who introduced me to the theory and practice of social history, discussed with me the earliest germs of the ideas that led eventually to this book, read every chapter in their early forms, and gave invaluable advice at many stages. Rick Halpern and Arthur Schmidt also read early versions and improved the work immeasurably with their suggestions. Discussions with John Seitter and Philip Scranton at the beginning stage of this project helped me see the possibilities in the study of the Campbell Soup Company and its workers. More than anyone else, Sharon McConnell Sidorick (a historian of another consumer industry in the city across the river from Camden) read and discussed every part of this book through every revision; many of the insights in this work are really hers. Other members of the faculty (especially David Bartelt) and graduate students at Temple University, and undergraduate students in my classes there, also helped in many ways directly and indirectly. Informal discussion with many people over the years, especially Jim Cleary, helped keep my thinking straight. The foremost historian of cannery women and their union, Vicki Ruiz, graciously shared with me the materials John Tisa gave her from the early years of the union at Campbell's Camden plant. Other historians, as should be evident from the book, had important influences on the formation of the ideas expressed here.

Central to the success of any work in history are archivists and librarians. In my case I want to extend my heartfelt thanks to the librarians at Temple University's Paley Library and to Margaret Jerrido and her staff at the Urban Archives there. I also depended directly on the help provided by the staffs of the Wisconsin Historical Society; the Reuther Archives at Wayne State University; the Southern Labor Archives at Georgia State University; the National Archives and Records Administration in Philadelphia and College Park, Maryland (especially Tab Lewis); the Camden County Historical Society; the Historical Society of Pennsylvania; and the Campbell Soup Company Archives.

When it came time to turn my unwieldy manuscript into a book, I could not have had a better editor than Fran Benson at Cornell University Press. Many others there provided essential help as well, especially Susan Specter, Brian Bendlin, and Mary-Anne Gilbert. And thanks to David Prout for a great job on the index.

Finally, I must extend my deepest gratitude to my family. My mother, Jeanne Sidorick, and my late father, Daniel Sidorick, have given me support, encouragement, and love my entire life, even if they sometimes wondered about the wisdom of my endeavors. To future generations—to Michael, Brianna, and Dante—I hope a better understanding of the past might contribute in some small way to a better future, and I thank you for helping me remember what is really important in life. Most of all, none of this would have been possible without my companion in this adventure, Sharon McConnell Sidorick. Beyond her work as a historian, her passion for justice has been an inspiration. And her love and support have kept me going.

✇ INDEX

Page numbers with an *f* indicate figures; those with a *t* indicate tables.